Torpedo Terror

Richard F

'Ther
Admirals

ie Vice
hill, April

© Richard Freeman 2022.

ISBN: 9798792339910
Imprint: Independently published

This print edition is published by the author and is available from Amazon.com and other book stores. A Kindle edition of this book is published by Lume Books.

The right of Richard Freeman to be identified as the author of this work has been asserted in accordance with the Copyright, Designs and Patents Act 1988.

Cover image: Lume Books. Cover text: Marcus Freeman.

Other books by Richard Freeman

The Great Edwardian Naval Feud. Pen and Sword 2009.

Admiral Insubordinate: The Life and Times of Lord Beresford. Endeavour Press 2012.

'Unsinkable': Churchill and the First World War. History Press 2013.

Tempestuous Genius: The Life of Admiral of the Fleet Lord Fisher. Endeavour Press 2015.

Operation Armageddon (novel). Independently published 2017.

Atlantic Nightmare: The longest military campaign in World War II. Lume Books 2020.

Be Very Afraid!: The scurrilous history of the invasion-scare novel. Independently published 2020.

Contents

PRELIMINARY NOTES 2
MAPS 4
A MOMENT IN HISTORY 7
1 THE KAISER WANTS A NAVY 12
2 A WILD GAMBLE 17
3 IN SEARCH OF A ROLE 26
4 LAND WAR TURNS TO SEA WAR 36
5 WARSHIPS UNDER SIEGE 48
6 SKIRMISHES 64
7 CHANGE OF COMMAND 70
8 BLOCKADE 86
9 NEUTRALS BEWARE! 96
10 PATROL LIFE 109
11 A NEW TARGET 116
12 LUSITANIA 126
13 INDECISION 135
14 MEDITERRANEAN DIVERSION 150
15 IN THE SHADOW OF THE UNITED STATES 164
16 THE END OF THE BIG SHIPS 179
17 ONLY U-BOATS REMAIN 191
18 LAST THROW OF THE DICE 205
19 WAKING THE GIANT 212
20 THE BATTLE FOR CONVOYS 227
21 UNSTOPPABLE SINKINGS 239
22 EARLY CONVOYS 249
23 THE BATTLE OF THE BREAKFAST TABLES 260
24 CONVOYS ON TRIAL 272
25 CONVOYS VINDICATED 280
26 OLD MEN DEPART 290
27 THE DARKEST HOUR 296
28 THE TAMING OF THE U-BOATS 308
29 DOWNFALL OF THE U-BOATS 324
30 SURRENDER 329
APPENDIX 1 STRATEGIC ERRORS AND SUCCESSES 342
APPENDIX 2 PEOPLE 344
SOURCES 348
INDEX 356
REFERENCES 368

Preliminary notes

Ships' genders: In line with modern ideas on gender neutrality, except in quotations, all ships are referred to as 'it' rather than 'she'.

British pre-decimal currency: £1 was worth 240 pennies (240 d); one shilling (1 s) was worth twelve pennies (12 d).

Historical currency conversions used in this book: Pound conversions: https://www.nationalarchives.gov.uk/currency-converter/; US dollar conversions: https://www.officialdata.org/

Currency values: £1 in 1915 was equivalent to £59 in today's money. $1 in 1917 was equivalent to $21 in today's money.

Measures: Weights and distances are generally given in Imperial units to match the measures of the time. 1 cwt (1 hundredweight) = 112 lb (51 kg). As a guide to today's units, 1 oz is just under 30 grams; 1 lb is just under half a kilogram. Loose goods (e.g. peas and beans) were sometimes sold by the pint. One pint = 473 ml. 1 fathom = 1.8 m.

Ranks: Ranks and titles are generally given as at the date of the events under discussion.

Rounding: Gross tonnages, cargo weights and other measures have generally been rounded for ease of reading.

Statistics: Ships' weights are given in gross tons.

Times: Except in quotations, times are given in twelve-hour format.

British Admiralty: The political head of the British Admiralty was a Cabinet Minister, holding the title of First

Lord of the Admiralty; the professional head of the admiralty was an admiral with the title of First Sea Lord.

German Admiralty: The political head of the German Admiralty was the Head of the Naval Cabinet: Admiral Georg von Muller held this post from 1906 until October 1918. The professional head of the German Admiralty was the State Secretary. Admiral von Tirpitz held this post from 1897 until March 1916. He was replaced by Admiral Eduard von Capelle.

German ranks: Oberleutnant zur See: Lieutenant.

Abbreviations: German warships – SMS: Seiner Majestät Schiff (His Majesty's Ship).

British warships – HMS: His Majesty's Ship; HMHS: His Majesty's Hospital Ship; HMT His Majesty's Transport.

Civilian ships – P&O: Pacific & Orient; RMS: Royal Mail Ship.

Other abbreviations – ASW: Anti-submarine warfare; BEF: British Expeditionary Force; RNVR: Royal Navy Volunteer Reserve; HVB: Handelsverkehrsbuch – German cypher key; SKM: Signalbuch der Kaiserlichen Marine – a German signals book; U: Unterseeboot.

Illustrations: Unattributed illustrations are believed to be public domain.

Maps

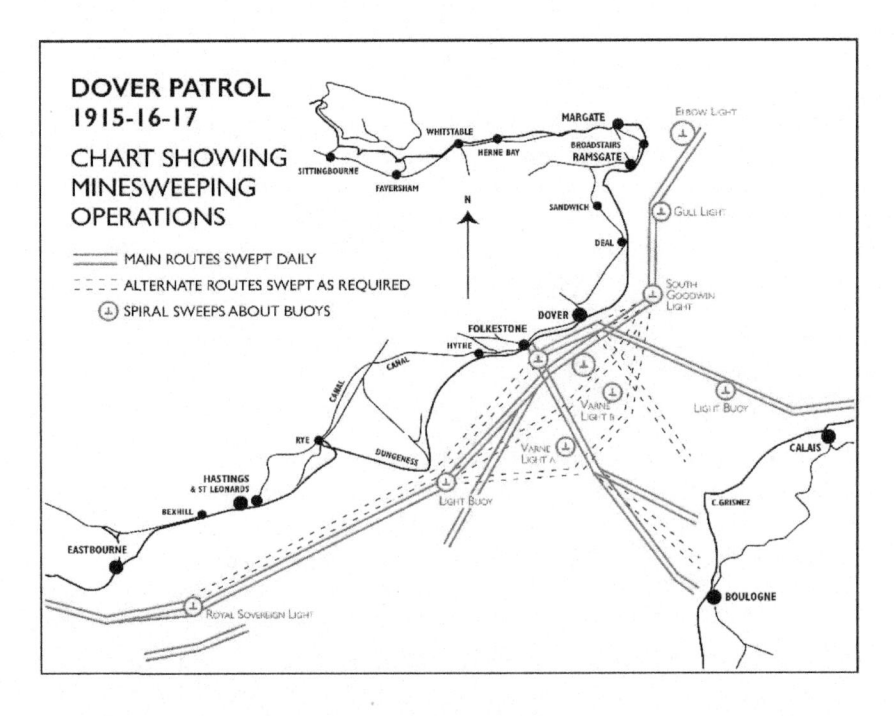

Dover Patrol, showing the swept channels around the waters of the Dover Barrage.

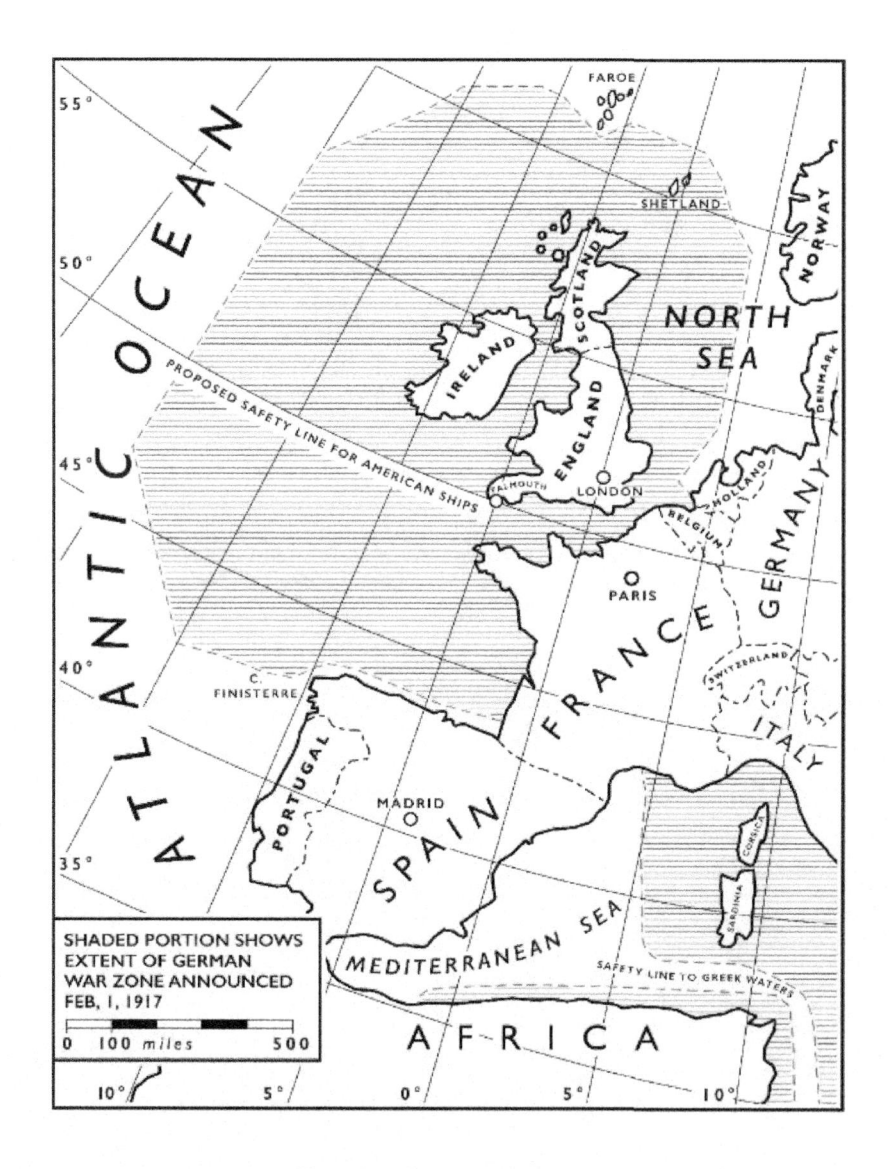

The 1917 German War Zone.

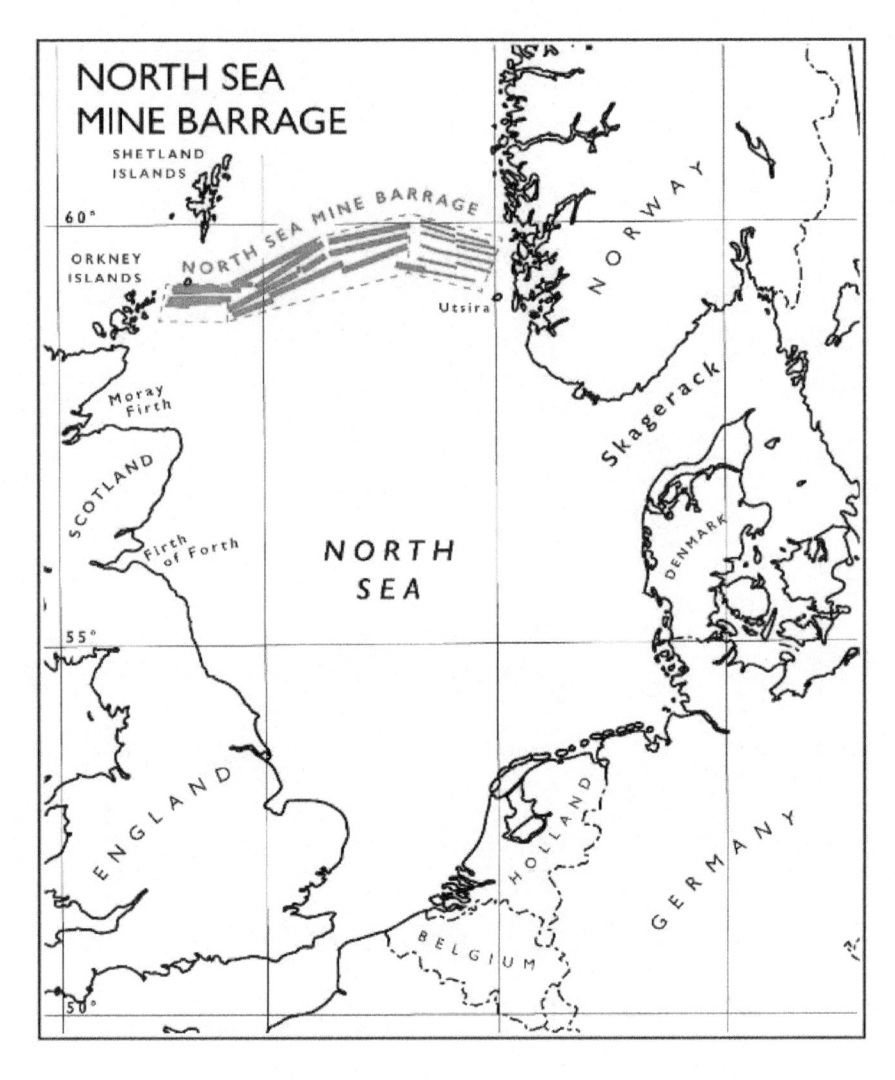

The American-built North Sea Barrage, 1918.

A moment in history

Early on the morning of Wednesday November 20, 1918, the submarine depot ship HMS *Maidstone* and the destroyers HMSs *Melampus* and *Firedrake* lay with steam up alongside Parkeston Quay at Harwich. On the deck of the *Maidstone* was a mass of British submarine officers. On the quayside below stood an expectant crowd of reporters, photographers and cameramen. They had arrived on the previous evening to be royally entertained by jubilant seamen in various ships' messes. (The lone female reporter had had to sleep on the billiard table of one of the ships.) Now they were ready for the great drama of the day.

In the dawn light, sailors on the *Maidstone* were readying the gangway – a sign that Vice Admiral Hugo Meurer in Kiel had confirmed that the great event was on. At 7.00 am the civilians were asked to board the destroyers. They had high expectations as they prepared to witness a momentous occurrence: the surrender of the first 20 U-boats.

On the previous evening, light cruisers and destroyers from the Harwich Force had disappeared into the night to rendezvous with the incoming U-boats. They were to meet at the formal point of surrender: Sledway, a few miles off the Suffolk coast.

Now at sea, the line of *Maidstone*, *Melampus* and *Firedrake* approached the rendezvous point, the vessels brushing their way past the Cork lightship, while its occupants cheered at the triumphant pageant. The stars were just fading and the rosy dawn in the eastern sky began to anticipate the day of victory. In the still of the morning, Rear Admiral Reginald Tyrwhitt of the Harwich Force ordered the bugler in HMS *Curacoa* to sound 'action stations'. At that moment a ship loomed out of the thin mist and a dozen binoculars swivelled in search of the nearing U-boats. First, HMS *Dragon* came into view, ahead of some indistinct grey shapes, low in the sea. *Dragon* took up its station at the rendezvous point. The ratings, officers, commanders, journalists and cameramen on the various ships held their breath.

Then the first U-boats came into sight ... one ... two ... They came slowly, with the twentieth appearing four hours later. *Dragon* turned to lead the boats into captivity. It was a staggering sight: the recently commissioned warship, with its spotless new paint, leading a destroyer with five U-boats in its wake. Then more destroyers and more U-boats. Overhead, a watchful British airship at 800 feet sailed down the line of ships. It was followed by two blimps and some low-flying aircraft. No one wished to miss this historic moment. With the first sightings of the enemy, *Firedrake* healed-over as its passengers rushed to one side of the ship to see and photograph the spectacle.

In shame, the defeated submariners had painted out the numbers of their boats. Their commanders laid no claim to honour in their blackest hour. Only one boat defiently flew a German engsign.

As the U-boats neared the rendezvous point, they passed under the gaze of the men on the *Dragon*. The lower deck, in clean sweaters, looked down contemptuously on the grubby submariners.

Checking the surrender documents, boat by boat. The men's baggage lies on the deck in front of the conning tower. (Wikimedia Commons.)

Thus ended the U-boat's lives. In each boat a British officer took command in the conning tower while the German crew moved forward on deck. Below, British engineers supervised their German counterparts to bring the boats to their appointed moorings.

There were a few brief exchanges between British and German naval personnel. As Rear Admiral Roger Keyes was taking the surrender of *U-98*, he noticed the huge pair of Zeiss binoculars around Kapitänleutnant

Rudolf Andler's neck. He asked whether they were government property. Andler replied: 'They are official glasses. Please have them.'[2]

After the surrender at sea, the U-boats – now British property – were led by destroyers into harbour in groups of five. Four distrustful light cruisers followed in the rear. At one mile from Harwich, the escorts and guards peeled off, leaving the U-boat crews the dignity of sailing alone for the last mile to their allotted moorings.

One by one, the boats edged into Parkstone Quay. Some of the surrendered craft bore the ravages of their last patrols. All were dirty, many were in a foul state, having come straight from lengthy patrols. A *Scotsman* reporter noted the earie hush: 'No sirens, whistles, or hooters were permitted ... It was a silent entry into captivity.'[3]

Amongst the crowds watching the U-boats coming into harbour were some British submariners who, as *The Manchester Guardian* journalist put it, had searched the seas for these vessels 'through privations, fastings and dangers'. One of them despairingly exclaimed: 'Oh, God! Oh God! Look at them, look at them!'[4]

With the boats tied up at the quay, the German sailors disembarked and were taken to their transport vessel for their return to Germany.

During their passage into harbour, the submariners had appeared dejected. Now, as they began their journey home, they cheered up. Singing began in one group but was quashed by an officer. Another group produced a gramophone.

Lieutenant Stephen King-Hall shared the work of supervising the disembarking of the German sailors. On one boat, as the men stood clutching their few possessions, the commander saluted his vessel. 'We,' said King-Hall, 'returned his salute.'[5]

King-Hall had been struck by the unexpectedly correct behaviour of the German seamen: 'In nearly every case the German officer has seemed genuinely anxious to assist in every way possible way, and give as much information concerning the working of the boat as was feasible in the time at his disposal,'[6] he recalled.

Tyrwhitt, though, saw a foretaste of Germany's nascent revolution as he noted that the men 'did not treat their officers with the respect and servility which one usually associated with the German Navy'.[7]

Compliance with the British orders for surrender was near total. One boat 'lost' the white ensign that the British required to be flown. It, and other pilfered items, were later found hidden in the belongings of a submariner. Other boats had already been looted by mutineers at Kiel, who had taken most of the portable items. One boat, though, was in mint condition: it had only been commissioned in October and had never put to sea on patrol.

A U-boat ignominiously flies the white ensign while two British officers stand warily to one side. (Harwich Haven.)

This first batch of surrendering boats included *U-9*, which had begun its patrolling on August 1, 1914, and had notoriously sunk three 12,000-ton warships in one day in that year. Another notable arrival was *U-55*, which had sunk 64 ships totalling 134,000 tons. It was boats like these which had brought Britain so near to defeat at sea.

A few defiantly proud officers had refused to sail with their boats, including Kapitänleutnant Lothar von Arnauld de la Perière. As the ace amongst the aces, he had good cause to disassociate himself from lesser commanders. (He was one of the few commanders still making regular sinkings in the last few weeks of the war, having made five hits in October.)

Oberleutnant zur See Freiherr von Wangenheim had sailed with his boat, but refused to take it into harbour, handing it over to his engineering officer in the last few hours of his command. 'I hate you, and England,' he said to the escorting officer. '[I shall] fight against you in the next war.'[8] His arrogance was hardly based on any innate superiority: he had been in *U-25* since December 1917 and had only sunk a 260-ton naval trawler.

At the end of the day King-Hall stood on the quay 'as the sun sank in a splendour of crimson and gold' and looked down on the U-boats 'harmlessly swinging round their buoys'.[9] James Bone from *The Manchester Guardian* was there, too. In his mind's eye he saw the 'ghosts of women and children and merchant seamen looking down upon the machines of death'.[10]

1
The Kaiser wants a navy

1899-1914

'[I]f we permanently lose command of the sea, whatever may be the strength of the home force, the subjection of the country to the enemy is inevitable.' – Committee of Imperial Defence, 1908.[11]

IMPERIAL AMBITIONS

Before 1898, Germany had never felt the need for an ocean-going navy. Its security lay in its armies. All this changed when throat cancer ended the 99-day reign of Frederick III of Prussia in 1888. His son, Wilhelm, was obsessed by a fervent desire for an empire to rival those of Britain and France. But his dreams of sun-drenched colonies, dispatching rubber, metal ores, precious stones and exotic foods to the homeland, depended on his first having an ocean-going fleet. That fleet was to bring death and destruction to the high seas on a scale previously unimagined.

Three men were to provide Wilhelm with the ideas and the means to realize his imperial ambitions. First, Wilhelm came under the influence of the American historian Alfred Mahan and his 1894 book *The Influence of Sea Power on History*. In its pages, Wilhelm learnt how Britain's world power status was dependent on the combination of its naval strength and its trade. He seized on this assertion and determined to have a navy to rival that of his grandmother, Queen Victoria. It was to be so large as to 'make it difficult for Britain to pick a quarrel with us'.[12]

Having found his vision, Wilhelm turned to the man who would provide the means: Admiral Alfred von Tirpitz. He shared Wilhelm's high ambitions and was soon at work. By 1899, the first of Wilhelm's naval bills had set the German shipyards cutting and bending steel, while the foundries were hammering and boring massive gun barrels. Soon, Wilhelm was signing himself 'Admiral of the Atlantic' when writing letters to his cousin Tsar Nicholas II in Saint Petersburg.

The third influence on Wilhelm was Field Marshal Alfred von Schlieffen, Chief of the Prussian General Staff from 1891 to 1906. Schlieffen told Wilhelm that Germany's route to world power status lay in the destruction of France. His proposed method, the Schlieffen Plan, involved an attack to the north-west through Belgium before wheeling south to encircle the entire French army. So fast would be the action that there would be no need for Wilhelm to risk his precious fleet in this opening encounter.

Kaiser Wilhelm, who signed himself 'Admiral of the Atlantic', in an admiral's uniform around 1900.

An anxious onlooker

By 1901, the British Admiralty was watching anxiously as German warships sped down the slipways at Kiel, Bremen and elsewhere. In 1900 the 11,880-ton SMS *Kaiser Wilhelm II* had been commissioned, followed by the SMS *Kaiser Wilhelm der Grosse* and the SMS *Kaiser Barbarossa* in the following year. Wilhelm had imagined that this show of force would cower his rivals. Far from it. The First Lord of the Admiralty, Lord Selborne, warned his Cabinet colleagues in November 1901: 'The Emperor seems determined that the power of Germany shall be used all the world over to push German commerce, possessions, and interests.'[13]

Britain and France, perennial antagonists for centuries, saw the common threat and decided to make-up. On April 8, 1904, Lord

Lansdowne, British Secretary of State for Foreign Affairs, and Paul Cambon, French Ambassador to Britain, signed the *Entente Cordiale* at a ceremony in London. The *Entente* itself was trivial, being no more than an agreement to recognize each other's colonial possessions in Egypt (British) and Morocco (French). But, when neighbours stop quarrelling over their back gardens, friendship follows.

A NEW POWER

The *Entente* might have served as a warning to Wilhelm. Instead, two months later, he chose the Kiel Regatta in June 1904 to flaunt his growing sea power under the nose of his Uncle Bertie. Not only was King Edward VII to admire the Kaiser's warships, but he was first to be humiliated by being made to arrive at Kiel by the back door of the Kiel Canal.

Edward VII's yacht, *Victoria and Albert*, docked at Brunsbüttel at the southern end of the canal on the evening of June 23, 1904. Next day, at 6.00 am, the *Victoria and Albert* began its ignominious slow passage through the canal, reaching Holtenau Lock at 3.00 pm, where the royal party were welcomed by the triumphant emperor. Edward's subsequent uneasy inspection of the rival fleet was tempered by balls and dinners, but nothing could disguise the fact that he had seen the future. And that future was war.

For all the festive glamour, British officers found the atmosphere restrained. An Admiralty intelligence report noted that, despite the surface curtesy: 'it was obvious that the general tone and feeling, more especially on shore, was decidedly anti-English'.[14] *The Times* drew similar conclusions: 'we feel that it is our duty to watch the progress of German naval power, and to consider the possible purposes for which it might be used'.[15] The *St James's Gazette* was less reticent as it openly declared that 'this growth of rival construction can only have one object ... ourselves'.[16]

Few commentators realized that the feverish building of warships both in Britain and in Germany was the last flourish of a redundant technology. The future belonged to the submarines, as Lieutenant Colonel Charles à Court Repington was to warn in *Blackwood's Magazine* in June 1910. The accuracy of his 1910 naval forecast reflected his deep understanding of war and defence: 'the great ships ... will, within a limited period of time, become useless for most operations in the North Sea'.[17] In consequence, Repington argued, 'Our great and costly battleships and cruisers must be stowed away safely in some distant, safe, and secluded anchorage – Scapa Flow and Portsmouth today, Berehaven and Lough Swilly perhaps tomorrow.'[18] As to submarines, 'Nothing that we can effect by naval means can, with any certainty, prevent German submarines putting to sea when they please.'[19] It was an extraordinarily discerning prediction for the naval war of 1914-1918.

It was not until 1912 that the Admiralty began to test Repington's thesis in exercises in which submarines attempted to penetrate blockaded ports. The official report made alarming reading: every single submarine had passed undetected through a line of blockading destroyers. For centuries, Britain had relied on close blockade to keep enemy warships in their ports – that was what Nelson's fleet was doing outside Cadiz on the eve of the Battle of Trafalgar. Now, close blockade was to be a memory. In the coming war, Britain had no prospect of confining German submarines to their bases. The Kaiser had spent a fortune on warships to strike terror into the French and British, but the true terror was to come from the cheap and humble U-boat.

June 1914 saw the last Kiel Regatta before war broke out. The Kaiser, dressed in the uniform of a British admiral, swaggered across the deck of the British flagship HMS *King George V,* declaring, 'I'm simply in my element here.'[20] Meanwhile, recalled Kapitänleutnant Johannes Spiess, the German submariners did everything possible to deceive the British as to the capabilities of their boats. This included taking down the radio aerials on the U-boats in order to make the British think that boats did not have radios. They also scattered the U-boats to remote moorings to disguise their number. In return, the British were making circumspect notes on the details of the newly enlarged canal. All the while, German machinations were concealed by days of sports, feasting and drinking. Even so, the German seamen could not shed their competitive spirit: they won all but one of the inter-navy sporting events.

The British delegation went home, not understanding that they had just been served an aperitif to war.

While the seamen in the Imperial Navy confidently anticipated their imminent destruction of the Grand Fleet, the Royal Navy was reeling from a January 1914 study of the submarine threat. It concluded that, because submarines could neither capture merchant crews nor take ships as prizes, their threat was 'a truly terrible one for British commerce and Great Britain alike'.[21] Prime Minister Herbert Asquith suppressed the report when it came before the May meeting of the Committee of

Imperial Defence. In consequence, the Admiralty failed to initiate any research into anti-submarine warfare. A nation, paralysed by the fear of underwater attack, simply decided that no enemy would ever stoop to such a level of depravity. No defence was therefore needed. Even the bellicose First Lord of the Admiralty, Winston Churchill, concurred, saying that he did not believe 'a civilized Power' would ever sink merchant ships.[22]

British warships at Kiel in July 1914. (Contemporary postcard.)

But, if Germany were *not* a civilized power? No major nation was more dependent on the sea than was Britain. Nearly 80 per cent of the wheat and flour consumed in Britain was imported, along with 35-40 per cent of the meat sold in British shops. Such high import levels were sustained by Britain being a major exporter of manufactured goods. In 1913 it accounted for 13.5 per cent of all world exports and a staggering 26 per cent of all world manufactured exports. This trade – and Britain's capacity to feed its 36 million people – depended on its 'command of the sea'. This command had been unchallenged since the Napoleonic wars of 1803-1815. Now, the British Admiralty was about to go to war knowing that every one of its warships and all the British merchant vessels were at risk of a torpedo attack.

2
A wild gamble

July 1914

'I perceived ... that the new submarine weapon, whose laws had to be discovered, opened up prospects for the militant qualities of the German nation to rival the larger navies of older and richer states.' – Tirpitz.[23]

WAITING

July 1914 was unusually hot and sultry. The weather was ideal for the annual holidays of the British working people, who had exchanged their smoky towns for the hedonistic pleasures of beaches, fairground rides and end-of-the pier risqué comedy. Ice creams and candy floss were in great demand. Deckchairs were hard to come by; donkeys were being ridden to exhaustion.

In Berlin, Horace Rumbold had just arrived to take up the post of Counsellor in the British Embassy. Given the quiet state of Europe, the Ambassador, Sir Edward Goschen, had gone home on leave. Day after day there were dark clouds in the Berlin sky and the air was charged with the electricity of a storm that refused to break. In the office there was nothing to do: political Berlin was on leave.

At home nothing disturbed the royals' summer rituals, one of which was the Fleet Review. At 6.30 am on July 20, Admiral Prince Louis of Battenberg, Britain's First Sea Lord, boarded the royal yacht *Victoria and Albert* at Spithead, where he was greeted by King George V. A procession of the Trinity House yacht, the royal yacht and the Admiralty yacht then moved off to the Nab Elbow buoy where the King was to witness the greatest display of naval power that the world had even seen.

After a night of rain the skies were heavy with cloud and a cold easterly wind swept over the sea. As the two men peered over the dull ocean they saw the towering form of HMS *Iron Duke* approaching – the flagship of the ageing Commander-in-Chief, Admiral Sir George Callaghan, the man who was to be Britain's first line of defence if war were to come. Not that any of the spectators had any expectation of war. That was something they left to the Continental powers.

Behind *Iron Duke* were the First and Second Fleets, followed by a parade of 22 miles of the ships of the Royal Navy: 55 battleships, 4 battle cruisers, 27 cruisers, 28 light cruisers and 78 destroyers, not to mention vast numbers of minelayers, minesweeping gunboats, repair ships, and depot ships for torpedo craft. Their 460 pennants were an expression of a self-confident empire at the height of its power.

A gullible public watch the Fleet Review, believing in its power to protect the British way of life. Few, if any, realized how defenceless the big ships would prove to be in the presence of submarines.

As if the gods wished to bless the enterprise, the sun broke through as the first ships passed the royal yacht. The King observed the thin scarlet line of the marines who stood to attention around the forecastles of the ships. As each vessel passed the yacht its band thundered out triumphal airs and the men gave three cheers for their monarch. It took an hour for the First Fleet to pass under the King's gaze, by which time the leading vessels were disappearing over the horizon. The Second and Third Fleets, which had been specially mobilized for the occasion, followed. In the lead were their mighty, but not-so-new, battleships. These were followed by their cruisers and auxiliaries.

Years later, Winston Churchill, who was at the King's side in his capacity as First Lord of the Admiralty, was to recall: 'One after another the ships melted out of sight beyond the Nab. They were going on a longer voyage than any of us would know.'[24]

Back in the Admiralty, on that same day, the Assistant Director of Operations, Captain Herbert Richmond, was drafting a memorandum on the threat – or lack of a threat – of submarines to trade. Like all naval officers, he could never conceive that a submarine would sink a merchant ship by torpedo and, '[since] she does not carry a crew which is capable of taking charge of a prize, she cannot remove passengers and other persons if she wishes to sink one'.[25] His misplaced optimism would soon be shattered by an enemy which, unbounded by tradition, was to make its own rules.

While Richmond was indulging in delusions, the enemy was making its own preparations for war at sea. On July 23, Austria-Hungary issued its notorious ultimatum to Serbia, effectively demanding the surrender of its neighbour by return of post. Four days later, the German High Seas Fleet under Admiral Friedrich von Ingenohl was sent to its war stations.

Ingenohl's orders were based on the assumption that the Royal Navy would seek to blockade the coastal waters off Germany – an area of the sea known as the German Bight. He was directed to use all means – raids, mine-laying and U-boat attack – to weaken Britain's naval power.

Foreseeing the triumph of this strategy, the chief of the admiralty staff, Admiral Hugo von Pohl, went on to extend his orders to the time when 'equality of strength had been realized'. That would be the time to concentrate the High Seas Fleet and 'to seek battle under circumstances unfavourable to the enemy'.[26]

With these vague war orders, which reflected Tirpitz's hazy idea as to the purpose of his fleet, the sailors of the High Seas Fleet, lying at the Jade, heard the news of mobilization on the evening of August 1. It was greeted 'with loud cheers,' recalled Vice Admiral Scheer in command of the Second Battle Squadron.[27]

By July 27, the British Admiralty recognized that war was near to inevitable. Cables went out from Admiralty House in London to far-flung ships, urgently recalling them to Home Waters.

The mighty ships of the Grand Fleet were still at Portsmouth when Winston Churchill ordered their departure to the Scapa Flow mooring in the Orkneys on July 28. That afternoon, Midshipman Oram and his friends had gone motorcycling on the hills inland. After dozing in the warm sunshine high above the sea, they made their leisurely way back to the ship. As they boarded the battleship HMS *Orion*, they found the crew feverishly preparing the ship for war. That night, as the ship passed up the Channel, everything inflammable – furniture, pianos, carpets – was tossed overboard. Even Oram's motorbike was pitched into the waves by an over-enthusiastic seaman.

A wild gamble

TO SEA

Commodore Roger Keyes, in command of the Eighth Submarine Flotilla, mobilized his vessels without even waiting for a call from the Admiralty, cancelling his men's leave from his home telephone on July 26. He then rushed up to London and demanded to see the Chief of the War Staff and the First Sea Lord. With their retrospective blessings for his action, Keyes' flotilla prepared for war. After his hectic day, Keyes attended a dance at Goodwood. Someone suggested to him that the event recalled the Duchess of Richmond's ball, held three days before the Battle of Waterloo. But the Goodwood dance would not be followed by swift victories and peace. Instead, Keyes and his fellow officers, faced the prospect of years of relentless conflict on the high seas.

Oberleutnant zur See Johannes Spiess was one of thousands of German sailors eager for war. In the bright sunshine of August 1 he was waiting anxiously for news as the bustling engineers worked on preparing the U-boats for war. His spirits rose when, in late afternoon, he heard that Russia had failed to meet Germany's 12-noon deadline to pull back from war. In Berlin, the War Minister, Major General Falkenhayn, called on Chancellor Bethmann Hollweg for his support in asking the Kaiser to mobilize Germany's mighty war machine. At the Stadtschloss, the Kaiser stood at the old table made from timbers from Nelson's *Victory*. Before him lay the fateful order. Without hesitation he signed his nation into war. 'God bless Your Majesty and your arms,' said Falkenhayn. 'God protect the beloved Fatherland.' Far away at Heligoland, Spiess' lusty voice was just one of hundreds that fulsomely greeted the arrival of war.[28]

Elsewhere, the German sailors were readying their U-boats for action. Kapitänleutnant Otto Weddigen in *U-9* was ordered to Kiel, where he found the ships massing for war. His boat was to take on board all such armaments as were needed for mobilization and then to proceed to Heligoland via the Kiel Canal. That night, at 3.00 am, the sound of U-boat hooters rang out in the darkness. One after another the boats slipped into line and passed under the Holtenau High Bridge, making for the Holtenau Lock. In the anonymity of the night, Spiess mused on the men's silent, unwarlike departure. An army send-off would have seen a spectacle of grand marching-tunes, fluttering standards and cheering crowds. For Spiess and Weddigen, and the rest of their flotillas, all that awaited them was the lonely vastness of the mighty seas and the constant watch for hostile vessels. Hearth, home, and humanity was now behind them.

The U-boats, though, were barely ready for war. Kapitänleutnant Hans Rose's VIIth Flotilla was typical of their state, having a total stock of only 55 torpedoes, of which only 21 were ready for action. (In comparison, on land Germany sent 2,070,000 men and 118,000 horses to war in 208,000 rail transports.[29])

Although Britain had made no decision to enter the war – that would come in the House of Commons on August 3 – Sub-lieutenant Alexander Scrimgeour and the rest of the crew of the ageing Edgar class cruiser HMS *Crescent* had been recalled to barracks at Portsmouth. Momentarily, he was dismayed at his truncated leave, but the excitement of war soon took over. The next day found Scrimgeour and a few of his shipmates at the theatre in Portsmouth, watching Alfred Sutro's *The Clever Ones*. When the curtain came down for the interval, an official came onto the stage to announce the immediate recall of the sailors. As the young men departed, never to see the next two acts, the audience cheered them on their way. Within the hour, Scrimgeour was stepping onto *Crescent*'s deck, his mind still on the 'several nice girls' who were now beyond his further acquaintance.[30]

For others, mobilization was more complicated. When the call came to Rear Admiral Wester Wemyss he was on half-pay and playing patience in the lounge of his hotel in Germany. He looked up to see Dr Philipp Heinecken, President of the Nord Deutscher Lloyd shipping line, hurrying towards him. Wemyss could see that something was seriously wrong from the pale and fearful look on Heinecken's face. 'The Russians are mobilizing,' said Heinecken, 'and the British Fleet are beginning to move.' Before Weymss could respond, a lift-boy handed him a telegram from Churchill's Naval Secretary, Admiral Horace Hood: 'Return immediately.' With no cash to hand, Weymss rushed out into the night in search of a money changer. By 3.00 pm Weymss, with his wife and child, was on a train for Calais.[31]

For Commander Kenneth Dewar the approaching war put an end to his plans for his honeymoon. He had married Gertrude Stapleton-Bretherton on July 28. Not only did the war disrupt Dewar's marriage but it was to bring further complications to his family: his wife's sister, Princess Blücher, was to spend the war in Berlin. Blücher would suffer greatly from the food shortages created by men like Dewar in the line of duty. (She will have much to say in her diary later in this book.) Four days after his marriage, Commander Dewar was on his way to Portsmouth, where the Second Fleet was assembling. By the time that he boarded the pre-dreadnought battleship HMS *Prince of Wales*, the crew were well advanced in dumping all superfluous material in anticipation of imminent battle. Although Dewar was not to face the enemy's guns, he would soon be engaged in one of the most critical tasks of the war: guarding the passage of the British Expeditionary Force (BEF) to France against U-boat attacks.

In the midst of these fevered preparations, Churchill had second thoughts about retaining the 61 year-old Callaghan as Commander-in-Chief of the Grand Fleet in a war command. He was summarily removed, being replaced by Admiral John Jellicoe.

At Plymouth, Scrimgeour, freshly out of Dartmouth Naval College, was getting to know his first ship. HMS *Crescent* would never threaten Tirpitz's guns, but, within a few days, it would be on the front line enforcing the shipping blockade in the far north. 'Hope war will be declared soon,' Scrimgeour wrote in his diary on August 2.[32]

WAR

The reality of the impending catastrophe came late on the evening of 3 August when the politicians Lord Beaverbrook, Lloyd George, Bonar Law and Lord Birkenhead paid a visit to Churchill at Admiralty House in London. They found Churchill calmly chatting with some friends. He suggested a game of bridge. The cards were dealt and the game began, but the players were soon interrupted by a messenger bearing a large box, which he presented to Churchill. He took a key from his pocket and opened the box to reveal a single sheet of paper. After reading its brief message, Churchill turned to his visitors and said, 'Germany has declared war against Russia.'[33] All those present knew that this meant war for Britain, too. Churchill passed his cards to Beaverbrook, rang for a servant, and departed. A few hours later he had mobilized the navy.

On the following day, Britain formally declared war on Germany. The King published his message to the new Commander-in-Chief of the Grand Fleet, expressing: 'the assurance of my confidence that under your direction they will revive and renew the old glories of the Royal Navy'.[34] (As Prince George, the King had served in the navy from 1877 to 1892.)

A wild gamble

The sudden arrival of war found people far from their native lands, and ships far from their home ports. The German liner SS *Kronprinzessin Cecilie* had sailed out of New York and was on the high seas when Captain Charles Polack heard that his country was at war with Britain. His 19,000-ton ship was a big enough prize for the Royal Navy to make huge efforts to track him down. Added to the valuable vessel, it was carrying 1216 passengers, over ten million dollars in gold and three million dollars in silver. He ordered lights out and canvas covers for the portholes as the ship veered 180 degrees to return to America. On arrival, he was ordered to dock at Bar Harbor in Maine, from where the passengers had to take a 300-mile train journey to return to New York. The *Kronprinzessin Cecilie*'s hasty retreat from the high seas showed how weak the German navy was in the waters that mattered for a country with imperial ambitions.

Winston Churchill at his desk with Admiral of the Fleet Lord Fisher in the Admiralty. Churchill dismissed the U-boat as a threat to merchant shipping while his First Lord viewed the boats with great alarm. (Illustrated London News)

On the pre-dreadnought battleship HMS *Prince of Wales* coaling was in progress when the call to war came. A bugle sounded 'still' on the busy ship. Every man froze at his task as the ship fell silent and the shrill whines of the winches died. The bosun's awesome words passed from man to man around the ship: 'Hostilities will commence against Germany at midnight.'[35] Over 700 men burst into loud cheering. As the uproar died away, the winches returned to their squealing, while the repeated thuds of coal bags falling on the deck reminded the men that they were earnestly preparing for war.

Although the officers and men in the British warships were enthralled by the excitement of war, many feared that they would never see action in what they assumed would be a short conflict. Wemyss was one of many half-pay officers who were delighted to have a command, but who had no expectation that their return to active service would last. Indeed, just as Wemyss was leaving the Admiralty, the retired Admiral Sir Reginald Custance warned him: 'These things are generally over in a few months.'[36]

Young Scrimgeour was equally sure that the war would be over in weeks. In his haste to join HMS *Crescent* he had left almost all his clothes in a trunk which he had deposited at the naval outfitter Gieve & Co. By mid-September he would be urgently asking his mother to retrieve 'one pair sea-boots (important)' as well as 'half-a-dozen shirts and handkerchiefs'.[37] And, perhaps foreseeing the winter to come, he asked her to knit him a scarf and gloves.

Earlier that day Maurice Hankey, Secretary of the Committee of Imperial Defence, had observed the naïve reaction of the public to the disaster that had befallen their nation. As he left Whitehall and walked through St James's Park to his hotel, he mused on the magnitude of the hour. After years of tireless preparation for this moment he felt assured that all that had to be done to defend the island had been done. But his mood was sombre as he threaded his way slowly through the excited crowds in Whitehall and the Mall. Arm-in-arm in their thousands, they sang jingoistic songs as they danced their innocent way towards Armageddon.

Late that night in the Admiralty, staff were despatching hundreds of telegrams to recall officers, requisition ships and put bases and units onto a war-footing. At the same time, the niceties of Britain's unwritten constitution had to be observed: the Lords Commissioners of the Admiralty petitioned the King for permission to call the men to active service.

A VULNERABLE NATION

Neither Germany nor Britain had reason to be sanguine about the coming naval war. Germany had neither land forces strong enough to win a decisive war in weeks, as foreseen by von Schlieffen, nor a navy strong enough to drive Britain's Grand Fleet from the oceans. Wilhelm would soon find that, with his army confined to muddy trenches and his navy holed-up in port, he had no choice but to fall back on an unplanned submarine war.

Britain's weakness lay in being an island nation which was massively dependent on imported food and raw materials. This made the country particularly vulnerable to attacks on its merchant shipping. Whatever the fate of the BEF in France, the war could only be lost at sea. And that was all too likely. As we have seen, the British Admiralty had made no preparation for a U-boat war, placing its faith in Germany not turning its boats onto the merchant ships. In these circumstances we have to ask: 'How did Germany manage to lose the U-boat war?'

3
In search of a role

Early August 1914

'The days of the dreadnought are numbered.' – ex-Prime Minister Arthur Balfour, 1913.[38]

ENOUGH FOR PEACE – TOO LITTLE FOR WAR

As the BEF prepared for war in Flanders, Britain's 10,123 merchant vessels of over 100 tons, totalling 20½ million gross tons, prepared for war at sea. These ships exactly matched Britain's peacetime needs. Over the next four years they would additionally have to transport 33 million troops, nurses, refugees and prisoners; 2.4 million horses and mules; and 554 thousand vehicles. Britain could not spare a single ship to the deep.

A BRUTAL START

With the ink of the signatures on the war declarations barely dry, minelayers of the German navy sortied into the North Sea to begin Germany's naval war. In the deep of the night they began sowing vast numbers of mines off the Thames Estuary. Germany was to turn the waters of the British trade routes into a graveyard for the thousands of merchant vessels that ran in and out of the London docks. But Britain's first sea casualty was not to be a merchant vessel.

The scout cruiser HMS *Amphion* had been in commission for under two years when it set out with a flotilla of destroyers to search for German minelayers in the area between Harwich and the Dutch island of Terschelling. It was not long before a trawler reported sighting a ship acting suspiciously as it threw overboard what appeared to be mines. Even more suspicious was the ship's livery: the yellow and black of the Great Eastern Railway's ferries. But what the Germans saw as a clever disguise was, to the British, an obvious cover for some nefarious activity. Captain Cecil H Fox in *Amphion* gave the order to chase the interloper with all possible speed.

The mines had been laid by the SS *Königin Luise*, a converted German ferry. It had finished its night's work by the time the chase began. In the lead were the destroyers HMSs *Lance* and *Landrail*. With the *Königin Luise* within range they began firing, but their guns failed to halt the fleeing ship. It seemed that the enemy would soon gain the safety of German waters. When *Amphion* reached the battleground, Fox ordered 'open fire' at 7200 yards. The first three salvos fell short. Fox raised the range to 7900 yards and was rewarded with the sight of *Königin Luise*'s foremast disintegrating. Up to this point *Amphion*'s gunners had calmly followed Fox's commands. Now success went to their heads as they fired as fast as their guns and keen training permitted. Fox calmed his excited men. Sights were corrected and he ordered three rounds of rapid independent firing. In his battle report Fox claimed that two out of three shots hit their target 'beautifully'. This was despite the difficult angle of fire since neither the *Amphion* nor the destroyers could directly follow the *Königin Luise* for fear of the mines that it might have left in its wake. The damaged minelayer was still under way and it was twenty minutes before its engines stopped, at which point its captain ordered it to be scuttled. The men on the *Amphion* burst out cheering at the first sinking of the war. Fox reprimanded his enthusiastic sailors and ordered them to stay alert. He was right to be wary. Their mission was far from over.

On the following day, August 6, Fox was still at sea, searching for more minelayers. His men were in high spirits as the day's work began. Knowing that the *Königin Luise,* had dropped all its mines on the previous day, Fox proceeded with caution, taking a route seven nautical miles to the west of where he thought the mines had been laid.

At 6.35 am, with many of Fox's men still at their breakfasts, *Amphion* was rocked by a tremendous explosion under its bridge. *Königin Luise* had had its revenge. *Amphion*'s keel broke. The destroyer HMS *Linnet* moved in to effect a tow, but, before a line was in place, *Amphion*'s forward magazine exploded. It was every man for himself as the sea poured through the massive holes in the shattered hull.

The official report on the sinking noted that 'with the same composure that had marked their behaviour throughout. All was done without hurry or confusion, and twenty minutes after the mine had struck, the men, officers, and captain left the ship.'[39]

One officer and 131 ratings were killed by the explosions. In addition, around 20 German prisoners from the *Königin Luise*, who were breakfasting in the mess, died alongside the British seamen. Fox, 16 officers and 135 ratings were rescued. With the deaths being amongst the first in the war, the newspapers took a special interest in the men's stories. One survivor said, 'I have been spared a most terrible death. It is the nearest I have been to the end, and the experience will last me a lifetime.' Another recalled: 'It is too terrible to relate.' And a third remarked: 'I cannot say whether I shall go to sea again, but if they stand in need of my poor services, I am quite ready to go, and, if necessary, go altogether, for it is for the King, Country, Home and Loved Ones that everyone is fighting for.'[40] This was no brash boast: on land and at sea, survivors would be brought safely home, only to return to the battle lines as soon as they were fit to do so. On both sides, life was cheap and heroism brought neither relief nor rewards.

> **THE KING AND THE DISASTER.**
>
> **His Majesty Profoundly Grieved.**
>
> The Press Association says—The King was profoundly grieved to hear of the disaster to the Amphion. He is displaying the deepest interest in all the details of and preparations for the war, and the latest official despatches are promptly and regularly transmitted to his Majesty.
>
> Yesterday evening the King held another Privy Council which was concerned with the issue of further Royal Proclamations contingent on the state of war and following upon the Proclamations already issued.

With no troops yet in France, the sinking of HMS Amphion was the lead war news.

For Captain Fox, there was a little glory. His triumph in sinking *Königin Luise* stood out at a time when there was little significant action on land or sea. This led him to being selected to be one of 144 people of note to appear on the commemorative stamps issued by the Lord Roberts Memorial Fund. He appeared on sheet number three along with Lloyd George, Winston Churchill and Vice Admiral Beatty. In addition to selling the stamps (which were not legal for postage) collectors could buy special stamp albums. These ranged from 'Red cloth' at 1 s 6 d to 'Royal blue and gold' at 5 s 0 d.[41]

The Admiralty took *Amphion*'s sinking calmly – perhaps too calmly. On the following day, Churchill told the Commons: 'The Admiralty are not at all alarmed or disconcerted by such an incident. We have expected a certain number, and we continue to expect a certain number of such incidents.'[42] This was surely a failure to recognize the significance of the *Amphion* episode. The scout cruiser's sinking revealed the true nature of the changed world of naval warfare. The *Königin Luise* had laid its mines as close as possible to the British shore. From now on, the North Sea was to be the site of four relentless years of hour after hour, day after day patrolling and minesweeping.

Blockade

Britain had dominated the world's seas since the Napoleonic wars when it successfully blockaded the key French ports. Now, Britain was to use blockade to choke off Germany's imports of raw materials, manufactured goods, oil. It was to be the biggest blockade in history.

This blockade would be complicated by its dubious legality. In theory, the uncertainties of contraband law had been resolved by the 1909 *Declaration of London*. Almost all the powers that would be drawn into the war had signed the treaty, including Austria-Hungary, France, Germany, Great Britain, and the United States. But, having signed, not one nation had ratified the treaty. Was it valid or not?

If valid, the treaty meant that Britain would be unable to interfere with neutral ships trading with Germany, except when carrying contraband of war. Such leniency was unthinkable for Britain. It would mean compelling Royal Navy ships to stand by as hundreds of neutral ships made their way to German ports, carrying raw materials, food and manufactured goods.

Nevertheless, Britain initially broadly accepted the contraband categories in the treaty. Absolute contraband covered items which were exclusively for war use, such as weapons and ammunition. Conditional contraband referred to items that could be used in peaceful or warlike manner, including fuel and animal fodder. The third category, free goods, included all raw materials. Maurice Hankey called this list 'most disastrous' from Britain's point of view.[43] That hardly mattered, though. As the war progressed, Britain abandoned any attempt to abide by the *Declaration* as it developed its own contraband listings. Item after item was added until Britain took the momentous step of including food as contraband.

The British blockade was to prove an effective instrument of war: a study by Professor Albrecht Ritschl found that the Allied blockade of

German trade was more damaging to the Germany economy than the U-boat campaign was to the British economy. German output fell by around 60-70 per cent during the war and the German economy shrank by 27 per cent. By contrast, the British economy *grew* by seven per cent during the war.

German openings

In the first days of the war, 750,000 German soldiers crossed into the small neutral country of Belgium. With such numbers, no one could doubt that Germany was intent on a scale of land warfare not seen since the times of Napoleon.

By contrast, the German U-boat fleet was nonsensically small. Britain possessed 77 submarines in August 1914. France had a respectable 60. Germany had a mere 28. All were obsolete, except for the ten most recently built boats (*U-19* to *U-28*). There were five additional boats under construction on the day that war broke out, although the arms manufacturer Krupp was busy selling them to the Greek navy. It was clear that the Imperial Navy had no understanding of the potential of submarines to destroy Britain's capacity to wage war.

This lack of understanding was the saving of the BEF as its first contingents began the hazardous Channel crossing on August 9. The lookouts on the troopships and their escorting destroyers scanned the seas for tell-tale signs of periscopes and the deadly silver streaks of approaching torpedoes. Yet not a single German vessel lay above or below the waters to the east of the BEF's passage. This would have been the perfect moment for the Kaiser's Imperial Navy to justify the millions of Marks spent on its construction. If capital ships were to be lost in any cause, no cause would be greater than frustrating British troops landing in France. Instead, Germany gave safe passage to four infantry divisions and one cavalry division, including their horses, guns and vehicles. The last of 120,000 troops reached France on August 22.

Amongst all the nervous onlookers at the passage of the BEF, none matched the vigilance of Rear Admiral Tyrwhitt with the destroyers of his Harwich Force, and of Commodore Roger Keyes with his Eighth Submarine Flotilla. As day followed day without a whisper of a German attack, their anxiety grew. On August 12, Churchill warned Jellicoe that '[the] extraordinary silence and inertia of the enemy may be a prelude to serious enterprises' and ordered him to bring parts of his fleet further south. Yet, Churchill later recalled, 'Not a ship was sunk, not a man was drowned'.[44] It was Germany's first strategic error. (See Appendix 1 for a summary of the strategic errors of the two sides in the U-boat war.)

On that same day, Britain declared war on Austria-Hungary, creating a combined enemy known as the Central Powers.

First Prizes of the War

While German forces held back in the Channel, in the far North Sea British patrols were engaging in the unglamorous game of blockading. It was the antithesis of Britannia ruling the waves in the spirit of Trafalgar, as the newly promoted Acting Sub-Lieutenant Oram found at Scapa Flow on the second day of the war. He was at gunnery practice in the dreadnought battleship HMS *Thunderer* when a German fishing vessel came into view. Oram, 'feeling self-consciously warlike with revolver in hand', took charge of the ship's cutter as it sped out to intercept the vessel.[45] The terrified fishermen in their pitiful craft shrank from the approach of the aggressive young officer. They knew nothing of the war and had limited English, as Oram found when he tried to explain that they had to gather their belongings and board the cutter to be escorted to *Thunderer*. With the fishermen and a good part of their catch on the warship, the fishing boat was taken in tow. As the captives sailed to internment, *Thunderer*'s gunners shredded their boat in a rare chance of target practice on an 'enemy' vessel. It wasn't heroic. It was hardly war. But this was how it was to be during four years of Britain's ruthless blockade of Germany.

A Warning from America

Two days after the major belligerents had begun hostilities in Belgium, Britain received notice that its dominance of the seas was to be contested by a third party: the United States of America. Secretary of State William Bryan had instructed Ambassador Walter Page in London to find out whether Britain would abide by 'the laws of naval warfare' as set out in the 1909 *Declaration of London*. An acceptance of these laws 'would prevent grave misunderstandings'.[46]

Eyre Crowe, an assistant under-secretary at the Foreign Office, replied on August 22 to say that Britain would abide by the *Declaration of London* 'subject to certain modifications and additions'.[47] These changes referred to goods that Britain was determined to treat as contraband. This was Britain's early warning to America that it would stretch and stretch the meaning of the word 'contraband'. It was not what the free-traders in America wished to hear.

(Crowe was another man for whom the war would test strained loyalties. He had been born and brought up in Germany, with German as his first language. Additionally, his wife's uncle was Henning von Holtzendorff – the Chief of the German Naval Staff.)

AN ABORTIVE RAID

The U-boats continued to hold back in the Channel because of the difficulty of distinguishing between legitimate war targets and innocent cargo vessels. (It would be months before the war-winning potential of sinking merchant vessels was recognized.) Meanwhile, the Imperial Navy's search for a role made a false start with a mass sortie. The sortie's target was to be the ships of the Grand Fleet. Perhaps fearing a short war, the Imperial Navy invested a high proportion of its U-boat service in this experimental operation: nine U-boats (a third of the force). With Scapa Flow being 500 miles from the U-boat bases, this was a bold move for craft that had been previously confined to coastal waters.

The nine boats slipped their Heligoland moorings at dawn on August 6 for their first hostile operation of the war. Johannes Spiess, second-in-command in *U-9*, recalled that, when the escort of torpedo boats pulled back, 'For the first time in the war we were absolutely alone on the high seas.'[48] The boats were still rather primitive and the men had yet to learn the difficult art of crash-diving under war conditions.

On August 8, just as the submariners were acclimatizing themselves to the demands of the battlefield, *U-9*'s engines began to malfunction. Kapitänleutnant Otto Weddigen reluctantly ordered a return to base. But *U-9*'s abortive passage had not been without value. The Imperial Navy had learned an important lesson: at no point had *U-9* found a single target. As Spiess noted: 'You need to sail a submarine under war conditions to understand how large the North Sea is, given how small it looks.'[49] As to *U-9*, it was soon back at sea and was to sink 14 merchant vessels and 4 warships, totalling 53,000 tons. It survived the war, to be broken up by the British at Morecambe in 1919.

A second U-boat on the sortie, *U-13*, disappeared without trace. It is possible that it was sunk by one of the vast number of mines that German ships had deposited in the southern waters of the North Sea. With it went Kapitänleutnant Hans von Schweinitz, who had only begun his career as a commander on August 1, along with 24 other officers and men.

The remaining seven boats proceeded northwards. Only one is known to have made contact with British warships: *U-15*. When Kapitänleutnant Richard Pohle reached the waters surrounding Scapa Flow he could not have wished for a better opportunity to prove the power of his war machine. As his periscope went up, he found three dreadnought battleships exercising at sea: HMSs *Ajax*, *Monarch* and *Orion*. Pohle tracked the warships throughout the night, but the best he was able to do was to fire one torpedo (which missed) at *Monarch*.

At some point after the failed attack on *Monarch*, *U-15*'s engines broke down. It was in this condition that HMS *Birmingham* found the boat in the swell off Fair Isle in heavy fog at 4.00 am on August 9. Hearing hammering noises coming from inside the boat, Captain Arthur Duff (later Admiral Sir Arthur) concluded that urgent repairs were under way. He ordered his guns to open fire. The salvo of six shots missed the U-boat, which responded by an attempt to crash dive. Luck was now on Duff's side. He knew that ramming was his only chance of sinking Pohle's boat – there were no depth charges at this stage of the war – but *Birmingham* was ill-positioned for an attack. The U-boat would surely be far below by the time Duff had hauled round *Birmingham*'s 5400 tons of steel. Nevertheless, he ordered full speed with the helm hard over. *Birmingham* turned as all eyes were on the disappearing prey. Pohle's men must have cursed the slowness of their dive as *Birmingham* smashed into their unresponsive boat, slicing it in two. It was the first U-boat sinking of the war. Not one man survived. This proved to be a prescient sinking: around ten per cent of U-boat sinkings would be by means of ramming – the oldest and crudest method of attack in naval warfare.

Tirpitz's fruitless grand sortie bade ill for the future of his U-boats. Despite British warships being out in the North Sea, only *U-15* had found a target (or, rather, three targets) and not one of these was even damaged. Two boats failed to return. These were replaceable but losing trained men to no purpose was a serious matter in war. Forty-eight seamen and two commanders with 13 years' service (Pohle) and 12 years' (von Schweinitz) were gone. Replacing seamen took 6-12 months. Replacing good commanders took years.

But the sortie was not a total failure since the U-boat service learnt some useful lessons. Of these, the most important was the fact that the boats had reached the battleground, 500 miles from their bases. The previous assumption that the U-boats were too frail to operate on the high seas had been proved wrong. As Scheer put it, 'from being merely a coastal defence machine, as was originally planned, [the submarine] became the most effective long-range weapon'.[50]

Scapa Flow – a challenge too far for the U-boats.

And yet, what was the value of this sea-endurance if no sinkings were to result? It was this negative result that most influenced the U-boat service. This early mass sortie was to be the first and last of the war. Within a week of the attack, von Ingenohl had redefined the Imperial Navy's role: 'Our immediate task is … to cause our enemy losses by all the methods of guerrilla warfare and at every point where we can find him, so that we can thus compel him to join battle with us.'[51]

This decision to use the U-boats to harass and reduce the Grand Fleet was a strategic error. The Grand Fleet was relatively harmless: it couldn't attack Germany's huge armies on land. Its primary function was to sink the High Seas Fleet. If the latter stayed in harbour, the Grand Fleet was deprived of its purpose. From the outset, the Imperial Navy should have focused on Britain's greatest strategic weakness: its dependence on imported food and raw materials. Defeating Britain's armies in Flanders did not guarantee Britain's surrender. Sinking a good proportion of Britain's merchant fleet was an absolute guarantee of surrender.

How long would it be before Germany turned this British vulnerability to its advantage?

4
Land war turns to sea war

Mid-August to mid-September 1914

'I don't think it is even faintly realised the immense, impending revolution which the submarines will effect as offensive weapons of war.' – Admiral Lord Fisher, April 10, 1904.[52]

Target: Minelayers

With the U-boats in suspense for lack of warship targets, the British Admiralty's immediate concern was mines. These were to sink around 300 ships in the various navies during the First World War. Of the estimated 235,000 sea mines laid, 190,000 were placed in the North Sea and the Dover Strait.

Sinking minelayers was an urgent necessity. This was no easy task since mines were laid at night, sometimes by U-boats, sometimes by surface vessels. Given that it was exceedingly difficult to catch minelayers in action, Commodore Roger Keyes conceived of a method of catching them and their accompanying destroyers as they returned to their bases at dawn.

The idea had come to Keyes in August after studying the patrols of his submarines in the Heligoland Bight area. He observed that the Imperial Navy was sending out destroyers on a strict timetable, with the patrol coming out at around 5.00-6.00 pm and returning to base at daylight. He suggested that British light cruisers could attack the German destroyers as the latter made their return. There would be enough daylight for a swift battle before the British ships would need to withdraw – the proposed battleground was frighteningly close to the German coastline. Even so, Keyes reckoned that, by the time that any large German ships had been sent out to support the embattled destroyers, the British cruisers would be safely away. Churchill enthused at the plan, which he called 'simple and daring'.[53]

The details of the raid were soon settled. Commander Tyrwhitt would lead two flotillas of his Harwich destroyers along with nine submarines. Three of the submarines were to hover as bait, while the other vessels were to keep well out of sight. When the German destroyers approached the bait, the full British contingent would sweep from east to west across the Bight taking what prey they could.

German mines ready for laying by a U-boat.

Although pleased with their plan, Keyes and Tyrwhitt had second thoughts on the risk of attacking so near to the German coast. They asked the Chief of Staff, Vice Admiral Sir Frederick Sturdee, for the support of the First Light Cruiser Squadron, plus the precaution of bringing the Grand Fleet south, just before the raid. When Sturdee declined this request, Keyes and Tyrwhitt protested to Churchill, who refused to overturn Sturdee's decision. It seemed that the two commanders were to undertake the raid against their belated second thoughts. It was their good fortune that Jellicoe, at Scapa Flow, heard of the plan. (He was not officially informed; the Admiralty were parsimonious in their communications with him.) He immediately saw the folly of the operation as planned and ordered Rear-Admiral David Beatty and his battle cruiser squadron, plus Captain William Goodenough with his light cruisers, to act in support. Jellicoe's intervention was to prove crucial.

The Battle of Heligoland Bight was the Royal Navy's first battle in which massive steel ships moved at high speeds while firing huge guns at long ranges in waters infested with submarines. *And*, because it was the first battle in the age of wireless, it was, to its detriment, to be the first naval battle with multiple command posts. Planned in London, Harwich and at Scapa Flow, different commanders had different understandings of the proposed action.

As the ships put to sea, the various commanders had no idea of the jealousies that were behind the chaotic planning. Jellicoe, who resented Sturdee trying to stop him sending his ships to sea, never told the Admiralty that he was dispatching Beatty and Goodenough. Beatty was given no instructions as to his role. And Tyrwhitt and Keyes never received the signal informing them of the Grand Fleet's participation.

On top of all these complications, Keyes, ever over-confident and inclined to arrogance, decided to proceed in his new flagship, the light cruiser HMS *Arethusa*, despite it not having finished its trials. Only in battle did he find how inexperienced his crew were, and that the 4-inch guns had a habit of jamming.

Rear Admiral Roger Keyes in 1917. He made a bad start, but later mastered the art of anti-submarine warfare.

A detailed account of the battle is hardly needed to illustrate the highs and lows of the first naval battle of the war. Tyrwhitt successfully found a group of German destroyers shortly after 7.00 am and began his attack. Two destroyers were put out of action, but the exchange alerted the Imperial Navy to the presence of British ships. Soon, enemy light cruisers were on their way to the scene. As Tyrwhitt was chasing the German destroyers, he found the cruisers SMSs *Stettin* and *Frauenlob* blocking his path.

The arrival of the German cruisers so early in the action put the British ships in difficulties. Tyrwhitt, by now aware of Beatty's hovering presence, radioed for his urgent assistance. It took Beatty just over an hour to arrive on the scene, where his powerful battlecruisers outgunned the German ships, sinking the SMSs *Mainz, Cöln*, and *Ariadne*. Additionally, three more German cruisers were damaged. After five hours of chases, turns, mistaken enemy ships and muddles, the big German ships were nearing the battleground. Beatty ordered the confused British ships to retire.

No one will ever know how close Tyrwhitt and Keyes came to firing on Goodenough's and Beatty's ships. Had they done so, they could hardly have been blamed for what would have been an almighty Admiralty blunder.

The battle was a British triumph, with three German light cruisers sunk and a fourth severely damaged. German losses were 712 men (one being a rear admiral) along with 336 prisoners in British hands. On the British side there were just 35 men killed. Beatty's ships had also successfully held off three U-boats which had attacked his ships at 11.00 am: 'The attack was frustrated by rapid manoeuvring and the four destroyers were ordered to attack them [the U-boats].' Beatty added, 'the smoothness of the sea made their detection comparatively easy'.[54] This was not a surprising result. U-boats could sink stationary or near stationary warships, but in a fast moving battle they were too slow to catch the large ships.

Von Tirpitz described the day as 'fateful, both in its after-effects and incidental results, for the work of our navy'. Kaiser Wilhelm was shocked at the losses. Without informing Tirpitz, he summoned Pohl and told him that ship losses were to be avoided. In future, he would personally authorize 'fleet sallies and any greater undertakings'. Tirpitz dubbed this a 'muzzling policy'.[55] As Churchill recalled in his *The World Crisis 1914-1918*: 'Except for furtive movements by individual submarines and minelayers not a dog stirred from August till November.'[56] Captain Herbert Chatterton concluded: 'The High Seas Fleet never got over the shock which it received at the Battle of Heligoland.'[57]

For the British, the battle was a welcome – and misleading – early success in the war. *The Times* called it 'a brilliantly successful engagement', which was 'evidence that the spirit of the old Navy still inspires our seamen'.[58] Beatty, though, showed no interest in the lessons to be learned from the engagement. Instead, in his typical egotistical fashion, he complained to his wife that he had not 'received an expression of their appreciation from their Lordships'.[59] A better judgement than these came from Keyes, who dismissed the action as a 'small affair'. He could not understand why so much fuss was being made of it, especially when he thought of 'what a complete success it might have been' had he been given the cruisers that he had asked for.[60]

The big ship men: Tirpitz greets the Kaiser on his birthday.

At the end of the month another opportunity arose to obstruct German minelaying. It illustrated both progress and stagnation in anti-submarine warfare.

Scrimgeour in HMS *Crescent* had had a wearying day on August 31: firing practice had gone badly, the captain was in a grouchy mood, and Scrimgeour had had a row with one of the other officers over slack deck-work. Meanwhile, he was wearied by the tedious routine of boarding and inspecting Norwegian cargo ships. Then, at a stroke, excitement beckoned. An urgent signal warned of a planned German minelaying operation off the Scottish coast between Pentland Firth and Rathsay

The land war turns to sea war

Head. (This warning was the result of one of the earliest wireless intercepts from Admiralty intelligence work, based on the newly-installed coastal listening stations.)

HMS *Crescent* joined other vessels in a night search for the minelayers and their escorts. Scrimgeour was energized by his anticipation of a thrilling night battle, running down unsuspecting enemy vessels as they dropped their payloads into the North Sea. Finally, at 4.00 am, reports came of three unidentified vessels. Scrimgeour's anticipation rose, but the shadows in the dark proved to be dreadnoughts from the Fifth Battle Squadron. It was daylight when the searchers finally found some of the German destroyers that had accompanied the minelayers. The scout cruiser HMS *Boadicea* led the chase but, even with its 25 knots, it was outrun. Scrimgeour in the slower *Crescent* had been deprived of the chance to satisfy his lust for some action more exciting than blockade boarding. Writing that day to his mother, he described his disappointment: 'all [in *Crescent*] wish that the "Grosse Deutsche Hoch-See Flotte" could be induced to come out and fight, instead of indulging in the glorious pursuit of sinking harmless neutral merchant and fishing vessels by mines'.[61] His wish came true on May 31, 1916, when the fleets met at the Battle of Jutland. Scrimgeour was among the 1026 officers and men who went down with the inappropriately named HMS *Invincible*.

A REDUNDANT FLEET

Both Rear Admirals Wemyss and Beatty were convinced that the High Seas Fleet would not be returning to the North Sea in force. As Wemyss, in command of the Twelfth Cruiser Squadron in the Channel Fleet, told his wife: 'Their game is surely to lie locked up in their harbours ... [and to] catch us unawares ... it will probably mean their ruin in the long run.'[62] Beatty, in the First Battlecruiser Squadron, came to a similar conclusion a week later, telling his wife: 'I fear the rascals will never come out.' He was itching for a decisive Trafalgar-style battle but the thought that the German ships might never come was 'more than I can bear'.[63]

Both were right in their predictions. Apart from the Battle of Jutland in mid-1916, the German fleet largely remained at its moorings. Meanwhile, the Imperial Navy took to minor U-boat attacks and sowing minefields. Additionally, it mounted surface craft hit-and-run raids on east coast towns such as Scarborough. Wilhelm was indifferent to his fleet's inaction. While he tracked every trench gained or lost on the battlefields, for him the surface fleet was more decorative than functional. As Vice Admiral Sir Peter Gretton has suggested: 'The Emperor, and the Chancellor, saw the Fleet as a valuable bargaining counter at the peace conference.'[64]

BIG SHIP VULNERABILITY

In the midst of this inactivity, one commander was to show that there was still some life in the U-boats.

With nothing significant sunk since the *Amphion* on August 6, the U-boats had been left to wander in the North Sea in the hope of finding a target of some consequence. *U-21*'s wanderings were to succeed.

The boat was commanded by Oberleutnant zur See Otto Hersing. At 29 years-old, and with a naval career dating back to 1903, Hersing was to be one of the 37 U-boat commanders to sink more than 100,000 tons during the war. (He reached 114,000 tons.) His boat was also a star performer. Launched in 1913, it was still afloat at the Armistice, meeting an ironic end as it sank in an accident *en route* to internment in 1919.

Hersing was on his second patrol of the war, out in the North Sea between Norway and Scotland. (He had already made an audacious attempt to sail up the Firth of Forth to attack the fleet base, but had turned back for lack of targets.) Now back out in the North Sea, Hersing spotted the 2900-ton scout cruiser HMS *Pathfinder*.

Hersing's attack was aided by the coal shortage in the Royal Navy at that time. With near empty bunkers, *Pathfinder* was proceeding at 5 knots. (Its top speed was 25 knots.) This was a suicidal pace for a warship in an area where U-boats were known to be active. The fatal moment came off St Abb's Head in Berwickshire on the afternoon of September 5. When Hersing had first located *Pathfinder* it was in the company of some destroyers. Later, the destroyers peeled off, leaving the great ship to patrol alone. Hersing could hardly fail in his attack. Indeed, so confident was he, that he decided to fire just one torpedo.

On board *Pathfinder* the lookouts spotted the torpedo's wake at 3.45 pm, coming straight for the ship's starboard bow. Officer of the Watch Lieutenant-Commander Ernest Favell had joined the navy in 1900 as a fifteen-year-old. His service record described him as 'zealous', 'capable', 'hardworking' and 'very trustworthy'.[65] He was now in his fifth ship. All this counted for little in the face of undersea warfare. As soon as Favell heard the lookouts' shout of 'Torpedo on starboard bow!' he ordered full-astern on the starboard engine and full-ahead on the port. The wheel came hard over as *Pathfinder* tried to evade its approaching fate. The ship's miserly 5 knots gave it little chance. At 3.50 pm the torpedo slammed into *Pathfinder*'s midships and exploded under the bridge. Favell, directly above, would have had no chance of survival.

Captain Francis Martin-Peake could see that there was no time to lower the boats. He pleaded with his men to abandon ship, shouting: 'Jump you devils jump!'[66] To gain their attention he ordered the firing of the stern gun. Unknown to Martin-Peake, its king-pin had been damaged in the attack. As soon as the charge detonated, the gun was torn from its mountings and tumbled down over the quarterdeck to fall into the sea, taking the gun crew with it.

Oberleutnant zur See Otto Hersing – the first U-boat commander to sink a warship.

Then came a second explosion when the cordite in the forward magazine went up. *Pathfinder* was torn in two as it plunged under the waves, taking down 259 men. Martin-Peake and his secretary had stayed on the bridge throughout the attack. They both survived. Staff Surgeon Thomas Smyth had a lucky escape. After sliding across the sloping deck he found himself 'jammed beneath a gun'.[67] All his efforts to free himself failed. Then, as the ship sank under the waves, the rising water lifted him free. An hour-and-a-half later Smyth was plucked unconscious from the water by the crew of a reserve torpedo boat.

The land war turns to sea war

Pathfinder had been near to land when it went down, so its sinking was clearly visible from the shore. Aldous Huxley (the writer-to-be) was then a student at Oxford University and was amongst those who witnessed the scene from the shore. Writing to his father, he described 'a great white cloud with its foot in the sea' and the 'appalling accounts of the scene' as told by the crew of the St Abbs' lifeboat. 'There was not a piece of wood, they said, big enough to float a man.'[68]

U-21 has the dubious record of being the first submarine to sink a British warship. Robert Whitehead, inventor of the self-propelled torpedo, had demonstrated his first torpedo in 1866 and had been selling his weapon to various navies since 1868. Yet still, nearly 50 years later, no means of protecting warships against these weapons had been found.

A SUBMARINER IN THE MAKING

One minor incident in the early months of the war is of special note for its consequences in the Second World War. Lieutenant Commander Max Horton had already made himself known to the Service when his 1907 service record described him as '*good* at his boat and *bad* socially'.[69] In his long career he never overcame his abrasive manner, but nothing could detract from his brilliance as a commander. He had been present in *E-9* at the Battle of Heligoland Bight but had found no opportunity to fire his torpedoes. Now on patrol in the same area, he seemed equally destined to see no action. Then his luck changed.

On the night of September 12-13, *E-9* was sitting on the bed of the North Sea, six miles south-southwest of Heligoland, oblivious to life on the surface. At dawn, Horton ordered his boat to surface. When he had dived on the previous day, visibility had been poor. Now Horton could clearly see a 2000-ton German warship less than two miles distant. The SMS *Hela* was proceeding slowly, and its lookouts had failed to spot Horton's boat. With his two forward torpedoes readied, Horton took *E-9* down again and moved in, reducing the range to 600 yards. By 6.30 am *E-9* was perfectly positioned for attack. Horton bellowed 'Fire!' in his commanding voice. Then 'Dive!' Down went *E-9* as the crew held their breath. The sound of an explosion suggested success. Horton ordered the periscope up. Shots from an unidentified ship greeted the boat but, in the distance, Horton could see the *Hela* with a heavy starboard list. *Hela*'s crew were getting into the boats while other vessels were coming to their aid. Further shots from the unseen ship ended Horton's chance to make a more detailed assessment of *Hela*'s condition. He ordered a crash dive.

Later, when *E-9* surfaced, Horton could see no sign of the *Hela* nor any other vessel. (All but two of *Hela*'s crew had survived.) *E-9* was now in dangerous waters. It was time to go. Later, as *E-9* edged into Harwich, Horton raised the Jolly Roger – the navy's traditional way of announcing success in battle.

The Admiralty were delighted at Horton's success. *E-9* and the destroyers involved in the action were rewarded with a brass plate to record the sinking. Horton will return in our story, as he was to return in Britain's story when he became Commander-in-Chief, Western Approaches Command, on November 17, 1942. In that role he turned the Battle of the Atlantic from a looming catastrophe to an astounding rout of the infamous Atlantic U-boats, as I recount in my *Atlantic Nightmare*.

THE THIRST FOR ACTION

With the war about a month old and with so little action at sea, naval life was increasingly unrewarding. For most of the naval men, their war was dominated by watching. The ships at Scapa Flow rarely sortied now that U-boats had shown that the northern seas were within their range. Blockade patrols searched for merchant ships carrying contraband, directly or indirectly, to German ports. Anti-submarine patrols searched for U-boats. It was lonely and unrewarding work. Day after day, night after night, the same sea, the same horizon, the same lack of action. There was also the torment of thinking that the war was elsewhere.

Rear Admiral Rosslyn Wemyss, after only a few days at sea in the cruiser HMS *Charybdis* and on patrol in the Channel, was distraught at the thought that he was missing out on the real war: 'I feel rising within me sometimes a feeling of despair that I cannot be there to share it with them.' Just as hard to bear was the lack of news: 'It is rather awful being here and knowing nothing.'[70] On the following day Weymss correctly foresaw how the big ship war was to develop: 'It's weary, weary work waiting and waiting and I am much afraid the Germans don't mean to come out.'[71] He echoed what so many men on patrol would say throughout the war: 'My days are busy but monotonous.'[72]

Beatty was equally frustrated, writing to his wife: 'This waiting is the deuce ... For thirty years I have been waiting for this day ... Three weeks of war and [we] haven't seen the enemy.'[73] On the German side, Tirpitz had a similarly jaundiced opinion of the naval war, writing to a colleague: 'The navy has no success to record. If the fleet would only come into action, and no blunders were made, it would fight brilliantly.'[74]

It wasn't just the senior officers who were wearied by the waiting war. Scrimgeour's days were filled with stopping merchant ships to question masters and inspect cargoes, and, if necessary, escort suspect vessels to Kirkwall in the Orkneys or Lerwick in the Shetlands. He found it unutterably draining, as he told his mother on September 1: 'we are having a very trying time, as I have only been on shore for two hours since we left Portsmouth over a month ago, and we only get about five or six hours' rest in twenty-four hours'. He added: 'all the luxuries of life such as sugar and butter and bread are things of the past'.[75]

ENTER THE ENTRENCHING TOOL

Six weeks of war had left the North Sea as deserted as an end-of-pier pavilion on a wet winter's day. The two great fleets lay silent in their harbours. Germany's smaller craft were unwilling to risk raids. And the U-boats had near to withdrawn from the war. All that was about to change, thanks to the entrenching tool.

The war was just under three weeks old when Field Marshal Sir John French gave the order to pull back from the Battle of Mons on August 23. By First World War standards it had been a sideshow, lasting only one day and with fewer than 2000 British dead. But it marked the end of the Allied advance. Since that day, the German armies had driven the retreating French and British westwards towards the River Marne. And there the Allied forces had halted on September 6 to make a last stand. If they failed, Paris would be in German hands within a day or two. If they succeeded, there might still be a chance of winning the war.

Two days later, Helmuth von Moltke, Chief of the German General Staff, could see that the Battle on the River Marne was lost. Under the cover of continued defensive fighting, he began to peel off the first units. Two days later he gave the order to cease attacking. His 900,000 men, diminished by nearly 70,000 dead, began the demoralizing trek back over the land that they had so triumphantly conquered since the start of the war. The Schlieffen Plan had failed. There had been no great arc of encirclement. No trapping of French armies trying to escape westward. No massive surrenders.

Harassed by French and British forces, Moltke's soldiers marched east. He is reputed to have said to the Kaiser, 'Majesty, we have lost the war.'[76] He, at least, lost his post, to be replaced by Major General von Falkenhayn on September 14. Falkenhayn's first operation was the humiliating task of ordering his armies to halt on the north side of the

River Aisne and dig in. Soon the first troops had taken up defensive positions in shallow trenches on the Chemin des Dames ridge.

British troops, still in pursuit, were briefly halted by heavy shelling as they tried to cross the river. The war diary of the 1st Battalion Hampshire Regiment recorded on September 12: 'the enemy were entrenched about 1500 yds to our front'. Later that day, the diary continued, 'we began digging ourselves in' despite being under artillery fire. The rain came down relentlessly and there was no sign of any rations. The land war had failed. Mobile warfare was to be replaced by static stand-offs.

As the great armies skulked in trenches and peered at each other through periscopes, Germany was to turn to war at sea. All that Germany could call on was its two dozen U-boats. But how to use them? What were they to sink? When? Under what international rules? The sea war promised much. But the decision to move to U-boat combat would eventually be the undoing of the German war.

5
Warships under siege

Autumn 1914

'As the motor vehicle has driven the horse from the road, so has the submarine driven the battleship from the sea.' – Admiral Sir Percy Scott, June 5, 1914.[77]

THE LIVE BAIT SQUADRON

The unnatural reticence of the U-boats in the first seven weeks of the war came to an end with a formidable demonstration of their destructive power in late September. The result was a catastrophe that shook the British Admiralty and its commanders out of their nineteenth century complacency over the threat of underwater war.

In early September, Churchill had been indulging in one of his favourite wartime activities: getting as near to the Flanders battlefield as his host, Field Marshal Sir John French, would permit. On his return to London, he boarded a train to Scotland for a visit to the Grand Fleet at Scapa Flow. Amongst the party was Commodore Keyes, who told Churchill that three ill-protected Cressy-class cruisers of the Seventh Cruiser Squadron were patrolling in the Broad Fourteens off the Netherlands coast. (The Broad Fourteens are an area of shallow water just 14 fathoms deep.) For a month, Keyes told Churchill, he had been protesting at the stupidity of allowing these nine-knot cruisers to work so near to the U-boat bases. (The squadron had been established to 'keep the area south of the 54th parallel … clear of enemy torpedo craft and minelayers'.[78] There had been no mention of U-boats.) In this perilous state the ships had acquired the sobriquet of 'the live-bait squadron'. Churchill was horrified. On his return to the Admiralty the next day he ordered the removal of the cruisers. That was on September 18.

Kapitänleutnant Otto Weddigen in *U-9* had been at sea since August 1. Not having found a single target, he and his crew of 34 men were impatient to see some action. It was 6.00 am on September 22 – four days *after* Churchill had ordered the removal of the cruisers – when Weddigen first saw the 'live bait'. *U-9* was 18 miles off the Hook of Holland at the time of the sighting and was partly submerged, with five feet of periscope showing. 'Dive!'

Weddigen easily manoeuvred *U-9* into a firing position. At a depth of 12 feet, off went his first torpedo, aimed at the middle ship. An avalanche of water poured into *Aboukir*'s engine room, stopping the ship dead. The reverberations of the thunderous detonation were felt throughout *U-9*. (Weddigen assumed that one of *Aboukir*'s magazines had exploded, but some accounts don't support this.)

Since no one in *Aboukir* had seen *U-9*'s periscope, all on board assumed that the ship had struck a mine. No action was taken to locate an enemy submarine.

With one successful sinking accomplished, Weddigen took *U-9* down to periscope depth to survey the scene. He could see the two remaining cruisers rescuing men from *Aboukir*. On its deck some of the crew were standing, waiting for orders as the ship slipped into the sea. Weddigen had no time to linger in watching: two more targets, sitting motionless on the calm sea, awaited him. Their failure to disperse had left them in perfect positions for his attack: 'The English were playing my game,' he later said.

First, though, Weddigen's crew needed to place one of the two reserve torpedoes into a stern tube. This complex operation involved clearing everything out of the officers' quarters while the torpedo was manhandled through the boat. While the torpedo passed along the boat, cries of 'Everyone forward!' and 'Everyone back!' rang out as men ran up and down the boat to maintain its horizontal balance. At the same time, one of the navigators wrestled with the diving planes, trying to trim the oscillating boat. So hard was this work that he had to be relieved before the torpedo was in its firing tube.

Weddigen waited anxiously as he itched to take his next ship. 'Tube 1 recharged! Boat trimmed!'

Hogue was an easy target. It received two torpedoes and sank in ten minutes.

On board HMS *Cressy* the truth now dawned. This was no minefield. Close by – very close by – was a U-boat. And then, as if to gloat, *U-9* burst through the surface. In fact, *U-9* was in trouble. With two torpedoes gone, the reduced weight left the boat's buoyancy out of control. *Cressy*'s Captain Robert Johnson saw his chance. With his boats still out rescuing men from *Aboukir* he tried to ram *U-9* before Weddigen could regain control of his boat.

But *U-9* escaped the cheese-cutter of *Cressy*'s 12,000 tons of steel. Back down below, with the boat trimmed, Weddigen fired two torpedoes 'to make the strike doubly certain' but only one struck the cruiser. His shot hit a vital area: *Cressy*'s boilers exploded and the sea poured in. Ten minutes after Weddigen's torpedo had ripped into *Cressy*, the ship was gone, sinking 'with a loud sound, as if from a creature in pain'.

There had never been anything like this speed of destruction on the high seas in all the history of naval warfare. At first, Weddigen and Spiess were dumbfounded at what they had done. 'Weddigen and I watched ... with a sense of tragic horror ... For long minutes we were lost as if in some kind of a trance,' said Spiess.[79]

U-9 surfaced to find the sea strewn with wreckage and not a sign of the three great ships. Lifeboats were dotted around, picking up men. Survivors were still swimming towards boats. Some men were desperately clinging to pieces of wreckage. One survivor recalled: 'the sea was literally alive with men struggling and grasping for anything to save themselves'.[80]

Sixty officers and 777 men from the three Cressies were saved. Just under 1500 men died when the three cruisers went down. Amongst the dead, were two out of three brothers, serving on *Cressy*. The unnamed survivor stood on the deck with his brother Alfred as the ship was about to go down: '[We] shook hands and told each other that whoever was saved to tell our dear mother that our last thoughts were of her.'[81] They jumped into the sea, but the survivor never saw Alfred again. His other brother, Louis, went down with the ship.

Amongst the survivors was the 15 year-old Kit Wykeham Musgrave. He was in *Aboukir* when it was torpedoed. When he knew that the ship was going down, he jumped into the sea and desperately swam to escape being sucked down in the sinking. He reached the *Hogue* and was about to board it when it was torpedoed. Once more he swam for his life, now making for the *Cressy*. In turn, it was torpedoed, and Musgrave was back in the sea, clinging to a piece of driftwood before being rescued by a Dutch trawler.

Weddigen and Spiess had watched the horrendous scene under a 'radiantly beautiful sky'. Then the British destroyers approached, catching *U-9*'s crew relaxing from the stress of battle. *U-9*'s crash dive was clumsily executed. That night the boat sat at the bottom of the North Sea while, above them, horrifically injured men awaiting rescue gave their last breath and slipped below the surface.

The news of the sinking of three British warships so early in the war was greeted with wild enthusiasm in Germany. On his boat's return to base, Weddigen was awarded the Military Order of St Henry (Saxony) for bravery. Meanwhile, he and his men hid *U-9* in a remote mooring in an attempt to escape the crowds of sightseers. But their refuge offered Weddigen no protection from the flood of fan mail that arrived at his boat. Crouched over his miniscule shelf-table he sat, hour after hour, writing letters and dispatching autographs.

A German celebration of Otto Weddigen's sinking of the Cressies. His action showed how defenceless warships were in the presence of submarines. (Contemporary postcard)

While Weddigen's admirers extolled his audacity, the truth was that he had been the beneficiary of the British Admiralty's stupidity. As early as 1904 Fisher had warned that warships could no longer cruise in submarine-infested waters. No one listened. Repington repeated these warnings in 1910. Still no one listened. Instead, the Admiralty had waited for proof. It now lay in three improvised steel cemeteries on the floor of the cold North Sea. From here on, warships belonged at their protected moorings except when needed to chase the High Seas Fleet back into port. The North Sea was abandoned by the Admiralty. Its new emptiness was a silent testimony to the power of the torpedo.

The military significance of the loss of the three Cressies was trivial, but the effect on British morale was devastating. Prime Minister Asquith, writing to the socialite Venetia Stanley, described the news as 'the worst

... since the war began'.[82] Maurice Hankey recalled that these sinkings (along with two others in October and November) 'caused great heart searchings in the Cabinet'. He could not recall 'any events in this part of the war which caused such an atmosphere of depression'.[83]

The Times, though, was more realistic when it warned its readers: 'We must expect more occurrences of this character.'[84]

SAIL ALONE, SINK ALONE

The warships, though, were small in number compared to the thousands of merchant vessels that were at sea at any one time. The Admiralty had no means of protecting them. Instead, Admiralty House simply advised the masters to choose their own routes, since, they argued, set routes would provide easier prey for the U-boats. It was a 'sail alone, sink alone' policy.

A MISSED CHANCE

While wasting resources on pointless patrolling in search of U-boats, the Allies were ignoring a significant opportunity to frustrate the boats' activities: the Belgian ports – perfect bases for U-boat operations – were still in Allied hands. As the German armies marched inexorably across the Belgian fields towards the coast, the British took no steps to demolish the port facilities. Locks and cranes could have been destroyed and channels blocked. Instead, when the U-boat service moved in at the end of September, they took command of fully-functioning ports. Hundreds of U-boats would sally forth from these ports over the next four years.

LISTENING IN

Elsewhere, the Admiralty had taken prompt action to gain one advantage over the German naval forces. The Grade II listing of a humble brick and rendering building in Marley Close, Stockton-on-Tees, testifies to its once having been an Admiralty listening station. Stockton was the first of the Admiralty's Y-stations for collecting naval intelligence. In September 1914 the men and women inside were fiddling with tuning knobs as they searched the airwaves for signals to and from Imperial Navy ships and boats. The building has since been converted into a house, so there is now no trace of the bulky equipment, the huge batteries and the bunks on which the off-duty staff slept. The towering aerials that surrounded the building have gone, too. Each station was connected by landline to

Admiralty House in London, where their teleprinter messages dropped from pneumatic tubes into an in-tray in Room 40. Very few of the First World War listening stations now exist, but archaeologists have found evidence of 215 sites in England, of which 87 were coastal intercept sites.

Marley Close, Stockton on Tees: one of the Admiralty's First World War listening stations that tracked the wireless messages of the ships of the Imperial Navy. (Historic England)

HORTON AGAIN

In early October, Horton once more displayed his skill as a submariner when he sank the German destroyer *S-126*. He had been patrolling off the Ems estuary on the German-Dutch border and had been hiding in the shallow water for a few hours while he entertained his men with music from his phonograph. As soon as he took *E-9* back to the surface he found the destroyer. It was, though, too close to risk sinking with a torpedo since the explosion might have also damaged *E-9*. Patiently, Horton tracked *S-126* until it was 600 yards distant. Away went two torpedoes. One found its mark and *S-126* was soon sinking. *S-126* had been patrolling in a body of destroyers, so discovery was highly probable for Horton and *E-9*. He took his boat down and crept away. Just eleven days later, Keyes was drawing up a submission to the Admiralty detailing the exploits of those of his men who deserved recognition. Horton's actions since September 13 were listed, concluding with: 'He is a most enterprising submarine officer, and I beg to submit his name for favourable consideration.'[85]

Max Horton (left) at the time of his commanding E-9. On the right is Noel Laurence, who commanded E-1.

ADMIRALTY JITTERS

While Keyes, Beatty and Wemyss (along with thousands of less well-known sailors) longed for action, their Admiralty suffered a bout of nerves in mid-October. Troop transports to France had run smoothly since early August until a U-boat turned up near the Isle of Wight. There was panic at Admiralty House. Even Churchill lost his nerve as he reported to an astounded Cabinet on October 15 that 'the Admiralty could no longer guarantee the safety of the transports'. It was, he continued, 'impossible to block in the German submarines at Heligoland and impossible to shut them out of our harbours'. The Prime Minister took careful aim at Churchill's ego: 'You mean we have lost command of the sea?' In his diary, the Postmaster General, Charles Hobhouse, noted that Churchill 'took great umbrage' at this.[86] He backed down and never again did Churchill's Admiralty suggest that the U-boats would ever get the better of the warships which were screening the troop escorts.

Target warships

The Imperial Navy's strategy of sinking warships gathered pace as Otto Weddigen roamed the seas in *U-9* between Orkney and the Shetland Islands on one side, and Norway on the other. After several days of searching, his men had nothing to show for their efforts other than the stress of numerous crash-dives as *U-9* evaded unattackable targets. At breakfast on October 15, with the boat submerged, the men breathed in the foul air and hoped that hot coffee would boost their energy levels and banish their headaches. Then, just before 5.30 am, the chief quartermaster at the periscope shouted: 'Three British cruisers ahoy.'[87]

Spiess was barely awake when he heard the cry. As *U-9* submerged he caught a glance of a warship before the waves closed over the boat. His first reaction was of trepidation. Surely the boat was too close to the cruisers for safety? Surely someone must have spotted the periscope? But not one lookout was to see *U-9* during the next five hours as it tracked the zigzagging Edgar-class protected cruiser HMS *Hawke*.

Later in the morning, the men grabbed what lunch they could while remaining at action stations. Could this, thought Weddigen, be a repeat of the action of September 22? His daydreams were interrupted when two cruisers pulled away from *Hawke*. Now, with only one cruiser in the vicinity, Weddigen felt confident enough to fire a single torpedo. His first attempt was cut short when a collision with *Hawke* seemed imminent. Then came a perfect angle for firing. As the torpedo sped from the boat, *U-9* lost its equilibrium. It took some time to stabilize the boat before Weddigen could look through the periscope: *Hawke* was already capsizing.

Only after the torpedo had torn into *Hawke* did the men on its deck notice *U-9*'s periscope, sticking out 'like a broomstick'. On the ship, the damage was immense, with a hole above the engine room and the plates 'twisted and torn', recalled a surviving stoker. The men tried to turn the

Warships under siege

guns onto the U-boat, but the increasing slope of *Hawke*'s deck left them firing too high in the air. Then an oil tank burst into flames, forcing the men to abandon the guns. One seaman recalled, 'I determined to make a dash for it. I scrambled precipitately up the iron ladder to the main deck. All this had happened in less time than it takes to tell.'[88]

Just after the torpedo had ripped into *Hawke*, Captain Hugh Williams called for 'Still'. The bugle rang out and, for a minute or two, every man stood at his post. Then *Hawke*'s increasing list persuaded the men that it was a lost vessel. It was every man for himself. The few witnesses of the ship's final moments testify to seeing Williams and his companions 'standing on the bridge as calmly as if they were on a fleet manoeuvre in the Solent' before 'the ship finally plunged bow first amidst a maelstrom of cruel, swirling waters'.[89]

No one in the other two cruisers heard or saw anything of the attack. Later, *U-17* attempted to sink HMS *Theseus*. This resulted in an all-ships signal to leave the area with all despatch. There was no reply from the *Hawke*. Out of a complement of 544 men there were only 70 survivors. Fifty-two of these were picked out of the water by the trawler *Ben Rinnes* under Captain John Cormack. So scarce were rescue boats that men were still being plucked from the freezing water six hours after the attack.

Spiess only saw one lifeboat when he surveyed the scene: 'At the rudder the boat officer hoisted a distress signal on the boat's staff. That little dory with half a dozen men aboard was all that was left of the proud warship.'[90] That same day Scrimgeour in HMS *Crescent* noted: 'At midday we passed a large number of pieces of wreckage and saw some lifebuoys floating about ... The wreckage may be possibly that of the *Hawke*.'[91]

The dead included three fathers-to-be from Ulster: Able Seaman Albert Wilson whose daughter Frances was born only four weeks later; Able Seaman James Gorman, whose brother Charles had gone down with HMS *Pathfinder* seven weeks earlier; and Stoker Martie Donald.

The press was still coming to terms with the war when the *Hawke* went down. The sinking was reported more as an anomalous event than a portent of the maritime massacre that was to come. *The Manchester Guardian* mildly opined: 'We have to deplore another success by a German submarine.'[92] Deaths of the very young, though, were another matter. One cadet from Kings Norton School in Birmingham was rumoured to have been only 14 years-old when he died. 'He was far too young to die in such a way,' said a local journalist.[93] In the light of what happened in the next four years that now sounds a naïve comment.

Young Stephen King-Hall took a more considered view of this episode, recording in his diary: '*Theseus* reports that she never even saw a sign of a submarine, save the track of a torpedo.' This led him to rightly surmise: 'I am reluctantly forced to the conclusion that the day of the surface warship is over.'[94] His remarks were reinforced by Charles Hobhouse, who noted in his diary: 'It is not reassuring to know that the Admiralty have at present no scheme of dealing with submarine attacks.'[95]

Australian and Russian gold

One advantage that the British Admiralty had over other navies was its world-wide spread of bases and coaling stations, plus the resources of the Empire. Australia was the first dominion to come to the aid of Britain in the new sea war, with a prompt capture in August.

Andrew Fisher, the Australian opposition leader, had already promised in the on-going election campaign that 'should the worst happen ... Australians will stand beside the mother country to help and defend her to our last man and our last shilling.'[96] Within days, Australia had a chance to show its support when the German collier SS *Pfalz*, loaded with 200 tons of coal, and destined for the Pacific Squadron of the Imperial German Navy, tried to flee Melbourne. Captain Kuhlken initially ignored a warning shot from the guns of Fort Nepean across *Pfalz*'s bow. The pilot boat commander then warned Kuhlken that he would shoot to hit if the *Pfalz* did not stop. Germany's first surrender quickly followed.

Having dealt with a minor vessel in port, Australia now turned its attention to the Imperial Navy's ships at sea. The Australian Navy was determined to capture as many German vessels as possible before the ships could warn other vessels of the state of war.

Australia's first impounding was the 6000-ton SS *Hobart*, which arrived at Victoria on August 11. Hobart's captain saw nothing suspicious as a boarding party of well-dressed civilians approached his vessel. Only when Captain John Richardson opened his overcoat to reveal his naval uniform did the captain realize the truth. Although Richardson had a pistol in his hand, he took no steps to arrest the captain or the crew. Nor did he restrain their movements as his deception plan unfolded. He discretely withdrew and hid in the captain's cabin. Night fell. Then, in the early hours of the morning, came the sound that Richardson had been waiting for: the door being gently opened. Two men tiptoed across the cabin and opened a hidden panel. Richardson shone his torch and brandished his gun as he seized the documents that the men had retrieved. These included the German HVB codebook, used by the Imperial Navy for communicating with its warships and those merchant ships equipped with radio. It would be the end of October before a copy of the codebook would reach London. According to an Australian source, the Australian's used a copy of the book to decode signals for London until London had received its copy.

With the aid of the navy's listening stations and the codebreakers in Room 40 at Admiralty House, thousands of HVB messages would be read by the British Admiralty in the four years of war. Since the Imperial Navy never suspected that the Admiralty was reading its communications, German ships were carelessly promiscuous in their signals. For example, on departure, the port authorities radioed vessels to inform them of which exit channel to use; on arrival, the ships called in to request their incoming channel. Room 40 thus had a detailed knowledge of which vessels were at sea and which were in port. Often, the Room 40's code-breakers were able to identify each boat's operational area. Their report of April 29, 1915, was typical, revealing that *U-35*, *U-36*, *U-39* and *U-41* had left Heligoland and were to go North around Scotland at 12½ knots. On the following day, Room 40 reported that *U-20* and *U-28* had left the naval base on the island of Borkum. Captured U-boat commanders were astounded at the British intelligence on them, which often included their names, their boat's complement and details of their boat's construction history.

The next codebook capture came via the Russians from the German light cruiser SMS *Magdeburg*. The ship, along with SMS *Augsburg*, had joined a group of destroyers and submarines to search for Russian warships sheltering behind a minefield at the entrance to the Gulf of Finland. Early on August 23 the vessels entered the dangerous waters. The sailors on the *Magdeburg* were on edge, being convinced that Russian armoured cruisers were lying in wait for them. Even so, the day passed uneventfully, with no sightings of Russian vessels. Ominously, no one seemed worried when the commanders ignored a difference of a mile between the navigational plots of the *Magdeburg* and the *Augsburg*.

Then the fog fell. By 9.00 pm the bridge lookouts on *Magdeburg* could no longer see the ship's stern. Lieutenant Commander Richard

Habenicht ordered soundings to be taken. The successive readings of 190 feet and 141 feet, followed by 112 feet at 12.30 am were alarming. Seven minutes later, *Magdeburg* made a course change; the tiller went over 20 degrees. *Magdeburg* replied with a dull thud and a few shudderings before coming to an abrupt halt. It was now firmly stuck on the north-western tip of the island of Odensholm, which was then Russian territory.

Desperate efforts failed to refloat the vessel so Habenicht decided to abandon ship. The captain called for three cheers for the Kaiser and ordered the ship's two boats to be lowered. Radioman Third Class Kiehnert grabbed the radio shack's codebook and cipher key and jumped into the freezing waters. When he surfaced, he found the cypher key had gone. Ten minutes later the charges blew, and *Magdeburg*'s hull was torn in two.

Lieutenant Galibin, the first officer of the Russian torpedo boat *Lieutenant Burakov*, was one of the men assigned to search the stricken ship. A locked compartment in Habenicht's cabin caught his attention. Forcing it open, he found a forgotten codebook.

Some days later, Count Constantine Benckendorff, a Russian naval officer serving on the battleship *Poltava*, was ordered to report to St Petersburg. He was handed a leather satchel, weighted down by a sizeable piece of lead. Inside was the precious codebook. Clutching his irreplaceable catch, Benckendorff boarded HMS *Theseus* at Alexandrovsk. After some delays, *Theseus* sailed on October 1, reaching Scapa Flow nine days later. Churchill completes the story in his *The World Crisis 1914-1918*: 'I received from the hands of our loyal allies these sea-stained priceless documents.' (Churchill's additional colourful description of the cypher being found 'clasped in the bosom' of a dead sailor was good journalism but high fiction.[97])

The *Magdeburg* codebook was a copy of the *Signalbuch der Kaiserlichen Marine* (SKM) which was used for German naval operations. Now the Admiralty had two of the three main code books used by the Imperial Navy.

The codebooks were destined for Room 40 in the Old Admiralty Building, which towers over the eastern end of Horse Guards Parade. This room was the centre of the Admiralty's intelligence operations. The Intelligence Department had been established in 1913 under Rear Admiral Henry Oliver and, in November 1914, Captain Reginald Hall had been appointed Director of Intelligence. This is not the place to explore the growth and development of Room 40, but its role in codebreaking is critical to our story. Day after day, Britain's listening stations telegraphed their latest intercepts to Room 40. By the end of the war Room 40 had received around 20,000 Imperial Navy signals from the listening stations. (The French had listening stations on the other side of the Channel but had no copy of the German cyphers. The British stations provided a de-cyphering service by courier each night.)

Code-breakers in Room 40 during the First World War. (University of Aberdeen.)

The Imperial Navy had quickly mastered the technicalities of radio, while remaining innocently naïve about the risks they ran in using it so prolifically. The British Admiralty intelligence staff, on the other hand, were just as quick to become master codebreakers, so turning the Imperial Navy's technological success against them.

Not that the Admiralty limited its intelligence gathering to wireless intercepts. Land-based direction-finding stations helped locate ships at sea; agents in German dockyards reported on shipbuilding and sailings; neutral vessels often proffered information on sightings of German vessels; and many consular agents around the world sent in reports on local warship activities.

AN UNSAFE MOORING

From the eighteen-eighties until the eve of the First World War, hardly a year had passed without a new round of lobbying for increased naval expenditure. A public agitation in 1888-1889 had yielded an additional £10 m for shipbuilding over several years. A 'Needs of the Navy' campaign in 1893-1894 saw the Naval Estimates increase to £17.4 m. Within seven years the estimates had leapt to £28.8 m as they ate up ever more of the nation's output: between 1880 and 1900 British Gross Domestic Product had risen by 25 per cent while naval expenditure had risen by 58 per cent. Yet still the navy could not find the millions that it needed to provide safe harbours for its warships on Britain's east coast. So, when the Grand Fleet was secretly dispatched to its war station on July 29, its destination was not a modern harbour with first class workshops, recreation facilities, communications systems and defences. Instead, the fleet was to lie at Scapa Flow: a desolate body of water in the Orkneys. It, and the surrounding land, had few visitors, although the Imperial Navy was ever keen to leave its visiting card.

Acting sub-lieutenant Scrimgeour described the anchorage in his diary as 'one of the most deserted parts of the British Isles'. He found the low hills 'wild and fine', but he noted that his shipmates had not seen one human being in seven-and-a-half miles of barren terrain.[98]

Every lookout on the ships of the Grand Fleet knew how vulnerable the Flow was. Jittery nerves ruled the day when out on exercises or at target practice. A piece of floating debris was enough for the shout of 'Periscope!' to ring round a ship's bridge. The first serious scare came on September 1 when three dreadnought squadrons and some light cruisers were preparing for an exercise. The rain and mist provided ideal conditions for a U-boat to slip into the Flow unseen. The Town-class light cruiser HMS *Falmouth* was on look-out duty near the entrance to the Flow. Although there were still two hours of daylight left, visibility was poor. The inevitable happened as a seaman cried 'Periscope!'; not far away, the armoured cruiser HMS *Drake* found its own U-boat. No attempt was made to confirm these sightings. *Drake*'s guns simply opened up and fired at the phantom craft. The offending target was later identified as a group of seals.

There was another bout of U-boat nerves on October 17, as King-Hall dramatically recorded in his diary entry: '[A] tremendous submarine attack has been launched.' He noted that '*Swift,* had several torpedoes fired at her at the scene of *Hawke*'s earlier loss, and a tremendous upheaval is going on at Scapa Flow, as submarines have actually got inside. One torpedo missed the *Leda* by 10 ft. The whole place is being evacuated.'[99]

King-Hall had witnessed the point at which Jellicoe could no longer support the strain of guarding his fleet at Scapa Flow. He told Churchill that he was taking his ships off to sea and would not return to Scapa 'until the Submarine Defence was placed'.[100]

Jellicoe led the Grand Fleet out of Scapa Flow and sailed round the north of Scotland to take it to an anchorage at the Isle of Mull on the west coast. This was no more secure than Scapa, but was more difficult for the U-boats to reach.

Beatty was not happy with the new arrangements, as he told Churchill on October 17 in a letter marked 'Private': 'we have no base where we can go with *any* degree of safety [to] lie for coaling, replenishing, and refitting and repairing, after two and a half months of war'. Meanwhile, every ship had to take the utmost precautions to protect itself: 'My picket boats are at the entrance, the nets are out, and the men are at the guns, waiting for coal which has run low, but ready to move at a moment's notice.'[101] The forced departure from Scapa Flow was a coup for the U-boats. Without even mounting an attack, Jellicoe's mighty ships had fled the North Sea and the dreaded boats.

Contraband

With the North Sea empty of any significant naval activity, and the competing armies facing years of indecisive trench warfare, Britain's blockade of Germany realized a new importance. Depriving Germany of fuel and raw materials was now the most effective way of emasculating its capacity to wage war. At the heart of this operation was the Northern Patrol, which cut off access to the North Sea at its northern end. The patrol was a vast operation involving, in October 1914, the Third Battle Squadron, the Second Cruiser Squadron, the Third Cruiser Squadron, and some armed liners. Any ship found to be carrying contraband was impounded or turned away from entry to the North Sea. Most vessels made no attempt to resist inspection. Others were less willing. One of the earliest patrols chased a German vessel for three hours before overhauling it. Beneath its hatches was a cargo of food, destined for German dinner tables and, no doubt, army rations. A prize crew from HMS *Crescent* turned the ship around and took it to Lerwick. Stopping American-owned ships was more controversial, but they were still challenged. By mid-October four American fuel tankers bound for Germany had been taken into Lerwick by prize crews. German war planners knew that their country was ill-positioned to fight a long war when its trading routes were severely disrupted. The blockading ships had to be sunk. HMS *Crescent* seemed to be a suitable candidate.

It was 6.30 am on October 18 when lookouts on HMS *Crescent* saw a U-boat sitting on the surface at a distance of five miles. Captain George Trewby, who had only taken command of the ship at the end of July, called for 14 knots. The command 'Repel torpedo attack' sounded through the 400-foot length of the cruiser as the men loaded the guns and closed-up the turrets. Five minutes after first being spotted, the U-boat submerged, but only to periscope depth.

As *Crescent*'s lookouts anxiously watched the periscope nearing their ship, shells from the warship's six 6-inch guns were falling into the water, seemingly around the U-boat. Then a second U-boat made its presence felt as a streak of white bubbles, ran broadside to *Crescent*. The port batteries swung round to fire on this new target. The shots fell short. *Crescent* was still closing fast on the first U-boat. The range would soon be too short for the depression of the guns. Trewby prepared to ram. As *Crescent* tore down on the U-boat, its commander recognized the peril of his boat's position. Down went the periscope. With one enemy gone, the second U-boat showed on *Crescent*'s starboard side. The boat submerged before *Crescent*'s guns could fire. Some said the boat then fired a torpedo; others thought not. Meanwhile, a third U-boat was spotted, although it did not attempt to attack. The episode had lasted 20 minutes. For Scrimgeour those minutes were 'perhaps the most exciting I have ever spent'.[102] *Crescent* sailed on and survived the war.

And so the war might have continued: the Imperial Navy attacking Allied warships while the Allied ships enforced the blockade. But two sinkings within seven days were about to change the course of the naval war in a direction that few had believed possible.

6
Skirmishes

Late October 1914

'As usual, we did nothing except meet with filthy weather.' – Lieutenant King-Hall.[103]

THE HUMBLE 'GLITRA'

For Germany, failure was now piling on failure as its war strategy collapsed under the resilience of the French and British armies on the Western Front and the intractability of the defensive posture of the Grand Fleet. The Schlieffen Plan had proved flawed. Germany's attacks on British warships had driven them from the North Sea rather than sink them. What next?

'Next' was what had been deemed unthinkable at the start of the war: sinking unarmed merchant vessels. Britain had always assumed that no power would ever stoop to such a cowardly action. Nor had the Imperial Navy ever imagined that it would engage in the unheroic act of seeking out *unarmed* foes. The change in strategy began with the modest 900-ton *Glitra*.

This British merchant ship was over 30 years old in 1914. Under Captain Johnson it had left Grangemouth in passage to Stavanger in Norway with a cargo of oil, iron plating and coal. The ship was within 14 miles of the Norwegian coast when it encountered *U-17* and its commander Kapitänleutnant Johannes Feldkirchner on October 20. Unarmed, Johnson had no choice but to stop *Glitra*'s engines and await boarding.

Five submariners, armed with pistols, were soon on *Glitra*'s deck. They ordered Johnson to lower the flag, with the threat of being shot if he failed to look sharp about it. As Johnson clutched the dishonoured flag, a submariner tore it from his hands, threw it to the deck and trampled on it. The ship's papers that Johnson was holding were ripped from his hands as he and his crew, shorn of their possessions, were forced down into the boats.

Before departing, *U-17* towed the lifeboats 500 yards nearer the Norwegian coast. They were soon met by the *Hai*, a torpedo boat of the Royal Norwegian Navy, which towed them into the harbour of

Skudeneshavn. *Glitra*'s crew had been lucky. Courteous tows by U-boats were not to be the order of the day for long.

The *Glitra* was the first merchant vessel to be sunk by a submarine in the war. It was a small affair, which neither side saw as worthy of comment. Feldkirchner had stuck to prize rules, so there was no loss of life. No norms of naval warfare had been breached. At this stage of the war, he was taking little risk in sticking to these rules. The sinking was, though, the start of the slow drift to sinking on sight, with no concern for the dead and injured. This strategy would lead Germany into ever more labyrinthine attempts to legally justify what, before the war, both sides had considered to be illegal and morally abhorrent.

The SS Glitra – the first merchant ship to be sunk by a U-boat.

The sinking of the *Glitra* was part of the beginning of the people's wars of the twentieth century. Until then, war had been seen as an occupation for soldiers and naval personnel, to be read about in newspapers, and, later, talked over around homestead hearths and in smoke-filled inns. Now, the unarmed civilian mariner was on the front line. The change in German strategy could not have been clearer: armies were to stand impotently in trenches while merchant ships were to be sunk and the British starved into surrender.

It is hard for us now to see what a significant event the sinking of the *Glitra* was. Even a U-boat man such as Spiess was flabbergasted at the news of its sinking. He, though, soon accepted the headquarters' argument that the action was justified by Britain's allegedly illegal blockade. He looked on approvingly as 37 mm cannons began to be mounted on the decks of the U-boats.

A LESSON IN RAMMING

As the big ships on both sides retreated from the North Sea, the U-boats still had to face the destroyers. The first destroyer to take on a U-boat was HMS *Badger*. The experience showed how much the Royal Navy had to learn if the blockade was to be effective.

Kapitänleutnant Constantin Kolbe in *U-19* was in search of prey in the Heligoland Bight area in late October. He was much in need of a target, given that his boat had been operational since the beginning of August without sinking a single vessel. Unknown to Kolbe, the destroyer HMS *Badger* from Harwich was patrolling near the Terschelling Lightship. It was dark and the sea was rough. No doubt *U-19* was struggling in the heavy sea and had its periscope obscured, so it is not surprising that Kolbe never saw any sign of *Badger*. It is equally likely that Commander Fremantle in *Badger* cursed the foul weather as his lookouts strained to spot the speck of a periscope in the swirling darkness. Then came the belated cry of 'Periscope!' *Badger* bore down on the unsuspecting boat and smashed into 650 tons of steel at 13 knots. With no sign of the U-boat after the collision, *Badger* was joined by HMSs *Hydra* and *Hind* in the search for survivors. Finding neither wreckage nor bodies, the boat was assumed to have sunk.

Some sources say that *U-19* was severely damaged; others that the damage was superficial. The latter is more credible since *U-19* returned to base and was back at sea in early 1915. *Badger*, on the other hand, was seriously damaged, with its bow crushed back to the forward bulkhead. With ramming being Britain's sole means of attacking a submerged craft at this stage in the war, this was a serious weakness. If every sunk U-boat resulted in a severely damaged destroyer, the anti-submarine war would soon lead to a dearth of warships. Orders were given for the rest of the Acheron-class of destroyers to have their bows strengthened.

Kolbe overcame his disaster and went on to sink 43 ships with a total tonnage of 42,000 tons in three boats. *U-19* went on to sink 57 ships, totalling 98,000 tons before surrendering on November 24, 1918. Both sets of figures show the disastrous consequences of Britain's failure to sink even those U-boats that came into physical contact with a warship.

SLOW WAR

In late September Captain Arthur Duff in the light cruiser HMS *Southampton* was detailed to search for a reported minelayer. Duff was sure that the culprit was disguised as a merchant ship. This assumption led King-Hall to fume in his diary about such a pointless exercise: if the minelayer *was* disguised as a merchant vessel, Duff would be unable to apprehend it since cruisers were forbidden to stop and search merchant vessels, for fear of a U-boat attack. King-Hall's report on the incident was bluntly dismissive: 'As usual, we did nothing except meet with filthy weather.'[104] The Royal Navy, it seemed, was being outmanoeuvred by the Imperial Navy's new form of warfare: mines on and under the seas; U-boats beneath the waves. As a result, battleships and cruisers had been relegated to by-stander status. Young men such as Scrimgeour raged at the serious lack of challenge.

At sea, the men in HMS *Crescent* had a rare interruption in their stop and search operations as the greater enemy – the winter weather – mocked the ship's 7700 tons of steel in late October. The table in the gun room (home of the midshipmen) had been smashed. Two anchors were careering at will across the deck, and the booms were thrashing from side to side. The starboard guns were under water while 36 men lay injured. The few small comforts in the harsh life of a sailor did not escape the storm as the gramophone lay shattered on the deck amidst the remains of the brittle shellac records which had played their last airs. When patrolling recommenced, the two steamers hauled-to by *Crescent* yielded no more than harmless Russian rubber goods destined for the Russian port of Archangel and a mass of fish on its way to Tromsø.

The minor success of the supposed sinking of a U-boat was not enough to lift the spirits of a navy in search of a role. Far away in the Admiralty, Churchill was also yearning for action as much as the men at sea. The Grand Fleet was near to being mothballed. 'I have never seen him so despondent,' wrote Captain Herbert Richmond, Assistant Director of Operations, in his diary. Churchill himself lamented 'the impossibility of *doing* anything'.[105]

A SINKING TOO FAR

Within days of Scrimgeour, Churchill and King-Hall despairing at the navy's lack of a heroic role, the war at sea took a sinister turn.

From the earliest weeks of the land war, Belgian refugees had been fleeing the terror of German occupation. By late October, around 250,000 of these refugees had arrived at Folkestone to take shelter in Britain. Now, a further 2500 had boarded the French steamer *Amiral Ganteaume* at Ostend, bound for Le Havre. After calling in at Calais on October 26, the ship put to sea again and was quickly sighted off Cap Gris-Nez by Kapitänleutnant Rudolf Schneider in *U-24*. He had commanded the boat since December 1913 but had not yet seen any action. Keen to justify his command, he willingly identified the 4500-ton vessel as a troopship and moved in for his attack. His first torpedo struck the ship between the engine room and the stokehold.

The mighty frame of the *Amiral Ganteaume* shook and thundered with the noise of the exploding warhead. The passengers rushed to the deck, fearing for their lives. By good fortune, the passenger ship *The Queen* was nearby. Its captain, Robert Carey, saw *Amiral Ganteaume*'s distress signals and gave orders to bring *The Queen* alongside the stricken vessel. Time was of the essence since Carey could see passengers in the *Ganteaume* already jumping into the sea. Onlookers in *The Queen* shouted, 'Ne sautez pas! Ne bouges pas!'[106] (Don't jump! Don't move!)

Seeing their rescue at hand, the terrified passengers on the *Amiral Ganteaume* began shouting, crying and waving hats and handkerchiefs to draw attention to their individual plights. The 67-year-old journalist, historian and translator Wentworth Huyshe, who happened to be on board *The Queen*, said that 'the whole mass of refugees were frantic with terror' but when they saw the red ensign there was a 'joyous shout of "Vive l'Angleterre!"'[107] Huyshe watched in anguish as boats tried to reach those in the water, but several passengers had already sunk beneath the rough sea before they could be plucked to safety.

Despite the threatening sea, Captain Carey brought his ship alongside the *Amiral Ganteaume*. As the two ships finally lay together, the refugees rushed forward. Women clung desperately to small children as the sides of the two vessels lurched up and down like sparring monsters, ready to grind and smash anything that came between them. For half-an-hour, the refugees jostled, pushed and grabbed each other in a heaving mass of desperation. There were fights and wounds. Two men were killed in the fray. One had an arm crushed between the two vessels. A woman with a baby in her arms fell between the two ships and was crushed as hull ground into hull.

Finally, a sort of calm was restored as the last survivor in the water was taken into *The Queen* and those still on board the *Amiral Ganteaume* realized that their ship was not sinking.

Four men in the engine room had died, along with twenty passengers. Seventeen passengers received hospital treatment at Folkestone. Had the torpedo done more damage, the deaths might have run into hundreds. The *Amiral Ganteaume* reached Boulogne and was later repaired. Two years later it was sunk by German destroyers at Varne Bank in the Strait of Dover.

Belgian refugees on the torpeoed Amiral Ganteaume transferring to 'The Queen' in October 1914. (Contemporary postcard.)

The first great atrocity of the sea war was over. Had this been a mistake or were U-boats to now sink not only unarmed ships, but ships carrying nothing but passengers?

7
Change of command

Late autumn 1914

'He still has fine zeal, energy and determination, coupled with low cunning ... He also has courage and will take any responsibility.' – Beatty re Fisher.[108]

A SIGNIFICANT SINKING

By the time of the attack on the *Amiral Ganteaume* the Imperial Navy had given up hope of defeating Britain through U-boat attacks on warships. No new strategy was in place, but thousands of German mines in sea lanes and off estuaries lay in wait for victims. One of these mines was about to show the vulnerability of the big ships to this often invisible weapon.

Early on the morning of October 27, Vice Admiral Sir George Warrender's Second Battle Squadron left the Grand Fleet's temporary moorings at Loch na Keal and made for the open sea. Amongst his ships was HMS *Audacious*. It was just 14-months old and was one of the most powerful war machines on the planet. Its 25,000 tons of steel carried five twin 13.5-inch guns as well as smaller calibre guns and torpedoes. It could race through the oceans at 21 knots and take on any warship that came within range. Its vital areas, such as the steering gear, were behind 4-inch armour plate. Below the waterline, it had an armoured belt of 12-inch plate. To the innocent eye *Audacious* was both unsinkable and impregnable. Captain Frederick Dampier had little to worry about, although his lookouts were at the ready should any vessel dare to approach his all-powerful war machine.

It was 8.45 am when the squadron, accompanied by cruisers and destroyers, turned into the strong swell of the choppy sea under a dull grey sky. On *Audacious* the men were already at battle stations. From prow to stern, from the crow's nest to the deepest bowels of the ship, over 800 men were calmly going about their allotted duties as they anticipated hearing the reassuring thundering roar of *Audacious*' guns at practice.

In the tense silence of anticipated activity, the low steady throb of the warship's steam turbines confirmed that all was well. This calm was disturbed by a strange sound. Sub Lieutenant H E Spragge thought he had heard a gun firing. Dampier had reached the same conclusion.

Lieutenant Thomas Galbraith had heard nothing, he told Dampier, as they walked towards the standard compass on the bridge. Just as they reached the compass, *Audacious* abruptly rolled to port. 'Close all watertight doors,' bellowed Dampier. Galbraith repeated the order, although he thought it rather pointless since the ship was already at action stations, which meant the doors were already closed. Nearby vessels watched as Dampier signalled that *Audacious* had been struck by a torpedo or a mine.

Down below, water was pouring into parts of *Audacious*' engine rooms. Soon the ship began to list to port and the swell on its beam was proving troublesome. Dampier gave orders for the ship to be turned to head into the swell. The ship's starboard engine was still running at full power, so he decided to beach *Audacious* on the coast which was just 25 miles away.

On hearing that the ship was severely damaged, Jellicoe ordered every destroyer and auxiliary vessel to the scene – he could not risk sending another large warship for fear that there was a U-boat in the vicinity.

At first, Dampier's planned beaching seemed to offer some hope. But, by time the ship's list had reached ten degrees, the engine compartments were flooding at an alarming rate. The sole working engine was already beginning to struggle. When the list reached 15 degrees Galbraith noticed that *Audacious* was making little headway. Then the ship came to a halt. It was, said Galbraith, as if *Audacious* was dying. It was now 10.00 am and the beach was still a long way off.

Audacious' boats had been readied, poised to evacuate the ship. With the loss of power, the now useless main derrick was swinging dangerously from side to side as the ship tossed helplessly in the unwelcoming sea. The warship's only hope lay in a tow.

The first chance of rescue came from the Atlantic liner RMS *Olympic* – sister ship of the ill-starred *Titanic* – which had responded to *Audacious*' distress calls. It had left New York on October 21 and was bound for Liverpool on its last peacetime run before taking up war service. *Olympic* only had 153 passengers, but, as they photographed and filmed the warship's plight, they were soon to prove to be 153 too many.

On *Olympia*, Captain Herbert Haddock offered to effect a tow. A destroyer carried a six-inch hawser over to his ship, but it parted from *Audacious* before the towing could begin. Dusk was now falling. With

Audacious wallowing deep in the water it was time to evacuate all but the minimal crew needed for managing a tow.

Vice Admiral Lewis Bayly, commander of the First Battle Squadron, came on board to supervise a tow from the Town-class light cruiser HMS *Liverpool*. This, too, failed when the cable fouled in *Liverpool*'s screws. It was now the turn of the collier *Thornhill* to take up the hawser. At last, it was in place. Then, as *Thornhill* prepared to take up the strain, the tow parted.

The windblown sea was no place for boats and rafts that night. One by one the destroyers had already come alongside and taken men to safety, leaving all but the executive officers and around forty seamen on *Audacious*. The ship's end was nearing. With the quarterdeck awash, the order came to abandon ship. The time was now 6.30 pm. In the dark, the sea water was washing over the forecastle and quarterdeck.

As Galbraith stepped into the whaler of the last destroyer to take men off, he looked back at the mighty ship. The commander's white sweater stood out as he paced the upper deck. The destroyer's guns hailed him, but he appeared not to hear them. When the whaler pulled away, the men continued shouting to the commander. At last, he responded. The whaler pulled back to *Audacious* and took Dampier off.

The ship survived for a further 45 minutes. Then, from deep down in the vessel, several explosions tore *Audacious* apart, spewing torn metal far into the night sky before it showered down on the attendant vessels. One chunk of steel brought about the only death from the sinking when it spun out of the night and felled a senior rating on the light cruiser HMS *Liverpool*.

At the Isle of Mull, Jellicoe had telegraphed to Churchill at 11.15 am to tell him that *Audacious* had been struck and that he feared that it was sinking. Churchill initially took the news calmly, telling Jellicoe: 'I am sure you will not be at all discouraged by *Audacious* episode.' He added: 'We have been very fortunate to have come through three months of war without the loss of a capital ship.'[109] But, when he saw Prime Minister Asquith shortly afterwards, Churchill was 'in a rather sombre mood,' as the Prime Minister told Venetia Stanley later that day.[110]

By late afternoon, Jellicoe had had time to brood on the loss of one of his precious dreadnought battleships. These were the ships that the public had demanded in 1909 when they cried 'We want eight and we won't wait!' at the Croydon by-election. Never a man to take a courageous lead, Jellicoe telegraphed to Churchill at 4.35 pm: 'Submit every endeavour should be made to keep AUDACIOUS incident from being published.' Churchill shared Jellicoe's concern as to the effect of the sinking on public morale. He temporized with the suggestion that Jellicoe send a signal to the Admiralty advising that *Audacious* 'will take at least three weeks to repair'.[111]

HMS Audacious sinking after being struck by a mine.

Asquith's Cabinet was stunned when Churchill reported the sinking of a dreadnought so early in the war. For his ministers, nothing in the gloomy daily diet of war news to date compared with this loss of a 25,000-ton ship to a single mine. The Chancellor of the Exchequer, Lloyd George, joined War Minister Lord Kitchener and Churchill in demanding that the news of the loss should be suppressed. Charles Hobson, the Postmaster General, was inclined to agree, but pointed out that the passengers on the *Olympic* had witnessed the attempt to tow *Audacious* to safety. Other leading Cabinet members argued that the government would soon lose the trust of the public if they failed to tell the truth about the war. Asquith accepted the case for suppression, although he later told Venetia Stanley that he had been '*very* reluctant' in his agreement.[112]

Soon, photographs and film clips of the sinking *Audacious*, taken by the passengers on the *Olympic*, reached the offices of foreign newspapers. Berlin knew the truth that the Cabinet had tried to suppress, but the British public were not told of the sinking until November 14, 1918, when an Admiralty press statement headed 'HMS *Audacious* A delayed announcement' reached the newspaper offices.[113]

The sinking was of little importance in the naval war, but had two unintended consequences. First, Jellicoe was more reluctant than ever to expose his fleet to mines or torpedoes, so further depriving the High Seas Fleet of an opportunity to seriously reduce the Grand Fleet. Second, the Imperial Navy found that its apparent triumphant success in sinking a battleship brought no strategic benefit. The High Seas Fleet was more redundant than ever. All that was left for the Imperial Navy was to despatch its U-boats to sink merchant vessels. It was far from clear whether such cloak-and-dagger operations could win the war that the army was failing to win on land.

Resurrection

Back in late August, the Civil Lord of the Admiralty, Arthur Lee MP, and the retired bombastic Admiral Lord Charles Beresford, had been standing in the entrance hall of the Carlton Club in Pall Mall, holding a heated conversation. As other members gathered round, they heard Beresford talking about German spies: a subject on which he acknowledged himself to be more expert than the security services. The conversation moved on to German residents in Britain: '*All* Germans, including highly placed ones, ought to leave the country,' Beresford declared. Arthur Lee pointed out that the head of the Admiralty – Prince Louis of Battenberg – was German born. Was he to go too? Yes, said Beresford, 'He keeps German servants and his property is in Germany.'[114] And so began a scandalous press campaign to drive Prince Louis from office.

It was two months before Beresford's campaign reached its crescendo. So public was his crusade that news of it even reached Scrimgeour at the extremities of Scapa Flow: 'All sorts of weird rumours floating round about Prince Louis of Battenberg being in the Tower with [the socialite] Mrs. Cornwallis-West as a spy,' he wrote in his diary. Loyally, he added, 'If this is true it must be a terrible calamity in our midst, but I don't believe it.'[115]

On October 28, Prince Louis, a broken man, sat down to write his resignation letter. He told Churchill that 'my birth and parentage have the effect of impairing in some respects my usefulness on the Board of Admiralty'.[116] Churchill had no choice but to accept Battenberg's resignation, vile as he considered the Prince's detractors to be. Admiral of the Fleet Lord Fisher, who had previously held the post of First Sea Lord from 1904 to 1910, was recalled to duty. Aged 70, Fisher's powers were waning. That there was no younger, better qualified man to fill this critical war-time command was a severe indictment of the navy's failure to breed dynamic, strategically-minded commanders. Beatty, writing from HMS *Lion* to his wife, correctly foresaw that Fisher was not the man for the job: 'I can't see Winston and Jacky Fisher working very long together in harmony. They will quarrel before long.'[117] (They did, in May 1915, over the Dardanelles operation.) A few days later Beatty told Ethel, '[W]e want a Kitchener at the head. We are only playing at war.'[118] In reality, not one of Jellicoe, Fisher and Kitchener was to prove up to the job of dealing a decisive blow against the German forces. All would have to go before victory could be secured.

No entry

With the Grand Fleet now a hostage to mines, the Admiralty responded by declaring the North Sea to be a 'military zone'. Its announcement of November 2 accused Germany of having 'scattered mines indiscriminately in the open sea on the main trade route from America to Liverpool'. Germany had 'wantonly and recklessly endangered the lives of all who travel on the sea'. From now on, merchant and fishing vessels were to be warned not to enter the area 'except in strict accordance with Admiralty directions'.[119] To simplify the navy's enforcement of the military zone, ships bound for Norway, the Baltic, Denmark and Holland were advised to approach the North Sea via the English Channel. In peacetime, the legality of closing off large areas of international waters would surely have been challenged, since the embargo sought to prevent neutrals from trading with Germany, which was contrary to international law. The Admiralty, though, valued short-term utility over long-term consequences.

A sort of outing

Early November saw one of the Imperial Navy's occasional attempts to sink elements of the Grand Fleet when Admiral Franz von Hipper led three battlecruisers, an armoured cruiser and four light cruisers to the sea off Great Yarmouth in the county of Norfolk. British intelligence intercepts ensured that he was met by Beatty with four destroyers, a minesweeper and three submarines. The brief firing from Hipper's ships left a few shells strewn on the beach; not one shell hit any of the buildings. The brief encounter between the warships left 235 German and 21 British dead. The Norfolk citizens looked on the raid with disdain, with the *Eastern Daily Press* observing: 'If it was a bombardment of the town it was a very poor half-hearted effort.' At most, it caused 'breakfasts to be left almost untouched'.[120] Hipper understandably never wore the Iron Cross that he was awarded for his part in this unheroic enterprise.

The raid's outcome further emphasized the irrelevance of the High Seas Fleet to Germany's war, and so strengthened the case for the more aggressive deployment of the U-boats.

A HARSHER REGIME

Five days later, the Imperial Navy was mulling over introducing a U-boat blockade of Britain. In his memoirs, Tirpitz quotes several documents that showed him to have wavered between ambivalence and opposition. It is now impossible to check this account, but we do have other firm evidence of his support in an interview he gave to the American journalist Karl von Wiegand on November 21. (Wiegand, despite his name, was American and was then working for the United Press agency.) When Wiegand asked Tirpitz whether Germany was considering introducing 'a U-boat blockade' of England, the admiral replied: 'If pushed to the limit why not? England wants to starve us; we can play the same game, lock in England and destroy every vessel that tries to break the blockade.' Wiegand then asked whether Germany had enough U-boats to enforce such a blockade. 'Yes,' boasted Tirpitz, 'in big U-boats we are superior to Britain.'[121] In his memoirs Scheer emphasized that this policy assumed that British merchant seamen were to be specifically targeted: 'a U-boat cannot spare the crews of steamers, but must send them to the bottom with their ships'.[122]

In the context of 1914, this was a momentous step. It was only four weeks since Feldkirchner was shivering in his sea boots at the thought of the dressing-down he would get for his callous sinking of the *Glitra*. (This was despite his having put the merchant ship's crew into boats.) Now, it would seem that any U-boat commander who treated merchant seamen so gallantly would be seen as too lily-livered to command.

An unneeded patrol?

By October the British blockade was having serious consequences for everyday life in Germany. Jellicoe, though, saw it differently. He had been analysing the list of ships that had been brought into Kirkwall since October 5, and had concluded that the Northern Patrol was a waste of resources. With only one out of 25 merchant ships being permanently detained, he argued in a telegram to the Admiralty that: 'The Squadrons now employed on this patrol work are much required for other duties ... Submitted whether the practice of boarding should continue or not.'[123] The long Admiralty reply concluded by telling Jellicoe that the work of the blockade 'has already produced most valuable results'.[124] Critically, they pointed out, the very fact that ships were being intercepted was a deterrent that ensured that many ship owners did not even endeavour to run the blockade.

The proof of the blockade's effectiveness could be seen as Germany moved towards food rationing. With its explosives industry making ever greater demands on oil products, cooking oils became hard to find in shops. Grain supplies were diminishing, forcing the government to set maximum prices to discourage the black market. Then, on December 28, came the first sign of the future for the German people: bread rationing. The initial ration of half-a-pound a day was a harsh cut from the average consumption of three-quarters of a pound a day. From now on the German people were to face food of ever decreasing quality and quantity as the blockade tightened and tightened. The British, meanwhile, would not see rationing until early 1918.

Big target, small results

On October 22, Falkenhayn's drive to break through to the Belgian coast came to a halt as the last attacks at the First Battle of Ypres faded into the November rains and mists. The unforgiving battle terrain sucked down every hoof, every boot, every gun-carriage wheel. All hopes of the 'over by Christmas' war were now shattered. The German armies would have to wait until spring to redeem their failure to live up to the high promises and bold ambitions of the first days of August. Until then, only one battlefield remained open: the sea. And, for the Imperial Navy, still dreaming of the annihilation of the Grand Fleet, that meant Scapa Flow. If the British ships would not come out, the U-boats must go in.

Change of command

There was no attempt at coordination between the high commands of the German army and navy, so it was pure coincidence that, on the very day that the Ypres battlefield fell silent for winter, Kapitänleutnant von Hennig in *U-18* was approaching Scapa Flow.

After the war, Churchill described the welcome that he imagined a U-boat would face had it tried to penetrate the Scapa defences. In addition to the navigational hazards, he said, the commander would have to avoid 'all the patrolling craft which for many miles kept watch and ward on the approaches' and would need 'to brave the unknown and unknowable terrors of mines and obstructions of all sorts, with which it must be assumed the channels would become increasingly infested'.[125] That was not how von Hennig found Scapa. He was almost welcomed in.

It was dark when von Hennig surfaced in the far north to survey the low barren Scapa landscape in the distance. Searchlight beams briefly lit up patches of the night sky, but there was no sign of any forward defences. From the presence of the blazing lights, Hennig concluded that the fleet was at its moorings. The omens looked good. Here was his chance to turn the naval war.

U-18 was now level with the Skerries – a group of small islands at the southernmost end of the ring of larger islands that surround the Flow. Ahead of *U-18* was Hoxa Sound, the main southern entrance into the mooring. Everything was going Hennig's way as he ordered 'Dive!' Up went the periscope. Hennig could barely believe his luck: right ahead of him was a steamer entering the Flow. He tucked in neatly behind the vessel before the boom nets closed. *U-18* was now in the Flow. What tales Hennig would soon be able to tell when he and his men were back in Kiel!

Except ... the Flow was empty. There was not a warship to be seen since Jellicoe's fleet had decamped to the west coast of Scotland. Twenty minutes later, Hennig faced the truth: there would no sinkings, no triumphant return. It was better to leave now, while the boom was still open, than to risk a more hazardous exit with the boom restored.

Unknown to Hennig, *U-18*'s periscope was spotted by the armed trawler *Tokyo* as he left the Flow. One brief radio message put the patrol vessels onto the highest alert. Hennig, unaware of the danger, repeatedly used his periscope as he negotiated *U-18*'s passage past the various low-lying islands to the south of the Flow. Then, up came the periscope once too often.

Chief Skipper Alexander Youngson in the minesweeper *Dorothy Gray* saw the periscope at 12.10 pm, 1¼ miles off Hoxa Head. With the U-boat submerged, Youngson resorted to ramming. Heading his Aberdeen trawler towards the U-boat, its engine picked up speed. The boat was on top of *U-18* before Hennig could take any evasive action. As the two vessels collided, the boat rose three feet into the air before falling back to lie helpless on the calm sea.

Hennig listened to the damage reports from up and down *U-18*'s 62 m length. The results were clearly terminal: the steering gear was unworkable; the hydroplanes were damaged; and the periscope, bent at a right-angle, was unusable. Yet Hennig was not a man to give up without trying. He took the boat down as if he still intended to make an escape. The boat's descent was barely controllable. It crashed with a thud onto the seabed. This second collision damaged the propellers and started a fire in the battery room. Hennig now knew that *U-18* would never sail again. Its last task was to take him and his men to the surface.

Robert Wilson, an Orkney Territorial, on lookout duty at Brough Ness at the tip of the island of South Ronaldsay, watched as *U-18*'s crew came up on deck and raised a white flag attached to a broom handle. His fellow territorials refused to credit his sighting, declaring that he did not know the difference between a whale and a U-boat. He retorted: 'Well, if it's a whale it's got 25 men standing on its back!'[126] On board the 'whale' the men found themselves surrounded by the destroyers HMSs *Erne* and *Garry*. Hennig ordered his men to scuttle their boat as they passed into captivity.

The sinking brought a bonanza for the crew of the *Dorothy Gray*. The Admiralty Prize Court considered the sinking to be of such importance that it paid out £500 (£29,000 today) instead of the normal £200. Individual shares varied from £70 for the master to £6 for the deckhands, engine-hands and the coal trimmer. In May 1919, Youngson was also awarded an OBE 'For valuable services in minesweeping operations throughout the War.'[127]

Hennig, desperate to get back to service in U-boats, took part in an escape attempt in August 1915 from the Dyffryn Aled Hall prison camp in Wales, known as the 'Colditz of North Wales'. He was one of three German prisoners of war who, on the night of August 13, 1915, got through the barred windows of the eighteenth century mansion to walk to Llandudno 20 miles away. Their pick-up – Kapitänleutnant Max Valentiner in *U-38* – turned up three nights in succession, but the three fugitives never made contact with the boat, even when, on the second night, they lit a huge bonfire on the rendezvous beach. Tired, cold and wet, they gave up the attempt to escape via the sea. One by one the submariners surrendered to the local police. Hennig rejoined the German navy after the war, retired, and then joined again in April 1940.

The British authorities suppressed the news of *U-18*'s sinking since the Imperial Navy had sent the boat to test Scapa's defences, which were still nine months off completion. The deception worked: *U-18*'s failure to return was taken to mean that the base was impregnably defended. As to the inglorious *U-18*, it had completed three patrols and had sunk nothing before its own sinking.

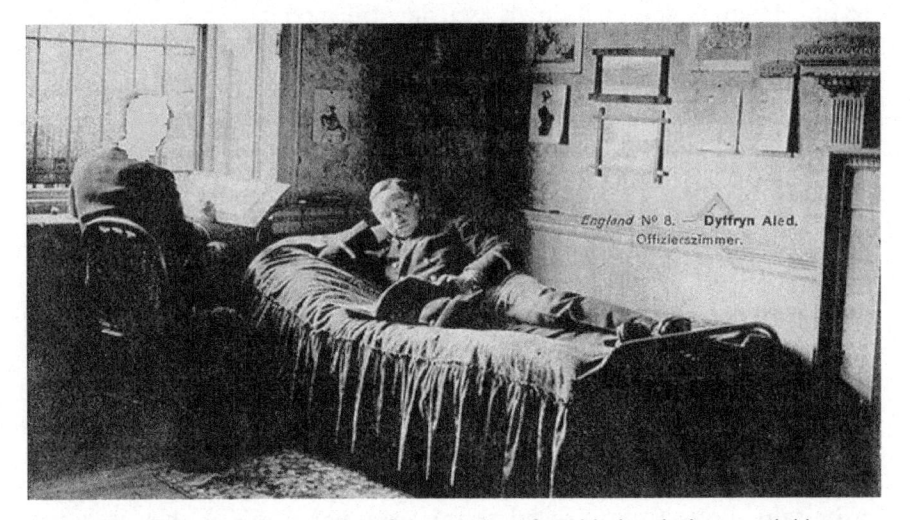

Inside Dyffryn Aled camp – a far more comfortable berth than a stinking, claustrophobic U-boat.

WAR BY MAIL ORDER

The spy mania that had gripped Britain in the years before the First World War had faded by the end of 1914 so the Committee of Imperial Defence was surprised when Captain Hall reported that messages 'in some abundance' were being posted from Britain to neutral countries.[128] On the verge of panic, the Committee gave orders for the outgoing mail to be censored. Censors were rapidly recruited and trained and the first 170 were at work by the end of the year. (There were to be 4861 censors by the end of the war.) To the Committee's surprise, the censored letters showed not a trace of any espionage. Instead, the letters revealed something just as important: they were being sent out of Britain to suppliers in neutral countries, placing paid orders for goods to be delivered to Germany via neutral vessels.

The scale of this cunning evasion of the blockade was near to industrial. The Admiralty were over-joyed at this further justification of their controversial stop and search policy. (It will be recalled that Jellicoe had attempted to end the searches.) But, just as they were about to draw on this treasure trove of intelligence, the move was threatened by a scandalized Member of Parliament. Who he was is not clear, but he was outraged at the introduction of mail censoring which, he said, was illegal. Technically, he was right. Censorship had been introduced so speedily and so secretly that no one had thought to officially authorize the mail tampering. When Hall was summoned to the office of the Home Secretary, Reginald McKenna, one glance from the minister was sufficient for him to know that he was in deep trouble. McKenna asked Hall how he had dared to interfere with the mails. He, McKenna, had little option but to send Hall for trial. Fortunately, Hall was a strong and persuasive character. The Home Secretary was soon on Hall's side, although even he had no authority to approve the censorship operation.

The next day it was McKenna who was the supplicant as he tried to persuade Prime Minister Herbert Asquith to give his assent to censorship. But Asquith, too, dared not approve the iniquity of opening people's private letters, even in wartime: it was the Cabinet's job to take that momentous decision. (Asquith's reluctance to see private letters being opened may have been influenced by his own highly indiscrete daily correspondence with Venetia Stanley. Many of these letters revealed details of secret matters.) Hall duly attended the Cabinet meeting on the next day, ready no doubt with persuasive retorts to fend off a third-degree ministerial inquisition. But no one asked him to speak and there was no discussion as the Cabinet approved the censorship of all out-going letters from the United Kingdom. It was another step towards total war, where the battle-front and the home-front meld into an indissoluble whole.

THE GREAT BLOCKADE LEAKAGE

At Christmas, Asquith's government received an unwelcome present from the United States in the form of a formal remonstration from the Secretary of State William Bryan. The Secretary's note protested against the stopping and searching of American ships carrying cargoes to neutral ports. He expressed America's 'deep regret' at 'the peaceful pursuit of lawful commerce', which Britain 'should protect rather than interrupt'.[129] Although the note was superficially polite, it was clear that America was not going to tolerate the interruption of its trade.

At the Foreign Office, Sir Edward Grey thanked Bryan for 'the most friendly spirit' of his note before pointing out to the Secretary of State the suspicious nature of much of the so-called neutral trade. The figures were damning. In 1913 New York exports to Denmark had valued $558,000. This figure had leapt to $7.1 m in 1914 – a rise of 1173 per cent. Similarly, Sweden's trade with America had increased by 658 per cent, and Norway's by 386 per cent in the same period. There was only one possible explanation: American goods were reaching Germany under the pretence of being destined for neutral countries.

Sir Edward Grey making the case for war in the House of Commons on August 3, 1914.

Grey then turned to a particularly alarming aspect of this trade: American exports of copper to European countries. These countries had imported American copper worth $37 m in 1913, while their 1914 imports were $335 m – a rise of over 800 per cent. Grey naturally concluded that most of this copper was destined for Germany. It was imperative, he told Bryan, that 'His Majesty's Government should do all in their power to stop such part of this import of copper as is not genuinely destined for neutral countries.'[130]

Elusive anti-submarine warfare

As the year came to an end, the U-boat war remained small scale. There was one last sinking when *U-11* was caught by a mine on December 9 off the Belgium coast, going down with all hands. Neither the boat, nor Kapitänleutnant Ferdinand von Suchodoletz ever sank or damaged a single vessel.

Just five U-boats had been sunk since the start of the war. *How* they were sunk foretells much of the story of the 1914-1918 anti-submarine war. *U-13* and *U-5* were sunk in unknown circumstances; *U-11* struck a mine; and *U-15* and *U-18* were sunk by ramming. In other words, the only two boats sunk in an action were on the surface. The British navy still lacked any viable means of detecting submerged boats. Nor did it yet have depth charges for sinking submerged boats once they were located. British shipping remained spectacularly vulnerable to a large increase in U-boat numbers – especially if the boats were to attack when submerged.

From the German point of view these first five months had put an end to the hubris of the Schlieffen 'over-by-Christmas' war. Nothing had gone to plan, either on land or at sea. Germany's battle-fleet lay idle and its U-boats were failing to throttle Britain's trade. Captain Zenker, Pohl's Staff Officer, noted: 'In spite of the successes of our submarines and minelaying vessels off the enemy's coast, no appreciable damage has been done to his heavy forces.' Nor had the cruiser attacks on the English east coast brought any useful result.

Of the over 300,000 tons of shipping sunk in 1914 only around one-third had been sunk by U-boat attacks – mines and surface craft had sunk the other two-thirds. This poor performance was at the cost of losing five U-boats. Kapitän zur See Zenker of the naval staff realistically summarized the position saying, 'our submarines have not succeeded now for a long time in gaining any results worthy of note'.[131]

Admiral Pohl had not been misled by the minimal impact of the U-boats. He knew that there was only one weapon that could defeat Britain: blockade. This was 'one of the most effective measures to secure our war aims with respect to Great Britain'. The sooner it began, the better, he wrote, 'so that its effects may not be minimized by the [British] accumulation of food-stuffs and raw materials which has begun'.[132]

There was, though, one snag in this plan: the Kaiser. So certain was he that there would be an early political resolution to the war, that he ordered the postponement of U-boat actions against merchant ships 'until the present ambiguity of the political situation is cleared up'.[133]

Admiral Pohl, who vigorourously supported unrestricted sinking.

On the Allied side, the Grand Fleet was as idle as the High Seas Fleet. British merchant losses at sea were well within its capacity for building replacement vessels, with losses from all causes totalling 313,000 tons. There was no sign that the U-boat menace might become serious, let alone a war-winning strategy.

Meanwhile, on the Western Front thousands of men squatted forsakenly in waterlogged, rat-infested trenches. Trench foot attacked their feet while their numbed minds turned to dreams of coal fires, Christmas trees and distant families. With no war to fight, yet no release from their hell, a few men played football with the allegedly infernal foe. Meanwhile, back home, Prime Minister Herbert Asquith, First Lord of the Admiralty Winston Churchill, and the Secretary of the Committee of Imperial Defence, Maurice Hankey, were all of one mind: the beleaguered Western Front was a pit of despair. Neither more men nor more guns could overcome the impassable tangle of barbed wire. Designed to contain harmless cattle, the wire now held at bay the mightiest armies the world had ever seen. Separately, the three men spent the post-Christmas week brooding on the bleak prospects of the imminent New Year.

Their broodings bore fruit in the New Year. The three men were of one mind; Britain should abandon the enigmatic Western Front to fester in its immobility and leave the U-boats to nibble at the edges of the mighty mercantile marine. Instead, Asquith and Hankey turned to the brighter prospects of a lightening victory at the Dardanelles. For them, the U-boats could be safely ignored. For the moment, Churchill demurred, favouring an attack on the island of Borkum.

8
Blockade

January 1915

'England wants to starve us; we can play the same game,
bottle her up and destroy any ship trying to run the blockade.'
– Tirpitz.[134]

A NAVY ON NOTICE

By the turn of the year the Royal Navy had had five months to work up its anti-submarine forces. Officers and ratings with only peace time experience had now learnt the routines of war. Men from the reserve had had time to shake off civilian ways and hone forgotten skills. The navy should have been at its peak performance. Yet the reality was otherwise. The men in the Grand Fleet had perfected the art of hiding from the enemy, but not that of destroying his forces. On the anti-submarine patrols, there were pitifully few men who had seen a periscope or fired a gun at a surfaced U-boat. With these deficiencies unresolved, the U-boats were to remind the Admiralty that the war was not to be fought on the Allies' terms.

A SIGNIFICANT SINKING

On the last day of the year, Admiral Sir Lewis Bayly's Fifth Battle Squadron had put to sea for battle practice off the Isle of Portland in the Channel. His eight battleships steamed at 10 knots in line-ahead with a light cruiser to each side. When Bayly heard that the flanking destroyers had been recalled to Harwich he concluded that the Admiralty were sure that there were no U-boats in the area.

In fact, Rudolf Schneider in *U-24* was on patrol and desperate for something to sink. (All he had to show for his efforts since war broke out was his attack on the defenceless *Amiral Ganteaume*, and he hadn't even managed to sink that.) Schneider had been chasing Bayly's ships for much of the day, but the 10-knot warships repeatedly outran him. As night fell, he brought his boat to the surface to recharge its depleted batteries. He assumed that he had seen the last of the warships. He lit a cigar and relaxed after a wearying day of fruitless hunting.

Bayly changed course after dark, as required by Admiralty orders. At 2.00 am he made a second course change towards Portland. Unknown to him, his squadron was now heading straight for Schneider's surfaced *U-24*. Schneider was staggered to see, in the feintest light, a complete line of eight battleships, offering itself to his boat. A tweak of the tiller and away went Schneider's first torpedo, racing for the lead ship. His men held their breath as they listened for the sound of a detonation. Silence. Somehow, a perfect, unmissable target had been missed. The desperate Schneider was now prepared to take risks.

Ordering his boat to surface, Schneider ran *U-24* down to the end of the line of ships, turned and caught up with the vessel in the 'coffin position': HMS *Formidable*, which was trailing HMS *London* by over 400 yards. It was 2.20 am when *U-24*'s second torpedo sped through the darkness, crashing into the starboard side of *Formidable*. Within minutes, water was flooding into the boiler rooms and the great battleship was beginning to list. Its captain, Arthur Loxley, pulled *Formidable* out of line and prepared to head for the nearby shore.

Loxley ordered the boats to be lowered. But *Formidable* was still well afloat so his men focused on getting it to the shore. On the bridge, Loxley encouraged his crew, shouting: 'There's life in the old ship yet' and urging them 'to be British'. The Chaplain, Rev George Robinson, braved going below to retrieve cigarettes for the men on deck.

Shortly after 3.00 am a second torpedo tore into the ship's starboard bow. The squally weather was worsening. HMS *Formidable* now had little chance of reaching the shore. It was time to abandon ship. The combination of a 30-foot swell and *Formidable*'s increasing list created impossible conditions for taking to the boats. Some could not be launched. Some smashed to splinters as the waves tossed them against the side of the ship, sending the occupants to their deaths. On *Formidable*'s deck, men heaved wooden objects overboard – including a piano – for use as make-shift rafts. Others stood silently smoking as they braved their fate. Finally, at 4.45 am, *Formidable*'s bow dipped into the sea. And then it was gone. Captain Loxley's last words are reputed to have been, 'Steady men, it's all right. No panic, keep cool. Be British.'[135]

Thirty-five officers and 512 men died when *Formidable* went down. These included Captain Loxley (and his dog Bruce), Commander Charles Ballard and the Rev George Robinson. Many men in the boats died from exposure before the shore could be reached. Most of those who survived were plucked from the boats the next morning, although one boat was not found until 22 hours after the sinking.

Schneider went on to sink 46 ships, totalling 143,000 tons. He met his death in October 1917 when he was swept off the conning tower of *U-87*. Although he was pulled from the water ten minutes later, he never responded to efforts to revive him.

The Illustrated London News' dramatic imagining of the end HMS Formidable. Captain Loxley's dog Bruce patiently waits to share the fateful conclusion. The sinking was to cost Admiral Bayly his squadron command.

Formidable was the first battleship to be lost to a U-boat, fulfilling the predictions of Admiral Fisher, Charles à Court Repington and others on the vulnerability of capital ships to torpedoes. Churchill recalled: 'The melancholy news reached the Admiralty with the light of New Year's Day.'[136] Even so, the Parliamentary Recruitment Committee attempted to turn the tragedy to good purpose by making use of Captain Loxley's last words in a recruitment poster: 'Boys! Be British! Enlist Now'.[137]

Bayly was hauled before the Admiralty and accused of 'failing to take adequate precautions against submarine attack', despite having been told to exercise without accompanying destroyers.[138] He was relieved of his command (which implied that he was to blame) but, at the same time, the Admiralty declared that 'conducting training exercises in the Channel without destroyer protection was excessive and should not be continued' (which implied that he was not to blame).[139] (Later in the war Bayly would distinguish himself with his energetic and imaginative command of the defences of the Western Approaches.)

On February 4 Churchill was challenged in the Commons by William Joynson-Hicks over the absence of destroyers at the time of *Formidable's* sinking. The backbencher received the only answer that a minister could give in wartime: 'I cannot undertake to discuss the conduct of naval operations during the progress of the War.'[140] For all the Admiralty's equanimity in the face of this loss, the fact was that, yet again, the navy had been forced to recognize that it had no answer to the U-boat threat. This was underlined by the next intervention when Lord Charles Beresford rose from his seat in the Commons to ask whether the Admiralty would provide 'naval defence' for convoys of slow merchant ships. Churchill replied: 'Sir, all these matters receive careful attention in the proper quarters.' In fact, it would be over two years before the Admiralty would give any serious thought to convoying merchant shipping.

Debacle at Dogger Bank

In January, Admiral Friedrich von Ingenohl was worried about the large number of fishing boats in the Dogger Bank area of the North Sea which, he suspected, were there to spy on the movements of his ships. He ordered Admiral Franz von Hipper to put to sea on January 24 to reconnoitre the area. It seemed like a low-risk operation that might yield useful results. Hipper's First Scouting Group set out with seven warships and 18 destroyers to observe or attack the small boats. It looked like overkill, and so it would have been, but for British intelligence.

Ingenohl's signals to Hipper had been intercepted by the coastal listening stations and forwarded to Room 40 at the Admiralty. Fisher immediately ordered Admiral Beatty to put to sea. As Beatty's forces approached Dogger Bank, they encountered Hipper's screening forces. Hipper realized that, in place of the anticipated impotent fishing vessels, he now faced a vastly superior force. He had no choice but to fight his way home.

Beatty had five large ships to Hipper's four. He planned that *New Zealand* and *Indomitable* should take on the slow *Blücher* while *Princess Royal*, *Tiger* and *Lion* dealt with *Derfflinger*, *Moltke* and *Seydlitz*. In the confusion of battle, *Tiger* engaged *Seydlitz* instead of *Moltke*. *Moltke* took advantage of the error to concentrate its fire on *Lion*, badly damaging it.

Even so, Hipper dared not take advantage of this weakening of Beatty's force. He abandoned the seriously damaged *Blücher* and fled the field.

Midshipman John Ouvry in HMS *Tiger* watched as two torpedoes 'at point blank range' hastened *Blücher*'s end: 'I saw the foremost turret blow up and the mast come down, she'd stopped and was listing. We then turned away back home leaving *Blücher* sinking and she actually sank within view.'[141] Around 800-1000 men died with the ship.

The dying Blücher at Dogger Bank demonstrated the Royal Navy's dominance of surface warfare in the North Sea.

The Admiralty counted the battle as a great victory, which it was in the sense that ships from the High Seas Fleet had once more fled the seas in the face of detachments from the Grand Fleet. Churchill, though, was deeply disappointed with only one large ship being sunk. But the significance of the battle lay in its consequence: the Imperial Navy finally turned away from dreams of mighty fleet clashes and decided to exploit the capacities of the humble U-boat. It was a key turning point in the U-boat war.

The bold *Laertes*

With merchant ships now being sunk as routine, the British public needed inspirational stories in which their brave sailors outwitted the enemy. *The Times*' ran one such narrative under the headline 'Chase by submarine – Escape of British steamer'.[142] The attack had taken place on February 10 when the 4500-ton steamship *Laertes* was near the Maas lightvessel off the Dutch coast. The *Laertes* under Captain William Propert was on its way from Liverpool to Java, calling at Amsterdam. As the ship neared the coast, Propert and his second officer were on the bridge, while lookouts were stationed on the poop and in the crow's nest. The inevitable U-boat appeared, three miles off the starboard bow. Almost immediately, the boat signalled 'Heave to', but Propert was determined on escape. Although *Laertes* was running at full speed, the U-boat gradually gained on the ship and, around 4.15 pm, it opened fire. Bullets were whistling through the air, most being aimed at the bridge. They pinged and bounced off the ship as the U-boat endeavoured to close on *Laertes*. This continued for nearly an hour, during which time Propert hoisted various signals designed to fake an intended surrender. The relentless U-boat paid no heed to the signals as its merciless gunfire continued. Then, just as Propert was making an evasive move, he saw a torpedo streaking through the water. He held his breath as the weapon passed astern and, simultaneously, the U-boat was engulfed in a cloud of steam and seemed to falter. The action had ended.

Not one person had been injured on *Laertes*, although the ship was riddled with bullet holes. Propert won a DSC and a gold watch for his 'gallant and spirited conduct'.[143] He never knew which U-boat had shamefully to report having been outrun by a mere cargo vessel.

> **The KING has been graciously pleased to award the Distinguished Service Cross to Lieutenant William Henry Propert, Royal Naval Reserve, of the Steamship "Laertes," for his gallant and spirited conduct in command of his unarmed ship when attacked by the gunfire and torpedo of an enemy submarine on the 10th February, 1915.**

Morale boosting in the meandering war at sea: the London Gazette's *February 1915 announcement of Captain Propert's DSO.*

AN ACCIDENTAL TARGET

The U-boat war took a serious turn at end of January when Otto Hersing's *U-21* turned up off the coast of Cumbria. Since sinking HMS *Pathfinder* in September, Hersing's successes had been limited to two small steamers, totalling only 2000 tons, both foundering off the French Channel coast. Now Hersing was ready for something more ambitious: Britain's west coast. *U-21* passed through the Dover Barrage on the night of January 21-22. From there, he proceeded along the English Channel and then turned north into the Irish Sea, arriving off Walney Island in Barrow-in-Furness on January 29. The island was heavily defended by coastal batteries since, amongst other industries, it boasted the Vickers submarine factory. (Whether Hersing chose the island for this reason is not known.)

U-21 surfaced at around two to three miles off the island. The boat was quickly spotted by the local garrison, but they failed to suspect that it was an enemy craft. The boat's allegiance was confirmed when it fired two shells at an airship shed on the island. The men of N°·7 Company of the Lancashire and Cheshire Royal Garrison Artillery were thrilled to find that the war had come to their doorstep. For once, they could fire at a real enemy target. A dozen rounds were enough to compel *U-21* to submerge. The authorities suppressed the news of the attack, so it was never reported locally, other than over pints in pubs.

Hersing's attack on Walney Island was no more than a display of bravado: a U-boat could never seriously threaten shore-based facilities. He followed his moment of frivolity with the more business-like job of sinking three steamers. Having so forcefully advertised his presence, Hersing took the wise decision to return to Wilhelmshaven. In doing so, he became yet another boat to pass back unnoticed through the Dover Barrage.

Hersing's raid on Walney Island led to panic in the coastal forces. *U-21* had penetrated into the seas off Liverpool – a major port for both Atlantic trade and warships. On the last day of the month all warship sailings were cancelled, and the port was closed to other shipping. Amongst the ships held back from sailing was HMS *Crescent*, which should have left that night to re-join the Northern Patrol. Scrimgeour looked forward to its departure 'which will be exciting, especially as we know three submarines are waiting for us'.[144]

Hersing's patrol was a significant moment in the U-boat war. In August 1914 U-boats had reached Scapa Flow, so demonstrating that they could threaten the full length of the British east coast. Now Hersing had shown that the west coast was equally vulnerable. And that was where most of the larger merchant ships were to be found.

Vickers publicity material for its factories, including the one that U-21 attacked in early 1915. (Contemporary advertisement.)

AMERICAN SPARRING

Towards the end of January the British Admiralty advised merchant vessels to fly neutral ensigns when nearing the British Isles. This did not please America. Writing to Ambassador Page in London on February 10, Secretary of State William Bryan said that he accepted the age-old principal of flying a neutral flag 'to deceive an approaching enemy' but he denounced the explicit encouragement of using neutral flags 'in portions of the high seas which are presumed to be frequented by hostile warships'. Such a practice, he told Page, put all neutral ships at risk. Bryan was particularly concerned about the misuse of the American flag. He asked Page to impress on Sir Edward Grey America's 'grave concern … in regard to the safety of American vessels and lives'.[145] (The King also strongly objected to the suggestion that British merchant ships should fly the American flag on approaching British waters, but he never made this public.) The ploy was, though, supported both by the ship insurers at Lloyd's of London and by the Customs Service: 'the use of false colours and simple disguises … [was] a well-established custom … not in any way dishonourable'.[146]

President Wilson's cabinet. Wilson (on the far left) faces Bryan (on the right, his hand on the table). (Library of Congress)

BLOCKADE SUCCESS

While the British armies in France had nothing to recompense them for their 104,000 casualties in the first six months of the war, the navy was having great success in enforcing the blockade. So much so, that the Northern Command teleprinter in the Orkneys was overloaded with problematic seizures being referred to London. Telegraph capacity was limited: it took an operator two hours to punch 5000 words and the transmission rate to London was around 60-100 words per minute. Every doubtful case was an urgent matter, since hours spent in punching, transmitting and reaching a decision in London translated into costly delays for ship owners. Excessive delays increased the temptations of masters to attempt to run the blockade.

Success, though, was an elusive concept for the blockade commanders. Did thousands of words of teleprint to London signal success? Was the number of vessels brought in for search a good measure? All this was exacerbated by a profound misunderstanding – near enough, a rift – between the blockade command and the Admiralty.

It had begun when Jellicoe had written to the Admiralty in November 1914 to complain about the blockade's waste of resources. The patrols repeatedly brought in ships laden with contraband which, when reported to London, were released. He gave as recent examples: '[ships] bound for the Baltic and Dutch ports ... allowed to proceed with complete cargoes which included 1 ship with copper, 11 with grain and foodstuffs, 5 with petroleum, 1 with magnetic ore, 1 with sulphur, 1 with coal and 2 with general cargoes.'[147] The Admiralty's reply on the following day explained that they had obtained adequate guarantees that these cargoes were not bound for Germany.

Jellicoe compounded these misunderstandings about the role of the patrol ships by his failure to share the Admiralty's replies with his commanders. They never received any feedback on which of their prizes had been retained, which released, and why. This left the commanders unsure as to what was and what was not contraband. Not surprisingly, this information vacuum was dispiriting for the boarding parties. They took great risks in dangerous seas, but felt neglected by the Admiralty and senior officers.

9
Neutrals beware!

February to March 1915

'All the waters surrounding Great Britain and Ireland, including the whole of the English Channel, are hereby declared to be a war zone.' - German Admiralty Declaration, February 4, 1915.[148]

GERMANY AT WAR

During the first five months of the war the British blockade had been steadily tightened. For Germany, this was a monumental threat. The Berlin government had been compelled to introduce bread rationing at the end of December; food shortages were affecting daily life. Germany's factories and armies needed oil, metals and chemicals to produce the weapons for the land war. In this same period, the U-boats had sunk 313,000 tons of shipping. Such sinkings had little effect on Britain's trade. In the blockade battle – British patrolling versus U-boat hunting – the British blockade was a success while the U-boat operations were no more than an irritation for Britain. It was time for a change of strategy.

This issue came to a head just at the time of a change of command in the High Seas Fleet. Following the poor performance of the German ships at the Battle of Dogger Bank, von Ingenohl was removed and replaced by Hugo von Pohl, who was an enthusiastic advocate of unrestricted submarine warfare. Pohl acted immediately by announcing on February 18 that: 'The waters around Great Britain and Ireland, including the whole of the English Channel, are hereby declared to be a War Zone.'[149]

The declaration brought opportunities for the U-boats, but at the risk of making enemies elsewhere, as Von Pohl recognized in his announcement. He warned, 'every enemy merchant vessel encountered in this zone will be destroyed, nor will it always be possible to avert the danger thereby threatened to the crew and passengers'. But the War Zone policy had a much more serious weakness: 'it may not always be possible,' said Pohl, 'to prevent attacks on enemy ships from harming neutral ships'. He blamed this aspect of the policy on the British for their 'misuse of neutral flags'.[150] It was a hazardous strategy, which rested on sinking merchant ships fast enough to knock Britain out of the war before angered neutrals (particularly America) yelled 'Cease and desist!'

Rather than intimidate American shippers, Pohl's War Zone declaration reset America's view of the Allied war. Gone were the accusations that Britain's blockade was as bad as German U-boat warfare. *The New-York Tribune* said that Germany was 'playing with fire'. *The Herald* declared that the sinkings policy was 'a crime of the high seas' and the *Evening Sun* prophetically said: 'The destruction of a neutral ship with its crew and passengers in the so-called war zone would set the world aflame with wrath.' In Britain *The Times* reported that Germany had 'created an unexpectedly favourable atmosphere for the settlement of Anglo-American trade difficulties'.[151]

Within a week the United States government added its official voice to the journalists' debate. Despite Germany's claim to retain 'sincere and most friendly sentiments' the President warned that the War Zone policy had created 'a critical situation'. The portentous note continued: 'the sole right of a belligerent dealing with neutral vessels on the high seas is limited to visit and search'. Then came America's first warning to Germany: 'To declare or exercise the right to attack or destroy any vessel entering the prescribed area ... would be an act so unprecedented in naval warfare that this Government is reluctant to believe that the Imperial Government of Germany ... contemplates it.'[152] In the world of diplomacy this was strong language, a fact that was recognized by the German Foreign Office, which knew how to decode threats veiled in diplomatic camouflage. On reading the United States statement the German Foreign Office began attempts to disown the War Zone policy before it had even been implemented.

Two days later, U-boat commanders were told that 'for urgent political reasons' boats already at sea were 'not to attack ships flying a neutral flag, unless recognized with certainty to be enemies'.[153] Pohl pounced on the flaw in this pronouncement: 'This order makes success impossible as the U-boats cannot determine the nationality of ships without exposing themselves to great danger. The reputation of the Navy will ... suffer tremendously if this undertaking ... achieves no results.'[154] Then, as if regretting the whole War Zone initiative, the following day U-boat commanders were told that the new sinkings plan was suspended until they received orders from the 'All Highest' [the Kaiser].[155]

After this muddle, the new policy went into force on February 18 with the proviso that the U-boats were not to attack ships flying neutral flags unless they were obviously enemy ships. Also, hospital ships were not to be sunk unless they were carrying troops. The announcement merited a characteristically pithy entry in Margot Asquith's diary, describing the War Zone policy as 'a form of naval warfare – piracy, indeed murder – unheard of in the world's History'.[156] (The Prime Minister's wife was never short of a forceful comment.)

And so began two fruitless years of Germany's attempts to find a U-boat strategy that could force Britain out of the war without bringing America into it.

The War Zone strategy was typical of Germany's incoherent naval war. The Kaiser and his advisers knew that a few high profile sinkings of neutral ships (particularly if American) could result in an enlargement of the war. Against this risk, the U-boat operations offered little in compensation since the Imperial Navy still had only 37 U-boats, of which only about 25 were available for North Sea operations.

Germany's intention was to starve Britain into submission. But, just as Germany was announcing the War Zone policy, Lieutenant-Colonel Sir Harry Verney, Parliamentary Secretary to the Board of Agriculture and Fisheries, was reassuring the House of Commons on the security of Britain's food supplies. There would be, he said, 'a substantial increase in the acreages under grain crops' in 1915.[157] Three weeks later he told the Commons that grain stocks were slightly up on their September 1914 level. Tirpitz and the U-boat commanders had not yet made any impression on Britain's capacity to wage war.

NEUTRALS UNDER FIRE

Germany's War Zone declaration proved problematic from its second day as the 7000-ton Norwegian tanker *Belridge*, in passage from New Orleans to Amsterdam, demonstrated. The ship was four miles south of the Varne lightship in the Dover Strait at 1.00 am on February 19 when it was struck by a torpedo from *U-16* under the command of Kapitänleutnant Klaus Hansen. *Belridge*'s crew took the detonation of the warhead to be an explosion in the oil tanks and immediately launched three boats. One boat, containing the pilot and 17 men, was quickly picked up by an American vessel. Meanwhile, Captain Olsen realized that *Belridge* was not sinking; he called for volunteers to reboard it. They volunteered to a man, so Olsen took the men from just one of the boats. He and his volunteers boarded the vessel and succeeded in taking it to shallow water off Walmer in Kent.

In Norway there was outrage at one of its ships being attacked on the high seas. Its government declared that it expected full compensation to be paid. If prompt payment was not forthcoming, it would seize German ships moored in Norwegian harbours. This was the first sinking of a neutral vessel under the new War Zone regime. Germany paid up, but the sinking was a harbinger of troubles to come.

Although the Imperial Navy tried to excuse the *Belridge* incident as a mistake, it was an inevitable consequence of the orders given to the U-boat commanders. 'The first consideration is the safety of the U-boat,' they were told. Hence 'rising to the surface to examine a ship must be avoided'. In other words, the full extent of a U-boat commander's assessment of a target was to be limited to what he could see through a periscope.

In a clarification of the sinking rules issued on February 22, commanders were told that 'Neutral ships are to be spared.' How, was not made clear. On the one hand, merchant ships with neutral flags in convoy, ships of the Belgian Relief Mission, and hospital ships were not to be sunk. On the other hand, commanders were advised that 'there is no guarantee that one is not dealing with an enemy ship even if it bears the distinguishing marks of a neutral'. The instructions concluded with the enigmatic advice that a sinking 'will therefore be justifiable unless other attendant circumstances indicate its neutrality'.[158] This reads like permission to 'shoot on sight'. Far from clarifying the sinkings policy, these instructions were bafflingly ambiguous. Unsurprisingly, Scheer claimed that 'the U-boat campaign was in fact ruined' by the restrictions placed on commanders.[159]

The Imperial Navy's casual attitude to identifying neutrals was in evidence when an unknown U-boat torpedoed the Swedish steamer *Hanna* in passage from the Tyne to Las Palmas with a cargo of coal at 1.40 am on March 13. The ship's name and nationality were clearly displayed on its side, but this was no protection against an aggressive U-boat commander. The *Hanna* was in the North Sea off Scarborough at the time of the attack. The second mate had seen the trace of the torpedo as it raced towards the steamer before it careered into the beam under the foremast. Six men, who were below at the time, died when the steamer went down about half-an-hour after the impact. The fourteen survivors, including the captain and officers, were able to get into a boat. For ten minutes they lay alongside the *Hanna* calling, 'Is there anybody aboard,' but no answer came.[160] They pulled away and were found by the collier

Gyller, which landed them at the Alexandra Dock in Hull. Whether the U-boat commander knew what sort of ship he had attacked is not clear. But an attack in which there was no prior contact with the ship and at 1.40 am when it was too dark to assess the *Hanna* suggests that he simply sank it because it was there. The *Gyller* continued coal-carrying throughout the war until foundering on September 9, 1918, with all hands lost.

Germany's complex relationship with neutral vessels deepened two weeks later when *U-28* blatantly ignored the 'neutral ships are to be spared' order of February 22 by sinking the 1200-ton Dutch steamer SS *Medea* off Beachy Head in the English Channel. *Medea* was flying the Dutch flag, had a Dutch crew, and its name was clearly displayed on its side. It was Korvettenkapitän Freiherr von Forstner's fourth of what were to be 24 sinkings. Forstner ordered the unarmed ship to stop and to send over a boat with the ship's papers. He then ordered the *Medea*'s crew into boats, while refusing to return their papers. As the crew rowed away, they saw Forstner's boat opening fire on the *Medea*, dispatching it and its London-bound cargo of Valencia oranges to the deep. HMS *Teviot* of the Ninth Destroyer Flotilla from Portsmouth soon picked up the stranded sailors and took them to Dover.

Despite the difficulty that the U-boats had in taking prizes, they occasionally succeeded. Forstner managed to do this with the Dutch *Batavier IV* in March 1915. The passengers in *Batavia IV* had only just woken when *U-28* took over the ship. On coming up from below, not fully dressed, to enquire why their ship had stopped, they saw *U-28* lying alongside. Forstner put one officer and one sailor on board the 1600-ton Dutch ship and then prepared to lead it to Zeebrugge to claim his prize. His men quickly adapted to their new command, with the officer signalling to *U-28* that 'There are a great many ladies on board.' Later he taunted his crew mates in the U-boat, signalling: 'We are having a delicious breakfast.'[161] Meanwhile, Forstner was getting a taste for prize-taking. Since he was port-bound, why not add another steamer to his tally? Stretching his crew to the limit, Forstner decided that he could spare one more officer and a stoker. The two men boarded the unarmed 1600-ton *Zaanstroom* and diverted its cargo of British breakfast eggs to Belgium. The Prize Court released *Batavia IV* in September so Germany gained little by this risky operation. It returned to sea only to be sunk by *UC-6* in May 1916.

The first two months of the Kaiser's War Zone policy had passed relatively quietly. The March sinkings of 81,000 tons were lower than the 98,000 tons of September 1914 so there was no sense of an acceleration in the U-boat campaign. But a subtle change was taking place as commanders became more careless in what they sank. Neutrals were being drawn into the war. No ship was safe. No nation was above being a target – not even the United States of America.

A TOO SANGUINE ADMIRALTY

Britain had few means of directly retaliating against the new German sinking policy. All that the navy could do was to make the blockade even more stringent in the hope of further weakening the German war effort. New rules were announced at an Order in Council on March 11: everything was now effectively contraband. British patrols could seize any ship carrying a cargo which might have Germany as its destination. Additionally, any ship that legitimately left a British port for a neutral destination, but on a subsequent voyage called at an enemy port, would be liable for seizure. The new policy's aim was the complete isolation of Germany from any seaborne trade. The patrols were not slow to enforce the enhanced blockade. In the following ten days the Northern Patrol took in 120 vessels for close inspection at Kirkwall.

At the political level, Asquith was relaxed about the enemy's determination to sink Britain into submission. In a Commons debate on a motion for further war expenses of £37,000,000 on March 1, he made the first official statement on Germany's War Zone policy. It had replaced 'regulated capture' with 'indiscriminate destruction', he told Members of Parliament. Britain's blockade of Germany was justified, Asquith argued, because '[we are] dealing with an opponent who has openly repudiated all the restraints, both of law and of humanity'. He continued: 'we are not going to allow our efforts to be strangled in a network of juridical niceties', but he assured the House that 'we shall carefully avoid any measures which violate the rules either of humanity or of honesty'.[162] The words were high sounding, but what did they mean? Britain had no answer to the War Zone campaign and was compelled to retreat behind a wall of Admiralty bravado and government waffle.

Freedom of the Seas

The U-boat war had brought a challenge to the centuries-old doctrine of the freedom of the seas. Since the seventeenth century there had been a general acceptance between nations that national rights over the seas were limited to coastal waters. America remained unyieldingly wedded to this principle: President Wilson would include it in his famous 'Fourteen Points' in January 1918. A peace settlement, he then argued, should recognize the 'Absolute freedom of navigation upon the seas, outside territorial waters, alike in peace and in war.'[163]

The determination of the United States to uphold the concept of the freedom of the seas was on the minds of British ministers when the Cabinet met on February 16. They struggled to reconcile the need to win the war – which meant stopping ships for inspection on the high seas – with the imperative necessity of not upsetting the United States. Charles Hobson noted in his diary that the Cabinet's determination 'to detain all ships carrying cargo useful to Germany, or likely to arrive there, directly or indirectly' might well involve stopping American ships. How would America react? Sir Edward Grey suggested that America would simply send its cargo ships under naval escort. The Cabinet found this more than credible and were unanimous in their view that 'we must take that risk'. Should American ships arrive under escort 'we should have to let them pass through'.[164]

The Cabinet's deliberations resulted in new regulations, which were announced by Asquith in the Commons on March 1. 'The British and French governments,' he said, would 'detain and take into port ships carrying goods of presumed enemy destination, ownership, or origin'.[165] In an attempt to pacify neutral countries, only goods already classified as contraband would be seized (a list that covered everything of any importance). Britain had now taken the blockade near enough to its limits.

A Touchy Friend

The new regulations brought clashes with America within days, especially over the interpretation of 'the freedom of the seas'.

The *Dacia* incident had begun in January 1915 when a Mr E N Breitung of the American shipbroker Breitung & Co proposed to buy the ex-cable-laying steamer SS *Dacia* and sail it to Germany with a cargo of cotton. The Germany-bound cotton was in clear breach of the British blockade rules. Sir Edward Grey was desperate to find a way of stopping the ship without upsetting the Americans. His rescue came from Ambassador Page, who turned up at the Foreign Office having already solved the problem in his own mind. Rather than tell the British government what to do, Page used a series of hints to help Grey to a resolution. After some chat about the British Fleet, Page continued: 'But have you ever heard of the French fleet? France has a fleet too, I believe.' Sir Edward Grey agreed. 'Don't you think that the French fleet ought to have a bit of advertising?' continued Page. Grey, now bemused, asked, 'What on earth are you talking about?' 'Well,' said Page, 'there's the *Dacia*. Why not let the French fleet seize it, and get some advertising?'[166]

Grey took the hint and asked the French government to intercept the *Dacia*. The seizure was declared valid by a French court on March 22. This was a satisfactory outcome to resolve one troublesome case, but it was no long-term solution to the conflict between the rights of Americans to trade and Britain's life-and-death necessity to enforce its unwavering blockade.

Other American attempts to break the blockade around this time included the SS *Trondhjemsfjord*, which was found passing north of the Faroes. It was taken into Kirkwall in July 1915, where its cargo was found to contain fuses and one million detonators. Another American-backed runner was the Swedish *Oscar II*. Its radioed call to Norway was picked up by a British listening station and the ship was intercepted at 3.00 am on February 14. Its 'cargo' included German reservists from America, all under false names. The ship later sank after a collision with the patrol ship HMS *Patuca* at 12.35 am on July 1, 1915, by which time it had established a reputation as a regular blockader runner.

U-BOATS UNDER ATTACK

One of the first close engagements between a U-boat and a merchant vessel occurred soon after the introduction of the War Zone. Captain John Bell of the 500 ton SS *Thordis* was in passage from Newcastle to Saltash in Cornwall with a cargo of coal. The ship was off Beachy Head when the attack came on February 28. A periscope was sighted: 'I immediately ordered all hands on deck in case we had to abandon ship,' Bell noted in the logbook. He stopped his ship and watched as *U-6* crossed in front of the *Thordis* at only 30-40 yards. To his horror, Bell saw the track of a torpedo heading straight for *Thordis*' beam. A sudden wave lifted the stern and the torpedo passed under the ship. Bell threw over the wheel and turned *Thordis* along the path left by the torpedo: 'I and all the crew heard and felt a crash under the ship's bottom,' he recalled, as the U-boat scraped its way under the ship.[167] Bell saw oil coming up from the sea but there was no a sign of the boat. Oberleutnant zur See Reinhold Lepsius had been lucky. The *Thordis* had ripped off his boat's two periscopes but there was no other major damage to *U-6*. It limped home to fight again. Lepsius and the boat made their first sinking – the *Folke*, a 1400-ton Swedish steamer – on April 14.

Bell thought that he had sunk the boat, so he neatly fulfilled the role of a much-needed-hero at that stage of the war. He and his crew shared a reward of £860 (£51,000 today) for being the first merchant captain to sink a U-boat. For Bell, there was also a visit to Buckingham Palace to receive a Distinguished Service Order medal from the King.

Captain John Bell receiving a reward from the Lord Mayor of London for his supposed sinking of a U-boat. (The Manchester Guardian History of the War.)

U-boat captures were rare, so the taking of *U-8* in early March was to be another boost to the morale of the anti-submarine forces. Kapitänleutnant Alfred Stoss had been in command of the boat since September 1 and had spent nearly six months on fruitless patrols. His luck changed in late February when he sank five merchant ships in two days, totalling 15,000 tons. That luck reversed when he attempted a westbound passage through the Dover Barrage on March 4.

The recently installed indicator nets at the barrage were about to claim Stoss as their first victim. Having resupplied with torpedoes at Ostend after his string of sinkings, Stoss began *U-8*'s passage through the nets of the supposedly impenetrable Dover Barrage, weaving between the buoys and lights. The foggy conditions helped mask the boat, but not enough to escape the lookouts on the destroyer HMS *Viking* Commander Evans opened fire at 1000 yards, precipitating *U-8*'s dive into the tangle of nets

Neutrals beware!

below. The hunt was now on. Soon, nine additional destroyers had joined in the search. *Viking* was the first ship to make contact with the boat when its sweeping gear detonated against *U-8*'s periscope, although no damage was done. *U-8* pressed on. Later, the destroyers HMSs *Maori* and *Ghurka* began sweeping. *Ghurka*'s explosive sweep soon caught on the boat and detonated against its hull. In *U-8*, the lights shattered and rivets in the pressure hull popped. As water trickled down the insides of the boat, the main switchboard caught fire. Then the motors went dead. *U-8* was overwhelmed. The boat surfaced and surrendered.

U-8's crew were marched under guard to Dover Castle and later transferred to a prisoner of war camp. Five days after the sinking, a curious Admiralty announcement appeared in *The Times* under the heading 'No honours of war.' Until now, said the Admiralty, German prisoners 'have received treatment appropriate to their rank'. This would not be the case for the men from *U-8*. 'There is strong probability that she has been guilty of attacking and sinking unarmed merchantmen and firing torpedoes at ships carrying non-combatants, neutrals and women.' Until their guilt or innocence could be established, *U-8*'s crew 'cannot be accorded the distinctions of their rank, or be allowed to mingle with other prisoners of war'.[168] How the Admiralty resolved this matter is not known.

U-8's capture reinforced the Dover Patrol's confidence in the supposed impenetrability of the barrage. In fact, all *U-8*'s five sinkings had taken place in the Beachy Head area, which showed that the boat had passed through the barrier at some earlier date. Indeed, it had returned to base through the barrier to re-arm and was only caught on its second attempt to pass Dover into the Channel. The barrage was a challenge to the U-boats, but not a deterrent, particularly since the boats could pass underneath the nets. Nor were the surface obstructions a major deterrent since storm damage often left navigable gaps.

Kapitänleutnant Freiherr von Spiegel's *U-32* was one of the boats that succeeded in escaping from initially being trapped in the nets. (*U-32* appears in Spiegel's memoirs as the fictional *U-202*.) The crew's nightmare began in early April 1915 when, through the periscope, Spiegel saw a group of vessels sweeping a channel, and a French destroyer standing off. This was no time to attempt to pass the barrage. He ordered a dive to the seabed. Spiegel watched the depth indicator while the boat began its slow descent. At a depth of nearly 60 feet he felt a massive blow. The boat rocked and shook. The lights went out and the men were thrown around like coins rattling in a near-empty charity collection tin.

The blast from a mine had triggered the boat's electrical cut-out system. In the pitch-black, men rushed to restore the power while Spiegel brooded on the likely damage. Yet, when the lights came on, there was not a leak to be seen. The boat looked completely normal. And then *U-32*'s bow plunged for no apparent reason.

The boat now had a life of its own. The men at the diving planes reported them to be already at their extremity. *U-32* stubbornly refused to answer to any of the controls: it was trapped in the barrage's indictor nets. Worse, the boat's stern began to rise towards the minefield above them. Spiegel ordered full speed ahead, shouting, 'Don't let her come up! Keep her down!'[169] The boat lurched ahead, only to bury itself deeper into a tangle of intractable wire netting. The men worked furiously at the rudders as they willed the boat to dive. *U-32*'s 1200 hp engine tugged and tore in its battle of steel on steel. And then, suddenly, the boat began to respond. The netting was shredding under the wrenching of the 900-ton vessel. Spiegel, his men and the boat had won. The depth gauge began to report their steady descent to the safety of the deep.

The nets which had caught *U-8* and *U-32* had been designed by Commander F R S Bircham RNVR. The net itself was made of wire mesh and hung to varying depths. Attached to the nets were glass buoys fitted with calcium lights, which automatically ignited when the buoy was fouled. Once snagged on a net, an unsuspecting U-boat dragged one or more of the lit-up buoys with it, so revealing its line of passage. According to Winston Churchill, 17 miles of this netting had been laid across the Dover Strait by mid-February 1915.

The first U-boat to be sunk by an anti-submarine vessel in 1915 went down in March. *U-12* was known to be off the North coast of Scotland in early March after having made a failed attempt to torpedo the armoured cruiser HMS *Leviathan*. The boat then disappeared until it was sighted outside the Firth of Forth on March 10 by the trawler *Man Island*. HMSs *Acheron*, *Attack* and *Ariel* were dispatched to the area. *Attack* was the first to locate *U-12*. Two minutes later *Ariel* also had it in view, by which time *Attack* had opened fire. *U-12* rapidly submerged to periscope depth – presumably Kapitänleutnant Hans Kratzsch was intending to torpedo one of his assailants.

Commander James Creagh in *Ariel* saw his chance. Ordering full speed ahead, he drove *Ariel* towards the periscope. The ship smashed into

Neutrals beware!

the boat, which promptly surfaced. All three warships now fired at the cornered craft. One shot damaged the conning tower, leaving the hatch jammed in a half-open position. Another shot tore the boat's gun off the deck. Inside, the men scrambled for their lives. Those near the conning tower, including Kratzsch, had no chance. Just ten men emerged from the other two hatches. As they stood on *U-12*'s deck, the boat sank under them.

Hans Kratzsch, had had an unimpressive war. He had first commanded *U-39*, in which he had made no sinkings. Within a month he had transferred to *U-12* and managed to sink one vessel of 1000 tons before encountering HMS *Ariel*.

All but one of the surviving crew were destined to spend the rest of the war in a prisoner of war camp. One man, though, escaped from his Maidenhead camp by digging a tunnel under a flower bed. He made his way to Hull, where he signed on to a Swedish ship. In late 1915 the ship was stopped by *U-16*, which soon had him back in Germany. He then sailed in *U-44* until, on August 12, 1917, it was rammed by HMS *Oracle*. There were no survivors.

The *U-12* story illustrates the serious consequences of a navy lacking any means of finding and sinking submerged boats. The sighting of *U-12*, and that of another U-boat in this period, pinned down every warship at the northern end of the North Sea for four days as the search went on to locate and sink it. With no means of detecting U-boats, luck still remained the main ingredient in the Royal Navy's sparsely filled locker of anti-submarine technologies.

10
Patrol life

1915

'Continuous snow storm all day. Intensely cold, thermometer below freezing-point'; the ship looked like a great white iceberg.' – Scrimgeour, January 1915.[170]

TAKING PRIZES

The work of the patrols that enforced the blockade was crushingly tedious. It made no headlines, nor led to stories of high heroism in the popular papers. Even so, it called for exceptional young men, ready to take on great responsibilities.

All merchant shipping entering the North Sea at its northern end was liable to be boarded by the men of the Northern Patrol. The boarding party would be led by a young midshipman or lieutenant. This Prize Officer had to be polite but wary as he checked a ship's papers and examined its cargo. An insensitively conducted boarding and search might set off an international incident. To minimize potential conflict, the Prize Officers were provided with detailed boarding instructions from the Admiralty.

STOP COMMUNICATIONS

The Prize Officer's first task on boarding a ship was to sever its communications with the outside world in order to prevent its crew from divulging the location of the patrol. 'The Wireless Office should be locked and sealed,' ran the boarding instructions, 'and a guard placed over it, but immediate access should be provided for, in case of submarine attack or other emergency.'[171] (On some occasions, a patrol ship would jam the suspect vessel's radio to prevent attempts to signal before the boarding party had gained control of the vessel.)

GETTING INFORMATION

Once the boarding party had blocked the ship's communications, the boarders were to do their best to pump the officers and crew for intelligence of value to the Allies. For this purpose, each boarding party was issued with a set of questions to put to the ship's master, such as: 'Have you seen any men-of-war, seaplane carriers, submarines, airships or seaplanes, patrol vessels or trawlers, hospital ships or transports of neutral powers? If so state:- (a) Number and class of vessel seen. (b) Date, time and position seen. (c) If a submarine state what other vessels, if any, were in the vicinity.'[172] And, finally, the boarding party were to collect all possible information about any German passengers or crew. This action was followed by temporarily confiscating any arms and ammunition.

A boarding party on its way to inspect a suspect vessel.

SHARP EYES

Then came the inspection of the cargo, which needed a sharp eye. Hollow masts might conceal valuable metals. Heavy bags of what looked like coffee beans could turn out to be disguised copper. And secret military and diplomatic messages might be found hidden in cabins. Some ships made no attempt to conceal obvious contraband. The American SS *Sea Connet*'s cargo of rifles, copper, armour-plating and ammunition was readily visible to anyone on the ship. *Sea Connet* was promptly taken into Kirkwall.

Some ships attempted to escape the patrols, as was the case with the 3000-ton American *Dirigo* when it entered the North Sea in March 1916.

It was easily outrun by HMS *Orotava*. The subsequent boarding party was not satisfied with the master's claim that the cargo was barley and nothing but barley so the ship was escorted into Lerwick. There, aeroplanes and armoured cars were found under the innocent cereal. The *Dirigo* continued trading until its sinking by Oberleutnant zur See Hans Ewald Niemer in *UB-23* in May 1917. It was, though, a reformed character by then, carrying steel from America to France.

If a ship was to be taken in, those of its crew who did not wish to risk internment were free to leave the vessel. If several of the crew left, seamen from the patrol vessel would board as a temporary crew. (A patrol vessel carried two additional officers and twelve additional ratings for use in boarding and escort parties.)

Vigilance

The escort parties were trained to be aggressively vigilant during a vessel's passage to the Orkneys. They were to trust no one – this necessitated their bringing their own food for fear of being poisoned. At the practical level, the sailors carried cash so that, once landed, they could train to wherever their own ship could next pick them up.

Taking-in began with the Prize Officer informing the ship's master of their destination. From there on, the prize crew were under strict orders to never issue a sailing instruction during the passage – if the ship went aground or had a collision, the responsibility had to be clearly that of the ship's own commander.

The logbook of HMS *Changuinola* shows the boarding routine in operation on February 11, 1915. The Norwegian SS *Stralsund* was allowed to proceed, while the American SS *Pioneer*, which was carrying oil, was taken into Kirkwall. The strong gale, and the seven men on the sick list remind us of the harsh conditions of winter patrolling.

At Patrol
Lat 59.8, Long -7.5
4.20 am: Sighted Steamship bearing ESE
4.50 am: Slow, signalled HMS CAESAREA
4.55 am: Stopped, sent boat away for prize crew
5.35 am: Boat returned with Mid Pearse & prize crew
8.15 am: Sighted Steamship bearing WSW
9.00 am: Signalled one of Patrol ships, name not given
Crew employed painting on boat deck
Noon: Sighted Steamship bearing SW/S

1.40 pm: Stopped, boarded & examined Norwegian SS STRALSUND Reykjavik to Troon with fish
2.40 pm: Allowed Steamship to proceed, boat returned
3.45 pm: Sighted Steamship bearing SW0.5S, altered course to S11W
4.20 pm: Stopped & boarded SS PIONEER of Bayonne, New Jersey, oil cargo
5.00 pm: Boat returned
5.10 pm: Mid Pearse left with prize crew [to take the ship to Kirkwall]
5.25 pm: Boat returned
5.30 pm: Proceeded
Midnight: Strong gale
Sick list 7[173]

Under way

Once under way, the boarding party had only partial control of their destiny. The ship might be attacked or even boarded: the risk was real. Sixteen of the ships under escort by men from the Tenth Cruiser Squadron were sunk by U-boats while the prize crews were on board. The prize crew were forbidden to carry out any belligerent act while in charge of the prize. If the prize was attacked while the prize crew was on board they could only they defend themselves once all the ship's crew had left the ship. However, the prize crew were permitted to hide or to escape in a ship's boat if capture appeared otherwise inevitable.

Despite all these precautions, a few wily captains outwitted their boarding parties. The captain of one sailing ship took advantage of the fact that the prize crew party knew nothing about sail. He kept pretending that he was taking the sole course that the wind permitted. Only when, a few days later, the Norwegian coast loomed ahead did the prize crew realize that they had been duped.

Hazards of weather

Boarding parties had to cope with the hazards of weather, while being forbidden from directing the ship's navigation. When the Danish SS *Canadia* was boarded by Lieutenant Herbert Spencer together with six ratings on March 13, 1915, the weather was foul and the navigation difficult. At 3.30 am land suddenly appeared ahead out of the impenetrable squally dark. Before any evasive action could be taken, the *Canadia* had rammed itself onto the rocks under a 400-foot cliff, and then stuck there. The local lifeboat crew made valiant attempts to reach the ship, but the hazards of the rocky shore were too great. At dawn, men carried ladders down the cliff, which they used to make a bridge from ship to shore. Every man in the *Canadia* was safely taken off by 9.00 am, with the only casualty being the captain, who suffered serious injuries from a distress rocket.

A RARE ALTERCATION

The American 7,700-ton sailing oil barge *Navahoe*, belonging to the Anglo-American Oil Company, offers a rare example of an attempt to resist a boarding party. When its commander refused HMS *Ambrose*'s request to board on March 1, 1915, *Ambrose* called for support from HMS *Patuca*, the senior ship in the patrol. Young Scrimgeour, whose diary mixed actual events with additions from his vivid imagination, recorded: 'Shots were fired across the Yankee ship's bow.'[174] *Patuca*'s log merely records:

9.30 am: SS *Navahoe* arrived
10.00 am: Part of prize crew returned from SS *Navahoe*[175]

Clearly the senior officer in the *Navahoe* thought better of his refusal to accept boarding.

ARRESTING A SPY

Service with the Northern Patrol was one of the toughest naval assignments of the war, as ships and men were relentlessly battered, soaked and drenched by the hostile weather and untameable seas. The call to take in a spy rather than a cargo of beef or a hold-full of metal ore was a welcome diversion.

At the end of 1914, news had reached the Admiralty that the Norwegian passenger liner SS *Bergensfjord*, in passage to Norway, was carrying a suspected German spy. A radio call to the commander of B patrol ordered him to stop the *Bergensfjord* and take the suspect into custody. The search began on January 1, 1915, and the intercept was soon accomplished. The suspect, together with some other doubtful passengers, was taken off *Bergensfjord* by the patrol ship HMS *Viknor*, which dropped them off at Kirkwall. The identity of the spy was not revealed, which left the field to the rumour-mongers.

By the time the news of the capture had reached Scrimgeour, the 'suspect' was none other than the notorious Baron Von Wedel. (In Karl Grave's 1914 book *The Secrets Of The German War Office* Wedel appears as Count Botho von Wedel, privy counsellor to the Kaiser and head of the spy bureau.) Scrimgeour's excited diary entry continues: 'What his mission in America was is unknown, but it is of little doubt that only a tremendous bribe would have induced the Captain of the *Bergensfjord* to risk his all by contravening international law so flagrantly as to bring a man like Von Wedel across the ditch. ... [Wedel] was found burning incriminating papers. He was taken unawares, as he did not expect us to know of his disguise.'[176]

(The *Viknor* foundered on January 13 in the new year off Tory Island, County Donegal in heavy seas. There was no distress call and there were no survivors, so it is presumed that the ship had struck a mine.)

THE OTHER ENEMY

For much of the year, the weather in the North Sea compounded the men's boredom when out on patrol. In January 1915 Scrimgeour recorded 'Continuous snow storm all day' along with 'Intensely cold, thermometer below freezing-point'. The rough sea lashed the ship, tearing away one of the wireless aerial braces and leaving the vessel looking like 'a great white iceberg'.[177] These troubles were minor inconveniences compared to the worst of the sea's ravishing of the patrols. The logbook for HMS *Patia* on January 19, 1916, records: 'Shipped heavy sea over bows, causing much structural damage to bridge, wheelhouse, & forward bulkhead & ward room 3 pdr gun shelters smashed. Lieut Thompson, Officer Of Watch, badly injured.'[178]

HMS *Orotava*, steaming through a Force 12 gale (technically a hurricane), suffered a similar fate at 3.50 pm on January 21, 1916: 'Sea struck bridge making clean sweep of all fittings and smashing fore side of wheelhouse, disabling wheel and steam steering gear.'[179] On days like these, men were stretched to their limits as patrolling gave way to simply staying afloat and alive. In some cases, sea water got into the water tanks, resulting in outbreaks of gastric illness.

Even a 5400-ton warship could struggle in the gales and rough seas. On December 27, 1915, HMS *Southampton* was rolling 40 degrees, King-Hall told his parents. Lunch went from table to deck in 'an avalanche of plates' taking the curry with them. 'The bread, cheese, and pickle-pots flung themselves at the fiddles [battens on table edges]' and the sideboard crashed to the deck. Meanwhile, the floor of King-Hall's cabin was 'a heap of books, music, coffee-pots, toffee tins, photos, war games, ash trays, papers, socks, boots'.[180]

Even when the sea was calm enough for boarding, the short passage to the suspect vessel could be perilous. Lieutenant Commander H Phillips was helping to store a boat when he was swept off the deck of HMS *Almanzora* in January 1916: 'Body not recovered' recorded the logbook.[181]

For the seamen who maintained the blockade in these hard conditions there was little recognition and less glory. But, for the German people, the blockade was the source of their daily misery. For them, any action at sea was justifiable if it would put food back on their tables. It was time for Germany to resort to more desperate measures.

11
A new target

Spring 1915

'After loss of several submarines through traps, order that safety of our own boats is to come before all other considerations. No longer essential to rise to surface.' – Von Pohl, April 2, 1915.[182]

DISAPPEARING U-BOATS

Towards the end of March, Tirpitz was reviewing U-boat losses. When *U-8* had failed to return earlier in the month he had presumed it lost, but he had no confirmation of its fate. Then there was the loss of Weddigen's *U-29* three weeks later. Once again, Tirpitz had no report of its fate; he convinced himself that 'Widdigen [sic] was perhaps too confident!'[183] In reality, Weddigen had been too cautious. He had successfully braved the Dover Barrage and sunk four ships off Land's End. Realizing how lucky he had been in passing the barrage, he chose to take the long route home via the North of Scotland. Four days after his last attack, in which he damaged the peacetime 500-ton excursion steamer *Atalanta,* he had successfully circumnavigated Scotland and was heading southbound in the North Sea. Just as a smooth home run seemed guaranteed, *U-29* came face-to-face with HMS *Dreadnought.* On the battleship's bridge, Lieutenant Commander Basil Piercy sighted *U-29*'s periscope, 20 degrees off the port bow. *Dreadnought*'s helm went over and the massive battleship made a straight run for the doomed U-boat, slicing it in two. There was just time for the bridge officers to read '*U-29*' before the shattered remains of the boat slid under the waves. A single item of clothing amongst the scraps of wreckage was the only testament to the 35 men who had perished with the boat. One of them was the man who had sunk *Aboukir, Cressy, Hogue* and *Hawke,* and who had been the first U-boat commander to wear the Blue Max, as *Pour le Mérite* was called.

It was losses like these that led Von Pohl to conclude that the U-boat commanders were taking too many risks. It was time to put the safety of his boats before the niceties of identifying the nature of potential targets. It was, he announced on April 2, 'No longer essential [for the boats] to rise to surface.'[184]

Passengers, beware!

The sinking of the *Falaba* on March 28 is often said to have been the first passenger ship to be sunk by a U-boat. In fact, von Forstner had sharpened his skills on the SS *Aguila* on the previous day.

Captain Thomas Bannerman's 2000-ton British steamer was in passage from Liverpool to the Canary Islands when the attack took place. The *Aguila* was passing the Smalls Lighthouse on the Pembrokeshire coast when a lookout sighted *U-28* at 6.00 pm on March 27. Bannerman's first reaction was to attempt to outrun the boat. He called for full-steam of 14 knots, but *U-28*'s top surface speed of 16 knots was enough to seal *Aguila*'s fate. As *U-28* came into range, von Forstner fired a shot across the ship's bow. Bannerman conceded defeat and stopped the engines.

With no preliminaries, Von Forstner gave Bannerman's crew and passengers just four minutes to evacuate the ship. But, even before this impossible limit had been reached, *U-28*'s gun was firing on the unarmed vessel. Chief engineer Edwards, boatswain Anderson, and donkeyman McKirkman were all killed as they stood on the deck. Somehow the boats were lowered. One capsized, taking with it the sole female passenger and a stewardess.

By the time that *U-28* had ceased firing, twenty shells had ripped into *Aguila*. Its end came with a torpedo that rent the ship in two. It rapidly sank, taking down eight passengers and crew. The survivors were rescued by a trawler and then transferred to the steamship *St Stephen*. They later landed at Milford Haven. Accounts vary as to how many passengers lost their lives in the sinking, but their fate was soon forgotten when Von Forstner found a bigger target on the following day. It was to be a sinking that would usher in a new era of carnage on the high seas.

The public first learnt about von Forstner's next outrage from the newspaper headlines: 'Murder by torpedo – German pirates sink two liners.' His second victim had been the passenger steamer SS *Falaba*.

The 5000-ton British *Falaba* was in passage from Liverpool to the west coast of Africa and was 50 miles off the Welsh Pembrokeshire coast on March 28. On the bridge were the Chief Officer, Mr Baxter, and the Third Officer, Mr Pengilly. It was 11.40 am when Pengilly saw what he took to be a submarine flying a British ensign. When Captain Davies came up from the chart room, he was not deceived. He altered course to place the U-boat behind him and called for full-steam ahead. As *Falaba*

A new target

turned, the radio operator put out an all-stations signal: 'Submarine overhauling us. Flying British flag. 51° 32', 6° 36'.'[185]

When *U-28* caught up with the *Falaba*, von Forstner repeated his *Aguila* routine. Davies had ignored the first warning, but on the second 'Stop, or I fire' he ordered 'Stop engines'. Picking up a megaphone, he shouted, 'Abandon ship immediately.' On hearing this call the radio operator sent a second all-ships message: 'Position 51° 32' N. 6° 36' W torpedo going boats.'[186] It was now five minutes past twelve. Five minutes later a torpedo tore into the side of the *Falaba*, still laden with passengers and crew. The ship lurched and fell into a list. Eight minutes later the *Falaba* was no more.

Only two of the ship's eight boats got away safely; two were damaged in the attempt to launch them. Sergeant Hubert Blair of the Royal Army Medical Corps told a *Daily Mail* reporter that the first boat to be lowered had capsized as soon as it hit the waves, throwing 20 men into the water. He was in the fourth and last boat to be launched, which was blown to pieces by the torpedo that struck the ship.

Von Forstner and his men made no attempt to help the survivors, nor did they depart the scene. Instead, Sergeant Blair recalled, the men of *U-28* 'gathered on deck and laughed and jeered as the passengers and crew struggled in the water'.[187]

The wireless operator testified to the hysterical condition of many of the terrified passengers and crew as they saw all hope of survival slipping from them. One of the firemen jumped overboard in the hope of a quick end from drowning. Another crew member had to be restrained from slitting his throat. Meanwhile, those still on deck were looking down at the 30 or so people fighting for their lives after their boat had capsized. The wireless operator later declared: 'I shall never forget the agony of listening to their final and awful cries, and watching the heartrending look of horror as they sank from sight.'[188]

One-hundred-and-four passengers and crew were killed; some by the torpedo explosions; some drowned; others succumbing to hyperthermia. The *Falaba* was the first significant passenger ship sinking. It marked a turning point in the war. Germany, having failed to beat the Allies on both the Western and Eastern Fronts, and having failed to eradicate the threat of the Grand Fleet, was now taking its war to civilians.

Those who could not imagine what was yet to come, looked in stunned horror at the slaughter of civilians on an unarmed vessel. One journalist summed up the reaction of many British people: 'If this is not piracy and murder, I don't know what is!'[189]

The crew of U-28 in 1917.[190]

One death on the *Falaba* went unremarked: that of Leon Thrasher, a 31-year-old mining engineer and native of Massachusetts. He was the first American to be killed in the war. It would take another sinking – and one not long in coming – for American deaths to become a contentious issue.

Five days after the sinking of the *Falaba*, the drifter *Orient II* called at Milford Haven to unload an unusual cargo, fished from the sea. Skipper Ernest Solomon called at the Post Office to hand over 32 heavy cases of mail. Amongst many other items in his miscellaneous catch were some cases of onions, some tyres and a bicycle frame belonging to a Mr A Houston, who had lost his life in the sinking.

The, by now, banal horror of merchant sinkings was captured by the *Sydney Mail*'s reporting of ten recent torpedo attacks on small ships in late March 1915. The sinking of 1500-ton passenger ship *Fingal* on March 15 by *U-23* when on passage from London to Leith with its general cargo was reduced to seven lines of a news column, packed with similar sinkings. Of those that died, all that could be said was: 'Six persons, including the chief mate and the stewardess, perished' when their lifeboat was torn to shreds by a boiler explosion.[191] Civilian deaths at sea were rapidly ceasing to be a news item.

Barrage or sieve?

The Imperial Navy's very limited access to the oceans was a serious handicap for the U-boats. All hunting grounds other than the North Sea lay beyond the Northern and the Dover patrols. By April 1915 the Admiralty finally acknowledged the leaky condition of the latter patrol when it transferred Rear Admiral Horace Hood to the command of the Third Battle Cruiser Squadron of the Grand Fleet. (He would later lose his life in HMS *Invincible* at the Battle of Jutland.) He was replaced by Rear Admiral Reginald Bacon. It was not much of change. Bacon had not been to sea since he became Director of Naval Ordnance in 1907 and he had been in retirement since 1909. Churchill's remark to Fisher about 'a frightful dearth of first-class men in the Vice Admirals' and Rear Admirals' lists' was to be vindicated at the Dover Patrol under Bacon.[192]

The Dover Patrol.

The Imperial Navy had no idea how many U-boats had come to grief in the Dover Barrage netting since Britain did not report U-boat sinkings in a manner that would aid German intelligence. It seems likely that the U-boat service often wrongly attributed unexplained losses to the nets. By mid-April, they declared the Strait passage to be too risky and ordered all boats to sail via the North of Scotland. This was a significant blow to the efficiency of the service since the outward and inward passages to the boats' hunting grounds would now take many more days. This seriously curtailed the number of boats that would be in contact with shipping at any one time, although the effects were to be masked by better weather and a growing number of boats.

No room for charity

With only 36 merchant ships sunk in March, Germany's new sinking rules were not delivering a war-winning strategy. It was at this time that Oberleutnant zur See Karl Gross took up his first command in *UB-4*. Keen to make an impact, he was delighted to find a large target within a day or so of putting to sea.

Gross had sighted the 6000-ton four-masted cargo ship SS *Harpalyce* just before 10.00 am on April 10. This was no ordinary ship, as Gross would have found had he stopped it. Captain Frederick Wawn would have shown him the ship's safe conduct certificate, signed by the German diplomat Richard von Kühlmann, Secretary of State for Foreign Affairs. The *Harpalyce* was sailing under the flag of the American Commission for Relief in Belgium. Having called at Rotterdam to unload its cargo of 11,000 individual gifts of food and other comforts for destitute Belgians, the *Harpalyce* was now returning in ballast to Norfolk, Virginia. Its large flag displaying 'Commission for Belgian Relief' and the same words in huge white letters on its sides left no room for doubt about its status.[193] (The Commission, founded by the American politician and engineer Herbert Hoover, was purely humanitarian, supplying over five million tons of food to Belgium and northern France during the war.)

It was 10.00 am when Karl Gross's torpedo from *UB-4* thundered into the *Harpalyce*. A massive explosion sent debris and clouds of steam and water high into the air. So fast was the sinking – five minutes or so – that the crew were unable to launch any of the boats. One boat was floated off from the sinking vessel, but was then found to have a leak. Two crewmen kept it afloat by continual bailing while they hauled some of their shipmates out of the water.

First Officer Anders Johansson died after he had struggled to save Captain Wawn, who died in his arms. Chief Engineer Henry Harwood was a lucky survivor. He was in the engine room when the ship was struck. He hurriedly donned a lifebelt and escaped via a skylight, only to be sucked down under the ship. Bruised and in shock, he was shot back to the surface by his inflated belt. Horwood then distinguished himself as he dived into the sinking ship's wash in an attempt to save a cook and an apprentice. He pulled them to the surface, holding one in each hand as he fought to keep their heads above the water. The monumental effort proved too much for him and he lost consciousness. The two seamen then slipped from his hands and slid beneath the waves. Harwood remained on the surface and was pulled into a boat from the Dutch SS *Elizabeth*.

Gross had done nothing to help those survivors who were struggling in the water. Aiding them was left to three steamers which had appeared on the scene. They plucked 29 men, including some seriously injured, from the sea. The remaining 15 crew members drowned at the scene.

The Times described the attack as a 'particularly cold-blooded murder of some 17 [15] innocent men … Their stories only need repeating to show German conduct in a light which will still further increase, if possible, the indignation and contempt of the civilized world.'[194] The war against civilians at sea was growing more brutal. As it did so, journalists would struggle to find words to match the horrors which seemed to increase without limit.

The men who perpetrated these horrors were the products of the long-range gun and the torpedo, which had removed the man-on-man aspect of warfare. In the days when the whites of the enemy's eyes could be seen, it had seemed possible to portray warfare as heroic. Once the enemy became unseen, killing became impersonal. Few submarine commanders ever saw the men they torpedoed, just as no sailor manning a long-range gun ever saw his victims. Von Spiegel offers us a rare insight into a U-boat commander's emotions in war in his description of *U-32*'s attack on the 9700-ton transport HMT *Wayfarer* in April 1915. Writing about the attack after the war, Spiegel recalled the mundane activities on the ship as he prepared to fire: 'I saw the captain walking on his bridge, a small whistle in his mouth. I saw the crew cleaning the deck forward, and I saw, with surprise and a slight shudder, long rows of wooden partitions right along all decks, from which gleamed the shining black and brown backs of horses.'[195] After the ship had been hit, Spiegel watched 'the despairing mass of men [who] were fighting their way on deck' and their wrangling over lifebelts. 'The men left behind were wringing their hands in despair and running to and fro along the decks; finally they threw themselves into the water so as to swim to the boats.' It was too much for Spiegel: 'I could not bear the sight any longer, and I lowered the periscope and dived deep.' In the end – after Spiegel had left – the ship failed to sink and only four of the 189 soldiers, and three of the 763 horses died. It is ironic that Spiegel's only close up view of the terror caused by his torpedoes was an occasion when their deadly impact was minimal.

A FAR AWAY SEA

With the Grand Fleet beyond the reach of the U-boats, the U-boat service turned its sights to the warships gathered at the Dardanelles in the eastern Mediterranean. These were thought to be easy prey since they were moored in open water and patrolled in a small area. There was, though, the problem of sailing a U-boat the 3600 miles out into the Atlantic, passing through the supposedly well-guarded Strait of Gibraltar and then traversing the full length of the Mediterranean to reach the Dardanelles and Gallipoli. Such a voyage was thought to be impossible until Kapitänleutnant Otto Hersing took his *U-21* from Wilhelmshaven to the Mediterranean in April 1915.

Hersing's boat left Wilhelmshaven on April 25. He was tempted to take the direct route through the Channel, but he was under the impression that too many boats had met their end in the barrage nets. Instead, he set a northbound course to pass the Orkneys before rounding Scotland.

In the misty seas of the far north, Hersing faced his first challenge as his boat ran into ships of the Northern Patrol. One vessel signalled 'Heave to' to which Hersing's response was a dive to periscope depth. Taking advantage of the mist, *U-21* stealthily passed through the patrol boats as they searched for the elusive craft passing to the west. A week later, now under a warm Spanish sun, *U-21* was off Cape Finisterre where a supply ship was waiting. In the discreet shelter of the Corcubión estuary *U-21* took on 12 tons of fuel and large quantities of food. Hersing seemed set for some spectacular raiding in the warship-rich zone at Gallipoli. Then disaster struck: *U-21* had taken on the wrong type of fuel. The engines refused to burn it, even when it was mixed with the remnants of the earlier supplies. The boat had consumed 31 tons of fuel on its passage out. It only had 25 tons of usable fuel left – too little to make the return journey. Hersing was in desperate need of a safe haven. He chose the Austrian naval base at Cattaro (now Kotor) in Montenegro as his destination. He passed Gibraltar unchallenged, since the British patrols assumed that no U-boat could reach the Mediterranean by this route.

Hersing now faced a run of 2000 miles before he could refuel. Dodging surface vessels and keeping as far from the sea lanes as possible, he edged his boat forward. Dives were fuel-heavy and had to be avoided. But even Hersing's skills could only eke out fuel to a certain extent. By May 13, the gauges registered 1.8 tons of oil. He had lost the battle – except, just when he needed it, an Austrian destroyer came to his rescue and took *U-21* in tow. A week at Cattaro for rest and an exchange of fuel left the boat ready for action. Hersing headed east.

On May 25 the pre-dreadnought battleship HMS *Triumph*, with its anti-torpedo nets deployed, was bombarding the Turkish forts at the entrance to the Dardanelles when a lookout sighted a periscope. *U-21* was on *Triumph*'s beam at a range of 300 yards, with Hersing only seconds away from giving the order to fire. Before *Triumph* could take any evasive action, a tremendous explosion tore through the ship. It listed 10 degrees to starboard and seemed to settle in that position. A short while later, an abrupt lurch left the ship with a 30-degree list. Ten minutes later the *Triumph* sank into the shallow sea. Seventy-eight officers and men out of a complement of around 800 died in the sinking.

Two days later Hersing found a second pre-dreadnought battleship – HMS *Majestic* – off W beach at Cape Helles. Once again, the extensive anti-submarine defences failed. One torpedo from *U-21* was sufficient to cause massive damage to the vessel, which sank in nine minutes. Forty-nine men out of a complement of nearly 700 were killed.

Having sunk two battleships within two days, Hersing had to wait a while for his next success: sinking the 5600-ton requisitioned French steamer *Carthage* on July 4. He remained in the Mediterranean until the end of the year, sinking another 12 ships, including the French armoured cruiser *Amiral Charner* on February 8, 1916. Of the 426 crew there was only one survivor, who was found on a raft five days after the sinking.

At first glance, the sinking of three warships in such a short period suggests that the Hersing/*U-21* combination was a fearful threat. Closer inspection shows a different picture. The sinking of *Majestic* occurred so quickly after that of the *Triumph* that Rear Admiral John de Robeck, who had only taken command at the Dardanelles on March 15, had had no time to review the anti-submarine defences before this second sinking two days later. But, after that second sinking, despite the vast number of warships in the eastern Mediterranean, Hersing had to wait until February 1916 before he sank the *Amiral Charner*. Given that he was an exceptionally talented commander, his failure to sink more warships in such a densely-filled zone, is a testament to de Robeck's command.

A TASTE OF THINGS TO COME

By the late spring of 1915, the U-boat commanders were in the ascendancy. Despite the restrictions in their orders, it seemed that they were effectively permitted to sink anything that floated. Unarmed ships and neutral vessels were sunk as if they were all legitimate targets. Now, boldness was to change to audacity. The Americans were no longer to be off limits. The US tanker *Gulflight* was to be the taster. Something much bigger would follow soon enough.

It was May 1. The *Gulflight* was carrying lubricating oil to Rouen when it was stopped off the Scillies by the patrol boats HMSs *Iago* and *Filey* on suspicion of having refuelled a U-boat. The patrol commander ordered *Gulflight* into port for inspection. While the boarding party was

A new target

preparing to take *Gulflight* into port, *U-30* arrived. *Filey* turned its attention to the enemy and made to ram the U-boat. Korvettenkapitän Erich von Rosenberg-Gruszczynski had just enough time to plunge a torpedo into *Gulflight* before taking action to evade the patrol boat.

Gulflight remained afloat but the shock of the torpedoing proved fatal for the captain, who died of a heart attack. The two sailors who jumped overboard also died. This was the first German attack on an American ship in the war. Up to this point Leon Thrasher had been the only American killed by the U-boats. Now *Gulflight*'s men added to the total. President Wilson called the attack 'an act of piracy' but he delayed making any formal response until he had more details of the action.[196] Before he could decide how to react, he was faced with a far greater crisis: the sinking of the *Lusitania*.

12
Lusitania

May 7, 1915

'Germany has become "the enemy of the human race".' –
The Times[197]

On April 22 the German Embassy handed a New York advertising agency the text of a warning to Americans not to embark on transatlantic liners. For unexplained reasons, this warning did not reach the newspapers until May 1 – the day that the *Lusitania* sailed. The notice reminded Americans that 'a state of war exists between Germany and her Allies and Great Britain and her Allies; that zone of war includes the waters adjacent to the British Isles ... vessels flying the flag of Great Britain or any of her Allies are liable to destruction in those waters ... travellers ... do so at their own risk'.[198]

Despite this warning, the *Lusitania* left New York on May 1 carrying over 1200 passengers and a crew of just under 700. At the time when the great liner was approaching the waters off the southern Irish coast Korvettenkapitän Walther Schwieger in *U-20* was lying in wait for fresh targets. (He had sunk one vessel on May 5 and two on May 6 in these waters.) Turner would have known of these dangers since the British Admiralty regularly issued 'all ships' warnings of U-boat activity. Specific warnings were also sent to the *Lusitania* on May 6 ('7.50 pm To *Lusitania*. Submarines active off south coast of Ireland') and May 7 ('12.40 pm To *Lusitania*. Submarines five miles south of Cape Clear proceeding west when sighted at 10 am.'[199]) Despite the obvious danger, Turner kept the *Lusitania* on a steady course, making no attempt to zigzag, as ships were advised to do. It was in this negligent state that Schwieger found the ship on the afternoon of May 7 off the Old Head of Kinsale Lighthouse. His last two torpedoes were the 'not so good' bronze type, but he took a chance and fired just one at 400 yards. 'There was a rather small detonation,' he recalled, 'and instantly afterward a much heavier one'.[200] The time was at 2.10 pm when Schwieger's torpedo ripped into the *Lusitania*, striking its starboard bow. He watched for a few minutes, waiting to see if a second torpedo would be needed. He noted in his diary: 'Many people must have lost their heads; several boats loaded with people rushed downward, struck the water bow or stern first and filled at once. ... The scene was too horrible to watch, and I gave orders to dive to twenty metres, and away.'[201] His account continued: 'Nor could I have fired a second torpedo into this swarm of people who were trying to save themselves.'[202]

Charles W Bowring, general agent in New York of the Red Cross Steamship Line, was having a late lunch when the ship was rocked by a huge explosion. Leaving his lunch table (which was covered with shards of glass) he went straight up to the deck, where he found a throng of passengers calmly waiting for instructions. The ship was already listing as the crew tried to lower the boats. One boat lost a rope halfway down, tipping all its occupants into the sea. Another fell uncontrollably into the water, landing on top of the occupants of the first boat. Bowring now knew that the *Lusitania* and its passengers were in real peril. He went below to find a lifebelt. On his way down, he passed the American businessman Alfred Vanderbilt Sr 'just sitting, thinking, not a bit excited', who would go down with the ship, leaving an inheritance of over $15 m ($281m today).[203]

Bowring returned to the deck with seven lifebelts, which he shared with other passengers, placing one belt on a young girl: she survived. He was now keen to leave the ship before it took him down. His first attempt to escape via the port side was thwarted by the ship's list. Finally, when the deck rail was only eight feet from the water, he jumped. Bowring had left his departure perilously late. Behind him, the ship was turning as he attempted to swim away. Above him was the mainmast, about to crash into his path. He held back, and the mast smashed into the water ahead of him.

Bowring swam to an empty lifeboat, straining against the sucking of the sinking vessel, which was finally slipping under the waves. As he clambered into the boat, he was joined by one of the ship's officers. For the next few hours, they were in and out of the boat as they pulled survivors from the water. All around, they could see that most of the people in the water were already dead. But they had done good work: by the time a trawler came to their rescue, there were 20 survivors in the boat.

Bowring's last memory of the scene was 'of a young woman, sitting in a wicker chair, serenely riding the waves'.[204] When some rescuers approached her she was found to be unconscious. Later, as the Second

Viscountess Rhondda, she would become a well-known businesswoman and suffragette.

Alice Drury, an English nanny who was in charge of a boy called Stewart, was one of the few people to have admitted to panic. She and her charge were standing on the deck as the passengers were being herded into boats. A sailor grabbed Stewart, declaring the boat to be full: 'there's plenty of room in the next one,' he said. Alice panicked, screamed, bit the sailor's hand and jumped into the boat. She tumbled over its side and was pulled out of the water by her hair. As the oarsmen fought against the pull of the sinking ship, Drury saw *U-20* on the surface. On its deck the submariners were 'watching all those bodies of people and wreckage'.[205]

The *Lusitania* sank in just 18 minutes, a rapidity that gave rise to multiple conspiracy theories. Many people reported an explosion on the ship. This might have been from a second torpedo (despite Schwieger's comment); equally it might have been from the boilers or the munitions the ship was carrying. Some of these were declared on the manifest; others were not. (The British government did not admit to the presence of these munitions until 1982 when the Treasury warned a salvage company that the cargo presented a 'danger to life and limb'.[206])

The contents of the ship is, though, an irrelevance in interpreting the significance of the sinking. What matters is what Schwieger could *justifiably have thought* was the position. There is no way that he could have known whether the ship carried munitions in sufficient quantity to make it a legitimate target. What he did know, was that it was a passenger liner. And he still chose to sink it.

Schwieger claimed that he had only discovered that the ship was the *Lusitania* when he later read some foreign newspapers. Even so, he still spoke as if he did not really understand the repulsive nature of his action. Rather than seek to apologise, he said that he was 'appalled' at the outrage against him and wondered why he was 'an object of odium and loathing'.[207]

Just under 1200 people – six out of ten passengers and crew – died in the sinking. A major factor in this calamity was that only six of the 48 lifeboats were successfully launched. Amongst the dead was the 64-year-old Canadian Mrs George Stephens, whose relationship with Schwieger was not at an end: in September, when her body was being returned to Canada on the RMS *Hesperian*, Schwieger torpedoed and sank the ship.

It was, though, the 128 American dead that transformed a human tragedy of calamitous proportions into an international crisis.

German Ambassador Bernstorff as seen in an American cartoon after the Lusitania sinking. (New York Herald.)

On the evening of May 7, Johann Bernstorff, German Ambassador to the United States, was looking forward to a performance of Johann Strauss' *Die Fledermaus* in New York. At the Hotel Pennsylvania he bought a newspaper. One glance put an end to his evening's entertainment: '*Lusitania* sunk.' He hurried to the Ritz-Carlton Hotel, where he soon felt the strength of the American reaction. As he attempted to leave the hotel by a side door: 'an infuriated and howling mob of pressmen' laid siege to him.[208] For the next few days Bernstorff holed-up in his Washington home and spoke to no one. The ambassador was not the only target of American anger. German-Americans were stricken with terror by the hostility of their fellow Americans. The German liberal politician and banker Dr Bernhard Dernburg, who had defended the torpedoing, fled the country in fear. Clearly the sinking of the *Lusitania* was, for the Americans, a step-change in the war.

It is doubtful whether the Germans at home realized that the sinking risked war with America. One woman in Berlin naively told an

American: 'Better a thousand times that the *Lusitania* be sunk and Americans be killed than let American bullets reach the lines to inflict death on German soldiers.'[209]

In Britain, anti-German riots broke out in Manchester, Liverpool and London, with shop fronts smashed and their contents looted. German homes were attacked. In the growing displays of public outrage, special constables were called out, along with the Territorial Army. Even so, German butchers at Smithfield were beaten by a mob. Attacks were particularly fierce in the East End of London. A baker's shop was stripped of all its stock. Furniture was thrown out of the first floor rooms of some German homes.

The virulence of the editorial in *The Times* of May 10 marked a turning point in the war: 'It is universally seen now that the Germans are a nation apart, that their civilization is a mere veneer ... No nation has ever fallen so low in infamy ... Germany has become "the enemy of the human race".'[210]

The public reaction in America was fiercely hostile to the point that the German Embassy in Washington received a bomb threat. *The New York Times* shared the view of the London *Times* that this was a watershed moment: Germany had 'snapped her fingers at the laws of war as at the law of morality ... The time for protest has now passed.'[211]

The American government was more guarded in its response as President Wilson searched for a form of condemnation that would not the risk of precipitating America's entry into the war. Between May and July, America issued three notes addressed to Germany, culminating in Wilson declaring that America would treat any similar sinkings in future as 'deliberately unfriendly'.[212] The note asserted the moral principle that 'The lives of non-combatants may in no case be put in jeopardy unless the vessel resists or seeks to escape.'[213] The President's personal diplomatic trouble-shooter, Colonel House, advised Wilson that: 'We can no longer remain neutral ... America has come to the parting of the ways, when she must determine whether she stands for civilized or uncivilized warfare.'[214]

Tossing House's cable aside, Wilson made his famous 'Too proud to fight' speech on the following day at the Convention Hall in Philadelphia. He told his audience of 4000 naturalized citizens: 'There is such a thing as a man being too proud to fight. There is such a thing as a nation being so right that it does not need to convince others by force that it is right.'[215] House retaliated on the following day, warning Wilson that, if he failed to call Germany to account over the sinking, Germany would go on sinking passenger liners under the pretext that they were carrying munitions.

A looted German shop in Liverpool following the sinking of the Lusitania.[216]

Princes Blücher was one of the first people in Berlin to detect the profound effect that the sinking of the *Lusitania* had on German-American relations. On the day following the sinking she noted that the Berliners were staggered at the achievement of 'one little submarine'. At last, the Germans around her were saying, 'Germany must become the mistress of the seas.' But those same Germans, who only days before the sinking had enjoyed dinners and tennis matches with the Americans in Berlin, were now pariahs to their visitors. Blücher continued, 'Friendly intercourse was out of the question. Their rage and horror at the idea that Americans had been killed knew no bounds.'[217] Germany had won its chosen form of naval spurs and lost a tolerant neutral.

The *Lusitania* sinking provided Lord Derby, then Director-General of Recruiting, with copious copy for his recruiting posters. One read:

'Remember the *"Lusitania"* ... Avenge this Devil's work'.[218] In a rousing speech he declared: 'This country calls no longer for men to fight an honourable foe. It calls for men to go in to hunt down and crush once and for all a race of cold-blooded murderers.'[219]

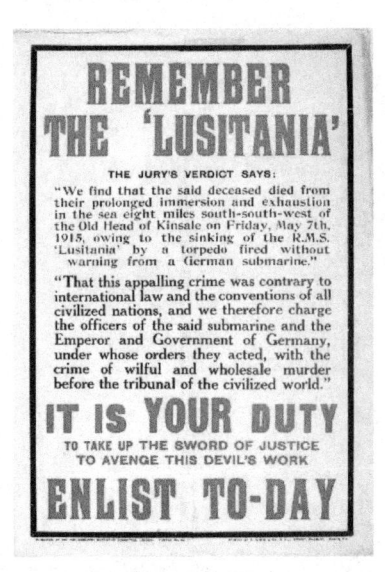

Lord Derby's use of the Lusitania sinking as an aid to recruiting. (Contemporary poster.)

American diplomacy saw the *Lusitania* moment as a last opportunity for Germany to change its sinkings policy. In Berlin, Ambassador Gerard tried to persuade the German government that it was impossible to sink commerce without ignoring the 'rules of fairness, reason, justice, and humanity'.[220] In London, House pleaded with Sir Edward Grey to lift the embargo on foodstuffs, on condition that Germany would 'discontinue her use of asphyxiating gases and the ruthless killing of non-combatants'.[221] This suggestion was rebuffed ten days later by Gottlieb von Jagow, State Secretary of the German Foreign Office. He refused to consider it unless the blockade on raw materials was also lifted. (In making this demand, Jagow confirmed that the blockade was causing crippling damage to German war production.) House knew that the Allies would never contemplate such a move. He had reached an impasse: 'I am terribly sorry, because the consequences may be very grave,' he told Gerard.[222] There was nothing more that he could do to influence European politics. House packed his bags and returned to the United States in the

American liner SS *Saint Paul*. In October 1917 it would be requisitioned by the US war department.

America, like Britain, was running short of ideas for thwarting the U-boat menace. That left Germany free to make the next move.

The German policy front was, though, less solid than it appeared to the Allies. When the Kaiser called a high-level meeting at Pless Castle in Upper Silesia at the end of May, Chancellor von Bethmann-Hollweg said that he refused to be responsible for the U-boat campaign. He demanded that it be 'conducted as to avoid any political conflict'.[223] General von Falkenhayn and the diplomat Karl von Treutler supported this view, but Tirpitz and the admirals declared that it was 'technically impossible' to conduct a U-boat war in the manner that Bethmann-Hollweg suggested.[224] The meeting broke up with no fresh ideas on how to defeat the blockade and no proposals for ending the daily risk of goading America into war.

Meanwhile, the German Ambassador in Washington had retired into seclusion 'so as to avoid any possibility of unpleasant incidents'.[225] He advised his government to issue a note of regret 'without admission of our responsibility'. Over the next few weeks, acrimonious notes were exchanged between Berlin and Washington. On June 2 Bernstorff feared that a declaration of war was imminent – a disaster that could only have one consequence. He demanded to see President Wilson that same day. At the White House, Bernstorff fell victim to Wilson's endless capacity to eschew straight-talking. He avoided all serious discussion of the implications of the *Lusitania* sinking, while talking at length about 'the humanitarian aspects of the matter'.[226] Lulled by a president who refused to look clearly at the horrific turn that the war had taken, Bernstorff was deceitfully reassured. Later that day he sent a lengthy cable back to the German Foreign Office. For all its verbosity, the core message was simple: 'it may now be regarded as certain, that neither the President nor the American people want a war with Germany'.[227] A week later, Wilson's Secretary of State, William Jennings Bryan, promptly resigned. At the same time, the 72-year-old American novelist Henry James, disgusted at Wilson's irresolution, resigned his American citizenship. In his application for British citizenship, James said that he had decided 'to throw his moral weight and personal allegiance' behind Britain's war effort.[228] Bryan was replaced by Robert Lansing, who was a strong advocate for US intervention in the war. But, for the present, both America and Germany had resolved to be irresolute. This was reflected in the most popular song in America at that time: 'I Didn't Raise My Boy to be a Soldier'.[229]

13
Indecision

Summer 1915

'Modern war is essentially a struggle of gear and invention.
Each side must be perpetually producing new devices.' – H G
Wells, June 1915.[230]

A NOD TOWARDS RESTRAINT

As President Wilson struggled to balance his high moral principles with the demands of everyday politics, it was the German government that made the first move to calm the situation. Admiral Ludwig von Schröder (Admiral Commanding Flanders) was determined to maintain an aggressive sinkings policy. He wanted authorization to permit warships to stop and search neutral vessels which, he said, were carrying 89 per cent of trade in the North Sea. For this purpose, he wanted large destroyers and cruisers for 'stop and search' actions under prize rules. Instead, on June 6, Chancellor Bethmann-Hollweg asked the Chief of the Naval Staff, Admiral Gustav Bachmann, to exempt large enemy passenger vessels from sinking. Bachmann refused. Bethmann appealed to the Kaiser, who ruled in his favour: passenger vessels (neutral and enemy) were not to be sunk. A furious Bachmann told colleagues: 'we should yield no ground in connection with the submarine campaign'. He concluded, 'To yield is to sacrifice the whole effect of submarines against England.'[231]

TORPOR AT ADMIRALTY HOUSE

While the Kaiser and his admirals wrangled over sinking policies, the British government was distracted by a crisis of leadership that was to have serious consequences for the naval war.

On May 15, the 74-year Admiral of the Fleet Lord Fisher resigned as First Sea Lord over a dispute with Churchill about sending more capital ships to the Dardanelles. This precipitated the creation of a coalition government and the ejection of Churchill from his post as First Sea Lord. (The formation of this coalition is invariably attributed to the 'shell crisis' – a shortage of shells on the Western Front. In fact it is clear that it was the news of Fisher's resignation that led Bonar Law, the Tory Party leader, to demand a coalition. See my *'Unsinkable': Churchill and the First World War I* and Blake's *The Unknown Prime Minister*, Chapter 15.)

The vacant posts were filled by the 66-year-old Arthur Balfour as First Lord of the Admiralty and the 60-year-old Admiral Sir Henry Jackson as First Sea Lord. The fiery Fisher and the youthful hyper-active Churchill, had been replaced by the contemplative Balfour and the lack-lustre Jackson. These appointments were a serious blow to the naval war. Churchill may have been too eager for action and Fisher may have been too ambitious in his mighty ship building programme, but these imperfections were no excuse for putting the Admiralty into a torpor.

The brains' trust

Balfour's 18 months at the Admiralty will be remembered for just one thing: his creation of the Board of Invention and Research (BIR).

The British people were to pay a heavy price for their belief that the war would be 'over by Christmas'. With victory seemingly so readily at hand, they had felt no need in the autumn of 1914 to manufacture mountains of ammunition or amass truckloads of guns. Nor did anyone think it necessary to research new weapons and new means of defence. The scientists in their laboratories and the engineers in their workshops heard no call to war. And then, as winter turned to spring in 1915, the mud-soaked battlefields dried out and the winter Atlantic storms abated, war returned in earnest. The same war. The same weapons. The same defeats.

In June 1915, the War Office Research Department was so short of work that many of its staff were turned over to production. Indeed, the department was so idle that a civilian had to kick it into life, as the novelist H G Wells did with a letter to *The Times* on June 11. 'Modern war,' he wrote, 'is essentially a struggle of gear and invention'.

Support for Wells came from a variety of scientists, provoked by the apathy of a government that understood nothing of science. Notable amongst these enthusiasts was Professor J A Fleming of University College London, inventor in 1904 of the thermionic valve. In a moving letter to *The Times* on June 15 he described how he had been visited by 'an eminent electrical engineer ... too old to enlist' but desperate to serve his country. The engineer could find no one ready to make use of his skills. As to Fleming, he too had been spurned: 'although a member of several scientific and technical societies and a Fellow of the Royal Society as well, [I] have not received one word of request to serve on any committee, cooperate in any experimental work, or place expert knowledge ... at the disposal of the forces of the Crown'.[232]

H G Wells playing a war game in 1911. By 1915 he was ready to show that he understood the realities of modern war better than the admirals and the generals. (Ilustrated London News.)

The silence from Whitehall during the next ten days confirmed Wells' thesis. He returned to the columns of *The Times* on 22 June. Officialdom, he argued, had neither the rapidity of action nor the imaginative leaps that war demanded. He attacked the proposals for committees 'of distinguished men', rejecting them as too slow and cumbersome for 'rapidly taking up, examining, testing and rejecting or developing new ideas'. Instead, he called for 'a small organization ... what I might call "a science and invention bureau".'[233] The result was to be the creation of the Board of Invention and Research, which began its work in July.

The Board was brought into being by Balfour at the Admiralty and was initially created to concentrate on research 'of urgent importance to the naval service'.[234] Balfour's languid manner and his air of disdain for the transitory, belied his capacity for resolute action when needed. An ex-Prime Minister, a philosopher by training, and the creator of the Committee of Imperial Defence in 1904, few British politicians understood defence as well as Balfour did. The Board could not have had a better midwife. June was not yet over when a letter from Balfour reached Fisher at the remote Dungavel House in Scotland. (He was skulking there with the Duke and Duchess of Hamilton, following the hullabaloo created by his controversial resignation in May.) The letter invited Fisher to become chairman of the new board: 'your great powers of original thought, combined with your unique experience, would enable you to do great service to the Navy and the Country'.[235]

Admiral of the Fleet Lord Fisher, who chaired the Inventions Board, conversing with Churchill on the steps of Admiralty House in 1915. (Wikimedia.)

Fisher's letter of acceptance showed how firmly he sided with the scientists: 'The war is going to be won by inventions. Eleven months of war have shown us simply as servile copyists of the Germans. When *they* have brought explosive shells into damnable prominence, *then* so have we. When *they* produced grenades for trench work, *then* so have we! ... Noxious gases made us send Professors to study German asphyxiation! German mines and submarines have walked ahead of us by leaps and bounds, although many years ago we were in a position of apparently unassailable superiority.' Fisher then listed three priority areas for the

Board, the second of which was 'Anti-submarine craft and anti-submarine devices including anti-submarine mines.' He concluded with a typical Fisher flourish: '*Man invents. Monkeys imitate.*' [236]

Fisher's letter marked an unsung turning point in the war. For the first time in British history, the armed forces were to enlist brains to match their brawn. Eminent scientists such as Sir J J Thomson, Sir Ernest Rutherford and Professor W H Bragg were amongst those on the Board or became its close advisers.

Deceit at sea

Decoy ships (known as Q-ships) had been in use since early in the war. Their failure yet to sink any U-boats is no surprise, given how few U-boats were at sea in the early stages of the war. The first sinking of a U-boat by a Q-ship was the work of the 250-ton steam trawler *Taranaki* working with submarine *C-24* in mid-1915.

Kapitänleutnant Gerhardt Fürbringer in *U-40* was on his first patrol as a commander; it was also the boat's first outing. By June 23 he was seeking prey off Aberdeen when he sighted the *Taranaki*. Owned by the Stepney Fishing Company, the *Taranaki* was the largest fishing vessel in the Scarborough area. At last, Fürbringer could prove his prowess as a U-boat commander. With *U-40* trimmed low in the water, he ordered the trawler to stop, but *Taranaki* continued on its way. Fürbringer does not seem to have thought it odd that an unarmed trawler should fail to stop. His insouciance was to cost him his life. Unknown to Fürbringer, *Taranaki* was towing the submerged submarine *C-24*. If all went to plan, he would attack the visible *Taranaki*, leaving the submerged *C-24* free to attack *U-40* in return.

C-24's tow-line incorporated a telephone cable to enable the two commanders to coordinate their actions. Via the telephone, Lieutenant Commander William Sanders in *Taranaki* reported his sighting to Lieutenant Frederick Taylor in *C-24* and waited for the submarine to let slip the cable. For ten terrifying minutes *Taranaki* sat in *U-40*'s line of fire, waiting for the line to drop free. Sanders assumed *C-24* was in some sort of trouble so he slipped the line at his end. Taylor was now free to manoeuvre, but *C-24* was trailing a hundred fathoms of heavy cable. One inadvertent tug might bring the cable to the surface and ruin the deceit. Meanwhile, *Taranaki*'s crew were doing their best to look like terrified fisherman as they rushed around launching boats and preparing to abandon ship. Fürbringer fell for this distraction and never noticed *C-24*'s menacing periscope. At 500 yards Taylor fired. His torpedo struck *U-40* under its conning tower and the boat disappeared. All that was left was smoke, flames and debris. Only the three officers who had been standing on its deck survived.

A concealed gun on a Q-ship.[237]

Taranaki served throughout the war, but was sunk by a mine, caught in its fishing net in 1920. Fürbringer spent the rest of the war in a prison camp. A month later, the same combination of a decoy ship and a towed submarine sank *U-23* midway between the Orkneys and Norway. Ten of its crew of 34 survived. Amongst them was Kapitänleutnant Hans Schulthess, who had sunk seven ships totalling 8800 tons between March and May. He was taken prisoner but, for reasons that are not clear, was interned in Switzerland from December 1916 to August 1918.

A month later, the 370-ton collier *Prince Charles* became the first Q-ship to sink a U-boat when not acting in consort with another vessel. Its peacetime crew of the master, Frank Maxwell, five deckhands, two engineers, and two firemen had volunteered to man the ship when it took up decoy work under Lieutenant Mark Wardlaw, accompanied by Lieutenant J G Spencer and nine ratings.

Indecision

The collier left Longhope in the Orkneys on July 21. Three days later, Wardlaw's lookouts sighted a stopped three-masted vessel with a U-boat nearby. Wardlaw studiously ignored the U-boat as *Prince Charles* maintained its air of innocent collier. Meanwhile, his men manned the hidden guns and the merchant seamen stood by, ready to lower the boats for a feigned 'abandon ship'. Kapitänleutnant Ernst Graeff in *U-36* took the bait as he gave the order for full-speed-ahead. With *U-36* at a range of three miles, Wardlaw raised the Q-ship's colours. Graeff responded with a shell which fell 1000 yards short, exactly as Wardlaw hoped it would do. Stopping the engines, he turned the ship into the swell and ordered the boats out. With the play-acting under way, Wardlaw held firm while *U-36* raced towards the *Prince Charles*. A second shell passed between the funnel and the foremast. Still Wardlaw held his fire. Then the U-boat stopped. Wardlaw now had to choose between running and opening fire. Firing it was to be. As soon as his port guns opened up, *U-36*'s gunners abandoned their weapon and scuttled down the conning tower. The boat began to dive, but a shell from *Prince Charles* caught it aft of the conning tower. Now, at only 300 yards from the Q-ship's guns, Graeff knew the battle was lost. The boat surfaced and its men were soon in the water. Fifteen of the crew of 33 were plucked from the sea.

The battle had been a spectacular success for the Q-ships. *Prince Charles*' 3-pounder and 6-pounder guns had taken on *U-36* armed with a 14-pounder and carrying seven torpedoes. Wardlaw received a DSO and was to end the war with the rank of lieutenant-commander. Later, he crowned his career as aide-de-camp to King George V in 1938, retiring with the rank of rear admiral. But Wardlaw's triumph was to prove hard to repeat as the U-boat commanders soon learnt to be wary of stopped merchant ships.

Q-ships took their name from their base at Queenstown (now Cobh) on the south coast of Ireland. Vice Admiral Lewis Bayly, rehabilitated after his loss of HMS *Formidable*, had taken over the post of Commander-in-Chief, Coast of Ireland, on July 20. His command stretched from the Sound of Mull in the north to Ushant off the Brittany coast in the south.

When Bayly took over the command he found it to be seriously compromised by its slack security. Ship to shore signals were by semaphore and sent in plain language, readable by any dockyard worker. Local people were allowed to board ships, and there were public entertainments at Admiralty House. Bayly immediately introduced a cypher code for messages, which were now to be by ship-to-shore cable. He also banned local people from boarding, and he ended the entertainments. Bayly paid similar attention to making efficient use of his ships and men. Before he arrived, ships spent five days at sea followed by a minimum of two days for rest and repairs. He told his commanders to report any serious defects while still at sea so that their ships could dock at the appropriate quay. Workers would be ready – stores to hand – to take over a ship and begin immediate repairs. Having the right materials to hand ensured that the Q-ships would usually be back at sea two days after docking.

It was from this command that the Q-ships were fitted with hidden armaments and given disguised profiles so that they had the innocent appearance of fishing vessels or merchant ships. To guard against spies in the dockyards, ships were given an additional temporary disguise, which they discarded once they were at sea. For example, a two-masted ship seen putting to sea might become one-masted once it was over the horizon.

Manning was problematic in these very small ships. Q-ship operations required a large crew, far in excess of that of a humble fishing vessel. Despite the augmented crews, the men had to maintain 'the strictest discipline', recalled Bayly with '[no] more than two or three people on deck at a time'. The naval men also had to learn 'to walk up ladders, not run' and were not to hang out their washing as if in a warship. A further complication was the role of commander. Taking a small ship to sea with the intention of using it to incite an attack was immensely stressful. According to Bayly, 'few could stand it for more than about nine months'.[238]

Q-ships have fascinated students of the First World War and have been the subject of many books. They offer drama and high courage as the seamen engage in their David and Goliath operations. Yet the more than 350 Q-ships in the war only sank 14 U-boats. In comparison, around 50 U-boats were sunk by mines, which tied-up far fewer men and vessels.

FAR FROM BATTLE

While Q-ships chased U-boats and merchant seamen died bringing food and materials to Britain, life on the home front was still almost unchanged for the wealthy. In London, the society hostess Lady Cunard gave a dinner party in July at which Cynthia Asquith was one of the guests. (Cynthia was a daughter-in-law of the Prime Minister.) It was,

Asquith noted in her diary, 'a fantastic dinner party'. Later they all played a game of 'imagining all our companions were lunatics'.[239] For them, the war was another world. Seven days later, Asquith had a full day of lunch with her friends, followed by a variety show at Her Majesty's Theatre and then dinner, all topped off by poker at the house of Edwin Montague MP. She made no mention of the war, but she worried as to how the impending marriage of her friend Vanessa Stanley to Edwin Montague would work out. (It was a most improbable matching.)

Even unassuming fishermen could find advantage in the war. With so many fishing boats having been requisitioned for the patrols, the remaining boats reaped a fine harvest. A short trip could yield a catch worth £100 – nearly £6000 in today's money. Even dog fish sold. Sprats, which fetched 6 s or 7 s before the war now sold for £2.00.

Meanwhile, the ever observant Ambassador Walter Page saw the sad evidence of the land war in the streets of London. On his daily walk to and from the Embassy at 123 Victoria Street he observed that 'the [Green] Park is full of wounded and their nurses'. All that the members of the government talked about was the war, he said. Even 'the man behind the counter at the cigar store' wanted to read him a letter from his son at the Front, describing 'how he advanced over a pile of dead Germans and one of them grunted'.[240]

A more vital change was the huge wholesale price rises for basic foods since the start of the war. Wheat prices were up by 80 per cent and meat by 40 per cent.

Contested sinkings

Neither home comfort nor civic calm was to be found afloat. Three months after the sinking of the *Lusitania* the war at sea was hardening, with three significant incidents in just seven days.

Not a single serviceman nor any medical staff had died in the cross-Channel transport of troops to the Western Front since the start of the war. In the Mediterranean, there had been less success in conveying troops to Gallipoli, where several troopships had been hit. The first such attack had occurred in August.

In late July, men were leaving depots in southern England to make their way to Avonmouth and Plymouth for the next transport to Gallipoli. Night and day, the trains carrying the Plymouth-bound men passed through Exeter, where they received refreshments from the Lady Mayoress' fund. Her hot tea, a sandwich, a piece of cake and an orange were accompanied by the inevitable packet of cigarettes. Poignantly, each man received a Good Luck card 'From the Mayoress of Exeter and Committee'. On July 28, a new batch of recruits who had enjoyed these comforts arrived at Plymouth and boarded *HMT Royal Edward*, already heaving with those who had boarded at Avonmouth.

Walter Page at his desk in the American Embassy in London.

Captain Peter Millman, a Plymouth man with 24 years of sea-going service, gave the order to sail two days later. Around 2000 men were now heading for Mudros harbour to take up positions in the shallow trenches of the Gallipoli Peninsular. After a call at Malta for coaling, the *Royal Edward* made for Alexandria, the main base station for Gallipoli. The sole – and so lucky – horse left the ship at this point. Then the ship slipped its moorings for the short run to Gallipoli and the Turkish guns.

The officers detected a melancholy atmosphere as the men approached the reality of war – they would have seen the injured in hospital ships at Alexandra and nurses by the hundred. A singsong was ordered, and song sheets were handed round. (The American Captain George Marshal would later observe the same comportment in an American embarkation. He remarked, 'The men seem very solemn,' to which an officer replied, 'Of course they are. We are watching the harvest of death.'[241])

Troops on Exeter station enjoying the Lady Mayoress' refreshments, on their way to boarding the HMT Royal Edward.[242]

On the morning of August 13, the men went about their daily tasks, including lifeboat drill and a foot inspection. All seemed well. Breakfast was served at 9.00 am and the ship saluted the sad sight of the hospital ship *Soudan*, loaded with wounded being taken to Alexandria.

Harry Ross, down near the engine room saw the torpedo through a porthole. At only 70 yards or so there was no time to warn his pals. It smashed mercilessly into the ship's side. Vast quantities of water rushed into the *Royal Edward*. The ship listed. The lights went out. Ross rushed to the deck. He dared not pause to put on a lifebelt. Instead, he grabbed a piece of timber and jumped into the sea. The water had appeared calm as the ship had cut through the sea. But, once in the water, Ross was tossed by heavy waves, which were picking men up and smashing them against the ship's side and against floating debris. He made for a capsized lifeboat and clung on until men from HMHS *Soudan* took him out of the water.

Arthur Sanders on the *Soudan* recalled seeing 'boats right way, wrong way up rafts, wreckage of all kinds, barrels, hatch covers' in the water. Terrified men were clinging to oars. With the aid of a crane the *Soudan* rescuers hauled up one end of a capsized boat to release two medical corps men who had survived by breathing through the drain hole in the bottom of the boat.

There has never been any agreement as to how many men died in the sinking. *The Times* reported around 1000 dead. The paper remarked: 'There is something peculiarly poignant in the circumstances in which a thousand gallant souls are missing without an opportunity to strike a blow for their own safety or defence.'[243]

The sinking was the work of Kapitänleutnant Heini von Heimburg in *UB-14*. (UB boats were small coastal submarines with a crew of around 15 men.) The *Royal Edward* was his third sinking. By the end of the war, he would sink 23 vessels, totalling 56,000 tons, plus another eight vessels damaged. Between the wars he was promoted to admiral and, in the Second World War, he became a Nazi judge. He died in 1945 in a prisoner of war camp near Stalingrad.

Six days later came the notorious *Baralong* incident, which has remained controversial to this day. It began as a simple U-boat attack, but evolved into an international affair.

Kapitänleutnant Bernd Wegener in *U-27* was proving to be a competent, if not ace, commander. His sinking career had begun in mid-October 1914, when he torpedoed the British submarine *E-3* off the Ems estuary. Two weeks later, he sank the 5600-ton seaplane carrier HMS *Hermes*. It was five months before Wegener's next sinking: the 6000-ton armed merchant cruiser HMS *Bayano*. Altogether he had sunk 12 ships totalling 37,000 tons when, on August 19, he came across the British steamer *Nicosian*, loaded with munitions and mules. With *U-27* surfaced Wegener opened fire at 600 yards. The outcome seemed inevitable as an unarmed liner faced a U-boat with a gun and torpedoes, but a third party was about to join the scene.

U-27 was on the starboard side of the *Nicosian* when it opened fire. Unknown to Wegener, the Q-ship HMS *Baralong* was approaching on *Nicosian*'s port side. Suddenly, *Baralong* appeared aft of the *Nicosian*, in full view of the U-boat. At 600 yards *Baralong* began to shower *U-27* with 12-pounder shells and rifle fire. As the boat became peppered with holes, and chunks of its fuselage were ripped open, the men on its deck dived into the sea. With the boat sinking, Lieutenant-Commander Godfrey Herbert turned *Baralong*'s guns onto the survivors in the sea. This, he later justified by saying that he feared the men were going to seize the deserted *Nicosian*.

The Admiralty knew a war crime when it saw one and sought to suppress the incident. There was not a word in the British press. Lord Milner obliquely referred to the incident in a session of the House of Lords in late 1915 during a debate on censorship. He argued that it was pointless to suppress accounts of the incident since it had been reported in newspapers around the world. 'The world would take our silence ... as an admission of guilt,' he said.[244]

Later, when the German government demanded that the commanding officer and 'other responsible parties' be tried for murder, Grey told Ambassador Page that it was 'the height of absurdity' for the German government to 'single out the case of the Baralong'. The offence was 'negligible compared with the crimes which seem to have been deliberately committed by German officers both on land and sea'. When Grey's letter became public in January 1916, *The Times* printed extensive sworn statements from Americans who had witnessed the episode. No one reading the newspaper would have been in any doubt that the crew of a British warship had fired on the crew of the sinking of *U-27*.

The incident failed to damage Herbert's career. He remained in anti-submarine warfare with his final First World War posting being with Admiral Bayly at Queenstown. He was recalled to arms in the Second World War to command the armed merchant cruiser *Cilicia* before retiring in 1943. The *Baralong* incident might have seriously damaged the Royal Navy's reputation had other events, just as deplorable, ensured that it was soon forgotten.

In August the U-boat commanders put Germany into another hopeless diplomatic situation with the deaths of more American passengers at sea. The British SS *Arabic* would be Kapitänleutnant Rudolf Schneider's twenty-first sinking. (At 15,800 tons the *Arabic* was even larger than HMS *Formidable*, which he had sunk on January 1.) On August 19 the *Arabic* was outward bound for the United States and passing Kinsale on the southern coast of Ireland – this was the area in which the *Lusitania* had been sunk, so shipping could expect to encounter U-boats there.

It was just after 9.00 am when Captain William Finch saw the torpedo, only 300 feet from his ship. The thundering explosion and the vast column of water that rose up left him in no doubt about the seriousness of the damage. He warned the passengers to put on the lifejackets that were ranged ready on the deck. At the same time, he ordered the launching of the boats.

The young Acel Nebeker was in his bathrobe when the torpedo struck. He raced up to the deck and made for the boats while fastening his lifejacket. He settled in a starboard boat, which quickly filled, but no one came to launch it. His terrified companions watched as the liner gradually sank. Nebeker knew he had to escape the vortex of the sinking ship. He jumped from the boat and swam vigorously away from the liner. A glance behind him showed that many of his recent companions were still in the boat when the ship took it down. When the ship's final moments came, he feared the towering vessel would crush him as it plunged into the sea.

With the great ship gone, Nebeker swam around for 20 minutes before a lifeboat picked him up. From the boat, he looked back over the ocean. Amongst the bodies was that of a child still in its lifejacket. The lifeboat was without a crew member so an engineer in another boat swam over to take charge until the minesweeper HMS *Primrose* arrived and took the boatload on board.

The 21-year-old Dorothy Kelk was one of the many who showed great heroism in the sinking. She was sitting in a boat when a young stewardess arrived in a state of great distress. Kelk insisted that the stewardess take her place and she returned to the ship's deck. As the ship sank lower in the water, Kelk looked anxiously for another boat, but none was launched. With the ship's list now at a dangerous angle, she dived into the sea and swam through the flotsam to escape the *Arabic*. She watched as it 'bobbed perpendicular like a cork, before filling to the brim and thundering to the seabed below'. She, too, was picked up by HMS *Primrose* and was landed at Queenstown with the other survivors.[245]

Captain Finch was another hero of the sinking. He went into the waves a minute or two before the ship disappeared and swam around for 40 minutes before rescuing a woman and her infant. Swimming on, he saved two firemen and a woman passenger. His heroic acts earned him an OBE, which he later received from King George V at Buckingham Palace.

One of the American survivors was especially careful when she later choose a ship to take her home. She settled for the SS *Saint Paul*: 'The American flag was painted all over the *St Paul*, and they played searchlights on those paintings all through every hour of darkness.'[246]

Three Americans and 44 other passengers, along with three of the crew, lost their lives in the sinking. Schneider maintained that he never intended to sink the *Arabic* and that his torpedo was meant for the 5000-ton steamer *Dunsley* which he also sank that day. He separately offered the excuse that he thought the *Arabic* intended to ram his boat.

Many Americans were outraged at yet another sinking of a passenger liner. Ambassador Page, on holiday with his son Frank in Derbyshire, remarked, 'That settles it. They have sunk the *Arabic*. That means that we shall break with Germany and I've got to go back to London.'[247] Johann von Bernstorff, German Ambassador to the United States, also saw the sinking as a step too far, telling the State Department: 'I fear I cannot prevent rupture this time if our answer in [the] *Arabic* matter is not conciliatory.'[248]

Meanwhile, the man who most mattered – President Wilson – was frozen in indecision as he struggled to keep America out of the war. He proposed to Colonel House that he should send a note to the German government, but House warned him: 'Further notes ... would cause something of derision abroad.'[249] In London, House found a fellow-thinker in Sir Edward Grey, who expressed his 'disappointment that the feeling in America is not more combative'.[250] Walter Page joined in the chorus that was calling for some stronger action from the President, telling House that if America did not act soon, it would be held in 'contempt' by the rest of the world.[251]

14
Mediterranean diversion

Late 1915

Berlin was 'enveloped in an impenetrable veil of sadness, grey in grey'. – Princes Blücher.[252]

MUCH TO LEARN

At the end of the first twelve months of hostilities Britain had much to be satisfied with the war at sea. The Grand Fleet had rendered the Kaiser's High Seas Fleet undeployable. New construction at 1.2 m tons had largely replaced the 1.3 m tons of sunk merchant shipping. Additionally, the navy had captured or detained 680,000 tons of enemy and other shipping. Of the merchant ships over 1600 tons, only 4 per cent had been lost in ship numbers and 3.5 per cent in tonnage. Germany had lost 17 U-boats to all causes, including accidents. Critically, Germany was failing to weaken Britain's capacity to import vital food and raw materials; nor was it threatening Britain's ability to export vital dollar-earning goods.

For the Imperial Navy, the performance of many of its U-boat commanders was disquieting. Of the 30 boats in commission only ten had sunk ten ships of more than 200 tons. Five boats (*U-20, U-28, U-38, U-39, U-41*) had sunk 20 or more vessels. Clearly, very few submariners could be turned into successful commanders. (Similarly, in the Second World, out of over 1400 U-boat commanders, the top 2.5 per cent accounted for 32 per cent of the tonnage sunk in the Atlantic.)

The performance of the Allied anti-submarine forces was equally unimpressive. Of the 20 U-boats that were sunk between the start of the war and the end of August 1915, 14 are known to have been sunk by anti-submarine action (four were sunk by gunfire, three by mines, one by being trapped in nets, four by ramming and two by torpedo). Of the remaining six, two were sunk by own-side incidents, with the fate of the other four being unknown. It was a discouraging result for the work of 2180 patrol vessels and the thousands of sailors who manned them. Something needed to change.

Unfortunately, the May changes at the Admiralty offered no prospect of radical thinking or vigorous action. Churchill, had he been kept in post, would have recognized the immensity of the U-boat threat. But, with Balfour and Jackson now installed in Admiralty House, all hope of bold initiative had gone. (The one significant innovation in this period – the greater use of Q-ships – owed nothing to the newcomers since decoy ships had been in use since November 1914 when HMS *Pargust* went on patrol. A second Q-ship, HMS *Antwerp*, had been commissioned in January 1915.)

Muddle

In Germany, the search for a successful U-boat strategy brought a crisis in the highest echelons of the state.

Having appeased America, the Kaiser faced the wrath of his three senior admirals, who were shackled by his restraints. Tirpitz, von Pohl, and the Chief of the Naval Staff Bachmann were all convinced that it was impossible to conduct an effective U-boat war if the boats were prohibited from sinking passenger ships. Bachmann refused to continue under this restraint, resigned and departed to command a base in the Baltic in June. Tirpitz attempted to resign, but the Kaiser demanded that he stayed in post.

Pohl showed his opposition to the Kaiser's policy of restraint in a more covert manner: he drastically cut back patrols from 15 boats in June to eight in August and five in September. This should have had a dramatic effect on sinkings, which might have enabled von Pohl to challenge the Kaiser's embargo. Unfortunately, Kapitänleutnant Max Valentiner in *U-38* wrecked Pohl's ploy when he sank 31 vessels totalling 82,000 tons, bringing his August total to 186,000 tons. Valentiner's contribution more than doubled the average monthly sinkings of 77,000 tons in the war to date. His spectacular performance left the Kaiser in a strong position. For now, any justification for all-out unrestricted sinking had gone. He was yet to learn that the U-boat war could only be won with hundreds of moderate performers. Relying on a few Valentiners was not a practical strategy.

Agreeing the latest policy on avoiding liners was one thing. Implementing it was to prove quite another. There was no reliable way in which the U-boat commanders could identify which ships were passenger liners. Vice Admiral von Holtzendorff, Head of the Imperial Admiralty Staff, recognized that the policy was unworkable and, on September 18, ordered the halting of U-boat operations in the English Channel and along Britain's west coast – the area where American vessels were most likely to be encountered. U-boats would continue to operate under Prize Regulations in northern waters.

The boats released by this yielding to American pressure were to go the Mediterranean.

Kaiser Wilelhelm (left) with Admiral Henning von Holtzendorff.

ANOTHER SEA

The first three boats in the new Mediterranean campaign – *U-33*, *U-35* and *U-39* – reached the Austro-Hungarian Navy's port of Cattaro in October. These boats came with a fearsome reputation: *U-33* had sunk 28,000 tons of shipping; *U-35*'s total was 34,000 tons; and *U-39*'s was 56,000 tons. In November Kapitänleutnant Max Valentiner arrived in *U-38* with his record of having already sunk or damaged 58 vessels.

The local situation was delicate since Italy was at war with Austria-Hungary but not with Germany. Hence, the U-boat commanders, who had proved unable to distinguish enemy from neutral ships around the British Isles, were now in peril of making a similar error in the Mediterranean.

Kapitänleutnant Konrad Gansser in *U-33* set the tone when he chose an Italian ship for the first sinking of the new campaign. The 185-ton SS *Tobia* was carrying olive oil and calcium carbide. By the end of the year, *U-33* had sunk or damaged 96,000 tons of shipping, including the passenger ship SS *Provincia*. Kapitänleutnant Walter Forstmann in *U-39* sank 65,000 tons of shipping in the same period, including the *H C Henry* – a 4000-ton tanker laden with tar oil bound for Alexandria and Mudros. Slightly behind, was Korvettenkapitän Waldemar Kophamel with *U-35*'s sinking record of 60,000 tons, including the 6000-ton British passenger liner *Californian*. With no casualties, *Californian*'s sinking merited only nine lines in *The Times*, seven of which reminded its readers that the *Californian* was the vessel that had failed to come to the aid of the sinking *Titanic* in 1912.

More serious was *U-35*'s sinking of the British troopship *Marquette* in passage from Alexandria to Salonika. The 700-plus people on board included 36 nurses from the 1st New Zealand Stationary Hospital. Nurse Jeannie Sinclair was taking a walk on the deck early on the morning of October 23 when she saw, 'a straight, thin green line coming through the water'. As the torpedo careered into the ship's starboard side, the ship 'quivered and then started to list', recalled nurse Edith Wilkins.[253] The nurses put on their lifejackets while one of port lifeboats was being successfully lowered. The next boat jammed in its davits before suddenly smashing down onto the previous one, causing the first deaths and injuries of the sinking. In the damaged boat one of the injured, Nona Hildyard, sang to keep up the spirits of her colleagues before dying of a heart attack. Mary Gorman, with two crushed legs knew she would not survive, and handed her lifejacket to another nurse. In total, 29 crew, 10 nurses and 128 troops died in the sinking.

The attack on the *Marquette* was a typical U-boat service public relations disaster, which came at a high cost to the German war effort: one more country had a reason to take up arms against it. In New Zealand, the deaths of ten nurses were used as propaganda to recruit troops under the heading:

> DROWNED WHEN PROCEEDING TO SERBIA. MEN ARE *NOW* WANTED TO AVENGE THEM.[254]

Mediterranean diversion

The early performance of the individual boats in the Mediterranean was impressive, but the overall U-boat war was faltering. In the four months prior to moving the boats south, mean sinkings per month had been 137,000 tons. In the first four months of the Mediterranean-focused operations the monthly rate dropped to 129,000 tons. In other words, the apparently easier sinkings in the Mediterranean failed to compensate for the lost sinkings in the northern waters. But, with the ever-present fear of American retaliation, the Imperial Navy continued to pour resources into its Mediterranean operations. By the end of the war, the Mediterranean would see 3.3 m tons sunk out of an all-sectors total of 11 m.

The Mediterranean U-boats relied on the Austro-Hungarian naval base at Cattaro for their servicing and repairs. Access to the base was only possible by passing through the Strait of Otranto, which separates the Ionian and Adriatic seas. For the Allies, blocking this passage was critical to reducing the threat of U-boats to merchant ships in the Mediterranean.

In the autumn of 1915, the Allies began work on building the Otranto Barrage to bridge the 45 mile gap between Brindisi in Italy and Corfu on the Albanian coast. With the might of the Austrian navy to the north and the peril of the U-boats to the south, the Otranto Barrage of indicator nets was to be partly patrolled by tiny North Sea drifters, manned by hurriedly-enlisted North Sea fisherman. At its peak of activity, it had 35 destroyers, 52 drifters plus 100 other vessels.

One of the first requisitioned drifters was the 99-ton *Garrigill* from Lowestoft, which went into service at the barrage on October 15. John Turner was a typical barrage man: a civilian fisherman, known as the 'gentle giant' in his village of Martham. He had enlisted into the reserve in February 1915 and was one of the first seaman in the Mediterranean to man the drifters, which towed nets to entrap U-boats. For over three years Turner lived day and night in a fragile wooden boat in a battle area were U-boats and destroyers could appear without warning. He did not return to his village until March 1919, bearing his Conspicuous Gallantry Medal for an action in 1917 to which I will return.

With the ever-present fear of American retaliation against the U-boats, the Imperial Navy allocated still more resources to its Mediterranean operations. By the end of the year, it was establishing a factory at Pola (now in Croatia) to build the new UB II boats (an enlarged version of the UB I). The parts were brought overland by train, along with German shipyard workers – a move which depleted the servicing and repair facilities for boats in northern waters.

Spurned Page

Back in London, Walter Page was in a subdued mood by the autumn of 1915. Living amongst the British, reading their newspapers, perusing their casualty lists and seeing their black armbands in the streets, meant that he knew how serious the war was. He also knew that the Allies were making little (if any) progress against their enemy. It was not easy reporting this to his masters in Washington. Page could have chosen the easy life by telling the Americans what they wanted to hear. Instead, he chose to tell the truth. In a letter of September 8 he told Colonel House that the British 'are laughing at Uncle Sam' saying that 'Uncle Sam is in the clutches of the peace-at-any-price public opinion [camp], that the United States will suffer any insult and do nothing'.[255] In another letter to House, written on the same day, Page commented that 'the President is fast losing in the minds of our best friends here'.[256] Two days later, Page told Wilson that the British think 'that the Germans have taken us in'.[257]

By late September, Anglo-US relations were at a low ebb. Page told House that 500 'insulting [anti-American] cartoons' had appeared in the British press in the last month. Living in Britain, the ambassador had to accept the brickbats that came his way. He was cold-shouldered by London society: 'It's the loneliest time I've had in England,' he told House.[258] A few days later, he visited an old friend on the outskirts of London, who had just lost two sons. 'Tell me, what is America going to do?' the man pleaded.[259] Page could offer no reply.

It's in the Post

Meanwhile, the British authorities continued to winkle out every German ruse for breaking the blockade, including a cunning use of small packages. It was in September 1915 that the postal service became aware of the enormous number of small parcels coming into the country. Sweden, which before the war was sending five parcels a week, was now sending 1000; in the case of Denmark, the leap was from 30 to 4500 parcels. Once opened, these packages revealed their secret: they contained small high-value items such as jewellery, violin strings and medicines, sent as a means of payment for illicit German-bound cargo that had evaded the blockade. Once exposed, these attempts to beat the blockade were easily cut off.

Desperation

Max Valentiner in *U-38* was having a busy November in the Mediterranean, having sunk 12 vessels during the first six days of the month. Of the 69 vessels that he had despatched since the start of the war, not one was a passenger steamer. He was now to mar that record of restraint.

Valentiner's first foray into sinking passenger liners went unnoticed in the wider world as he torpedoed the 4300-ton French ship *France IV* travelling from Mudros to Marseille on May 7. There were no casualties, nor did the British papers report the sinking. Perhaps the ease with which he sank a vessel that was so obviously not a warship emboldened him for his next day's work with a sinking that would shock the world.

The Italian liner SS *Ancona* had left Naples for New York on November 6. After picking up more passengers at Messina on the following day, it put to sea with 446 travellers bound for America. Flying under the Austrian flag, the *Ancona* could expect a smooth passage through the Mediterranean.

On the morning of November 8, *U-38* found the *Ancona* off Tunis. Ignoring the fact that the ship was clearly a passenger liner, Valentiner fired 100 rounds at the ship as it tried to flee. Cecile Greil, in her sworn deposition, estimated the firing to have lasted 'about 45 minutes'.[260] How much damage Valentiner did by gunfire will never be known since, fifteen minutes after the firing had stopped, Valentiner fired a torpedo.

When the torpedo struck the ship, Cecile Greil raced to the upper deck. Seeing the state of the ship, she knew she would have to leave. As she turned to go below to collect her passport, Greil saw that staircase that she had used on the way up had been shot away. After finding another staircase, she went below, passing through a cabin strewn with dead and wounded. While standing in her stateroom, the porthole glass was shattered as some object smashed through. It struck her maid, who fell dead with a severe head injury. Back on deck, many passengers were fighting over lifeboats. Some threw themselves over the side; others hurled themselves into the lifeboats, crashing down onto already seated passengers. Somewhere between 100 and 200 people lost their lives in the sinking. Amongst these were twenty Americans.

Two days later the American Ambassador in Rome, T N Page (no relation to Walter Page in London), told Washington that the American dead included an Alexander Patattivo with his wife and four children, a

Mrs Francis Lamura, plus 'about twenty other first-class passengers'.[261] While there is no accurate figure for the number of Americans lost in the sinking, Valentiner's action had swept away the diplomatic advantage that the Kaiser had sought in moving the U-boats to the Mediterranean.

Inured to sinkings: hundreds dead but no longer a splash-headline event.

The headlines and commentaries of the world's newspapers said all that needed to be said in response to Valentiner's insane choice of a target: 'Rome shocked by *Ancona* tragedy' ran *The Times*' headline of November 11. *The Manchester Guardian* spoke for many on the same day when it declared that the Germans 'had no more excuse in the Mediterranean than had the same scene of murder and bloodshed been enacted outside New York and in American waters'.[262] Meanwhile, a Rome newspaper warned its readers to expect more losses since 'the Germans have been compelled to transfer their activities from the North Sea to the Mediterranean'.[263]

The *Ancona* sinking was yet another diplomatic disaster for Germany. The U-boat service had scurried from the Western Approaches to the

Mediterranean in order to avoid the growing American anger at attacks on United States' citizens. Now, in the Mediterranean, Germany had rekindled American wrath *and* enraged the Italians. The message was clear: Germany could not win the war at sea without making new enemies. It could contain the war by a stricter sinking policy or widen it by a 'sink anything that floats' policy. Its oscillation between these options was to cost Germany the chance of victory at sea.

American opinion on how to respond to the *Ancona* sinking was divided. With just one year to go until the next presidential election, Wilson was determined to keep America out of the war. Meanwhile, Colonel House pleaded: 'The country is ready and waiting for action ... I believe it would be a mistake to send further notes.'[264] Wilson ignored this advice and sent a note of protest via Vienna. As far as America was concerned, it was 'business as usual' in a world where nothing was usual and respect for international law was at a discount.

The war had entered a new and dangerous phase, as Max Valentiner's torpedo had shown. No flag was now sacred. No neutral was now safe.

GREY'S DESPAIR

While Wilson endeavoured to keep America neutral, behind the scenes he gave the Allies what limited support he could without having to appeal to Congress. Just seven days before the sinking of the *Ancona* he had told his Cabinet: 'I will permit nothing to be done by our country to hinder or embarrass them in the prosecution of the war unless admitted rights are grossly violated.'[265] Despite this covert support, the United States continued to undermine the Allied blockade of Germany – the sole means of seriously damaging Germany at that stage of the war. Even as the *Ancona* was sinking, the American government had sent a thirteen-page protest note to the British government, packed with legal contestations of the blockade. *The Times* described these legal arguments as 'mostly capricious and sometimes inconsistent'. The paper declared: 'while the Allies are fighting for their lives and for all that they and America hold most sacred' the United States was claiming a right to be exempt from 'the inevitable consequences of a great maritime war'.[266] Grey was deeply upset by the American note, telling House that he was in such despair that he was tempted to abandon the blockade 'but that would go near to abdicating all chance of preventing Germany from being successful'.[267]

By coincidence, on the day of the *Times*' article, America announced export figures for 1914 and 1915 to Scandinavia and Germany. While exports to Germany had plunged from £31.2 m to £2.32 m – a decrease of £28.8 m – exports to Scandinavia had risen by £25.0 m. There could be no doubt that these increased Scandinavian imports were destined for Germany. Clearly, the blockade was less of an impediment to American trade than American businesses were prepared to admit in public.

A Baltic side-line

By this stage of the war, Britain had relaxed its objections to sinking merchant shipping without warning and was taking advantage of the opportunities to reciprocate in the Baltic Sea. This was perilous work since access to the Baltic was through the narrow passage between Denmark and Sweden. Lieutenant Commander Francis Cromie in *E-19*, who passed through the passage in September 1915, proved to be a skilful commander. He quickly sank eight merchant ships, including four on one day. He followed these actions by sinking two U-boats before the end of the year.

Cromie's greatest prize was the sinking of the 3000-ton German light cruiser SMS *Undine* in November 1915, despite its being protected by two destroyers. He fired one torpedo, but was unsure whether it had caused enough damage to sink the ship. His second firing proved more than enough as *Undine*'s magazines blew up. With its back broken, the ship sank rapidly. Surprisingly, only around 25 men lost their lives out of a complement of 14 officers and 256 men. Cromie received a DSO in May 1916, as well as French and Russian orders. (His prowess as a submarine commander was matched by his mastery of Russian. This was to prove his nemesis. In May 1917, Cromie was appointed naval attaché at the British Embassy in Petrograd (Saint Petersburg) and was still in Russia when the Revolution broke out. He was shot dead when the Bolsheviks attacked the Embassy on August 31, 1918.)

For those U-boats left in northern waters, the winter was as much a foe as the mines and the anti-submarine forces. Spiess in *U-9* was in the Baltic in December, having a thin time. In the last four months he had only sunk a steamer and an auxiliary minesweeper. Now, when he surfaced, his boat was encased in ice. The radio aerial towered rigidly above the water, an eerie icebound advertisement of the boat's presence. All the cables were frozen solid into their runners. The men hammered away at the ice only to find that, behind their backs, the conning tower hatch had frozen in the open position. A blowlamp came to the rescue and the boat submerged. But the submariners' woes were not over: all the mechanisms within the periscope were also frozen. The Latvian port of Libau served for a Christmas pause before Spiess returned to Germany, where *U-9* became a training boat. He was to miss the kinder spring and summer weather, not returning to sea until September 1916.

HOME FRONTS

On land and at sea, the war continued to demand more from men than they could readily give. Yet, on the home front in Britain, civilians were still barely troubled by the war. Food was plentiful, if sometimes expensive: fish prices had risen by 132 per cent in the first two years of war. In response, the Archbishop of Westminster had permitted Roman Catholics 'to eat cheaper cuts of meat instead'.[268] The upper classes still had the lowland covers and moorland shoots to enrich their fare with game. In October, Charles Hobson joined the Speaker of the House of Commons, the Duke of Marlborough and other dignitaries in the slaughter of 1,828 partridges at Nuneham House in Oxfordshire over four days. He then went on to the neighbouring Blenheim Palace to assist in downing 425 birds. It was a callous contrast to the 89,000 tons of merchant sinkings and the 25,909 casualties on the Western Front in the same month. (Much of that shipping contained food for those people who had no access to game reserves.)

The contrast on the German home front could hardly have been greater. From now until well after the end of the war, the citizens of the Central Powers (Germany, Austria-Hungary, Bulgaria and the Ottoman Empire) were never to forget the British blockade. It dominated their every waking hour. As the German people anticipated Christmas, ration coupons were issued for pork products, and bakeries were ordered to prepare only two varieties of Christmas fare. By the fate of the calendar, Christmas Eve fell on a meat-less day. With no Stollen in the shops and Christmas cakes forbidden, it was to be a frugal celebration. There was little of the Christmas atmosphere. Princess Blücher noted in her diary that Berlin was 'enveloped in an impenetrable veil of sadness, grey in grey'. Those who gazed into their Christmas trees did so 'with eyes dim with tears'. And the little joy that she could find at that Christmas was tempered by her 'heart-rending' visit to a home for blind soldiers.[269] By the end of 1915, restaurants were required to have two meatless and two fatless days each week. In the new year, news came that Hungary had introduced rationing for flour and bread, while Germany announced the rationing of potatoes from the spring.

Meanwhile, there was a severe shortage of metals. A War Resources Board was set up under the industrialist Walter Rathenau to procure and allocate resources. In the drive for metals, people began to strip copper from roofs, tear out lead downpipes and remove fixtures and fittings from buildings – and even from trains. Metal bathtubs and pails disappeared from houses. This was no enforced seizure: the people voluntary gave up not only useful household items, but also toys and treasured possessions such as inherited brass candlesticks. Princess Blücher described seeing 'cartloads of old pots and kettles and candlesticks, door-handles, chandeliers, etc' passing through the streets. '[The] Government pay well,' she noted. On the rumour-front it was said that, if necessary, 'even the telephone wires' would be requisitioned.[270] The people demonstrated their patriotic stoicism by buying 12 m marks worth of the latest War Bonds in 1915. The blockade was coming near to breaking the German economy, but not the people.

(There were no equivalent scrap metal collections in Britain during the First World War. The famous removal of house railings did not take place until the following war.)

As Page looked on the London scene, his faith in the French and British at war grew. In a private letter to friends in America he overflowed with admiration: 'the courage and the endurance of the British and the French excel anything ever before seen on this planet.' And, in the case of the British: 'They are financing most of their allies and they have turned this whole island into gun and shell factories.' But he rightly spotted a British weakness: 'they are slower than death to change their set methods'.[271] This was to prove true on the Western Front as failed frontal assault followed failed frontal assault. In the navy, courage would not prove lacking, but intelligent exploration of new ways to conquer U-boats would be beyond the Admiralty's capabilities.

WEIGHING THE BALANCE

At the approach of 1916 the achievements of the U-boats did not bear close examination. During the year, Germany had lost 19 U-boats in action, but new building had nearly doubled its fleet to 54 boats. Yet this increase in boats failed to show in tonnage sunk. The average monthly tonnage sunk for the second half of 1915 was 135,000 tons; the figure for the first half of 1916 would be lower at 133,000 tons. Neither of the two principal reasons for this fall in productivity offered any comfort. The move away from the rich pickings in northern waters could only be reversed at the risk of enraging the United States. And, more boats meant finding new commanders. The figures suggested that the best commanders were already at sea.

German donations of metal objects for the production of war materials.[272]

For the Allies, the critical issue in the U-boat war was the paucity of methods for sinking U-boats. Of the 25 boats lost up to the end of 1915, nine were sunk or grounded without any Allied involvement. Four were rammed, three sank to mines and five succumbed to gunfire. Only four were sunk while they were under water: one by net entrapment and three by torpedoing. The U-boats had only to remain submerged to reduce their chances of being sunk by two-thirds. Nothing was more urgent in the Allied cause than finding effective means of locating and sinking them.

While the Allied anti-submarine patrols had little to show for their long hours of staring across empty seas in the near futile hope of finding a U-boat, the Northern Patrol had succeeded in sealing Germany off from access to the North Sea for trade. (Apart from London's lenient release of dubious cargoes.) The scale of its work was impressive with 3098 vessels having been intercepted by Rear Admiral Dudley de Chair's Tenth Cruiser Squadron and associated vessels. Of these interceptions, 743 had been taken into Kirkwall or Lerwick as suspected blockade-runners. According to the Admiralty, only eight ships of any importance had escaped the blockade.

'THE SEA MURDERER'S LATEST CRIME'

Symbolically, the Imperial Navy rounded off the year by yet another provocative liner sinking: the British SS *Persia*, in passage from London to Bombay. *U-38*'s torpedo hit the *Persia*'s port boiler room, causing one of the boilers to explode. The resulting massive damage caused the ship to sink in minutes. With only four lifeboats launched, 343 of the 519 people on the ship died, making the sinking the P&O company's worst disaster of the war. Once more, Americans were amongst the victims, including the Aden Consul Robert McNeely, the missionary Rev Homer Salisbury and the newspaper magnate Frank Coleman. The *Daily Sketch* announced the sinking as 'THE HUNS' NEW YEAR GREETING TO THE WORLD'. For the *Daily Mirror* it was 'THE SEA MURDERER'S LATEST CRIME'. *The New York Times* declared 'WASHINGTON SEES A NEW CRISIS THREATENED'. At that time, President Wilson was on his honeymoon with his second wife, Edith, in Hot Springs, Virginia. (His first wife, Ellen, had died in August 1914.) An urgent telegram from Secretary of State Lansing brought their 'heavenly time' to a sudden end.[273]

It looked as if the New Year would just be a repeat of the old – only worse.

15
In the shadow of the United States

January to May 1916

'The day of reckoning with Germany is at last at hand.' – *The New York Times*,[274]

INDECISION

The Imperial Navy's policy of concentrating the U-boat services in the Mediterranean had failed to bring any conclusive results. All that could be said in its favour was that it had reduced clashes with America. But, by the end of 1915, the search for yet another U-boat strategy had begun.

For the Allies, the New Year began with the same set of useless tools for tackling U-boats. Yet no alarm bells rang. There was no sense of a growing crisis.

As to America, it had played the victim so far in the war. For all its protest notes, it preferred not to think about the slowly intensifying U-boat war. America was prepared to do almost anything to avoid war. Even to lose friends.

Walter Page had the difficult task of reporting the deterioration in British-American relations to his president. Writing to Wilson in early January, he described how, at a recent cinema session, the screening of the American flag provoked 'such hissing and groaning as caused the managers hastily to move that picture off the screen'.[275] More generally, he added: 'It is often made unpleasant for Americans in the clubs and in the pursuit of their regular business and occupations.'[276] Americans were being ostracized, and all because America had failed to act over the *Lusitania*.

Just at the time when Germany was preparing its next U-boat offensive, convoys came under consideration in the British Admiralty. The initiative had come from the Admiralty Trade Division, which was directed by Captain Richard Webb. Following discussions in the division, Webb issued a paper on February 24 which strongly argued against the introduction of convoys. The paper declared that 'scattering was the best policy'. After stating that the danger of attack 'is difficult to estimate' the paper concluded 'Probably, however, it is sufficiently great to make it undesirable to introduce convoy.'[277] Webb's paper was speculative rather than evidence-based, but such ways of thinking were common in the navy at that time. It would take a year of rear-guard argument and action by officers at sea to overturn this disastrous document.

DEATH OF A RAIDER

In late February a message reached Room 40 in Admiralty House from agents in Kiel, reporting that the 5000-ton German raider SMS *Greif* was preparing for sea. Its departure was a fearsome prospect since such a ship could despatch twenty or thirty substantial vessels once it was out on the oceans. First, though, the *Greif* had to pass through the North Sea.

The raider slipped its moorings on 27 February in the company of *U-70*. Two days later, just after midnight, the British Admiralty's wireless direction-finders reported a suspect vessel off the south-west coast of Norway. Jellicoe ordered cruisers from Scapa Flow and the Tenth Cruiser Squadron to begin searching for the mysterious intruder.

At that time, Captain Thomas Wardle in the armed merchant cruiser *Alcantara* was returning from a patrol of 50 days and was due to rendezvous with HMS *Andes* to handover secret documents. It was 4.00 am on February 29 when a signal alerted Wardle to the presence of an enemy ship in his area. Just over four hours later one of his lookouts saw smoke on *Alcantara*'s port beam. Yeoman of Signals Frank Coombes on the bridge examined the stranger through a telescope and saw a Norwegian flag. On her side was the Norwegian name *Rena*.

When ordered to stop, the raider replied, 'I am stopping my engines to adjust my machinery.'[278] Captain Wardle ordered a boat to be lowered, ready to board what he felt to be a suspicious ship. As the boarding party was being lowered over the side, Wardle noticed that the 'Rena' ensign had disappeared. At exactly that moment, a shell hit *Alcantara*'s bridge, smashing the steering gear and telephones, and killing some of the men. Flaps on the *Greif* fell open to reveal its guns. Fire was exchanged from 9.40 to 10.35, by which time *Alcantara* was sinking. On the *Greif* its magazine had been hit and the ship was engulfed in dense smoke, but it remained afloat for 40 minutes. The *Grief* was under the waves before its raiding career had begun, taking with it about 187 men. Sixty-eight men in the *Alcantara* died in the action.

The loss of the *Grief* indicated a crucial weakness in the Imperial Navy's raiding strategy: raiders had first to pass the British cruisers in the North Sea before they could reach the relative safety of the vast oceans. When it came to the big ships, the North Sea was still a British sea.

Easy targets

While the raiders had little future, the U-boats were a failing force. In an effort to redeem themselves, the U-boat commanders were now to redouble their efforts by the simple expedient of a callous disregard for the nature of their targets.

The Russian hospital ship *Portugal* was at anchor in the Black Sea on March 30, transferring wounded men in flat-bottomed barges to the shore. Meanwhile, Kapitänleutnant Konrad Gansser in *U-33* was in the mood to sink whatever he could find.

Nikolai Nikolaevitch, an official of the Russian Red Cross on the *Portugal*, heard the shout of 'Submarine boat!' at 8.00 am.[279] Those below rushed to the deck, not out of fear – they were certain that no one would ever attack a hospital ship – but out of curiosity. (The *Portugal* was clearly marked with Red Cross insignia and was flying a Red Cross flag from its masthead.) When about 200 feet off, *U-33* circled the *Portugal*, as if out of curiosity, rather than with deadly intent. As Gansser completed his second circling, the onlookers screamed in horror at the sight of a torpedo tearing through the water. It passed the ship, but another torpedo quickly followed, ripping open *Portugal*'s beam.

Nikolaevitch ran to the saloon to grab a lifebelt. Back on deck, he could hear the sisters of mercy screaming, some of them were even fainting. As the ship healed over, Nikolaevitch involuntarily slid off the pitching deck into the sea. By good fortune, he was thrown clear of the deadly swirl of the ship's vortex. When under the water he heard the dull sound of the exploding boilers. Back on the surface, Nikolaevitch swam amongst other survivors. Many of them were thrashing wildly and screaming for help as they battled with the waves. He soon clambered onto a raft along with 20 survivors, where he joined the French mate in organizing rowers to set out for the nearby shore. From amongst the debris they fished out a lifeless woman and then found that she had the faintest of heartbeats. Although blue, she responded to massage and came back to life. Twice, the Nikolaevitch party met motorboats, which offered to take them on board, but, on each occasion, they directed the boats to the many others still in the sea.

Fourteen nuns had been killed in the sinking, along with 101 other personnel. The sinking was Kapitänleutnant Konrad Gansser's forty-fourth attack.

There were attacks on troopships, too, at this time. In late February, it was seven weeks since Kapitänleutnant Lothar von Arnauld in *U-35* had sunk a vessel. When he finally found a target on February 26, it was too big to miss: the 14,000-ton SS *La Provence*. It's peace time run had been Le Havre to New York. On its maiden voyage in 1905 it had effortlessly broken the transatlantic liner record. Now, *La Provence* was a French troopship, taking men to Gallipoli and Macedonia. Its commander, Captain Vesco, had been in *La Provence* when, four years earlier, his radio operator had picked up the *Titanic*'s distress calls, so he had first-hand knowledge of the deadly power of the sea.

The ship was in the Mediterranean in passage from Toulon to Salonika when *U-35* struck. The crash of the torpedo and the fountain of water came without warning. The gun crews had been at their posts and numerous lookouts had been scanning the waves, but no one saw either a periscope or the wake of a torpedo.

The weather was clear and the sea was calm as *La Provence* began to list. Fourteen minutes later it was gone. Ten vessels came to its aid, taking 296 survivors to Malta and 400 to the French island of Milos in the Aegean Sea. In all, about 900 people were drowned. Contemporary accounts say that the serious damage below meant that few of the crew survived and that, in any case, there were only boats and rafts for 'a bare 700 and odd men'.[280]

The story of *La Provence* was simply another minor tragedy in a pitiless war. The deaths were quietly accepted as routine.

'Belligerent' Merchant Ships

On February 10 the German government announced a new sinkings policy. It reaffirmed its aggressive policy towards defensively-armed merchant ships, stating that 'a merchantman assumes a warlike character by armament with guns, regardless of whether the guns are intended to serve for defence or attack'. The merchant ships were to be treated 'as belligerents'.[281] In fact, the orders given to merchant ships by the Admiralty Trade Division in October 1915 clearly stated that 'armament was supplied solely for the purpose of resisting attack by an armed enemy vessel and must not be used for any other purpose whatsoever.'[282]

Secretary of State Robert Lansing challenged this British stance, saying that 'grave legal doubt exists as to the right of a merchant ship to carry armament'. He also denied that an armed merchant ship had a right to try to escape from a hostile U-boat. Instead, he said, the ship 'should stop if ordered'. Not so, said *The Times*: 'merchant ships have been armed from time immemorial, and their right to resist capture had never been disputed'. The paper continued: 'it is inconceivable that the British government should make any concession in this direction'.[283]

In the end, though, the legality or otherwise of defensive armament was irrelevant. It was the effect that counted. And that effect was to discourage U-boats from making surface attacks. The alternative – submerged attacks – made it impossible for a boat's commander to establish with certainty the nationality of a ship and the nature of its presence on the high seas. The way was now open for more 'accidental' and 'unintentional' sinkings of neutral vessels and passenger ships.

The Kaiser's continued refusal to adopt full unrestricted sinking brought the resignation of the 67 year-old Grand-Admiral von Tirpitz on March 15. He had been in post since 1896. The Imperial Navy was his navy, just as Britain's Grand Fleet was Fisher's navy. In the end, neither admiral stayed in post to see the triumphs and failures of his creation. But the two men are distinguished by their contrasting attitude to submarines. At the start of the war, Fisher had understood the power of the submarine, saying: 'The use of submarines in the last two annual manoeuvres has convinced most of us that in wartime nothing can stand against them ... the whole foundation of our traditional naval strategy ... had broken down!'[284] Tirpitz, for all his desire to introduce unrestricted sinking, failed to prioritise U-boat construction, so contributing to Germany's defeat. He was replaced by Admiral Eduard von Capelle, who saw no need to accelerate U-boat construction and argued for the continued construction of battleships, telling the Reichstag in March that he did not believe that unrestricted sinking would succeed in 'bringing England to her knees'.[285]

'GERMAN MILITARY ETHICS'

Having announced its new sinkings policy in one month, the German government was to renege on it in the following month.

The humble Folkestone to Dieppe ferry, SS *Sussex*, was quietly crossing the Channel on March 24 when it was sighted by Oberleutnant zur See Herbert Pustkuchen in *UB-29*. The *Sussex* was to be his thirty-second victim on the high seas. Why he chose to attempt to sink the ship is a mystery: he was not short of targets – he had sunk five ships in the previous four days. Had Pustkuchen known that the *Sussex* passengers included the United Press staff correspondent John Hearley, he might have hesitated. Instead, he handed a talented American journalist a scoop with a story that *The Times* described as 'The latest exhibition of German military ethics.'[286]

The *Sussex* was carrying 53 crew and 325 passengers. At the moment of impact, the ship lurched to one side and a violent explosion tore at its innards. Passengers panicked. Women and children slithered on the sloping deck as they made for the boats. Pustkuchen calmly observed his handiwork, writing in his logbook: 'The deck is filled with people. The steamer is a troop transport.'[287] It is hard to believe that he could not distinguish between young males in uniform and a mixed-ages, mixed-gender mêlée. One is left with the suspicion that the logbook entry was to cover Pustkuchen's unauthorized sinking of a ferry.

Many passengers were too badly injured to move. Passenger Edward Marshall recalled, 'I went among the wounded. Their injuries were freakish. Both of one man's legs were twisted till his feet pointed backward. Another's face had been blown in by the explosion.' Marshall went below to the steerage area, where he found passengers huddled together in fright, and women sobbing. Children were crying weakly and the lightly injured were moaning.

The chaos and the lack of any immediate aid gave rise to acts of heroism and solidarity. A young American doctor with a broken leg instructed a young woman on how to stop the bleeding of the severed artery of a Frenchman by pressing her thumb on wound, which she did for two hours. Another young woman, a nurse, refused to get into a boat, saying, 'No, give my place to a man with a family and children.' Some of the worst injuries were in the gentlemen's saloon. One man's legs were sliced off by flying debris. A Belgian aristocrat was thrown across the saloon by the blast. The American George Herbert Crocker was so badly injured that, three days later, the London surgeon Dr Clayton Green still dared not operate on him.

Marshall watched as men pushed women aside to reach the boats. Several women simply jumped into the sea. A deranged husband ran around, traumatized by the sight of the crushed bodies of his wife and son. Some passengers acted calmly as they sought the best way to survive.

Mr McHarg, an Australian merchant, was below when the torpedo struck. He stood to one side as his fellow passengers rushed in a mass for the boats. Later, on the deck, and wearing a lifejacket, McHarg was about to step into a lifeboat when he was thrown to the deck by a rival passenger. Providence was with him as he watched the boat drop into the sea and capsize under the weight of its passengers. McHarg joined another boat ten minutes later, but it soon became apparent that the *Sussex* was not going to sink, so the party in the boat returned to the ship.

Passengers on the Sussex anxiously await their rescue.

Of those lifeboats that were launched, at least two capsized. One of the empty boats was smashed into splinters by a huge fountain of water. Many passengers, though, remained on the crippled vessel as it wallowed in the cold sea. Then came a radio message at 7.00 pm from the Boulogne trawler *Marie Thérèse*, which was searching for the drifting *Sussex*. On reaching the *Sussex*, cold hands and tired bodies helped offload the wounded while the roughening sea buffeted the fragile trawler. McHarg finally slid down ropes into the *Marie Thérèse*. He and his fellow survivors landed at Boulogne, where they were later reunited with their luggage.

Of the 325 passengers and 53 crew, around 50 lost their lives. Some were simply swept from the ship's deck by a large wave – one witness claimed that most of the casualties were caused in this way. Amongst the 'if only' deaths was that of the Spanish composer Enrique Granados. He was much in demand in America at that time, having recently performed for President Wilson. Granados had delayed his planned departure for Spain in order to record some piano rolls, so missing his ship home. His return via England cost him his life. He and his wife (who was too heavy to get into a lifeboat) were last seen clinging to a life raft.

The presence of Americans on the *Sussex* guaranteed headlines over the water: '*Sussex* Torpedoed ... Six Americans Injured, One Still Missing', declared the *New-York Tribune*. Although no American lives were lost, the attack on the *Sussex* was an attack too far for many Americans. John Hearley took the lead with his assertion that the torpedoing was: 'The most serious situation since the *Lusitania* incident' and that it 'threatened German-American relations'. He was backed-up by *The Times*, which called the attack a 'crime'. 'No German,' the paper declared, 'can be dense enough to imagine that it could serve ... any military purpose'.[288] Four days later *The New York Times* was heralding America's hardening attitude towards German attacks on civilians. It suggested that the government should recognize that 'the day of reckoning with Germany is at last at hand'.[289] But President Wilson made no move, causing Colonel House to comment in his diary: 'He does not seem to realize that one of the main points of criticism against him is that he talks boldly, but acts weakly.'[290]

The torpedoing of the Sussex overshadowed many other attacks around that time, each reported by *The Times* as mere routine – the dull, anaesthetised, tedium of war. The 5000-ton Dominion liner *Englishman* had disappeared; the 3300-ton steamer *Salybia* had been sunk; the 4400-ton *St Cecilia* was also sunk, as had been the 3800-ton steamer *Fenay Bridge*. The *Sussex*, though, was about to make the headlines in the wrong way for Germany.

Before the American government had responded to the attack on the *Sussex*, Berlin issued a note denying that a U-boat had been responsible and blaming British mines for the damage to the ship. Over the next two weeks the American government investigated in depth the circumstances of the sinking. The affidavits taken and the submissions received ran to 47 pages. The evidence from these sources merited only one conclusion: Germany had torpedoed the *Sussex*. President Wilson, who had tolerated German sinkings of non-belligerent vessels on many occasions, finally acted. A packed and solemn Congress listened as the President declared: 'Again and again the Imperial Government has given this Government its solemn assurances that at least passenger ships would not be thus dealt with, and yet it has again and again permitted its undersea commanders to disregard these assurances.' He continued: 'We are in some sort ... the responsible spokesman of the rights of neutrals'. He warned that 'if it is still its [Germany's] purpose to prosecute relentless and indiscriminate warfare against vessels of commerce' America 'can have no choice but to sever diplomatic relations with the Government of the German Empire altogether'.[291]

Secretary Lansing's later response to the new sinkings policy showed that America was now determined on ending attacks on American vessels: 'If the commanders of the U-boats from the beginning of the war had observed the rules and principles ... there would have been no submarine controversy between the United States and Germany.' The United States demanded only one thing of the German government: that it conform to 'existing international law'.[292]

Germany – on paper – capitulated in the face of the American threat and, on May 4, it issued a memorandum that is now known as the '*Sussex* Pledge'. The long, rambling, document claimed that Germany was 'resolved to go to the utmost limit of concessions' in the U-boat war. Bowing to the demands of the United States, Germany agreed not to attack passenger ships, and to allow crews of enemy merchant vessels to abandon ship before their ships were sunk.

After the war, Tirpitz described the *Sussex* Pledge as 'the beginning of our capitulation' and 'a decisive turning-point of the war'. By 'rejecting the submarine campaign', he argued, Germany had lost its 'last chance of salvation'. Germany's withdrawal had 'strengthened the determination of the English to hold out'.[293]

A NEW NAVAL TARGET

In early February, Admiral Pohl had died from liver cancer, to be replaced by Admiral Scheer as Commander-in-Chief of the High Seas Fleet. By late April, Scheer was ready to take his fleet into action. He was convinced that the superior design aspects of the German warships, combined with his officers' meticulous training in tactics and aerial reconnaissance, could outperform the Grand Fleet. But first, he needed a tip and run raid to draw out and destroy elements of Jellicoe's fleet. His initial target, though, was to be innocent civilians.

At dawn on April 24 the townspeople of Lowestoft and Yarmouth on England's east coast awoke to the thundering roar of guns and the terrifying sound of shells shattering the houses of the two towns. In all, 200 houses were hit and 25 local people killed. The rapid arrival of ships from the Grand Fleet resulted in a brief exchange of fire with the raiders before Scheer fled the field. The results were inconclusive. One German and two British cruisers were sunk; both sides lost one submarine. This outcome was yet another demonstration of the irrelevance of the High Seas Fleet in a U-boat-dominated war. Scheer gained nothing, while Jellicoe moved seven King Edward VII-class battleships from Rosyth to the Thames, where they would more or less sit on Scheer's doorstep.

An easy, but hardly strategic, target for the High Seas Fleet: housing in Lowestoft, April 1916. (Illustrated London News.)

The raid had been timed to distract attention from German support for the Irish Easter Rising of April 24-29. With the failure of the rising and the inconsequential outcome of the east coast raids, the Imperial Navy's surface fleet was once more left searching for a role.

As Scheer pondered the futility of his raids, he brooded on the inoperable *Sussex* Pledge now that many British merchant ships were armed. He declared that the U-boats were being forced to operate under Prize Law, which 'must expose the boats to the greatest dangers' and 'could not possibly have any success'. If a U-boat commander wished to avoid the risk of being sunk by gunfire, Scheer argued, he had to attack while submerged. Yet in that state it was near to impossible to determine the nature of a target. The result would be many more *Sussex*-style incidents. In his despair at the German Admiralty's policy, Scheer acted unilaterally: 'I recalled all the U-boats [attached to his fleet] by wireless, and announced that the U-boat campaign against British commerce had ceased.'[294]

Scheer's view of the U-boats as a failing force was not shared by the British. The U-boat campaign in the Mediterranean, combined with the end of the winter weather around the British Isles, had brought an increasing number of sinkings. January to April sinkings (558,000 tons) were 128 per cent higher than those for the same period in 1915 (244,000 tons). At the Admiralty, Arthur Balfour was alarmed at the possible effect on morale should these figures reach the public domain. He called in the newspaper magnate Lord Riddell, who ran an informal liaison group of newspaper editors. Could he help? Such was Riddell's influence that his short note to his fellow editors ensured that the cumulative figures for shipping losses never reached the news-stands. (Riddell served the government so well that, despite his secret divorce in 1900, he was raised to the peerage by Lloyd George in 1918 – the first divorcee to enter the Lords.)

NET GAIN

In early 1916, anti-submarine drift nets towed by patrol craft brought one of their rare successes. Oberleutnant zur See Wilhelm Smiths in *UB-26* was attempting to enter the French port of Le Havre when his boat became entangled in the nets being towed by six auxiliary patrol drifters. Men on the drifter *Endurance* saw the bobbing indicator buoys and then heard a loud thud under their ship's hull: *Endurance* had caught a U-boat in its net. With a damaged rudder, *Endurance* was now at the mercy of the submerged boat. Other drifters moved in to surround the stricken vessel. They watched for 20 minutes as *Endurance* tried to haul in its catch, but the U-boat proved too strong a foe. To save his ship, Captain Wylie cut the net loose. The remaining drifters followed *UB-26* as it continued to attempt to wrestle free from the net. The arrival of a French destroyer brought *UB-26*'s antics to an end. Two depth charges found their prey. (At this stage of the war, a sinking by depth charge was a rarity since the charges were only available in very small numbers. It is possible that the two charges dropped by the French destroyer were the only ones on board.) The damage to the U-boat was massive. The compass was smashed. One of the batteries had caught fire. Some of the high pressure air lines were ruptured and the starboard electric motor was drowning in a massive oil leak. Then came a second explosion from an unknown cause. The forward hatch sprang open, as did the torpedo doors. With the compressed air now released, the boat was taking on water at an alarming pace. Smiths ordered the tanks to be blown. Surrender was inevitable.

Once on the surface, the crew scrambled out to stand on the deck before the boat dropped away beneath them. All were saved by the drifters. In his first boat – *UB-5* – Smiths had only sunk five ships, four of which were under 100 tons. The fifth was under 1000 tons. In *UB-26* he had sunk nothing in his two patrols. One more ineffective commander was now in captivity. There would have been cheering on the drifters at their success, but the seas were not much safer with the removal of the weaker elements of the U-boat fleet.

Kapitänleutnant Ralph Wenninger left a graphic account of his *UB-55* being caught in a net later in the war. With the boat's steering gear already damaged and the boat rolling in an uncontrolled manner, his crew twisted and turned their submerged boat for 90 minutes as they attempted to free it. As a last resort Wenninger took the drastic step of pumping six tons of water into the boat's tanks. Suddenly, the increasing weight wrenched the boat free and it plunged to the seabed. Eighteen hours later Wenninger tentatively raised the boat. There was no sign of any anti-submarine craft, but his torment was not over. Neither his compass nor his depth gauge was working, and the steering gear was damaged. Down went *UB-55* for six hours of repairs.

For the lack of a submarine

It was at this time – after a year's experimental work – that a rift developed between the Admiralty and its Board of Inventions. The Board's highest priority was its research on hydrophones, being carried out at the Hawkcraig Experimental Station (known as HMS *Tarlair*) near Aberdour on the Firth of Forth. The work was being held back by a lack of access to ships and a submarine for testing the experimental devices. Commander Cyril Ryan of the Hydrophone Service (who represented the Admiralty) told the Liverpool University physicist Albert Wood, that the researchers 'have no right to demand two ships'. As to their request for access to submarine *B-3*, Ryan was unable to tell Wood when it would be available. Wood also complained that equipment was being taken from the establishment without any explanation. This catalogue of Admiralty disruptions of a vital research project highlights how little faith the naval officers in Admiralty House had in new technology. We can only speculate as to how many merchant ships were sunk because of the Admiralty's failure to support the work at Hawkcraig. (Wood was no ordinary researcher: he was the key brains behind the development of asdic and would end World War Two with a string of honours and awards.)

Experimental towed hydrophones at HMS Tarlair.

BUSINESS AS USUAL

The home front in Britain in the spring of 1916 remained largely untouched by the ravages of the U-boats. With 7.5 m acres of pasture converted to cereal cultivation and yields up 40 per cent on those of recent years, food remained unrationed. The news in May of the failure of the North American wheat harvest left the War Council unperturbed: orders were placed for more wheat from Australia. When Lord Selborne, Minister of Agriculture, suggested growing yet more wheat at home, the council decided that the U-boats had not succeeded in interrupting supplies and rejected the proposal. (Growing more wheat at home used precious manpower needed by the army.) British dining tables would continue to defy the U-boats. As *The Times* remarked in May 'no one would believe that this country is at war'.[295]

For those coming home on leave, entertainment in abundance awaited them. King-Hall, now a lieutenant, was in London in early April. He recorded in his diary having a 'very good time' in a round of 'theatres, dances, dinners, etc'. London, he noted, 'seemed pretty gay'. The only signs of war that he saw were 'the wounded sunning themselves in front of the hospitals'.[296]

Peacetime normality was even possible in the larger ships. In late March, King-Hall was musing on the good dinner that he had just had in HMS *Southampton*: 'I could not help thinking how comfortable it all looked. Tulips on the table, nice white table cloth, a dozen or more officers smoking, drinking their port and coffee, the whole well lit up with electric lights shaded in yellow silk'. His cabin was 'well lit, well warmed ... (two radiators)'.[297]

BLOCKADE SUCCESS

Life was very different in Germany at this time. The blockade brought ever more misery to the towns and cities, while the battlefronts produced corpses and casualties rather than victories.

When the German people had paid their taxes in the early 1900s to build the Kaiser's warships, they never imagined that his mighty fleet would not even be able to guarantee putting food on their tables. Meanwhile, as Scheer mulled over the small outcome of his east coast raids, belts were tightened and stomachs rumbled in the homeland. Housewives stood for hours in queues outside the butchers', grocers' and bakers' shops. Some housewives were getting up in the night to head the queues, aided by camp stools for comfort and knitting for necessity. Princess Blücher even saw one woman queuing while operating a sewing machine. Daily rations had been cut to ½ oz of sugar, ½ lb of meat or lard, 1 lb of potatoes and a weekly ration of 4 oz of butter.

THE EVE OF JUTLAND

For the Imperial Navy, the first five months of 1916 had been months of standstill. The raiders on the oceans had had successes although they were never within sight of sinking or capturing a significant tonnage. The High Seas Fleet had limited itself to attacking civilians sleeping in their beds or sitting at their breakfast tables. None of this looked like a war-winning strategy. But there was worse news from the U-boat front. Average monthly sinkings for the first five months of the year were

137,000 tons, against 141,000 tons for the last five months of 1915. This drop was despite an increase in U-boat numbers, with 34 new boats commissioned against 7 boats lost. Meanwhile, on the Western Front, Falkenhayn was beginning to think that his latest offensive had failed.

If the Allies could not be beaten on land and were failing to succumb to the U-boats at sea, there was only one option left: the High Seas Fleet. Scheer prepared for the battle of his life: Jutland.

It was a confident admiral who led his fleet out to sea on the 31 May. Scheer fully expected to return a hero the next day, with a sizeable chunk of the Grand Fleet at the bottom of the North Sea. He only needed one day to turn the naval war around. It was the greatest chance of his life, and Germany's greatest chance of ending the hegemony of the Grand Fleet.

16
The end of the big ships

Summer 1916

'To-day we sold the effects of the men who were killed [at Jutland].' – King-Hall.[298]

BIG SHIPS AND SMALL RESULTS

From the very first days of the war, the High Seas Fleet had lain in harbour to await orders to engage the British Grand Fleet. It had been built with the fanciful purpose of ending Britain's dominance of the world's oceans. But, after just under two years of war, the only testaments to the might of that fleet were wrecked houses and shattered promenades in seaside towns such as Scarborough and Hartlepool.

With victory on land increasingly improbable, and Britain's breakfast tables still boasting unrationed bacon, butter and plentiful bread, the ships of the High Seas Fleet slipped their moorings in the small hours of May 31 to do battle with Jellicoe's fleet.

Admiral Scheer led out 99 war vessels, including 16 battleships and 5 battlecruisers. His aim was to engage elements of the Grand Fleet off the Skagerrak, sinking enough ships to significantly weaken Jellicoe's strength. Instead, thanks to British intelligence, he was to find 151 British ships, including 28 battleships and 9 battlecruisers hurrying south to greet him.

The outcome of the battle was crucial to the future of the U-boat war. From 3.48 pm on May 31 when the battlecruisers first opened fire to 7.18 pm when Scheer turned away from Jellicoe's dreadnoughts for the second time, the two fleets engaged in the first ever high-speed, big-gun naval action. As the smoke from the guns was carried away on the breeze at the end of the day, over 6000 British seamen were dead and 14 British warships had been sunk. With German losses of around 2500 men and 11 ships sunk, Scheer appeared to be the victor. But was he?

The British press had no trouble in answering that question: their billboards gave their screaming verdicts: 'Great naval battle', 'Six British cruisers sunk' and 'Eight destroyers lost'. The public drew its own conclusion: something calamitous had occurred. The returning seamen were the first to feel the opprobrium of a disillusioned public, convinced that its Grand Fleet had suffered a humiliating defeat. As the destroyer HMS *Obdurate* steamed home up the Forth, sub-lieutenant Harry Oram was devastated to hear the jeering workers standing on the great bridge while his ship passed underneath. Meanwhile, the press reports were a public relations disaster for the Admiralty. Instead of glorious claims of victory, many papers chose to stress the losses: 'Heavy British losses – three battlecruisers sunk' (*Daily Express*). Others quoted German accounts before British ones: 'German story of success' (*The Manchester Guardian*). In the case of the *Daily Mirror* its front page simply carried the bald summary 'Women who mourn and the men who have died' with no detail until the reader reached page 3. It was not until June 5 that papers such as *The Manchester Guardian* began to talk of the battle as a British victory.

In reality, Jutland was a clear-cut British victory. As Admiral Jellicoe said after the battle: 'Victory always rests with the force that occupies the scene after the action.'[299] More crucially, of the two protagonists, Jellicoe was the man who had achieved his strategic aim: to keep the High Seas Fleet out of the North Sea and to maintain the Grand Fleet in-being. (Two days after the battle, at 9.45 pm, Jellicoe telegraphed the Admiralty to declare that his fleet was ready for action again. One month later, the Grand Fleet was stronger than when it sailed to Jutland.)

Scheer, on the other hand, had totally failed in his aims. His strategic objective was simple: for the High Seas Fleet to gain mastery of the North Sea and unfettered access to the Atlantic Ocean. With such access, Scheer's powerful fleet could have wreaked such fearful havoc as to push Britain out of the war in months. But, to achieve this objective, Scheer first had to seriously weaken the Grand Fleet. Jutland was his chance to gain that dominion of the seas. It was a chance that he missed.

Nevertheless, in Germany Jutland was seen as a war-changing victory. A High Command general told his subordinates: 'As the victory flags of Jutland wave from the masts of our ships and our storm troops approach Fort Vaux [on the Meuse], the provisioning of the German people is assured. The successes on the war front and at home make our final victory an absolute certainty.'[300] None of this was to prove true. The Battle of Verdun was to see another six months of fruitless fighting before von Falkenhayn would withdraw his forces. Meanwhile, the U-boat war would be as inconclusive as the land war. Jutland had changed nothing. As to the assured provisioning, all that the Germans could look forward to was ever-diminishing food stocks of ever-decreasing quality.

The end of the big ships

For Jellicoe, Jutland was to prove to be the peak of his career. He was fortunate that British strategic needs in 1916 favoured preserving the fleet over destroying German warships. He had fought a defensive battle and had returned home with a still all-powerful fleet. But the need for a defensive stance ended there. Jellicoe would soon be First Sea Lord with a remit to take on the U-boats. The skills that won Jutland would prove inadequate in that greater battle to come. Also, he was already worn out, as Keyes noted in July: 'I had not seen him since my visit to Loch Ewe, I thought he looked tired and harassed.'[301]

'The big victory': A German view of Jutland in 1916. (Contemporary postcard.)

The Imperial Navy's assessment of the battle was delusional. The perceived victory bolstered its faith in battleships and battlecruisers. Before his resignation in March, Tirpitz had placed orders for 13 battleships and battle-cruisers and, back in September 1915, he had paused the building of new U-boats so as to give priority to surface vessels. This concentration on building ships that would never fight, distracted Tirpitz's successors from the one battleground where Britain was supremely vulnerable: the trade routes. It would be six months before the Imperial Navy finally let go of its warship fantasies and turned to the one proven war-winning weapon that it had: the U-boat.

The end of the big ships

AN OLD WARRIOR DEPARTS

In early June, the young diplomat Hugh O'Beirne heard that he had been picked to join a military mission to Russia, headed by Lord Kitchener. His experience as a former counsellor at the British embassy in Petrograd would be invaluable to the Field Marshal. Also, a successful mission would be a huge boost to his career. But, on his arrival at King's Cross station, O'Beirne found that the mission's train had already departed. Undeterred, he ordered a 'special' train, which sped him north to Scapa Flow. He was not going to miss the adventure after all.

A storm was raging when O'Beirne caught up with the party awaiting the arrival of HMS *Hampshire* at Scapa Flow. The mission included Kitchener's Military Secretary, Lieutenant Colonel Oswald Fitzgerald, and Brigadier General Arthur Ellershaw, as well as the munitions expert Sir Hay Frederick Donaldson. This was clearly a mission not to miss.

Out of the dusky mist on June 5 the huge form of the cruiser HMS *Hampshire* appeared. With the gangway in place, Jellicoe and Kitchener exchanged a few last thoughts before the *Hampshire* cast off into the wild sea at 4.45 pm. Five hours later the ship was off Orkney in a heavy sea when an explosion tore out its centre. It had struck a mine in a channel where mines had never previously been found. Twenty minutes later there was not a sign of the mighty vessel.

With only twelve survivors out of a crew of 735 and 14 passengers, little is known about Kitchener's last moments. Some said that the cry of 'Make Way for Lord Kitchener!' went up as men hurried to the boats.[302] Others said that he was on the bridge with Captain Herbert Savill, dressed in a raincoat and with a walking stick in one hand. The two men watched passively as vain attempts were made to launch the boats into the tempestuous sea. Only four boats got away but not one made land. It was not until June 9 that a few men, clinging to a raft, were plucked from the sea. In Colonel Fitzgerald's case, his body was washed up on the shore some days later.

The *Hampshire* had gone done in waters close to Scapa Flow, having struck a mine laid by *U-75*. The long reach of the U-boats had extended to waters that the Royal Navy expected to dominate. *Hampshire*'s sinking emphasized that the British navy continued to be powerless against this new form of warfare.

Kitchener's death was a coup for the Imperial Navy but of no consequence to Britain's war. As early as November 1915 the War

The end of the big ships

Council had sent him off to Gallipoli as an alternative to removing him from office. His visit to Russia was yet another device for keeping an ineffective War Minister out of the way. *The Times*' editorial on his death hinted at the prevailing view of Kitchener in 1916. His death 'in harness' was 'an enviable fate ... At a period when the cold shadows of advancing age begin to gather'.[303]

Jellicoe and Kitchener exchange a few last words before HMS Hampshire sailed to its – and Kitchener's – doom.[304]

EXPORT OR DIE

In Germany, the Allied blockade was an ever-increasing threat to its capacity to wage war. The country desperately needed rubber, metals and oils. It also needed to earn dollars to pay for imports. With imports by surface ship being exceedingly hazardous, the Imperial Navy turned to its latest submarine: the cargo U-boat *Deutschland*. At over 2000 tons it was 63 m long and had a 9 m beam.

The locals in Hampton Roads in Virginia stared in amazement when, on July 10, a mighty vessel appeared out of the ocean: the *Deutschland* was calmly sitting in the roads, awaiting a tug to take it into Baltimore Dock. The boat quickly became known as the 'super submarine'.

The *Deutschland*'s pioneering voyage had been captained by the sailor and businessman Paul König, who was in search of adventure rather than war. In its hold were 750 tons of valuable dyes and large quantities of precious stones. Rumour had it that the cargo was worth $1 m (about $25 m today). Selling this cargo would bring dollars with which Germany could purchase zinc, silver, copper and other raw materials. (The voyage also had an ulterior motive. America, cut off from importing German dyes, was rumoured to be planning to build its own dye factories. With luck, the *Deutschland*'s supply would discourage America from developing a competing dye stuff industry.)

The Deutschland arriving in America in 1916. (Contemporary postcard.)

The *Deutschland* was inspected by the Port Collector, William Ryan, who declared it to qualify as a merchantman since its only armament was a few pistols. With that approval, König gave a round of press interviews, declaring that voyages such as his would 'break the British blockade'. He referred to 'the British attempt to kill by starvation 100,000,000 German and Austrian children, women and non-combatants'.[305]

The New York Times welcomed the visit, describing it as 'a noteworthy *victory of peaceful character*, voyaging 4,000 miles through enemy waters ... without armed escorts'. Assuming that the vessel was only defensively armed, the paper said 'she may enjoy the use of our ports at her pleasure, and may take on cargo'. Nevertheless, when the paper discussed the war aspects of the voyage, it concluded: 'The pretence that submarines sent out with cargoes and passengers for a 4,000 mile voyage are primarily or exclusively engaged in commercial ventures would not deeply impress a court of law.'[306]

The *Deutschland*'s pioneering voyage was openly talked about in Germany. The people, wrote Princess Blücher, saw it as 'the commencement of a new era of commercial success enterprise and success'.[307]

The boat made one further voyage. The only other blockade-breaking U-boat to go into service, the *Bremen*, disappeared on its maiden voyage in September 1916. The cargo U-boats soon fell out of favour, so the large boats in production were converted to patrol work. The cargo boats had proved to be yet one more failure in the U-boat war strategy.

Dearth and plenty

The *Deutschland*'s voyage was a clear demonstration of the profound implications of Germany's many shortages. These, by June 1916, included serious food shortages. The British authorities had developed a wide range of tactics for preventing food from reaching German and Austrian ports. Ships that traded with these ports were denied coal when they called at British coaling stations. British traders were blacklisted if they were found to be assisting in goods reaching the Central Powers. And, in extreme cases, the British government would buy up and destroy food merely to prevent the Central Powers acquiring it. This was done with Norwegian herrings, which the British barely ate. At the same time as preventing ships from trading with Germany, Britain compelled neutral ships to keep trading with Britain by holding them hostage until another ship from the same country arrived. On a one-in-one-out basis few ships could escape the enslavement to serving British commerce.

In Austria and Germany food shopping had become a daily torture as the shortages were felt in every corner of the alliance. Even the great port of Hamburg was a place of harrowing suffering. Anna Kohnstern, who lived in the city, endured queues of up to 800 people on a daily basis as she sought sustenance for herself, her five daughters, and her son in the infantry. (Being in the army was no guarantee of an adequate diet. In one regiment in Posen the recruits lost 15 per cent of their weight in their first month of enlistment.) Everyone in the Kohnstern family was losing weight and Anna feared the coming winter.

Most of the queuing was orderly, but fights were not unusual. Riots broke out, with sixty bakeries being attacked and looted. One woman described how two housewives were killed in a dispute over food.

The end of the big ships

Matters were made worse when the potato crop was damaged by a fungus; bakeries were again looted. In the summer of 1916 a failure to distribute a new batch of potatoes in Hamburg led to much of the stock rotting.

By now, 'food' in the Central Powers meant adulterated food as the authorities stretched the meagre supplies. Bread contained any number of unidentifiable ingredients, often leaving a burning sensation in people's mouths and throats. Pepper was stretched with 85 per cent ash. Egg substitutes were concocted from grains. Wheat flour often contained gypsum. And 'coffee' was never authentic coffee but imaginative creations made from the roasted stones and kernels of walnuts, plums and other fruits.

It was not just food that was now in short supply. The blockade had crippled almost every aspect of domestic German life. The simplest things such as needles and thread were now almost impossible to find in the shops. A lack of rubber meant that gas masks had to be made from leather. Household goods and utensils were no longer available; bicycle spares were unobtainable. And attempts at substitutes did not necessarily ease matters. When sugar was found to be useful for making explosives, the result was less sugar in German kitchens.

In Britain, life continued much as it had done in peacetime, as it did for Keyes when his family moved north to be near to Scapa Flow in mid-1916. His wife and three children were accompanied by seven servants and 'about two tons of luggage'.[308] Once settled in the north, Keyes was able to indulge in grouse shooting on the Novar Estate in the Scottish Highlands, where he and his young officers engaged in some team-building by shooting 75 brace of grouse. Two signalmen on hill tops maintained communication with the fleet by means of semaphore flags on shore and a searchlight on the flagship.

A NEW BELLICOSITY

No doubt the hardships in Germany help to explain the increasingly heartless treatment of civilians caught up in the war at sea, as exemplified by the fate of Captain Charles Fryatt.

Fryatt had been with the ferries of the Great Eastern Railway since 1892, first as a seaman and, since 1915, as a master. Twice in early March of that year his ferry had come under U-boat attack, but, on each occasion, he had managed to outrun the enemy. Then, towards the end of the month, came Fryatt's encounter with *U-33*.

The end of the big ships

Kapitänleutnant Konrad Gansser was eager for a sinking since neither he nor his boat had yet despatched a single vessel. Yearning to prove himself, he decided to take what he could get: a passenger ferry. His boat was surfaced when he met the 1380-ton ferry SS *Brussels*.

When Fryatt's lookouts yelled 'Submarine!' he knew that his only hope of escape lay in forcing *U-33* to dive. He called for full-speed-ahead and ordered his crew to the back of the ship in case the U-boat should open fire. The *Brussels* lurched forward, striving to reach its maximum speed of 16.5 knots. As the ship surged towards the U-boat, the chief officer fired rockets to give the impression that the ship was armed. So far, Gansser had held firm. Now the *Brussels* was almost upon him. A collision seemed inevitable. Fryatt saw the periscope disappear beneath the waves and ordered his helmsman to hold a course over the spot where *U-33* had disappeared – it was imperative that the boat did not surface. When the *Brussels* came clear of the area of the action, Fryatt saw *U-33* surface briefly with a decided list. It then disappeared. He concluded that he had sunk the boat. *Brussels* proceeded on its way and Fryatt thought no more of the episode.

It was over a year later in June 1916 that Fryatt's spontaneous action to avoid a U-boat proved to be his nemesis. The *Brussels* was in passage from the Hook of Holland to Harwich when it encountered five German destroyers. This time, there was no point in calling for full-speed-ahead. *Brussels* hove to, and Fryatt was arrested. His court-martial at Bruges Town Hall followed on July 27, leading to his being sentenced to death by firing squad. (The official announcement of his execution said that he attempted 'to destroy a German submarine by running it down'.[309]) Beyond German shores, a different view was taken of the episode. Prime Minister Asquith described Fryatt's execution as an 'atrocious crime against the laws of nations'[310] while *The New York Times* called it 'a deliberate murder'.

TWILIGHT OF THE BATTLESHIPS

In the late summer of 1916 Scheer was struggling to find a purpose for his fleet. Only the tossing and pitching of thousands of tons of steel, cutting through a menacing sea, the pounding of naval guns, and the smell of cordite could satisfy the cravings of this battle-fleet man. In this mood, Scheer decided on another attempt to lure out elements of the Grand Fleet. Both sides were to learn hard lessons about modern naval warfare.

The end of the big ships

Fyratt and the SS Brussels. The ship was seized by the Germans and renamed Brugge. In November 1918 it was scuttled at Zeebrugge. (Contempary postcard.)

On August 18 radio traffic from Scheer's ships that were preparing to sail was intercepted by a British listening station and was promptly decoded by Room 40. By the time that Scheer's advance force of the battlecruisers *Moltke* and *Von der Tann* had put to sea, together with the three battleships, *Bayern*, *Markgraf* and *Grosser Kurfürst*, British ships were already on the move. With Jellicoe on leave, Admiral Cecil Burney led the Grand Fleet out of Scapa Flow. At the same, time Beatty's ships left the Forth, and Tyrwhitt's Harwich Force put to sea. With the rest of the High Seas Fleet following Scheer's advance party, there was almost enough steel afloat for a second Jutland.

What followed was farcical. Scheer had two Zeppelins to help him locate the British ships, but their reports were to sabotage the outing, rather than lead him to victory. The first Zeppelin-report told Scheer that the Grand Fleet was heading away from him, suggesting that an engagement would not be feasible. Then came a report from Zeppelin *L-13,* which had sighted the Harwich Force, but wrongly reported its cruisers as battleships. This was more than Scheer had bargained for. He broke off the attack at 2.35 pm without having sighted a single British warship.

The end of the big ships

Despite the failure of the big ships to even meet, two vessels were lost by the end of the day, beginning with the light cruiser HMS *Nottingham*. As the competing forces were nearing each other in the early morning of August 19, *Nottingham* was spotted by *U-52* at 6.00 am. (Kapitänleutnant Hans Walther had been lying in wait for the Grand Fleet as part of Scheer's plan.) When *Nottingham*'s lookouts first spotted the U-boat it was taken to be a small fishing vessel. Only when two torpedoes slammed into the warship did its crew realize the danger they were in. With the loss of all electric power the ship was an easy target for Walther's third torpedo. *Nottingham* sank in 25 minutes. Most of its complement of 480 men were picked up by two of Beatty's destroyers, but 38 men died in the sea.

At the other end of the day, another light cruiser, HMS *Falmouth*, was to suffer the same fate. It was caught at 4.00 pm by two torpedoes from Kapitänleutnant Thorwald von Bothmer in *U-66*. Bert Stevens, who had just come off the dog watch, was about to take a first sip of his welcome mug of tea when he heard an explosion. By the time he reached the deck, the ship had stopped. Looking up, Stevens saw flames and smoke belching from *Falmouth*'s funnels. Captain J D Edwards passed the ship back and forth over the attack area while dropping depth charges, but without any result. (*U-66* survived until September 1917.) With no sign of any debris from a wrecked U-boat, *Falmouth* limped for port at 2 knots, accompanied by eight destroyers. Despite this massive protecting force, *U-63* managed to fire two torpedoes at the crippled vessel, neither of which succeeding in hitting the ship. *Falmouth* struggled on but sank when five miles off Flamborough Head. Just one man had been lost in the action.

The Action of 19 August, as these events came to be known, was barely worth recording, except for its influence on the rest of the war at sea. Scheer had learnt yet again that taking the High Seas Fleet into the North Sea was both hazardous and unproductive. The Zeppelins had proved more of a liability than an asset since, of their seven reports, four were incorrect. But the hardest lesson for Scheer was that both the sinkings on that day were brought about by U-boats. The age of the battleship was over, and with it, Scheer's ambitions for glory in battle also died. Never again would he venture so far out into the North Sea.

As to Jellicoe, he was reduced to being the caretaker of a fleet that had no enemy. To 'win' the battle in the North Sea all he had to do was to sit still, ready to raise steam should Scheer ever come out again. Both men were to remain big-ship men at heart. Neither would be able to shake off the influence of his years of apprenticeship. Meanwhile, the U-boats would side-line them both.

FRIEND OR FOE ACROSS THE POND?

Towards the end of the summer, Britain was rapidly losing America's support as a result of clashes between Wilson's steadfast commitment to the concept of 'the freedom of the seas' and Britain's unswerving determination to prevent goods from reaching Germany by sea. It was Britain's treatment of the American steamer *Rizal* in August that next provoked American ire.

In August the *Rizal* had called in at Colombo in Ceylon (now Sri Lanka). Its captain's request to take on coal was bluntly rejected on the grounds that the *Rizal* was not on the list of ships permitted to receive bunker coal. In London, the American *Chargé d'Affaires*, Irwin B Laughlin, had the unenviable job of passing on to the British Foreign Office the indignation of the State Department. The American note accused Britain of 'arbitrary practices' with 'no grounds recognized by law'.[311] But this was no one off event. This was America demanding the right to trade where and when it wished, with no regard to Europe's life and death struggle. Matters were exacerbated by a belief in the State Department that Britain's contraband list was part of a clandestine plan to take over American markets. For Britain, a country reeling from the endless calamitous news of merchant sinkings, the prospect of an openly hostile America was devastating. President Wilson took no steps to discourage his countrymen from attacking British policy, telling Page that 'the hearty sympathy' that Americans had for the Allies at the start of the war 'had greatly changed'. He could find 'no one who was not vexed and irritated by the arbitrary English course'. Meanwhile, in that same month, the U-boats sank 163,000 tons of shipping – an increase of 38 per cent on the July figure.

In this atmosphere, President Wilson recalled Ambassador Page to Washington. Wilson gave no explanation for the withdrawal to the British government, nor to Page himself. Page and Sir Edward Grey, though, were in no doubt as to the reason for Wilson's abrupt informal severing of relations: Britain's aggressive blockade was preventing American ships from carrying cargoes to German ports. It was an unacceptable interference in America's right to trade.

17
Only U-boats remain

Late 1916

'No conclusive answer has as yet been found to this form of warfare; perhaps no conclusive answer ever will be found.' – Jellicoe, late 1916.[312]

SINKING AT WILL

For the British, the June to August increase in monthly sinkings from 109,000 to 163,000 tons was a crushing indictment of the performance of the anti-submarine forces. This increase could not be passed off as a minor variation. Then came the September sinkings of 230,000 tons – the highest ever monthly figure up to that time. This was a catastrophic level, indicating that the U-boats could more or less sink at will. The impotence of the anti-submarine forces was starkly revealed by one seven-day search operation in September when two (or possibly three) U-boats mocked 49 destroyers and 48 torpedo boats, working with 468 armed auxiliaries, in northern waters. Not one U-boat was sunk, while the U-boats themselves sank more than 30 merchant ships.

This particular week was not exceptional. Of the seven U-boats that had been sunk in the first five months of 1916, only one had been sunk by British anti-submarine forces. (French forces sank one other boat.) Worse, the one boat that the British had sunk – *U-68* – was one of the least offensive, having been on patrol since November 1915 without sinking a single ship. Although it was clear that the Imperial Navy's ruthless sinking strategy had nothing to fear from British anti-submarine patrols, the Admiralty persisted in the patrols, for lack of any other ideas.

Against this background, the anti-submarine forces were desperately testing various means of destroying U-boats. Explosive sweeps towed across the paths of the boats had been tried, but not one U-boat had been sunk in this way. Lance bombs had proved equally ineffective. Attempts at using hydrophones to locate U-boats would contribute to only two boat sinkings by the end of the war: *UC-49* on August 8, 1918, and *UB-115* on September 29, 1918. Additionally, the many forms of towed nets were as much a hazard to the towing vessels as they were to the U-boats. Overall, sinking U-boats was near to impossible with the available technology. It would take the arrival of depth charges in quantity before a surface vessel approaching a U-boat could expect to sink it.

By the end of October, Jellicoe, still with the Grand Fleet, was studying the lack of success in destroying U-boats. In a memorandum to the Admiralty he attributed the failure to four factors: 'increased size and radius of action of enemy submarines'; 'attacking more frequently with the torpedo'; 'the very powerful gun armament now carried by submarines'; and 'enemy awareness of Allied ASW methods'. He concluded that 'new methods of attack should be devised and put into execution at the earliest possible moment'. He called for a committee to be set up and to report 'not later than the spring of 1917'.[313] It is hard to credit that Jellicoe was proposing to wait four or five months before his proposed committee reported, plus the additional months before its recommendations could be put into action. But what really stands out in his 1500-word letter is his failure to understand the central conundrum in anti-submarine work. *All* methods of sinking were useless without a means of first locating submerged boats. Given this immutable fact, there was only one answer: provide the boats with some bait to compel them to come to the destroyers. That meant convoys. There was, though, not a word about convoys in Jellicoe's memorandum.

A MISSED OPPORTUNITY

In September, the inexorable rise in merchant sinkings led to a proposal to retake the French and Belgian coast as far east as Zeebrugge. This idea had first been explored by Churchill and General French in September 1914, but they were overruled by the French generals. Now, the plan had been resurrected by the French themselves. Haig, who fully supported the proposal, advised Admiral Bacon to use flat-bottomed boats to land tanks. By mid-December Joffre, the French Commander-in-Chief, was able to hand Haig a plan for a British-French operation for immediate action. Five days later, Lloyd George, Haig and Robertson backed the French proposal. Haig noted in his diary: 'The Navy are all in earnest to cooperate.'[314] And there the trail runs cold. As the merchant sinkings rose and rose in 1917 someone must have regretted this failure to even *attempt* to put the U-boat bases in Belgium out of action. They were to account for a staggering loss of ships, cargoes and men over the next year and a half.

Only U-boats remain

Thinking the unthinkable

By the end of August, Germany's naval and military commanders were in despair. Neither on land nor at sea could they discern any sure path to victory. On August 31, Chancellor Bethmann-Hollweg was joined by Generals Hindenburg and Ludendorff plus Admiral Holtzendorff and others at the Kaiser's headquarters in Pless Castle. Their mission was the search for the elusive war-winning move.

Holtzendorff set the tone for the meeting when he declared that the Allied war was being determined by England: 'it is therefore necessary for us to prevent England, by the use of all means in our power, from continuing to carry on the war'. This meant, he said, 'the destruction of England's ocean commerce'.[315]

Holtzendorff's vision of victorious U-boats annihilating British trade was tempting, but was victory as simple as that? Secretary of State Jagow thought not. He reminded the meeting that 'Unrestricted U-boat war would in any event mean the breaking of diplomatic relations with the United States, and, if American lives are lost, would finally lead to war.' The Secretary of State of the Interior, Karl Helfferich, pointed out that Britain had food stocks for four to five months and 'only 5 per cent of the arriving ships are destroyed monthly'. He concluded, 'I am not persuaded that England can be actually downed.'[316]

Having listened to all the arguments, Bethmann-Hollweg urged caution, both because of the threat of America entering the war and because 'We can lay down no iron ring around England.'[317] And so Germany pulled back from unrestricted sinking. As the admirals and generals and politicians left the meeting, they knew that they had only postponed the day of desperation, when they would be compelled to risk all by using the last weapon in their armoury: outright unrestricted sinking.

Provoking the giant

In October, the Imperial Navy took the hazardous step of taking the war to America's doorstep. Without going so far as to sink American ships, the U-boats were to mockingly prance within sight of its shores.

The first boat to taunt the giant was *U-53*, commanded by Kapitänleutnant Hans Rose. It was also Rose's first command, in which he already had one success to his name: the British *Calypso*, which he had sunk off the coast of Norway. Thirty seamen lay drowned as he headed for the Atlantic Ocean. In less than a year he would send 223,000 tons of shipping to the depths.

Perhaps Rose's mission was just the innocent boasting of a confident service, but it seems more likely that *U-53*'s visit was a carefully considered warning to America: stay out of the war or have more *U-53*'s on *your* doorstep, sinking *your* ships. At the same time Rose would be able to impress America with the power of his boat and the proficiency of his crew as he sank British vessels under American eyes.

With two of the boat's diving tanks filled with additional fuel, and two torpedo tubes holding three tons of additional fresh water, *U-53* set out for an epic voyage of 11,000 nautical miles. As Rose approached the American coast, he found a United States submarine ready to welcome him when three miles east of Point Judith on Rhode Island. He prepared to exploit the next few hours to the full.

The crew of U-53 boldly standing on America's doorstep.

U-53 had been welcomed by Lieutenant G C Fulker in *D-2* as he ran up the American ensign and signalled 'follow me'. Rose, who was about to score a diplomatic coup, signalled in return: 'I salute our American comrades and follow in your wake.'³¹⁸ *D-2* led *U-53* to Goat Island, where Rose dropped anchor within sight of the Naval War College. Nearby, was the cruiser USS *Birmingham*, flagship of Rear Admiral Albert Gleaves, commander of the Newport-based Atlantic Destroyer Flotilla.

Onshore, Rose relished the welcome, but accepted the warning that, if he did not wish to be interned, he would have to leave by 6.00 pm. There was still time for him to entertain some high-ranking American officers and their wives to drinks on board *U-53*. The guests eagerly accepted the opportunity to be the first Americans to see the inside of a modern U-boat. Back at their base, the officers quickly noted what they had seen and heard, including the 'novel third periscope' and the radio which, the submariners claimed, could receive messages at the then unimaginable range of 2000 miles. At this point, the authorities brought the fraternizing to an abrupt halt, ordering Gleaves to tell Rose to leave American territorial waters without delay. At 5.30 pm *U-53* was on its way, the crew lining up on the deck as they waved their goodbyes and saluted the American warships. It had been a never to be repeated moment of international acceptance of Germany at war.

Back in international waters, Rose returned to combat on the following day. A steady flow of SOS calls reminded his American hosts of the power of his boat. In short order, Rose and his crew stopped and sank five or perhaps six merchant ships: three British, one Dutch and one Norwegian, totalling 21,000 tons. (Their average tonnage – 4100 tons – was higher than Rose would have found in British coastal waters.) The presence of an American on board one of the ships enabled Admiral Gleaves to legitimately despatch 16 destroyers to rescue the victims, with the result that there was no loss of life from Rose's operations.

U-53 returned home to an exultant welcome at Heligoland on October 27. The coastal artillery fired booming salutes and a brass band thundered triumphal airs while the crews of the moored boats lined up on deck to salute the returning heroes. On landing, members of *U-53*'s crew were bombarded with a mass of fan letters from the general public. A similar welcome followed at Wilhelmshaven, where Iron Crosses were awarded to the crew. Rose received the Knight's Cross with Swords.

In London, *U-53*'s expedition was widely condemned. Lord Robert Cecil, Parliamentary Under-Secretary of State for Foreign Affairs, accused Germany of blackmailing America: see what we can do if you don't let us violate international law. In the House of Lords, Lord Sydenham, an acknowledged expert on defence, both condemned

Germany's provocation and lambasted the United States for taking no action: 'What must small neutrals think of their powerful representative?' he asked.[319] Sir Edward Grey, though, was more cautious. There was nothing Britain could do to stop U-boats crossing the Atlantic, so he calmly and realistically said that the incident 'was no affair of Great Britain's.'[320]

A HESITANT KAISER

While *U-53* was unnecessarily provoking the United States, the Kaiser was ruminating on another attempt to introduce unrestricted sinking without simultaneously drawing America into the war. As he juggled these two incompatible objectives, he lurched between itching to authorize the sinkings and issuing appeasing notes to the President. In October he sent a memorandum to Ambassador Bernstorff for presentation to the American government in which he implied that unrestricted sinking was imminent. Barely had he dispatched the note, than he took fright at the thought that he might have tipped America into war. He hastily telegraphed to say that 'the memoir is not intended to convey a threat of submarine warfare', adding 'Unrestricted submarine warfare is for the present deferred.'[321] Two weeks later, the French recaptured Douaumont Fort at Verdun. It was a reminder to the German High Command that they could not rely on the land war for victory. Around the same time, Scheer allowed his withheld U-boats to be deployed against merchant shipping once more. With four times the number of boats at sea since they were last deployed, the results soon came. Against average monthly sinkings of 145,000 tons in January to September, the last three months of the year brought average monthly sinkings of 340,000 tons – an increase of 134%.

A LEAKY BARRAGE AND A WEAK COMMANDER

With increased U-boat activity, the Dover Barrage took on a new importance. But all was far from well in Admiral Bacon's domain. The U-boat commanders were showing increasing confidence in their skills as they made repeated attempts to pass through the barrage. Between May and October, Bacon's patrol logged 12 U-boats attacks on the barrage, while his patrol boats came under air attack on 28 occasions. There were also nine attacks by German destroyers and monitors. Bacon, who meticulously recorded these figures, was less willing to divulge his estimate of how many boats had successfully passed through the barrage.

On October 24, Bacon sat reading a report from the Admiralty. It warned him that a flotilla of German destroyers had been moved from the Heligoland Bight to the Belgium ports. Trusting in his ill-founded faith in the strength of his barrage he dismissed the report, saying, 'No useful military purpose would be served by their entering the Straits.'[322] He did not have to wait long to see how misguided this judgement was.

The Dover Patrol: Captain Bowring (Chief of Staff); Admiral Bacon; Flag Lieutenant Morgan; Fleet Paymaster Gask. (Bacon 1919.)

Bacon's enlightenment came in the form of a force of 23 German torpedo boats which attacked the barrage's defences on the night of October 26-27. In the dark, the night action was a confusing mêlée in which the patrol ships spent more time trying to sort friend from foe and avoiding collisions than they did in actual fighting. Even so, two British destroyers succumbed to German fire.

The destroyer *Nubian* had its bow torn off by a torpedo. Despite the dark and the rising gale, it was taken under tow. The *Nubian* and its tow battled against the heavy waves for a short time before the cable snapped, leaving the ship to drift helplessly towards shore. *Nubian* beached itself, its gaping prow tilted upwards in the air like the mouth of giant sea creature pleading to be fed. Two men on the ship died and 13 others were missing, presumed to have been killed at the time of the torpedoing. (*Nubian*'s commander, Montague Bernard, would survive a second torpedo attack when his Armed Merchant Cruiser *Cheshire* was hit in 1940.)

The action also saw the loss of the destroyer *Flirt*. Its commander, Lieutenant Richard Kellett, had gone to the aid of the drifter *Waveney II*. While one of *Flirt*'s boats was in the water, a vessel loomed out of the darkness. Kellett's challenge was met by heavy firing. *Flirt* quickly sank. The only survivors were the men and the officer in the boat going to the aid of the drifter.

These losses were to be expected, given the size of the attacking force. The other significant sinking was the empty troopship *The Queen*, which featured in Chapter 6 when it rescued passengers from *Amiral Ganteaume*. A single torpedo sank the vessel. All its crew were saved, although the ship's cook, Lewis Dilmot, later died from scalding in the kitchen as a result of the exploding torpedo.

In addition to these sinkings, six drifters were also lost. Nevertheless, the Imperial Navy had failed to inflict any substantial damage on the barrage or its defences. For Bacon, though, the consequences were more serious. The Admiralty criticized his sending his destroyers into action 'without any previous formation or orders' – this had resulted in each acting as a lone vessel.[323] Bacon contested this judgement and, in doing so, perhaps sealed his fate. His endless self-justifying reports on the state of his command reflected complacency rather than perfection.

Try anything ... except convoys

Unable to stem the merchant sinkings, the War Council decided at the end of October to tighten the censorship on reporting them. The new guidelines were designed to obscure the scale of the sinkings, while still technically reporting them. Newspapers were only to quote Press Bureau information on the specific day of issue. Sinkings were not to be totalled over a period of time – not even over two days. Further, the papers were 'Not to disclose *when, where,* or *how* the vessels were sunk.'[324]

The government also indulged in obfuscation of the figures for the tonnage sunk. By slight-of-hand, Dr Thomas Macnamara, Parliamentary and Financial Secretary to the Admiralty, was able to tell the Commons in November that 'the net loss up to the end of the 30th September, 1916, is slightly over 2½ per cent'.[325] Admiral Fisher leapt to his pen when he read this outrageously disingenuous figure. Writing to the MP George Lambert, he said 'Macnamara told a big lie in spirit ... What has that [figure] to do with the present menace?' And how right Fisher was. Macnamara's figure related to the war to date. No juggling of statistics could hide the horrifying truth: the U-boats were sinking merchant shipping at a rate that far outstripped new construction. Fisher rammed this point home when he shared a taxi four days later with Lord Derby: '[I] gave him a fright, and he has gone off to Lloyd George!', he told Lambert.[326] That the Admiralty should have stooped to such a gross attempt to deceive Parliament shows how rattled they were about their own performance.

It was the October sinkings of 353,000 tons that triggered the next attempt to push the Admiralty into taking effective action. At a special meeting of the War Council (with Jellicoe in attendance) the Tory Party Leader Bonar Law, together with Lloyd George, jointly pressed the case for introducing convoys. They were virulently opposed by Jellicoe, who said that convoys 'offered too big a target'. When Lloyd George pressed his case further, Jellicoe switched his argument to claiming that the merchant ships would not be able to keep station in a convoy. The Council sided with Jellicoe, recording: 'The system of convoys had only been found successful where it was possible to allot a separate escort to each vessel.' And, for good measure, they added: 'merchant vessels straggled too much'.[327] With those words, and without even testing the use of convoys, the War Council lost the chance to stem the Armageddon that was rapidly approaching. Within weeks, Britain's food supplies would be plunging to the depths of the oceans at a devastating rate, while the U-boats mocked the impotent anti-submarine vessels. The British Admiralty was about to enter one of the most shameful periods of its existence.

Another easy target

In November, another hospital ship was the victim of a mine. HMHS *Britannic* was one of the *Titanic*'s sister ships. It had been requisitioned for work at the Dardanelles in 1915 and had been fitted out as a hospital ship by Harland and Wolff. The public rooms had become wards with 3309 bunks, which were placed as close to the lifeboats as possible. Below, the first class dining room had been replaced by a set of operating theatres. Finally, the funnels had received the yellow stripes of a hospital ship sailing under the 1907 *Hague Convention*.

In November, the *Britannic* was in the Eastern Mediterranean with 1065 people on board, sailing for home. Despite the precautions of the ship's livery and its obvious non-military demeanour, those on board could never forget that they were sailing through a war zone. Vera Brittain, who went out to the Dardanelles as a Voluntary Aid Detachment nurse in the *Britannic* in September, recorded her experience at sea in her classic 1933 *Testament of Youth*. She recalled 'the feelings of terror the dark hours used to bring us' and described how she used to look down over the ship's side, thinking 'Perhaps now – or now – or now!' At night, Brittain would lie awake listening to 'the thresh of the screws and the whistle of the wind above the mastheads and the rushing of the water against the side'.[328] Every crash or bang made her shudder at the thought that it might be a torpedo or a mine.

It was just before 8.00 am on November 21 when the *Britannic* had entered the Kea Channel between the island of Kea and mainland Greece. The sun was shining, the sea was calm, with the ship making a steady 20 knots. Breakfast was being served to the medical staff, when there was a loud roar and the ship shuddered. The breakfast crockery rattled. Cups and plates fell to floor. Captain Charles Bartlett ordered 'Stop engines.' The watertight doors slammed shut and the ship's radio broadcast a distress signal.

The damage from the explosion was massive and the ship was flooding rapidly. Within ten minutes it had taken on as much water as the *Titanic* had done in one hour.

With Kea Island close by, Bartlett thought he might be able to beach his ship. In the chaos of the disaster, boats were already being lowered as the ship began to move forward again. At the same time, the ship's list caused boats to crash into her side. Splinters of glass fell on the people in the boats. As the boats touched the water and attempted to move away from the ship, its 23-foot diameter screws drew the fragile craft towards their deadly lacerating blades.

By the time the fourth, dummy, smokestack had fallen into the water, only one man was left on board. Captain Charles Bartlett stepped into the ocean just before his ship rolled over and thrust its stern into the air. It plunged to the depths, giving a last cry from its exploding boilers. All that was left was the sea, a mass of lifeboats, and hundreds of terrified men and women struggling in the water.

Amongst the hands on the *Britannic* were some boy scouts from Southampton and Liverpool, who had volunteered to work on the ship.

George – just 15 years old – was one of those whose life was threatened by the screws. As the water attempted to suck him under, he held fast onto a davit line until the thrashing stopped. His only injuries were some rope burns.

Another scout – Pope – stayed on the ship almost to the end, running back and forth to collect valuables and mementos for the passengers in the boats. Other scouts operated the lifts during the evacuation, and sounded the steam whistle.

By good fortune, there were no patients on board when the mine struck, so the casualty numbers were low. Out of just over 1000 seamen and medical staff on board, there were only 30 dead and 38 wounded. Had the ship been carrying a full complement of stretcher cases, the deaths would have run into thousands. The sinking was, though, a foretaste of the desperation of the U-boat service as its ever-increasing sinkings failed to deliver the promised 'victory in six months'.

The German government justified the sinking of yet another hospital ship by arguing that it could 'no longer suffer that the British Government should forward troops and munitions to the main theatre of war under cover of the Red Cross.'[329]

Self-defence

In December, the War Council declared that the arming of merchant ships was to be made a high priority. (This decision reflected the British Admiralty's continuing hostility to convoys.) Guns for these ships, the Admiralty said, were 'indispensable [and] should be a first charge on our artillery resources'.[330] For the first time in the war, manufacturing guns for merchant ships was to take priority over supplying guns to the Western Front. Put in less concealing language, the Admiralty were abandoning the merchant ships: they were to take charge of their own defence. Eight days later, the War Council considered a proposal to transfer around 800 4-inch guns and around 600 howitzers to the navy.

There seemed to be a good case for arming merchant ships in the absence of introducing convoys. In the year January 1916 to January 1917 armed ships proved much less vulnerable to a successful attack. When attacked, unarmed ships escaped in only 22 per cent of attacks, whereas armed ships escaped in 76 per cent of attacks. However, the American historian Jan S Breemer took a closer look at the figures over time, rather than as a block. He found that 33 per cent of ships sunk in December 1916 were armed and a staggering 56 per cent of those sunk in

January 1917 were armed. It would seem that the U-boat commanders became accustomed to the risk of attacking armed merchant ships.

A MISTAKEN APPOINTMENT

In October, the U-boats sank 354,000 tons of shipping – an increase of 53 per cent on the September figure. Britannia, which had once ruled the waves, was impotent in the face of the ever-increasing sinkings. In Paris, the British Ambassador Lord Bertie listened as ambassador after ambassador told him how their countries had lost faith 'in British Naval supremacy ... They think something should be done.'[331]

Meanwhile, as the Allied anti-submarine forces grew, so, contrarily, the U-boats were getting harder to catch. The boats used torpedoes more frequently than at the start of the war and carried heavier deck guns to hold anti-submarine craft at a distance. They were also getting smarter at rapid sinking. In the Admiralty, passive acceptance of these sinkings was the order of the day. An Admiralty memorandum written around this time said: 'Of all the problems which the Admiralty have to consider, no doubt the most formidable and the most embarrassing is that raised by the submarine attack upon merchant vessels.' Then comes the clinching sentence, which Lloyd George italicized when quoting it in his memoirs: *'No conclusive answer has as yet been found to this form of warfare; perhaps no conclusive answer ever will be found.'*[332] The U-boats had nothing to fear from the Admiralty's fatalism. And then the Admiralty made a move – a wrong move.

Three men had been running the navy during this crisis: Arthur Balfour as First Lord, Admiral Sir Henry Jackson as First Sea Lord, and Jellicoe in command of the High Seas Fleet. All were utterly unqualified for their posts. Balfour was more of an intellectual than a man of action; Jackson was a man who never distinguished himself in any way; and Jellicoe both lacked the belligerent streak needed for war and was worn out. The inadequate duo of Balfour and Jackson were about to bow out. Balfour's last act was to appoint Jellicoe as First Sea Lord on November 30. In doing this, Balfour demonstrated that he had no idea of the qualities needed in a wartime First Sea Lord. But Jellicoe got the job, and the country was to pay the price.

In view of Jellicoe's October memorandum in which he had revealed that he had no new ideas for anti-submarine warfare (beyond appointing a committee that would report 'in six months' time') his appointment appears to be incomprehensible. What did Balfour expect of such a man?

In his post-war writings, Jellicoe admitted that 'I knew then that no fresh measures involving the production of fresh material could become effective for a period of at least six to twelve months.' This did not seem to bother him since he was ready to be 'the object of the same attacks as those to which my predecessor ... had been exposed'.[333] In other words, Jellicoe took up the post with a pessimistic view of what could be done and a self-pitying view of his own situation.

Jellicoe's move to the Admiralty found few champions. Keyes objected to the admiral's promotion because he thought the Grand Fleet could not manage without him: 'a terrible loss to the Fleet'.[334] Baron Bertie in Paris, was more astute in his prediction that Jellicoe would not 'discover a fresh remedy'.[335] Haig, too, had his doubts about the admiral, writing in his diary on December 15: 'I liked very much what I saw of Jellicoe though I should not look on him as a man of great power or decision of character.'[336]

Jellicoe was now the most powerful naval commander in the world. He had the means and authority to act, but not the flexibility of brain to match. For the next six months young officers *outside the Admiralty* would lead the fight to act against the U-boats. Jellicoe, meanwhile, was to prefer a rearguard action in favour of those very methods that he had implicitly rejected in his memorandum to Balfour.

A DIRE PROSPECT

Britain's failure to sink or contain the U-boats increased the German government's faith in sinking Britain into surrender. One-hundred-and-eight U-boats had gone into commission in 1916 and only 22 boats had been lost from all causes. Only half of those losses were the result of Allied anti-submarine actions. In brief, the Royal Navy's anti-submarine forces were near to useless. And the scale of those forces was staggering. Two-thirds of all British destroyers, submarines and other ancillary craft were engaged in anti-submarine work – that is around 3000 vessels. With 168 U-boats in commission at December 1916, each U-boat had 18 vessels searching for it. Or, to put it another way, with 11 boats lost to anti-submarine action in 1916, it had taken 273 search craft working for one year to sink one U-boat. And still the Admiralty insisted on defending this monumental failure.

Britain's position was threatened on all fronts. That guarantee of victory – the Somme offensive – had come to an end with one million killed or wounded from the three million men in the contending armies.

At home, the War Council members were in a panic as they desperately searched for 40 merchant ships to bring in Australian wheat supplies. The Wheat Commission warned: 'the shipments during the last fortnight to arrive this year have been nearly 200,000 quarters [50,000 tons] a week less than requirements'.[337] Meanwhile the Deputy Secretary to the Cabinet, Thomas Jones, fretted about the lack of civilian support for the work of the anti-submarine forces. He saw how the well-off lived comfortably while 'the weakest members of the community are not far from starvation'. What was needed was rationing 'with the object of equality of treatment for all classes in the matter of necessaries'. He also wanted to see a ban on 'the importation of non-essential commodities' and 'a ban on manufacture of certain items'.[338]

With not one piece of good news on the war front, urgent action was needed. The man who needed to act was Prime Minister Asquith. He, though, was not made for war. He hated it, squeamishly recoiling from the hard decisions that had to be taken. Cornered, weary, near to despairing, he had allowed disastrous decisions to be made by others. (Also, his eldest son, Raymond, had been killed at the Somme on September 15. Asquith never fully recovered from this loss.)

One man, though, knew what needed to be done. All that he needed was the power to act. His name was David Lloyd George.

18
Last throw of the dice

December 1916 to January 1917

'For the first and only time in the war I suffered sleepless nights.'– Maurice Hankey.[339]

A NEW WARRIOR

On December 1, 1916, the Secretary of State for War, Lloyd George, sat down to write a letter that would change the course of Britain's war. He had demonstrated his genius for radical action with his revolutionary budget of 1909. As Minister of Munitions, he had turned Britain's output from a trickle to a flood. But, all the while, he had sat in a Cabinet under a Prime Minister totally unsuited for war. Asquith was an exceptional peacetime prime minister. But his patient, intelligent, high-minded management of his Cabinet had proved a disaster in war.

Lloyd George's letter was short and simple. It was a masterpiece of cunning, with the aim of forcing Asquith to relinquish power. He simply proposed the setting up of a new War Council. But what a council! It was to consist of the First Lord of the Admiralty, the Secretary of State for War, and a minister without portfolio. One of the three would chair the meetings. Lloyd George's exclusion of Asquith was a calculated insult, designed to provoke the events that followed.

When Asquith rejected the proposal, Lloyd George resigned as War Minister. On December 5, Asquith resigned the premiership and the King sent for the Tory Party leader, Bonar Law, to ask him to form a government. When Law found that Asquith would not serve under him, he declined the offer and the King called on Lloyd George. By December 7, the Liberal Lloyd George was the Prime Minister of a three-party coalition with a Cabinet of 15 Tories, 12 Liberals and 2 Labour members. There were no startling new appointments (other than Lloyd George himself). His War Cabinet was to consist of Lord Curzon, Bonar Law, Arthur Henderson (a Labour MP) and Lord Milner. The change was, wrote the historian A J P Taylor, from 'a damp squib' to 'dynamite'.[340]

Within days of taking office, Lloyd George had changed the atmosphere in Downing Street from that of a gentleman's club, to that of a frontline headquarters under siege and with more than a whiff of cordite in the air.

Change of command: the squeamish Asquith gives way to the warrior Lloyd George.[341]

A WAVE OF HOPELESSNESS

The mood in early 1917, writes the historian Correlli Barnett, was 'a wave of hopelessness' which 'swept over the nations'. Joffre and Haig had failed on the Somme after 614,000 futile casualties, and Falkenhayn had nothing to show for his abortive attack on Verdun. Barnett notes how these failures had resulted in 'currents of pacifism and even tentative peace moves'.[342] He might have added the corollary that it was now more urgent than ever to decide the war at sea.

Jellicoe's in-tray was heaving with problems – some were new – most were intractable difficulties which had been resolved by the expedient of the pending tray. Although the Imperial Navy was failing to sink enough merchant shipping to bring a swift end to the war, the U-boats had wrought a terrifying devastation. The leap from 163,000 tons sunk in August to 355,000 in December was a staggering achievement. While advances of a single meaningless mile on the Western Front were hailed as evidence of military genius, even if the gain was then lost within weeks, the U-boats were breaking all records and shattering the Admiralty's strategy.

Alongside the unchecked U-boats, British shipbuilding was failing to keep up with sinkings. In 1915 the net loss of tonnage was 281,000. By 1916 tonnage sunk exceeded new construction by 954,000 tons. Shipping came under discussion at the new War Cabinet's meeting on December 22. It had often been discussed by the old War Council, but it had never been treated as a priority. Jellicoe told the members that current losses were 300,000 tons per month; replacements were projected to be 400,000 tons over six months. The new Shipping Controller claimed that output would be one million tons for the first six months of 1917 'provided the necessary labour and material were available'.[343] Yet, no matter how they manipulated these figures, there was only one interpretation: Britain's lifeline was about to be severed by simply having too few vessels to bring in the food and materials needed to wage war.

For the officers on the bridges of the patrol ships, future launches of fresh shipping were about as realistic as planning what to do in their retirements. Their minds were elsewhere. Around the coast they were meeting in clusters to discuss the merits of convoys. Every officer who had any convoy experience was convinced that they were the only means of taming the U-boats. Meanwhile, the Admiralty was ready to try anything – as long as it wasn't convoys. This included introducing the perilous 'approach routes' – cone shaped approaches for merchant shipping entering the major ports. It was thought that, with the ships less spread out, the U-boats would find them harder to locate. It was a calamitous mistake. The U-boats soon located the approach routes, where they found ill-defended ships, nicely herded for easy pickings.

Holy Terror

While there was no hint of urgency in the British Admiralty, in Germany there was a sense of despondency. Braced by the fear that the German armies could not hold out for more than six months, pessimistic minds were turning to perilous measures.

In December, Grand Admiral Henning von Holtzendorff, Chief of the Naval Staff, thought the unthinkable and composed a memorandum that was to determine the whole course of the rest of the war at sea: 'A decision must be reached in the war before the autumn of 1917,' he wrote. If not, the war would end through 'the exhaustion of all parties'. This, he said, would be disastrous for Germany. And, since victory could not be won on land, it had to be won at sea. All that was needed was five months of unrestricted U-boat warfare to drive England to sue for peace.

Holtzendorff's reasoning was partly based on how he thought the neutral countries would react. He assured his colleagues that, if unrestricted sinking were introduced: 'at least two-fifths of neutral sea traffic will at once be terrorized into ceasing their journeys to England'. For an even better effect, there should be no warning: 'the declaration and commencement of the unrestricted U-boat war should be simultaneous'. It was, said Holtzendorff, to be 'holy terror'.[344]

By December 23, Hindenburg was ready to give his assent to unrestricted sinking. Up to that point, he had been convinced that the army would win the war. Now he talked of 'our unfavourable military position' and his concern for 'morale in the army'. He concluded: 'The diplomatic and military preparations for the unrestricted submarine campaign have to commence immediately.'[345] Ludendorff was of the same mind, telling Holtzendorff: 'Unrestricted sinking' was 'the only means of bringing the war to a successful conclusion within a reasonable time ... the U-boat war should now be launched with the greatest vigour.'[346] Bethmann saw the move more clearly, saying that unrestricted sinking was 'a game of *va banque* whose stakes will be our existence as a Great Power and our entire national future.'[347] (*Va banque* is a high-risk card game in which players have to stake all. In 1940 Hitler would say of himself that '[*Va banque*] is the only call I ever make.'[348])

On January 8, 1917, the army, the navy and the politicians gathered again at Pless Castle to take the fateful decision. The case for unrestricted sinking was put by the Admiralty staff. They argued that Britain had access to 10.75 m tons of shipping for non-war cargo (6.75 m tons British; 1 m from its allies and the balance from neutral countries). If Germany could sink 600,000 tons per month, the neutral vessels would take fright and refuse to sail. Within five months British tonnage would be reduced by 39 per cent. Also, the poor American wheat harvest in 1916 favoured the German cause since Allied vessels would have to make longer voyages to South America, India and Australia to take on grain. These long voyages would not only tie up shipping but also use more fuel. In addition, planned increases in U-boat activity in local waters would reduce British imports of fats from the low countries, and of timber from Scandinavia.

Ludendorff spoke strongly in favour of unrestricted sinking, but Karl Helfferich, Secretary for the Treasury, said the decision would be 'catastrophic',[349] and the Secretary of State, Von Jagow, forecast that 'Germany will be treated like a mad dog against which everybody combines'.[350] Chancellor Bethmann-Hollweg called for unrestricted sinking, but only as 'the last card'.[351] He warned that it would push America into the war: 'her help will consist in the delivery of food to England, financial assistance, the supply of aeroplanes and a force of volunteers'.[352] He also warned: 'Certain success of the U-boat war, in my opinion, could be just as little proved as certain failure. If success was denied then the worst of all ends stood before us.'[353] Despite all these reservations, the decision for unrestricted sinking was agreed because no one could think of anything better.

One man was thoroughly pleased with this outcome: Scheer. As commander of an impotent fleet, he was delighted to find the army appealing to the navy to save it from defeat. He told his submariners that they should be proud to be trusted with the fate of the nation and 'the responsibility for exerting the decisive pressure on our main enemy'.[354]

It was left to Bethmann-Hollweg to announce the decision to the Reichstag, which he did on January 31. Any guilt in the policy, he said, 'falls alone on our opponents' because 'they decline peace negotiations with us'. From posing as a proponent of ruthless killing of civilians on the high seas, Bethmann-Hollweg then adopted the cloak of sweet peacemaker. All Germany asked, said Bethmann-Hollweg, was 'the freedom of the seas' and 'equal rights for all nations, and the open door to trade'.[355] He then reverted to warmongering. Germany had to fight on. The Allied Powers' peace terms, he argued, were totally unacceptable since they would mean the loss of Alsace-Lorraine (seized from the French in 1871) and the Ostmark provinces in the east. The speech was heard in silence. In Washington, President Wilson turned to his Private Secretary, Joseph Tumulty, and remarked: 'This means war. The break that we have tried so hard to prevent is inevitable.'[356]

Fregattenkapitän Hermann Bauer, Commander of the Submarines, gathered his U-boat commanders together on the *Hamburg* on February 1 to announce the decision for unrestricted sinking. He was met by a 'deathly silence' according to Hans Rose.[357] Even so, champagne was served, and the policy was christened with three cheers.

At least the announcement pleased the annexationists in the Reichstag such as Gustav Stresemann. For him, victory had to include the annexation of the ports in Belgium and the Baltic Sea. He hailed the new policy, saying: 'The Emperor's command for full battle for the U-boats has lifted a nightmare from the German people.'[358]

TESTING HUMAN ENDURANCE

That Christmas, one of the best-selling toys for boys in Germany was a U-boat with a dreadnought. The boat fired a torpedo, aimed at a dreadnought and, if the torpedo hit a red dot on the ship, the ship fell apart. (It could be reassembled to ensure endless sinkings of its dreadnought.) Girls were offered no more than peacetime favourites such as dolls. Toys, though, could do little to brighten the dismal everyday lives of the German people.

The winter of 1916-1917 came to be known as the Turnip Winter. The harsh weather and the lack of fuel for farm vehicles brought a serious shortage of potatoes. By December 1916 they were becoming a luxury. The ration of seven pounds per person per week dropped to five pounds plus two pounds of turnips. Within weeks that ration became three pounds of potatoes and four pounds of turnips and, by February, it was down to five pounds of turnips and two pounds of potatoes. Even the rationed potatoes were not guaranteed, as stocks disappeared in many towns. Other foods were in desperately short supply. Milk could rarely be found, and the fat ration of two ounces per person per week was pitiable. Vegetables and fruit were unobtainable.

That winter was particularly cold with temperatures in Berlin down to -22°C. Schools were closed because there was no coal to heat them. In the streets, Princess Blücher saw 'shivering throngs of hungry care-worn people'. She added, 'We are all gaunt and bony now, and have dark shadows around our eyes. Our thoughts are chiefly taken up with wondering what our next meal will be, and dreaming of the good things that once existed.'[359] By February 1917 there would be 2207 soup kitchens in German towns and cities.

The cold, the hunger and the despair at the never-ending war in which each day was more unbearable than the last, took their toll on the people's health. They lived in a state of permanent fatigue. At work, they found it hard to concentrate and were plagued by the minor illnesses of run-down constitutions.

By January 1917, the people longed for an end to their ordeal. Few now expected the army to bring them victory. Only the U-boats could save them by reducing the British population to the same level of a half-living, half-dead existence. They all knew that unrestricted sinking would be the last throw of the dice.

A bread queue in Germany in the winter of 1916-1917.

WILSON RE-ELECTED

For the Allied nations in the dark days of late 1916, when the U-boat war looked to be all but lost and relations with America were in the balance, two events on successive days presaged America's move to war.

First, President Wilson had been re-elected for another four-year term, which gave him the freedom to ignore his most acerbic anti-war critics and lean towards the Allies.

And second, on November 8, *U-49* had sunk the American cargo ship SS *Columbian*. American commentators remarked that Wilson now had 'the heaviest burden since Lincoln'. *The Times* noted that this sinking came on top of the sinking of the 5200-ton *Marina* on October 28 and the 7000-ton *Arabia* on November 6, both of which involved American casualties. Additionally, there were *U-53*'s audacious sinkings of non-American ships within sight of the American coast. The U-boat war was daily becoming harder for America to ignore. *The Times* revealed that Wilson intended 'to adopt a more strenuous policy' on the U-boats. It dared not openly express the hope that America would enter the war, limiting its comments to 'We should welcome from our hearts the vindication at American hands of the doctrines reprobating submarine atrocities.'[360] But the unwritten text was that America would soon be at war.

19
Waking the giant

February to 6 April 1917

'Those Prussians will realize that, when they made war on this country they woke up a giant which will surely defeat them.' – President Wilson.[361]

SINK! SINK! SINK!

While the British Admiralty pursued its 'anything but convoys' policy, the Imperial Navy was preparing for the battle of its life. Hermann Bauer was determined to get the maximum out of his fleet of U-boats in the minimum possible time. Commanders were to be ruthless and were not to fire warning shots; they were 'to fire their entire outfit of ammunition as often as possible' and were never to leave a ship afloat.[362] Speedy turnround was essential, commanders were told, with patrols being limited to 14 days. To this end, the boats were to pass through the short route of the Dover Barrage. The message was clear: sink anything by any means. Commanders now had no incentive to take the risks associated with surfacing to ascertain a vessel's provenance. Sinkings without warning would rise from 29 per cent in 1916 to 64 per cent in the first four months of 1917. The rate would be even higher later on.

DEATH OF A Q-SHIP

It was at this despondent time, when the U-boats seemed unstoppable, that Commander Gordon Campbell in the Q-ship *Farnborough* summoned extraordinary lengths of courage in order to sink a U-boat. In February 1917 Germany's unrestricted sinking had led to frequent sinkings off the south coast of Ireland, including the 2000-ton *Eudora* on February 14, carrying maize from Brazil, and the 3800-ton *Iolo* on February 17, taking coal to Italy. Campbell and the *Farnborough* were in the area, so it seemed inevitable that he would soon find a U-boat in this contested sea.

What made Campbell's encounter with *U-83* special was his standing orders for his ship. These contained the directive: 'Should the Officer of the Watch see a torpedo coming, he is to increase or decrease speed as necessary to ensure it hitting.'[363] The implication was clear: if the only way that *Farnborough* could sink a U-boat was to result in its own sinking, so be it. It was an extraordinary commitment to self-sacrifice, but one to which all his men had signed up.

On February 17, at around 9.45 am, one of Campbell's lookouts spotted a torpedo racing towards *Farnborough*. No attempt was made to turn away. Orders were orders. Campbell and his men let the weapon strike just abreast of the N$^{o.}$ 3 hold. A sub-lieutenant engineer was injured and huge hole was ripped in the side of the ship.

Following the well-honed practice of the Q-ship 'panic' procedure, two lifeboats and a dinghy were lowered and one lifeboat was left partially lowered. With most of his men sculling around in the boats, the ship had the air of having been abandoned. But, lurking behind the camouflaged shields, the gunners were ready to welcome the approach of their attacker. Campbell was lying hidden on the bridge, eyeing the scene, waiting for the perfect moment to open fire.

Hoppe was an experienced submariner, having already sunk 15 ships. We can surmise that he did not intend to be caught out by an ambush. Keeping *U-83* under the water, Hoppe circled round, edging closer and closer until Campbell could see the whole submerged U-boat. In the *Farnborough,* water was rising in the engine room, but Campbell ordered his men to stay below. Then, at 100 yards, Hoppe felt sure that *Farnborough* was his. Campbell and his men froze as the boat began to surface. The hatch opened and the triumphal Hoppe appeared. With Campbell's yell of 'Fire!' the flaps come down and the guns came out. Forty-five of *Farnborough*'s shells tore into *U-83*. The wrecked boat sank, leaving no survivors.

With the U-boat out of the way Campbell was left with a ship sinking beneath him. Its fate seemed inevitable. He signalled to Vice Admiral Queenstown: '*Q5* slowly sinking respectfully wishes you goodbye'.[364] But *Farnborough* survived and was towed to land to be beached. The American Admiral Sims, who met Campbell later in the year, described him as 'a Britisher of quite the accepted type … [He] was about as cool and determined a man as was to be found in the British navy'.[365] In June, Campbell used the same deception techniques to sink *UC-29* when in command of HMS *Pargust*.

THE GIANT AWAKES

While Allied anti-submarine forces struggled to contain the U-boat terror, America was edging towards war. On February 1, Colonel House was in the wood-panelled dining room of the New York Plaza Hotel, then only ten years old, and with rooms costing just $2.20 a night. His fellow diners included the rail magnate Frank Trumbull and Sir William Wiseman, Head of the British Intelligence Mission in the United States. (Wiseman was newly arrived to set up Britain's first secret service office in America.) House's digestion was challenged throughout the meal as he was repeatedly called from the table to deal with telephone calls, telegrams and even visitors. 'The excitement became intense,' he recalled, as newspaper after newspaper pressed him for news of the coming war.

Next day, Colonel House took breakfast alone in the White House before joining President Wilson and his wife to await the arrival of Secretary of State Lansing. Wilson fussed around with piles of books while he paced up and down the room. His wife asked whether he might play some golf, but House advised against such a trivial pastime at this historic moment. One of the party suggested a game of pool and they were into their second game when Lansing arrived to confirm that Germany had begun unrestricted sinking. There was little to discuss. The years of diplomatic gymnastics between America and Germany were over. The three men spent the next few hours honing the documents that would break relations between the United States and Germany. All that was left was to send von Bernstorff back to Germany (he left on February 15). It wasn't yet war, but it wasn't peace, either.

On February 3 Wilson addressed Congress, reminding its members of the previous commitments that Germany had made. Despite Germany's repeated failures to leave Americans and American ships free to sail the seas, the President still said: 'I refuse to believe that it is the intention of the German authorities to do in fact what they have warned us they will feel at liberty to do.' But if they did proceed, he told Congress, 'I shall take the liberty of coming again before the Congress, to ask that authority be given me to use any means that may be necessary for the protection of our seamen and our people in the prosecution of their peaceful and legitimate errands on the high seas. I can do nothing less.'[366]

February 3 was a long day in the American Embassy in London. Hour after hour Walter Page, his wife and his secretaries sat in the

Ambassador's room waiting for the much-anticipated news. The hours dragged until at 9.00 pm the front doorbell rang. Wilson's personal secretary, Eugene Shoecraft, 'excitedly left the room' and found Admiral William Hall hurrying up the stairs. On seeing Shoecraft, Hall simply said, 'Thank God!' Britain's long wait was over. Clutching a coded message that had been thrust into his hand, Shoecraft returned to the ambassador's room. The message from Captain Guy Gaunt in Washington was hardly diplomatic in its language but no one in the room failed to understand it: 'Bernstorff has just been given his passports. I shall probably get drunk to-night!'[367] With diplomatic relations severed, years of Anglo-American sparing came to an end. Bickerings over trade were to give way to building a war-winning partnership.

The consequence of unrestricted sinking. Roosevelt (on the left) could not be more delighted. Wilson's long face on the right shows a more realistic understanding of the horrors of war.

All that America could now do was to wait to see how long it would be before its shipping was in the firing line. An early warning came in Germany's reaction to the safe arrival of the American SS *Orleans* at Bordeaux from New York on February 27. A huge crowd welcomed the ship, waving handkerchiefs and cheering as Captain Allen Tucker and his crew were paraded through the streets. Mayor Gruetz praised the men for 'disregarding the insolent provocations of a nation of prey'. Arthur Zimmermann, the Germany Secretary of State for Foreign Affairs, retaliated: 'We make absolutely no distinction in sinking neutral ships within the war zone. Our determination is unshakable since this is the only way to finish the war this summer.'[368] Tucker was to find confirmation of this when his *Orleans* was sunk by Oberleutnant zur See Reinhold Saltzwedel in *UC-71* in July. As the ship was sinking, *UC-71* surfaced amongst the boats that were trying to rescue survivors still in the water. An officer asked for Saltzwedel's help, to which he replied, 'Can't help you. This is war. They've no business to be over here.'[369]

A French welcome for the American Captain Tucker.

While Germany was engaged in the niceties of diplomatic exchanges with America, dark forces were at work. A mysterious telegram intercept reached Room 40 in mid-January. With some difficulty, enough of the telegram was deciphered to reveal its monstrous content: a request from the German government to the Mexican government, asking Mexico to enter into an alliance 'to reconquer the lost territory in New Mexico, Texas, and Arizona'. In this way, the German telegram claimed, 'we shall make war together and together make peace'.[370] It took a good deal of ingenuity for Admiral Hall to find a way of letting the American government know the contents of the message without Germany realizing that Room 40 had broken its diplomatic cypher. (That story is well-told in books such as James' *The Eyes of the Navy*.) The so-called Zimmermann telegram brought an abrupt end to America's hopes of staying out of the war.

PROVOCATIONS

It was Wilson who took the next step when, on February 26, he asked Congress to give him 'the means and the authority to safeguard' the country by arming merchant ships. But Wilson was ahead of his nation. Anti-war senators organized a filibuster and the Congressional session ran out of time. Undeterred, Wilson was determined to act: he armed the merchant ships by executive order, using powers originating from an archaic anti-piracy law.

Germany obligingly sunk the 18,000-ton British steamship *Laconia* at this time, which helped to endorse Wilson's case. The liner was carrying 75 passengers along with a crew of 217 when Kapitänleutnant Gerhard Berger in *U-50* sank it with two torpedoes 160 miles off Fastnet and nearing the Irish coast. With headlines such as 'Chicagoans lost on the *Laconia*',[371] 'Ghastly death of Americans'[372] and 'Gave last rites to dying in his boat' it was clear to the Americans that the war was creeping ever nearer to them. *The New York Times* knew how to utilize the reports to rouse American ire: 'Mrs Hoy died in the arms of her daughter. Her body slipped off into the sea out of her daughter's weakened arms. The heartbroken daughter succumbed a few minutes afterward, and her body fell over the side of the boat.' The daughter had been 'In icy water up to her knees for two hours' while supporting her mother.[373] President Wilson later described the sinking as the 'overt act' for which he had been waiting.[374]

America did not have to wait long before another German provocation brought the war ever closer. The 1800-ton steamship *Algonquin* had left New York on February 20, carrying no weapons, but with a cargo valued at $1.7 m. On March 12 the ship was 65 miles off Bishop Rock lighthouse, nearing London at the end of its passage. At that point, *U-62* surfaced and opened fire. The four rounds all missed the *Algonquin*, but they were enough to send many of its terrified crew to the boats. Their disembarking was quickly followed by Kapitänleutnant Ernst Hashagen's men boarding the steamer. Armed with bombs, they despatched the ship to the bottom. Originally a British ship, the *Algonquin* had been transferred to American ownership in December 1916 and ten of her 27 crew were Americans. On arrival in London, Captain Nordberg said, 'There was no warning. I stopped the engines and then went full speed astern, indicating this by three blasts on the whistle. The submarine kept on firing, the fourth shot throwing a column of water up, which drenched me and the man at the wheel. It was a close call.'[375] *The New York Times* called the sinking 'very serious', but reluctantly admitted that there was nothing America could do to stop such sinkings 'unless it wishes to take the last step and declare war'.[376]

Meanwhile, on the day of the sinking, the United States Government announced the arming of all merchant vessels in the War Zone. This did nothing to deter the U-boats. The next American ship to go was the American 4100-ton SS *Vigilancia* on March 16. It was sunk by Otto Wünsche in *U-70* when in passage from New York to Le Havre with a cargo of sugar and other foodstuffs. *Vigilancia*'s voyage was nearly complete but, like so many vessels, it had been caught near Bishop Rock in the Isles of Scilly. (Wünsche was one of the most successful U-boat commanders of the war with 58 vessels sunk so far.) The 5200-ton *City of Memphis* was sunk by *UC-66* on the following day. It was Herbert Pustkuchen's eighty-second sinking. The ship's crew of 57 men were fortunate in being quickly picked out of their five boats by another steamer.

The German newspaper *Deutsche Tageszeitung*, much read by industrialists, bankers and ministerial officials, was thrilled at the news of the steady flow of sinkings. It opined that Americans had to learn that 'there is only one policy for the United States, as for the small European maritime powers, namely, to retain their ships in their own ports as long as the war lasts'.[377] Another German press comment said that the sinkings 'were certain to produce special satisfaction throughout the empire'.[378] Clearly, these commentators had no inkling of what might come next unless Germany ceased its attacks on American ships.

Three days after this spate of American sinkings, President Wilson summoned his Cabinet to ask them for their advice on how to respond to the German attacks. His Cabinet was in the mood for war. Secretary of State Lansing opened the debate by saying that 'in my opinion an actual state of war existed today between this country and Germany'.[379] Then Secretary of Labor William B Wilson, made the critical move as he called for America 'to employ all our resources to put an end to Prussian rule over Germany which menaces human liberty and peace all over the world'.[380] Wilson's policy of armed neutrality had failed. War was the only option left on the table, although no decision was taken that day.

In Britain, Ambassador Page took advantage of the 'war in the air' mood in America to maximize the role that America could play once it entered the war. In the short term, that meant aid to Britain. His staff visited all the key players in the ministries, asking each the same question: 'How can we help?' Jellicoe asked for 'More ships, merchant ships, any kind of ships' and for America to 'take over the patrol of the American side of the Atlantic'. Balfour wanted 'American credits in the United States big enough to keep up the rate of exchange.' And the army asked for 'An expeditionary force, no matter how small, for the effect of the American Flag in Europe.'[381] Britain had waited a long time for this day and was ready to welcome Americans and their aid in a handsome fashion.

MALTREATMENT AT SEA

The Imperial Navy's unrestricted sinking policy brought a new intensity to the war at sea. Gone were the days when a U-boat would tow lifeboats to safe coastal waters. From now on, stories of maltreatment at sea became more frequent. An early case was the sinking of the *Dalmata* in February 1917.

Kapitänleutnant Wilhelm Amberger in *UB-38* had found the 1800-ton Norwegian cargo ship 40 miles northwest of Bishop Rock in passage from New York to Le Havre on February 11. Before sinking the vessel, Amberger forced the crew to take to the two small lifeboats, but it was the presence of the Captain's wife that turned a routine sinking into a symbol of wanton German cruelty. The two were recently married and the wife was making her first voyage with her husband. The ship's complement and the wife spent three days in the boats, during which time one man died and three were frostbitten. On landing, the wife described her torment to the waiting press: 'The sea was extremely heavy, it was piercingly cold, and my two coats and blanket were soaked as a result of sea washing over the boats ... I lay down in the bottom of our boat and prepared to die. My arms and legs were like sticks and my eyes bloodshot from staring.'[382] *The Times* held back from a full condemnation, saying that it was not clear whether 'in perpetrating this outrage' Amberger was acting under orders or 'following his own inclinations and judgement'. Either way, the paper said, 'his act was one of gross callousness'.[383]

Shortly after the *Dalmata* incident, the British 2900-ton steamer *Thracia*, laden with iron ore and bound for Ardrossan in North Ayrshire, was passing Belle Ile on the Brittany coast on March 27. Without the least warning, a torpedo struck the forward stokehole. Its explosion wrought massive damage. *Thracia*'s boilers burst, causing the deaths of an engineer, two firemen and a greaser. Before anyone could begin to lower the boats, the ship was listing to starboard and beginning to sink bow-first. Midshipman Douglas Duff went down with the vessel but surfaced in the water, where he saw an upturned starboard lifeboat without its stern. He and seven other men clambered onto the hull. Two of them were badly injured and had not the strength to hold on. They soon slipped into the sea. Three others then dropped back into the water to swim to a steamer that they had sighted. Duff watched as the steamer pulled away into the distance. The swimmers never returned. Just two men were left, hanging onto the raft-like boat. Duff could not recall what happened in the next few hours but, at some stage, he found himself alone – the sole survivor out of seven boat-clingers. He had little hope of ever seeing another human being. In his desperation he made a promise to become a monk if he survived. Then the dark shape of a U-boat rose out of the sea. The hatch opened and its commander, his Luger in one hand, asked Duff which ship he was from and its destination. When the commander had no more questions he said, 'I am going to shoot you.' Duff told him to go ahead to which the commander said that he would not waste his powder on an Englishman: 'Drown, you swine! Drown!' The commander disappeared. The hatch closed. And the U-boat submerged. Next day, Duff was found by a French fishing boat, which later handed him over to a French torpedo boat. The 16-year-old Duff was the only survivor from *Thracia*. He later survived another sinking and a broken leg in a U-boat attack. After the war he kept his promise to join a monastery. Brother Lawrence, as he became, soon found the life was not for him. In the Second World War he was back at sea and rose to the rank of lieutenant commander.

A RAIDING FAILURE

In March, the Imperial Navy made one last attempt to send a raider to sea. (There were still some raiders operating in distant waters.) The auxiliary cruiser SMS *Leopard* set out for distant oceans in the middle of the month. Disguised as a Norwegian freighter, the *Leopard* reached the Norwegian Sea on March 16 where it was sighted at noon by HMS

Achilles from the Second Cruiser Squadron, working alongside HMS *Dundee*. There was nothing suspicious about the *Leopard*, but inspections were routine in this area, so *Dundee* and *Achilles* turned towards the unknown vessel. It took several hours to catch up with the stranger, by which time Commander Selwyn Day of the *Dundee* was uneasy. Why was the 'n' in the name *Rena* upside down? Why was this ship much larger than the registered *Rena*? Why did it appear to not have wireless ariels? It had to be a raider. Day ordered a boat to be lowered and Lieutenant Frederick Lawson set off to investigate.

While Lawson's boat made its slow passage through the sea, the stranger kept on the move, as if trying to keep away from *Dundee*'s guns. An innocent merchant vessel would have had no fear of *Dundee*. Day kept his men on high alert, ready to fire at the least confirmation of their visitor's malign status. Suddenly, the ship's Norwegian flag came down. Day gave the order to fire. Almost simultaneously, two torpedoes sped towards *Dundee*, but Day turned the ship away in time. Both vessels were now firing their guns. Soon *Achilles* joined in. The *Leopard* had no chance of surviving, but it never surrendered. As the ship finally settled into the water, it was a smouldering wreck. Not one of its complement survived. Amongst the dead was Lieutenant Lawson and the other members of the boarding party.

The Imperial Navy never sent a raider to sea again. Perhaps Grand Admiral Holtzendorff realized how little they contributed to sinking merchant shipping; or perhaps he feared that British patrols would sink further raiders as they attempted the treacherous passage through British-controlled waters before they could reach their raiding grounds. From now, on the Imperial Navy's entire efforts would be concentrated on U-boat attacks on merchant shipping, with the imperative of forcing Britain out of the war before the Western Front collapsed.

A RETURN TO EASY TARGETS

With merchant sinkings reaching levels never thought possible, more and more non-combatants faced the terrors of attack and the fearful power of the sea. Captain Benjamin Chave's report of the sinking of the British passenger ship *Alnwick Castle* provides a vivid picture of the nightmare that was shared by thousands of sinking victims in this war.

On March 19 Captain Chave was woken at 5.00 am according to his routine. He gave orders to his chief officer for the ship's daylight zigzagging to begin, together with the placing of lookouts in each of the crow's nests, plus one man on the fore bridge. Two cadets were stationed on either side of the lower bridge. Just over an hour later, when Chave was drinking his coffee, there was a huge explosion which blew the hatches off one of the holds. A towering column of water and debris shot into the air. Chave ordered the engines full astern.

All six lifeboats were safely lowered while the ship was steadily sinking by its prow. Meanwhile the radio officer, Mr Carnaby, was sending out SOS messages. Ominously, he received no acknowledgement. With the ship almost gone, Chave jettisoned secret Admiralty documents over the side, together with his code books. The occupants of his allocated boat pleaded with Chave to join them, but he waited until he and Carnaby were the only ones left on board. Together, they stepped into boat N°. 1 and the oarsmen pulled it clear of the sinking liner. At the same time *U-81* surfaced with a gun trained menacingly on the boat.

Alnwick Castle gave one last valedictory blast on its whistle as it slipped under the waves. The six boats were now alone on the sea, 300 miles from Land's End. The men's last sign of their enemy was a huge plume of water some way off: *U-81* had sent a second vessel to the bottom. (This was the steamer *Frinton*, in which four men died.)

With only three men capable of helping Chave to sail boat N°. 1, the boat's occupants faced days of battling against strong winds and a rough sea as they made for land. At times, the sea was too rough to permit sailing. At one point, the foot of the mast broke and Chave and his men had to improvise a repair. At intervals, food and water were shared out. Thursday – their fourth day in the boat – found some passengers to be light-headed; others were trying to drink sea water. There was some relief when that day's hailstorm brought welcome fresh water. Chave struggled to find passengers still willing to help with bailing out the boat: 'most of the men were now helpless and several were in delirium'. Fireman Thomas died in the night. 'The horror of that night, together with the physical suffering, are beyond my power of description,' recalled Chave.[384] On the Friday morning Fireman Tribe went too, followed by Buckley, Chave's steward. The last death was a cattleman called Peter. And then, at 1.30 pm, the survivors were found by the French steamer *Venezia*.

Not one of the twenty-four survivors in boat N°. 1 had the strength to board the *Venezia* so they were hoisted up one by one. Four dead bodies were left behind in the boat. When Chave wrote his report, he had no news of the other five boats: there would never to be any trace of two of them.

The experiences of those on the Chief Officer's boat were even worse. One of the 31 people became deranged, one jumped overboard and ten died. When they sighted the coast of Spain on March 26 the survivors were too weak to work the oars. They were rescued by some Spanish fishermen from the village of Cariño. The local priest led the townspeople in taking the survivors to their cottages before transferring them to the hospital at Ferrol. In total, 40 of the *Alnwick Castle*'s passengers and crew died in the disaster.

Chave returned to sea after a period of convalescence and served throughout the war, retiring as commodore in 1932. He remained in the Royal Navy Reserve and served again in the Second World War.

On the day following the sinking of the *Alnwick Castle*, another hospital ship was the victim of the insatiable U-boats. HMHS *Asturias* was torpedoed by *UC-66* when in passage from Avonmouth to Southampton. Although the ship failed to sink, its master ordered the medical staff into the boats, one of which sank. Only around 30 people were killed since the ship had disembarked 1000 wounded at Avonmouth earlier in the day. But Oberleutnant zur See Herbert Pustkuchen had shown himself willing to attempt to sink a ship that was potentially carrying hundreds of wounded. It was truly an act of 'unrestricted sinking'.

A NEW ALLY

By April, the Imperial Navy had sunk ten American ships starting with the 3000-ton freighter *Housatonic* off the Scilly Islands on February 3 and ending with the 3700-ton *Aztec* on April 1 off Brest. It was almost as if Germany were deliberately targeting American ships. The President's patience was exhausted. It was time to act. He hinted at this in his inaugural speech on March 5 when he said, 'We are provincials no longer. The tragic events of the thirty months of vital turmoil through which we have just passed have made us citizens of the world. There can be no turning back. Our own fortunes as a nation are involved whether we would have it so or not.'[385]

On Monday April 2 at 8.35 pm Wilson took the final step to take America into the war as he stood before a joint session of the Senate and the House of Representatives. In the gallery, 1500 people eagerly awaited the historic event.

Outside, the streets around the Capitol were seething with excited citizens. Searchlights played on the famous dome. The fluttering Stars and Stripes on its pole was caught in their powerful beams. Below, two troops of cavalry in dress uniform, sabres drawn, guarded the building. In the crowds, hundreds of uniformed and plain-clothed police kept order.

His address had taken the President ten hours to prepare. When he started to speak, he appeared nervous. His complexion was pale and his voice was weak, but his message was clear and strong. He began: 'I have called the Congress into extraordinary session ....' Within minutes there was clapping and cheering as he turned to the spate of sinkings: 'Vessels of every kind, whatever their flag, their character, their cargo, their destination, their errand, have been ruthlessly sent to the bottom without warning and without thought of help or mercy for those on board.' He continued: 'I was for a little while unable to believe that such things would in fact be done by any government that had hitherto subscribed to the humane practices of civilized nations.' Wilson then turned to America's response, asking Congress to accept America's entry into the war. He did this, he said, 'With a profound sense of the solemn and even tragical character of the step I am taking.' He then called for 'at least 500,000 men'. The President closed his address by reminding Americans of the reason for entering the fray: 'we shall fight for the things which we have always carried nearest our hearts – for democracy, for the right of those who submit to authority to have a voice in their own governments, for the rights and liberties of small nations.'[386] The atmosphere throughout his address was frenzied. The President repeatedly had to stop until the uproar died down. When he finished with his 'America is privileged to spend her blood' climax the great chamber went silent before the vast audience took to deafening applause. Back in the White House, Wilson sat in silence. Then, recalled his private secretary, Joseph Tumulty, 'The President put his head down on the table and wept.'[387]

The British relief at America's entry into the war was neatly demonstrated by a genuine 'man in the street' who approached Walter Page when he stepped out of his house in Grosvenor Square the next day. The man stopped and shook the Ambassador's hand:

'Thank God,' the Englishman said, 'that there is one hypocrite less in London to-day.'

'What do you mean?' asked Page.

'I mean you. Pretending all this time that you were neutral! That isn't necessary any longer.'

'You are right!' the Ambassador answered as he walked on with a laugh and a wave of the hand.'[388]

President Wilson asks Congress to declare war on Germany, April 2, 1917.

On hearing the news from America, the American socialite Viscountess Nancy Astor rushed to the Embassy to enlist Walter Page's help. She asked him for a copy of Wilson's speech to read to her servants in her St James's Square house, and for help in finding an American flag to place on her dining table.

Back in Washington, the Foreign Affairs Committees of both houses met on April 3 at 10.00 am to consider the resolutions that would enact the President's decision for war. These resolutions 'authorized and directed' the President 'to employ the entire naval and military forces of the United States and the resources of the Government to carry on war against the Imperial German Government'.[389] The 13-hour debate lasted until 11.00 pm, when a vote was finally taken. In the Senate six members opposed the resolution, to no effect. In the House 'amid resounding cheers' the resolution was approved by 373 votes to 50. America was going to war.[390]

The Times' leader on America's entry into the war was unrestrained in its approbation of the action. Quoting the words of Lloyd George, the paper declared that 'at one bound America has become a world-power'. And, rightly foreseeing the longer-term consequences of Americans marching onto the world stage, the paper opined: 'The intervention of America as the champion of right in a European controversy is an event so great in itself, and so pregnant with inscrutable results for the whole world, that it baffles understanding on both sides of the ocean.'[391]

The British public greeted the news enthusiastically. The Stars and Stripes were dug out from years of storage to hang exultantly from shops, houses and hotels. In the streets, rosettes in American colours sold briskly. From bandstands, the strains of the *Star Spangled Banner* filled the air. More formally, both Houses of Parliament flew the flags of the two nations in intimate unity. London men raised their hats to the fluttering symbols of hope.

On April 6, America opened its war by seizing 91 German-owned vessels. Before the port authorities could act Bernstorff had sent a coded message to the ships' masters ordering them to destroy the engines in their vessels. The sailors did little damage beyond sawing off bolt heads. But sawn-off bolts would not deter the woken giant. A new world power had been born. In that moment, all Germany's hopes of empire and glory died.

20
The battle for convoys

April 1917

'Jellicoe ... is feeble to a degree and vacillating.' – Haig.[392]

Paralysis

Chief of the Naval Staff Admiral Von Holtzendorff would have been elated if he had known just how successful his unrestricted campaign was to be in its first few months of 1917. Sinkings increased from 369,000 tons in January to 540,000 tons in February, and rose even further to 594,000 tons in March. These March sinkings amounted to one quarter of all in-bound shipping. This was near enough to the admiral's target of 600,000 tons for him to claim vindication for the controversial policy. His prediction that neutral vessels would be deterred from sailing proved true as well. The 471 neutral arrivals in January fell to 299 for February and March combined. It looked as if Germany's gamble was to pay off. The British Admiralty were demoralized by these staggering figures and concluded: 'we are faced with the certainty of an increase, month by month, in the number of hostile submarines'.[393]

Evidence of the increasing sinkings could be seen on the British High Streets. With the rising price of imported wheat, the less well-off turned to cheaper foods. Potatoes were soon in very short supply, despite government appeals for people to eat less. A greengrocer in London's Edgeware Road was fined £3 for refusing to sell them to shoppers who did not also buy greens. The potato shortage brought a rapid rise in the prices of substitutes: large swedes cost 2 d, bananas 2½ d and haricot beans were 8 d a pint. Many hotels introduced one or more meatless days; all were now legally required to ration meat portions to 5 oz at lunch and dinner. The First Lord of the Admiralty, Edward Carson, remarked that 'the situation threatens the food of the people to an extent that no one could have anticipated' – a comment which suggests that he had lived a very sheltered life.[394]

Rising food prices suited the government since rationing by price was politically more acceptable than rationing by legislation. Overall, the cost of living for working class families had risen by 65 per cent since 1914

The battle for convoys

and food prices were up by exactly 100 per cent. Formal rationing could not be delayed for much longer. For the troops, rationing had effectively begun when the War Cabinet decided that soldiers would have one day a week without potatoes.

In lieu of any firmer action, the government sort the King's aid. Ethel Bilbrough, a well-off housewife in Kent, heard the monarch's appeal 'exhorting the people to practise the most rigid economy, especially in bread'. (This call was read out four Sundays running in Bilbrough's local church.) In her diary she bemoaned: 'We are not allowed to feed our horses on corn any longer.'[395]

Rather than introduce rationing, the British Government urged restraint in cosumption.

THE FIRST CONVOYS

One of the most puzzling aspects of the Admiralty's objections to convoys in early 1917 was the great success that they were already having with the few actually in operation. Food convoys had been running between the Hook of Holland and Harwich since July 26, 1916. This 'beef trip', as it was known, had lost only one straggler before unrestricted sinking started in 1917. How Jellicoe and his officers could persist in saying that merchant masters could not keep station and match the speed of the convoy is a mystery beyond elucidation. Indeed, even

Jellicoe found his own position a mystery as he said in his *The Crisis of the Naval War* in 1920: 'The immunity of this trade ... from successful attack by submarines was extraordinary.'[396]

Then there were the highly effective convoys carrying coal to France. These had begun sailing on February 10 from Mount's Bay in Cornwall to Brest. In the period from March to May only nine ships had been lost from 4016 sailings, despite the escort being limited to armed trawlers. Here was resounding proof of the efficacy of even lightly protected convoys. This evidence left the Admiralty no excuse for not immediately introducing convoys on a large scale. But it buried its collective head in the sand and sneakily called the coal convoys 'controlled sailings'.[397]

These coal convoys had been approved by Jellicoe himself on January 16, but clearly against his better judgement since it would be 51 days before he admitted to their existence at the War Cabinet. Meanwhile, Jellicoe was to spend three months using every argument he could find to block the introduction of further convoys, including engaging in a dubious piece of 'market research' (see below) when he interviewed ships' masters.

Hankey's brainwave

On February 8, the War Cabinet met at 10 Downing Street. The meeting promised to be just one more tedious review of a stagnant war, a wearying nation, and an impotent Admiralty. Yet the meeting would lead to one man unlocking the solution to the U-boat's unrelenting sinkings of merchant ships.

The Prime Minister and his colleagues (Lord Curzon, Arthur Henderson and Bonar Law) together with the usual plethora of army and navy chiefs, plodded through the rather sparse agenda, which included submarines as item 5. Having discussed 'the serious situation threatened by the increased losses from submarines', they earnestly turned to intensifying food production, building more merchant ships and introducing more restrictions on imports. No one mentioned convoys. No one even suggested that there was anything that the navy could do to overcome the U-boat threat.

Meanwhile, another brain at the table set to work on the problem of defeating the U-boats.

Maurice Hankey, who had been present as secretary, returned home from the meeting in a despondent mood. That night he wrote in his diary:

The battle for convoys

'The submarine warfare has become frantic. We seem to be sinking a good many submarines, but they are sinking a terrible lot of ships.' It was all 'rather a gloomy business', made worse by the paralytic fear that had gripped the Admiralty and the War Cabinet. Hankey slept badly for three nights in a row. Then, on the Sunday morning: 'I had a brainwave on the subject of anti-submarine warfare.' Suddenly, everything was clear: why the current system was wrong; why the Admiralty's objections to convoys were mistaken; and what the solution was. After lunch, Hankey motored to Lloyd George's home at Walton Heath in Surrey to expound his brainwave to the Prime Minister. He modestly wrote in his diary that Lloyd George 'was very interested'. It is more probable that Lloyd George was ecstatic at Hankey's energy and imagination in place of Jellicoe's sullen acceptance that the U-boats were invincible. Hankey motored home and sat up long into the night writing his 'general scheme' for convoys which would involve 'ultimately an entire reorganization of the Admiralty's present scheme'.[398]

In his paper, Hankey foresaw how to make convoys work. 'It involves,' he wrote, 'the concentration on this service of the whole anti-submarine craft allocated to the protection of trade routes, excepting only those vessels devoted to the protection of our main fleets.' He intended to use 'every means of anti-submarine warfare – the gun, the submarine, the net, the depth charge, the mortar, the hydrophone, and wireless telegraphy.' And, crucially, convoys: 'To prevent the enemy from knowing when and where our merchant ships are to be found …; to debar the enemy from engaging without undertaking a serious attack and himself running great risks …; to concentrate our widely scattered craft on the immediate defence of the merchant shipping they are intended to protect; *to bait the trap* …'[399] (Emphasis added.)

The Tuesday morning found Carson, Jellicoe, Duff and Hankey at Lloyd George's breakfast table for a discussion on anti-submarine warfare. Suddenly, the Prime Minister turned to Hankey – a mere civil servant – and asked him to read out his audacious paper in front of the First Sea Lord and Rear Admiral Duff. The gold-braided admirals listened politely, but, wrote Hankey, in his diary: 'They resisted a good deal.'[400] He went on to note the anomaly that was to beset the Admiralty over the next few months: they were successfully convoying transports yet declaring that convoying was a bad idea *in principle*.

After two hours of bacon, eggs, coffee and Hankey's intransigent sagacity, Jellicoe still refused to run up his white flag. He left the meeting with his guns ever uselessly firing the blanks of inaction. His one concession was to consult some mercantile marine captains on their views on convoys. Jellicoe, as usual, was asking the wrong question. Whether merchant masters *wanted* convoys or not was irrelevant. The only point at issue was whether they *worked* or not. And, on that issue, the Admiralty already had all the evidence that was needed.

On March 2, Jellicoe reported on his consultation with ships' masters. (His report was the first time that he referred to convoys in the War Cabinet.) He said that he had consulted 'ten captains of tramp steamers who had had experience' and that their 'unanimous opinion had been strongly against convoy'. Their objections were remarkably similar to Jellicoe's including 'the difficulties of station-keeping' and inexperienced engineers and officers. But how reliable was such a small sample? And might the lowly masters have been overawed by the august gold-braided First Sea Lord and so told him what he wanted to hear?

After the war, Commander Henry Kenrick RNVR of the French Coal Trade was highly critical of Jellicoe's consultation. He pointed out that five of the nine (not ten, apparently) men whom Jellicoe consulted were masters of coastal vessels 'to whom the very idea of Convoy was anathema'. Of the remaining four, two were ludicrous choices for such a consultation: they had both been recently torpedoed while under escort. Additionally, Kenrick pointed out that the masters had been given only one day's notice of the meeting: 'Had more notice been given the attendance could have been secured of a fair number of Masters of large Ocean-going liners and cargo steamers.' At least Kenrick's account allows us to exclude Jellicoe from having tried to rig his meeting with the masters, but his understanding of how to draw a representative sample was woefully lacking. But, hard as Jellicoe had tried to close down the convoy debate, it had only just begun.

THE GREAT CONVOY DEBATE

With neither Duff nor Jellicoe showing the least faith in convoys, Britain's fate seemed sealed by the rampaging U-boats which, month after month, broke their previous sinking records.

Resolution came when two junior officers – Captain Herbert Richmond in HMS *Commonwealth* and Commander Reginald Henderson in the Anti-Submarine Division – decided to act. They were so determined to see convoys introduced that they stretched discipline to the limit and leaked confidential material to Lloyd George.

It was probably Henderson who made the first critical move. One of the Admiralty's objections to convoys was a lack of escort vessels to accompany the 2500 weekly sailings. But Henderson discovered that the figure of 2500 sailings was utterly bogus, since it included coastal sailings, for which convoys were not needed. The true number of sailings that needed to be convoyed was 140 ships per week. Henderson passed this critical figure to Lloyd George. It seems certain that these figures were what convinced the Prime Minister that Maurice Hankey was right. The final battle for convoys was ready to be played out as Lloyd George, Hankey and Henderson circled the obdurate Admiralty.

In the 43 days following Lloyd George's breakfast party, something around 800,000 tons of additional shipping had been sunk. Beatty was in his cabin in *Queen Elizabeth* at Scapa Flow, unburdening himself in a letter to his wife: 'The outlook on the sea does not improve ... *and the Admiralty will not introduce the system of Convoy.*'[401] (Emphasis added.) Two days later, Beatty realized that only backstairs methods would stir the Admiralty into action: 'I must see the Prime Minister and put my views before him,' he told Ethel on March 30.[402] (Appropriately, that was the day on which March sinkings set the new monthly record of 594,000 tons sunk. While Beatty would not have had a precise figure for such recent sinkings, he knew that the March sinkings had risen to a crisis level. And still, the Admiralty made no move to change its failing anti-submarine methods.)

It so happened that a meeting to discuss convoys had already been arranged at Longhope in the Orkneys, to take place just five days after Beatty had written to Ethel. It had been convened under pressure from Sir Eyre Crowe at the Foreign Office, who had reported that Norwegian shipowners were losing confidence in the Royal Navy.

Beatty had hoped that Lloyd George would be able to join the conference, but, even without the Prime Minister's presence, he got the result that he wanted. At the meeting he pressed the need for convoys and found immediate support from Sir Reginald Tupper, Vice-Admiral Commanding Orkneys and Shetlands. Tupper declared that 'a system of escorts would be more efficacious than a patrol system'.[403] Although there were differences amongst the admirals present, the meeting agreed to begin daily convoys to Norway with different rendezvous points on different days. Eastbound ships would be escorted to reach the

Norwegian coast at daylight. (The merchant ships had to sail the last few miles alone since the escorts were unable to enter Norwegian waters.)

Beatty's report to the Admiralty highlighted the need for 'an alteration in policy'. In an act of insubordinate defiance, he said 'patrols have given little, if any, security to shipping during the war'. He continued: 'Escorts have, however proved an effectual protection ... It is manifestly impracticable to provide an escort for each individual vessel, the only alternative is to introduce a system of convoys.'[404]

When the heretical Longhope report arrived at Admiralty House, where convoys were known to be useless, a grudging Anti-Submarine Division authorized some experimental convoys 'as an exceptional measure'.[405] Some experiment! Six-thousand vessels ploughed the Scandinavian route in 1917 under the protection of the contested convoys with a loss of only 70 ships – just over 1 per cent.

The Longhope Conference, though, had little impact on the overall sinkings of over 500,000 tons a month. Whatever the outcome for Norwegian trade, the vast majority of merchant vessels were to be left unprotected. The battle for convoys had not yet been won. An Admiralty that regarded convoys as 'an exceptional measure' had only one general policy for the merchant seaman: 'sail alone and sink alone'.

Nearly two weeks had passed since the Longhope Conference and the Prime Minister was at last in Admiral Beatty's quarters in the *Queen Elizabeth*. Here was Beatty's chance. In telling Ethel of this meeting, Beatty had said: 'This is secret, so don't mention it to *anyone*.'[406] (He feared that the Admiralty might forbid him from speaking directly to the Prime Minister.) What passed between them we do not know, but it is safe to assume that Beatty railed against the Admiralty's passive acceptance of the indomitable U-boats. Lloyd George would have returned to London knowing that he had the sea-going officers on his side. All that he had to do was persuade the Admiralty to put Hankey's paper into action.

Shortly after Lloyd George's visit to Scapa Flow, Rear Admiral Duff approved the Longhope Conference proposals, which Jellicoe endorsed, saying the 'system was to be tried, and a report sent fortnightly on its working'.[407] This, though, was not a Damascene conversion. Jellicoe still showed no thirsting for 'early-adopter' status. The driving force behind these initial convoys was Beatty, with strong political support from Hankey and Lloyd George. As to Jellicoe, as we have seen, he had told the War Cabinet on March 8 that ships' masters were 'strongly against' convoys and appeared to accept this as conclusive evidence against them.[408]

Sailors at Longhope, the site of the conference that goaded the Admiralty into accepting convoys.

Despite Duff having approved the Scandinavian convoys on April 11, he effectively opposed them in a confused minute on April 19 by saying, 'to be effective [convoys] must number two escorting vessels to every ship'. This same minute revealed that Duff was far from being converted to convoys, saying, 'an insufficiently guarded convoy passing daily over the same area must prove the easiest of preys to the submarine'.[409] Black, in his study of the Admiralty War Staff, concluded: 'The belief, that patrols deter and work, and convoys attract and fail, was one reason why Duff was unable for so long to make the imaginative leap from patrol to convoy.'[410] Rear Admiral Sir Henry Oliver, Chief of the Admiralty War Staff, shared Duff's reservations: 'I am very doubtful of its success as convoys invite torpedo attack and the available escorts are too few for the number of ships proposed for a convoy.'[411] In summary, in the second half of April the Admiralty was a bastion of opposition to convoys, based on two incompatible objections: convoys would not work because masters could not keep station; and convoys were impossible because there were not enough escort staff. No one in the Admiralty ever spotted that, if the first objection were true, the second objection was nullified.

While his staff were dismissing convoys, Jellicoe twice faced the War Cabinet on April 23. At the 11.30 am meeting he ruled out convoys until 'a much larger number' of destroyers was available. He had not one word to say about how the Admiralty intended to answer the 881,000 tons that were to be sunk that month. At 5.00 pm the War Cabinet convened again, and Jellicoe presented a paper on 'The Submarine Menace and the Food Supply'. The meeting also had the benefit of the more precise – and much more alarming – figures from the Ministry of Shipping. The Parliamentary Secretary, Leo Money MP, revealed that, after meeting the needs of the army and navy, the tonnage left available for trade in January had been 8.4 million tons. With the current rate of sinkings, the Ministry's estimate for December 1917 was 4.8 million tons available for shipping. Imports were forecast to drop from 3 million tons in January to 2 million tons in December. It would not be until the Second World War that a British Cabinet received a more terrifying report. Britain was on the verge of being starved into submission. Jellicoe recommended building more destroyers; appealing to the Americans for more ships; sowing more mines in the Bight; building up food reserves; and laying down 'unsinkable vessels'.[412] But he had not one word to say about convoys. Nor, to their shame, did a single member of the War Cabinet ask why the Admiralty had nothing to say about them.

This was surely the navy's lowest point in its history as it admitted that, rather than tackle the enemy, the country should offer him yet more bait.

Duff recanted on April 26 when he advised Jellicoe that 'the time has arrived' to 'introduce a comprehensive scheme of convoys'.[413] In the post-war 'battle of the memoirs' Jellicoe spent tedious page after tedious page justifying his opposition to convoys, while Lloyd George placed himself centre stage in their introduction. The American naval historian Arthur Marder declared Henderson to be 'the chief architect of the convoy system'. A better way of sharing the credit is to see Hankey as the imaginative genius, Henderson as the key operator and Lloyd George as the midwife.

Four days later, Jellicoe, knowing that he was fast being cornered over convoys by Hankey, Beatty and Lloyd George, got his defence in first with an apocalyptic memorandum that he wrote on April 27. He warned that *'our present policy is heading straight for disaster'* and then set out four demands if the disaster was to be averted: (1) withdrawal of British forces from Salonika; (2) troop convoy escorts had to also carry 'essentials from the Colonies'; (3) banning imported labour*; and (4) 'ruthless' suppression of the import of non-essentials.[414] (*Around 450,000 labourers and other workers were brought to Europe from the colonies and China during the war.) Only if these pre-conditions were met would the Admiralty be able to escort convoys. These absolute, irrevocable demands seem to have been forgotten when Jellicoe and Duff ran up the flag of truce a few days later.

The War Cabinet's exasperation at the opaqueness of the Admiralty's strategy was shared by Beatty at Scapa Flow, as he told his wife: 'Everything at present is given up to the defensive attitude, and even that is not being well done. I am terribly exercised over the question of getting neutral traffic across the North Sea and down the coasts, and hope to establish a system.'[415]

Jellicoe's response to the sinkings crisis at the War Cabinet meeting had unnerved the other members. Two days later, they noted that they were not 'sufficiently informed' on the issue and asked the Prime Minister to 'visit the Admiralty with a view to investigating all the means at present in use in regard to anti-submarine warfare'.[416] Lloyd George grasped this critical opportunity, for which he needed to be thoroughly armed. He asked Hankey to prepare a searching list of questions based on memoranda prepared by Viscount Milner (Minister without Portfolio) and General Robertson (Chief of the Imperial General Staff), together with his and Hankey's own papers.

Lloyd George's Admiralty meeting might well have resulted in Jellicoe's resignation, given the admiral's intransigence in successive War Cabinet meetings. But Jellicoe knew that he was cornered. A retreat – or, at least the appearance of a retreat – was required. In this mood, Jellicoe took the War Cabinet's broadside with a good grace and the meeting passed 'very pleasantly' said Hankey, who then worked into the night 'dictating a long report, embodying a large reconstruction of the Admiralty and more especially the Admiralty War Staff'.[417] This account comes from the most reliable source in the whole episode: Hankey. He was the only disinterested person in the debate, so we can take it as certain that it was at this meeting that Jellicoe finally began to acknowledge the inevitability of convoys. But, for all Jellicoe's being 'pleasant', he still nurtured a visceral antipathy towards convoys. As Vice-Admiral Kenneth Dewar wrote in his *The Navy From Within*, 'The idea that they [the Admiralty] were really in favour of convoy, and only awaited a favourable opportunity to introduce it, is neither borne out by the facts nor by their own memoranda.'[418] Beatty, Hankey and Lloyd George had won only half a battle.

Was it a coincidence that Duff passed his proposal for convoys to Jellicoe on the same day that Lloyd George had effectively said 'enough is enough'? We shall never know, but the timing is deeply suspicious. As we have seen, Jellicoe had sat through a War Cabinet three days earlier at which the crisis had been discussed. He offered a string of actions, none of which had the remotest chance in the short term of ending the relentless sinkings. Yet he said not one word about convoys. His preferred option was the building of the massive ships. (Or, a few weeks earlier, building lots of small vessels!) If convoys were just two days away from being a realistic option, surely Jellicoe would have mentioned them, even if only to say they were under active consideration. We are forced to the conclusion that Jellicoe correctly sensed the political atmosphere: his job was on the line. If he failed to introduce convoys, Lloyd George would find a more cooperative First Sea Lord.

At least, though, the crisis meeting compelled the doubting Duff to draw up a first tentative list of an initial 45 convoys for routes to Gibraltar, Dakar, Louisberg (Nova Scotia) and Newport News (Virginia). Two days later at Corfu, a naval conference of Britain, France and Italy agreed on a system of Mediterranean convoys.

In his post-war accounts of this period, Jellicoe offered a brazen attempt to re-justify his long-discredited views. In his 1934 *The Submarine Peril: The Admiralty Policy In 1917* he repeated the same arguments against convoys that he used in 1916 and early 1917. He referred to the 'time wasted' in assembling convoys; that a convoy has to travel at the speed of the slowest ship which '*adds greatly* to the delay'; the 'congestion' in ports when a large number of vessels arrive simultaneously; merchant ships not having facilities for being darkened at night; merchant ships being unable to keep station. He justified his repeating these objections, long debunked by the success of the convoys, by saying that their 'advocacy had been premature'.[419] Jellicoe went on to refer to a report in February 1918 about poor station-keeping in convoys, despite the fact that monthly losses had been reduced from their peak of 880,000 tons in April 1917 to 319,000 in February 1918. Not content with repeating these long punctured arguments, he went on to detail five 'naval difficulties' which made it impossible to have convoys before April 1917. Three of these reasons were ones that he never mentioned in April 1917.

The American historian Jan S Breemer discusses other evidence in support of the view that Admiralty were, at best, half-hearted about convoys. He argues that, if their only objection (as Jellicoe frequently claimed), was a lack of escort ships, then the Admiralty would at least have 'laid the foundation for carrying out the system' once the resources were available.[420] The British historian and intelligence officer Patrick Beesly comes to the same view: 'Jellicoe, Oliver and Duff – and indeed many other senior officers – were by no means converted to the idea, and the organization and extension of the convoy system proceeded with lamentable slowness.'[421]

21
Unstoppable sinkings

April 1917

'There is no time to be lost.' – Walter Page. [422]

THE THREAT OF FOOD CONTROL

In early April British food supplies were beginning to run down. Flour stocks, which had stood at 14 weeks' supply in December 1916 were now down to nine weeks'. In the War Cabinet, the Shipping Controller was urged to induce 'the United States Government to ship as much wheat as possible at the earliest moment'.[423] Even so, the members steadfastly refused to introduce rationing. Instead, the Food Controller, Lord Devonport, contrived to reduce consumption in hotels, restaurants and boarding houses by means of restrictions on what they could serve. There was to be a meatless day once a week together with five potatoless days, and portion sizes were to be controlled by law. Meat at lunch was not to exceed 2 oz, while at dinner a 4 oz portion could be served. More generally, bread prices were to be fixed, based on the price of flour. He also introduced a *Flour and Bread Order* which permitted mixing wheat flour with other grains. As he introduced these measures, Devonport studiously avoided using the word 'rationing' but the newspapers were not deceived. *The Times* called his scheme 'Rationing by Bulk'.[424] Even with these restrictions Spiegel, by now a prisoner of war, was more than satisfied with his rations, as he told his wife in April: 'One hardly notices anything of the war here, no [ration] cards of any kind, not even for bread.' Presumably thinking of all the U-boat men who had died in their attempt to starve Britain into surrender, he added: 'It is very sad, but it is true.'[425]

LIVING ON THE EDGE

In Germany, the massive April sinkings brought no dividend to its people. Clothing was in desperately short supply and could only be bought with clothing certificates, which were hard to come by. Women who owned two daily dresses and one Sunday dress were barred from extending their wardrobes. In schools, increasing thefts from cloakrooms led to clothing hooks being transferred to classrooms. Keeping clean was

Unstoppable sinkings

a daily struggle, with fatless soap made of sand and clay. Almost all public baths were closed. Coal was in such short supply that it was now called 'black gold'. Religion, too, bowed to weapons production. Church bells (having failed to ring out for victory) were melted down for armaments – in all 18,000 tons of bells were taken in 1917.

Morale both on the battle front and the home front was waning. Germany had nothing to show for the 2.8 m wounded and the deaths of 1.6 m soldiers. The people were compelled to survive on 1100 calories per day. Secret reports from the battle front showed a longing for the war to end. In the cities, workers struck in protest against the reduced bread ration. Ominously, there were the first stirrings of revolutionary protests as leaflets circulated, crying 'Down with the war! Down with the government! Peace! Freedom! Bread!'[426] In April, Hamburg's soup kitchens served six million meals. There could be no better testimony to the success of the Allied blockade.

Only the U-boats could end the blockade. The ever-increasing level of sinkings indicated that success was not far away. Just a few more months of sinkings at the April rate would suffice. Food would return to the kitchen tables; clothes would reappear in the shops; and the accoutrements of civilized life such as soap would let people feel human again. All it needed was one more push ... Meanwhile, even the better-fed submariners could be driven to desperate means to stock their larders, as the crew of *U-9* found in late April.

U-9 was rounding the north Scottish coast, when Spiess spotted the numerous sheep on the tiny island of North Rona. Here was food galore, although it could only be won with a certain ingenuity. With the aid of his binoculars Spiess identified a crevice in the sheer cliff face and despatched a hunting party to land on what was little more than a rocky outcrop. The five men – a watch officer, three seaman and the cook – beamed with joy as they dropped into the dinghy. On landing, throngs of terns voiced their resentment at the intrusion as they screamed in anger and flapped their wings. The hungry men were undeterred: the prize was too great for a retreat. Spiess watched as the men stepped onto the rocks, pulling up the dinghy behind them before climbing up the crevice and disappearing from view. Sometime later, several sheep carcasses lay on *U-9*'s deck. The stench of the butchery forced Spiess below. As for the catch, it proved to be meagre fare. The apparently fat and promising sheep turned out to be scrawny specimens, puffed up by fleeces that were teeming with maggots.

Later in the war, Edgar Spiegel had more success in his scavenging when *U-93* seized eggs from a cargo vessel: 'You can't imagine how tired a man can get of hard tack, pea soup, bacon and canned stuff,' he told the American broadcaster Lowell Thomas after the war. Having satisfied his hungry crew, Spiegel collected another 10,000 eggs to take back to Germany – no boat could have had a more welcome arrival in 1917.

Hungry German soldiers plundering the plentiful food stocks left by retreating Allied armies.

A NEW MAN

On March 31, the luxurious 10,500-ton SS *New York* docked at Liverpool as it had regularly done throughout the war. A man in civilian clothes presented his false passport to the immigration officers and was quickly waved through. A special train had steam up, ready to take him to London. Rear Admiral William Sims was the advance party of what would be the American contribution to anti-submarine warfare in the Western Approaches. Sims had been the first captain of America's largest battleship – the USS *Nevada* – and in February 1917 had been made President of the Naval War College. Both appointments were indications that he was regarded as a man with great potential. His despatch across the ocean was a sign of America's commitment to serious action in Europe.

In London, Walter Page was eagerly awaiting Sim's arrival. After three years of Washington's disdain for his reports on the calamitous state of Britain's naval war, he at last had a man who would share his sense of urgency. As he showed Sims the two rooms at the embassy that he had set aside for the admiral he said, 'You can have everything we've got. If necessary, to give you room, we'll turn the whole Embassy force out into the street.'[427] First, though, Sims needed to call on the Admiralty.

Admiralty House dated back to 1788. No other building in Britain – not even Parliament itself – was as great a testament to Britain's world power. Here, in heart of London, was the nerve centre of the world's premier navy. It was this navy that had built the world's largest empire. It was this navy that had defeated the French at Trafalgar – the last time that the French had dared to do battle with a British fleet. And it was this navy that had driven the Kaiser to paroxysms of jealousy, provoking him to construct a rival fleet. Sims must have sensed some of this past magnificence as he was escorted up the grand staircase towards the splendour of the First Lord's room. Inside, was to be another story.

Page had warned Sims that 'Only the help of the United States' could forestall 'calamity'.[428] Nevertheless, Sims was still stunned by his briefing from Jellicoe. After some customary preliminaries, Jellicoe reached for a drawer in his desk and pulled out a document. Sims ran his eyes over the astounding figures of tonnage sunk – three to four times the figures ever admitted in public. Jellicoe commented, 'It is impossible for us to go on with the war if losses like this continue.' When Sims asked, 'Is there no solution to this problem?' Jellicoe replied, 'Absolutely none that we can now see.'[429]

The British government had been so successful in suppressing the truth about the U-boat massacre that even a work-a-day admiral had never heard a whisper. (His own State Department had dismissed Walter Page's dispatches as panicky exaggerations.) Now, the American government was to receive a dispatch that far outdid anything that Page had written. It was to be the world's longest naval shopping list. Britain, Sims told the US Navy, needed every available 'floating craft that could be used in the anti-submarine warfare'. This meant 'destroyers, tugs, yachts, light cruisers, and similar vessels'. All these should be sent immediately to Queenstown 'where they would do valuable service in convoying merchant vessels and destroying the U-boats'.[430] He referred to the 50 to 60 destroyers patrolling the American coast and hoped to see them transferred to the real battlefield.

And then Sims waited in his two rooms at the American Embassy. Nothing had prepared him for his government's parsimonious response: just six destroyers were to be sent.

Sims was in a desperate mood when he sat down to draft a response to the woefully inadequate offer. Being an admiral rather than a diplomat, he asked Page to look over his draft. Page emphatically declared, 'Admiral, it isn't half strong enough!' and he offered to write something much more forceful. Headed 'Very confidential for Secretary and President' Page penned one of the most audacious dispatches imaginable from a diplomat to his own government. After repeating the details of Britain's precarious position, Page turned to the scale of response that was needed: 'our help is now more seriously needed in this submarine area for the sake of all the Allies than it can ever be needed again'. He went on, 'This seems to me the sharpest crisis of the war, and the most dangerous situation for the Allies that has arisen or could arise ... *There is no time to be lost.*'[431] Page's letter was shorn of all diplomatic etiquette. He wrote not as a servant of his government but as a friend of a beleaguered nation that had no other aid to turn to.

A week later, with no response from Washington, Page wrote directly to the President. He told Wilson how 237,000 tons of shipping had been sunk in the last week: 'the war will pretty soon become a contest of endurance under hunger, with an increasing proportion of starvation'. He now upped his previous demand for destroyers, saying that 100 were needed, but 'A third of that number will help mightily.' Without these, he said, 'At the present rate of destruction more than four million tons will be sunk before the summer is gone.'[432] There was no reply.

Unstoppable sinkings

After three months of the Imperial Navy's unrestricted sinkings policy, the ever increasing sinkings seemed to be unstoppable. From January's base of 368,000 tons, the toll had risen relentlessly: up 47 per cent in February; up another ten per cent in March; and then a leap by a further 48 per cent in April. Overall, the three months had seen an increase of 140 per cent. By April, the monthly total was 882,000 tons – the highest that the war would see. But the fastest rate of increase was in the Mediterranean where the number of ships sunk in April was treble that in

March. Hospital and troop ships were now regular targets, with April seeing three major sinkings in ten days.

In mid-April HMT *Arcadian*, carrying 1335 men, was in passage from Salonika to Alexandria under escort by a Japanese destroyer. It came into the sights of *UC-74* on April 15. A single torpedo fired by Kapitänleutnant Wilhelm Marschall caused massive damage to the vessel. Woodwork turned to jagged splinters, glass shards were strewn everywhere and steelwork was twisted into unidentifiable tangles. Meanwhile, the escaping steam from the ship's boilers hissed in seething anger. Those on board had only minutes to leave the ship. Trooper Reginald Huggins pulled off his army boots and put on a lifebelt as he prepared to make his escape. By the time that he was peering over the side, the over-loaded boats had already pulled away. His attempt to shin down a rope left him entangled in mid-air. Freed by two comrades, Huggins slid down the rope. The cool sea water soothed his rope-burned hands. He looked back to the ship and saw in horror the chaplain being sucked down a funnel before a boiler explosion shot him back out into the sea.

The last moments of the Arcadian.

Three minutes later, there was no sign of the *Arcadian*. Huggins had been dragged down to the depths by the dying ship, but his lifejacket propelled him back to the surface, where he was violently sick. He looked at his watch. It had stopped at 5.45 pm.

Hours later, Huggins joined others in clinging to one of the rafts: 'Darkness descended quickly, and the sea was bitterly cold.' From out of the night, he could hear some men on a raft singing 'Nearer my God to Thee'. Sometime later, he managed to clamber up onto the raft. At midnight its occupants spotted a small light. And then another. And then another. An officer pulled out a torch and began to signal in Morse code. As the searchlights on the rescue ships swung to and fro over the lonely darkness of the sea, the spirits of the raft's occupants grew. At times, a beam would come tantalizingly near. Then it would turn away. Eventually, a beam flashed over the men before it went dead. Out of the dark a distant signal lamp spelled out: 'Will pick you up soon as possible with other survivors.' The men waited in 'utter blackness' but 'with a hope'.[433] Finally, at midnight, Huggins saw the towering black mass of the Q-ship HMS *Redbreast* emerging from the darkness. Down came a rope ladder. His ordeal ended with hot grog, warm towels and a bunk.

Two-hundred-and-seventy-nine men had died in the attack. Three months later, 42 men in *Redbreast* died when it was torpedoed by *UC-38*.

For large vessels, mines were the deadly hazard. The 461-bed hospital ship *Salta* was caught in this way as it arrived at Le Havre on April 10. Captain Eastaway had brought his ship from Southampton to pick up wounded men from the Western Front. He was warned by the French port authorities that *UC-26* had laid mines the day before. Even so, the drifter HMS *Diamond* allowed *Salta* to proceed into the harbour by means of a buoyed channel. Once in the channel, Eastaway was seen to alter course, perhaps to let another ship pass.

At 11.43 *Salta* was rocked by a massive explosion. Water poured in through the torn hull. Ten minutes later the *Salta* sank.

Steward Frederick Richardson thought that just three boats had got away, although they had quickly filled with water as the waves crashed over them. In the ship's last moments, he saw the commander step off the bridge straight into the sea. Richardson himself was pulled to safety by a minesweeper after about one-and-a-half-hours in the water. On board, he watched several of the survivors die from exposure before the ship could return to land. Once refreshed and re-clothed, Richardson suffered the ordeal of identifying corpses in the morgue. Six days later, he attended the funerals of some of the crew.

Rescuers had tried to save the 205 passengers and crew on the *Salta*, but the high sea and the strong winds trounced their brave efforts. Fifty-one medical staff and 79 of the crew died. Many bodies were never recovered.

Seven days later, two hospital ships were sunk. On April 17, *UC-21* torpedoed HMHS *Donegal*, killing 29 wounded soldiers and 12 of the crew. That the same day, HMHS *Lanfranc* was torpedoed by Kapitänleutnant Hans Howaldt in *UB-40*. Amongst the 40 dead were 18 German soldiers. Princess Blücher met a nurse who had survived one of these sinkings. She told the Princess how she would 'be haunted to her dying day by the expression of agony on the faces of the helpless wounded men, unable to make the slightest effort to save themselves in their tight bandages'.[434]

A DAY OF PROMISE

Page had written his desperate plea to President Wilson on May 4. That day proved to be prescient as three events contrasted the apocalyptic terror that seemed indomitable with the hint that victory for the Allies was possible.

First came the reminder of the horrifying power of the U-boats when a torpedo from *U-63* ripped into the port side of the troopship HMT *Transylvania* in the Mediterranean. Walter Williams of the Army Service Corps was one of around 3000 men on board. He and his pals were assembling for parade at the moment of impact. None knew their boat allocation. All was chaos. Officers had to resort to firing their pistols into the air to regain order. With discipline restored, the men stood aside to allow the 60 nurses to get into the boats. The boats, though, were in poor condition and no one had been trained to launch them. Several boats were left hanging in mid-air, suspended by one rope. Faced with the choice between the peril of remaining on the ship and the jeopardy of the unmanageable boats, some men jumped down into the destroyers that were pulling survivors out of the water. Others dropped into the sea and were crushed between the boats and the ship. When the ship sank 50 minutes after being hit, hundreds of men were still on the deck. Knowing their own fate, they were compelled to watch the last of the overloaded rescue boats sail away from the impending vortex. Just over 400 hundred men and women died in the tragedy.

The horrific news of the *Transylvania*'s sinking was tempered by two encouraging signs on the same day. First, the Permanent Under Secretary to the Foreign Office, Lord Hardinge, reported some significant news on the situation in Germany. Bernhard Guttmann, Editor of the *Frankfurter Zeitung*, had revealed that the German government now recognized that the U-boat war had failed and 'that it would be impossible to reduce the Allies by hunger'. They were 'confident that the Western front could not be broken'. The war, Guttmann's sources said, could only be concluded by the 'complete exhaustion of all parties'.[435] The War Cabinet minutes make no mention of any discussion of this startling admission, but these revelations were manna to the Allies: Germany was admitting that its latest initiative – unrestricted sinking – was failing.

Troops boarding the SS Transylvania.

The second encouraging event of that day was the arrival of the first American destroyers at Queenstown. The six destroyers had sailed under sealed orders – although their crews would have easily guessed their destination. After battling Atlantic storms, Lieutenant Commander (later vice admiral) Joseph Taussig and his ships were greeted by the British destroyer *Mary Rose* which hoisted the signal 'Welcome to the American colours'.[436]

Later, on land, Admiral Sir Lewis Bayly asked Commander Taussig when his ships would be ready for service. Taussig replied, 'We are ready now, sir, that is as soon as we finish refuelling.'[437]

With those brief words a turning point in the war had been reached. While Germany floundered under its failing strategy, the Allies had gained the vigour and resources of the United States of America.

22
Early convoys

May 1917

'The Admiralty are now doing what I have been pressing them to do for months, but alas only in a half-hearted way.' – Beatty.[438]

CONVOYS TO THE RESCUE

The first convoys outside home waters set out from Gibraltar on May 10. Seventeen steamers took up their stations to be escorted by two Q-ships. An uneventful passage brought the ships safely to the Downs off the Kent coast 12 days later. Jellicoe failed to report this success to the War Cabinet until June 13 – over three weeks later – saying 'the only two British Convoys had been successful'.[439] It was a small-minded acknowledgement of a significant achievement.

Atlantic convoys began sailing two days later, although the Admiralty saved face by calling them 'protected sailings'. Ten merchant ships left Hampton Roads in Virginia on May 24 under the protection of the 11,000-ton armoured cruiser HMS *Roxburgh*. Although one straggler was lost off the Irish coast, the other vessels arrived without incident on the British coast on June 8. Captain Frederick Whitehead reported that the masters had been 'attentive to signals', station keeping had been 'good' and the ships' zigzagging had been 'satisfactory'.[440] So smooth was the operation that Whitehead volunteered to convoy 30 ships on his next run. (Captain Whitehead's pioneering role in convoying was rewarded by his appointment to Director of Mercantile Movements at the Admiralty in September.)

Suddenly, the so-distrusted convoys, 'known' by Jellicoe to be impracticable and rejected by his consultation with ships' masters, became routine. In June, four Hampton Roads convoys brought 60 ships across the Atlantic with the loss of only one vessel. Despite this good evidence that merchant ships could keep station in convoys and that convoys reduced the risk of successful U-boat attacks, a reluctant Admiralty insisted that these early convoys continued to be labelled 'experimental'. Such caution infuriated Beatty, as he told his mistress, Eugénie Godfrey-Faussett: 'the Admiralty are now doing what I have been pressing them to do for months, but alas only in a half-hearted way. J.J. was always a half-hearted man'.[441]

The first convoys were for inward bound shipping since the U-boats primarily attacked steamers as they neared their British destinations. The success of these early convoys led the U-boats to switch to attacking outward-bound shipping. In turn, this brought the introduction of outward-bound convoying in August 1917.

Mediterranean convoys began two weeks after the first Atlantic runs, when four merchant ships were escorted from Malta to Alexandria by four trawlers. In the first eight weeks of these convoys just two merchant ships were lost.

Jellicoe's brief, downbeat reports on the convoys to the War Cabinet were worthy of Eeyore in the Winnie-the-Pooh stories. While he perfunctorily reported the early success of the convoys, he made no mention of the significant drop in tonnage sunk. In May, monthly tonnage sunk in the Channel was down by 100,000 tons, with a further drop of 32,000 tons in June. Jellicoe was presiding over the first good news that the Admiralty had had since seeing off Scheer at Jutland in mid-1916. Yet, to judge by his tone, convoys were barely worth the bother.

Discontent with the Admiralty

Jellicoe lacked political antennae, so he never noticed the scheming behind the scenes to eject him from the Admiralty. Field Marshal Haig, one of Jellicoe's earliest critics, made a first move in the intimacy of his diary. Writing on May 7, he wondered how the Admiralty expected 'to win without fighting or running risks' and when 'old inefficient officers are seldom removed'. On that same day Haig told his wife: 'I met Jellicoe in Paris … I am afraid he does not impress me – Indeed, he strikes me as being an old woman!'[442]

Beatty, too, had increasing doubts about the value of Jellicoe at the Admiralty, telling Ethel: 'Jellicoe is very seedy and has had to go away for a rest.' He pointedly added: 'The submarine menace is no more in hand to-day than it was 3 months ago.'[443] Beatty's reaction to the sinking of a U-boat two weeks later summed up the dismal state of the navy at this time. One U-boat here or there was nothing in the immensity of the Imperial Navy's deadly onslaught, but Beatty could still remark to Ethel in July: 'You can have no idea what a fillip it is to score even a small success in times like the present.'[444]

Rather than dump their First Sea Lord, the War Cabinet opted for building more warships. To this end, they brought the civilian Sir Eric Geddes into the Admiralty to be Controller of the Navy – the traditional title for the admiral in charge of ship construction. (At that time, Geddes was the railway supremo behind the battle lines on the Western Front.) Geddes had made his name working for the North Eastern Railway (NER) where, says the Oxford Dictionary of National Biography, 'his energy, focus on the larger issues, and clear judgement were identified as ideal executive qualities'. These qualities, combined with 'his rigorous attention to statistical data' were just what the Admiralty lacked.[445] When *The Manchester Guardian* leaked the story, its headline ran 'CIVILIAN "GENIUS" FOR THE ADMIRALTY'.[446]

Joffre listens while Haig emphasises a point to Lloyd George. One of his key messages was the urgent need to remove Jellicoe from the Admiralty.

ANTI-SUBMARINE SUCCESSES AND FAILURES

May merchant sinkings brought some relief, falling to 597,000 tons – a 32 per cent reduction on the April sinkings. Even so, the latest figures remained frighteningly high.

One of the few promising developments in mid-1917 was the sinking in May of six U-boats. In no previous month had more than three boats been lost to anti-submarine actions. Two had been torpedoed; two rammed; one mined; and one bombed. The Imperial Navy also lost two boats from other causes. Five boats were commissioned that month, making a net loss of three boats. The signs were that even seasoned commanders and successful boats were now falling victim to a more experienced anti-submarine force.

Kapitänleutnant von Schmettow was one of the veteran commanders who succumbed to the more proficient anti-submarine forces – he had been in U-boats since August 1915 and had sunk nearly 110,000 tons of shipping. It was five days since he had sunk the 2000-ton steamer *Ussa* off Jersey when in *UC-26*. All he could now find for his last torpedo was the 75-ton *Iris* off Cherbourg. With his stock of mines and torpedoes exhausted, Schmettow turned east to head for Zeebrugge. At 1.00 am on the following day his boat was spotted by the destroyer HMS *Milne*. Insisting that his boat had not been sighted, Schmettow remained on the surface. He belatedly realized that HMS *Milne* was hurtling towards him. He shot down the conning tower as he ordered a crash dive. The hatch failed to close fully and water poured into the boat. *UC-26* sank uncontrollably and thumped onto the seabed. Men rushed to the conning tower and the engine room as the water rose up in the boat. Those in the engine room found they were trapped when the hatch stuck in its partly-open position. Von Schmettow and his men assumed the worst. He called for three cheers for the Kaiser as they all prepared to die. In one last bid to survive, Schmettow released compressed air into the boat. The water stopped rising and the engine room hatch opened. As it sprung back, the air pressure blasted all the nearby men out of the boat. How many men got out of the boat is not known, but only two survived.

It was now two years since the Inventions Board had been established under Fisher, but it still had nothing to offer to aid in the detection or the destruction of submarines. Its open approach of inviting the public to submit their ideas had not proved productive. The result was a flood of zany suggestions, but zaniness was no bar to an idea being taken seriously, as a May 1917 report reveals:

> In consequence of a suggestion made by the Board of Invention and Research to test the possibilities of attracting seagulls to the periscopes of submarines by ejecting food therefrom and thereby training them to follow and locate enemy submarines, the Admiralty have approved an experiment being made in submarine B3 and have asked BIR to provide a suitable food box for the purpose.[447]

Trials of stuffing bird feed into a dummy periscope went on for two months before the experiment was abandoned.

Seagulls aside, the most important area of the Board's research programme was the acoustic location of U-boats. An early version of a hydrophone had successfully detected *UC-3* in May 1916, but still, in mid-1917, hydrophones were far from ready for general use. As Jellicoe told the War Cabinet 'the trials were not proving satisfactory'.[448]

Commanders at sea were carrying out their own trials of novel methods of locating U-boats, including observing from tied balloons, and bombing by airships. There were few successes, although both methods compelled U-boats to submerge, as Spiess found in May 1917. He was in *U-9* heading for the Orkneys when he met some patrol vessels. Using the maximum magnification on his periscope he began to count off the coasters and their anti-submarine trawlers. Then his eye caught a movement in the sky, which he took to be a Zeppelin. He thought the location odd for a German airship until he realized that, hovering above him, were two British airships, searching for U-boats. Remaining submerged, Spiess took *U-9* further north. It had been his first encounter with this new type of U-boat hunter.

With monthly tonnage sunk remaining perilously high, and convoys still at an early stage, the Admiralty continued to prioritize searching for U-boats rather than using convoys to keep them at bay. It was not a productive use of men and resources. Only seven U-boats had been sunk in action in the first four months of the year – a hopelessly small number compared to the nineteen boats commissioned in this period. The action of the Q-ship HMS *Prize* on April 30 highlighted the futility of relying on finding and sinking U-boats rather than convoying.

Prize was to encounter Kapitänleutnant Edgar Spiegel. Now in *U-93*, Spiegel had had a good and a not-so-good day. He had sunk the 3200-ton Italian *Ascaro*, the 3000-ton British steamer *Horsa*, and the 3000-ton Greek *Parthenon*, but it was the *Horsa* sinking that seems to have upset him. After the ship had sunk, Spiegel and his men had helped some of the survivors. He recalled finding injured men clinging to an upside-down lifeboat: 'Some had arms and legs broken by the force with which they had been knocked down by the torpedo hit ... The sight of those poor fellows battered and broken on our deck touched them [the U-boat crew] sharply ... They put splints on legs and arms and administered drugs from our medicine chest.'[449] The submariners even rescued two men trapped under a lifeboat. It was in this sombre mood that Spiegel cautiously approached the apparently abandoned *Prize*.

Lieutenant William Sanders and his crew of 17 had only been in the newly-converted schooner for five days, so this was their first opportunity to carry out the Q-ships' 'panic stations' routine in the presence of the enemy. They did a good job, but Spiegel still sensed danger as *U-93* neared the lifeless, unkempt ship. Yet, the closer he came, the more abandoned the ship seemed to be. Its deck, he recalled, 'was a mass of wreckage' and there was not the least sign of life.

At 80 yards, Spiegel cried: 'Hit her at the water line and sink her.' *U-93*'s first shell scored a perfect hit. Water began to flood into the seemingly deserted hulk. In an instant, flaps crashed to the deck and *Prize's* 12-pounder gun erupted into vicious life. Before Spiegel could react, his fore gun had been shot to pieces and some of his gunners lay wounded on the deck. He ordered full speed ahead and a turn to port. Racing across the sea at over 16 knots Spiegel put 500 yards between the two vessels. Then his engine stopped dead. Even so, Spiegel was not ready to admit defeat. He still had one functioning gun. Along with three seamen, he raced down the deck and turned the second gun onto the *Prize*. Before they could fire a shot, one headless gunner lay at Spiegel's feet, while the sea began to rise over his boots. *U-93* was sinking. Discarding his heavy footwear, Spiegel and two seamen stepped into the sea as their boat disappeared beneath the waves.

The *Prize* was badly damaged, too, and its engines were stopped. Its inexperienced crew had to stoop to asking their prisoners for help in restarting the engines. The ship limped back to Milford Haven three days later. Sanders won a VC, while Spiegel was sent to the relative luxury of the Donnington Hall prisoner of war camp in Derbyshire. It was there that, three weeks later, he heard that *U-93* had limped home to its base. When *U-93* had sunk under Spiegel's feet, it had eight cavernous shell holes in its hull, and its upper works were a tangle of scrap metal. The starboard compressed air compartment was open to the threatening sea, as were five of the diving tanks. Precious fuel oil was leaking into the water and most of the boat's instruments had made their last readings. Both periscopes were no more. Perhaps the most alarming damage was the hatch, or rather, the lack of a hatch. Unable to dive, *U-93* returned to base using the 2000-mile journey via Iceland and the Arctic Circle to minimize the risk of being spotted. It was an agonizing nine days' navigation before, hugging the Danish coastline, the crew saw the friendly lights of a neutral nation. On reaching the safety of the German coast at the tiny settlement of List auf Sylt, *U-93* dropped anchor. A hospital ship took off the wounded, including two petty officers with shattered legs, their agony of nine days without morphine was finally over.

Donnington Hall prisoner of war camp for officers – a far more comfortable berth than the stinking confinement of a U-boat. (German Prisoners In Great Britain. Tillotson & Son 1916.)

Spiegel survived to return to waging war on the Allies in 1939, firstly in consular work and later as an SS Oberführer. *U-93* returned to sea in June and sank a further 26 ships totalling 75,000 tons before being recorded as missing in January 1918.

As to the *Prize*, it returned to sea after repairs, succumbing to *UB-48* on August 14, 1917. It sank without trace, taking Lieutenant Commander Sanders and his men with it. In its four months of service the ship had failed to sink a single U-boat.

In May 1917 Spiess returned to sea after a period of training new recruits. Although Allied anti-submarine operations were only slowly improving, he found a changed environment: 'The English, without pause or rest, had perfected their methods of attacking submarines,' he said.[450] He particularly disliked the new depth charges: 'This cursed invention was to play an important part in the daily events in the operational zone.' Nor was he keen on the Heligoland minefield, which he found to be 'extremely disagreeable ... it was impossible to enter or leave port without the aid of a minesweeper.'[451] Spiess overcame his loss of nerve and went on to sink 14 vessels in the remainder of 1917 and a further 12 vessels in 1918.

SMALL BOATS AND A BIG BARRAGE

The foci of the U-boat war were the North Sea and the Western Approaches, but operations continued on a smaller scale in the Mediterranean. The centre of the activity was the Otranto Barrage between Brindisi and Corfu. It was there that a typical action took place in May 1917, involving the small craft that patrolled the barrage against passages by the superior forces of the Central Powers.

The 22-year-old Joseph Watt was a typical guardian of the barrage. He came from the Scottish fishing village of Gardenstown near Banff and had enlisted at the outbreak of war. Now he was serving as skipper in the drifter *Gowanlea* – one of 120 drifters that maintained a 24-hour patrol of the barrier's 45 miles. The 85-foot wooden vessel boasted just one six-pounder gun. Watt was in the *Gowanlea* on the night that the Austro-Hungarian Navy attacked the patrol with four destroyers and a light cruiser.

Watt's *Gowanlea* was soon prow-to-prow with the Austro-Hungarian 3500-ton cruiser *Novara*. When the *Novara* demanded the trawler's surrender, Watt countered by calling for full steam ahead. *Gowanlea* with its lone gun was now pitched against the *Novara*'s multiple weapons: there was no contest. Shell after shell blasted into the drifter. One carried away the port railings, shattered the bulwarks and disabled the gun. Another blew a gunner into the water. More shells found their targets as the tiny boat fought on.

The shattered *Gowanlea* crept away and its remaining able-bodied seamen turned to rescue work. With 14 out of 47 drifters sunk that night, there was no shortage of wounded men to be plucked from the sea. Watt won a VC for his part in the action. Another 31 medals and awards were won that night.

THE THREAT OF RATIONING

The cataclysmic sinkings of the first few months of 1917 were putting an increasing strain on Britain's food supply. Once again, the War Cabinet discussed rationing and, once again, the members shied away from such intrusive state interference in everyday life. Instead, Lord Devonport, announced maximum prices for Burma peas and beans, of which over 50,000 tons were being imported annually. Only in a *Times*' footnote of May 2 did readers discover the more portentous news: 'plans for the adoption, if necessary, of compulsory food rationing ... are being pushed forward'.[452]

With food supplies now under threat, even the King could not avoid showing constraint, as Walter Page found when he spent an evening with the monarch: 'he gave us only so much bread, one egg apiece, and lemonade,' Page told Doubleday.[453] A few weeks later, the King appealed to his people 'to practise the greatest economy and frugality in the use of every species of grain', asking them to cut their bread consumption by a quarter.[454] This message was reinforced by the illustrative claim that a saving of one teaspoon of breadcrumbs per person per day amounted to 40,000 tons per year.

The first National Kitchen on the day of its opening by Queen Mary, May 21, 1917. (Imperial War Museum.)

With food prices rising, and some foods in short supply, Queen Mary opened Britain's first National Kitchen in Westminster Bridge Road on May 21. (Although called 'national' these kitchens were set up and run by local organizations.) Within days of that opening, the Women's Institute in the market town of Cullompton in Devon had opened its own National Kitchen and had sold 150 meals 'in minutes'. It then opened twice a week for full meals and one day a week for soup. By the end of the war, the kitchen had served 3000 meals. The *Western Morning News* reporter who visited the restaurant in February, found that 3 d bought 'an excellent plate of meat soup with vegetables and potatoes' with, to follow, treacle pudding. But a similar venture in Exeter closed within six months of opening. (Many National Kitchens were shunned by the poorer classes, who saw in them uncomfortable echoes of soup kitchens and Lady Bountiful condescension.)

While starvation, disease and shortages of every description were sapping the German home front, Walter Page marvelled at the changes taking place around him in London. 'This country and these people are not the country and the people they were three years ago,' he told his friend Frank Doubleday. 'They are very different. They are much more democratic, far less cocksure, far less haughty, far humbler.' The war, Page said, 'is making England over again. There never was a more interesting thing to watch and to be part of.'[455]

THE PROMISE OF CONVOYS

The ease with which the merchant masters took to the discipline of sailing in convoy surprised many people. Even the U-boat commanders were impressed at the skills of the convoyed masters. Spiess was one of the first to observe this new tactic when in his *U-19* 'They [the merchant ships] followed a perfect line, something that we had always judged impossible for merchant ships – particularly given their varying tonnages. Every ten minutes, the convoy changed course by 20 degrees behind the leader. The clearway was maintained by four escorts in a fantail in front of the convoy ... The whole formation gave the impression of a well-trained naval division.'[456] His admiration changed to despondency when he tried to attack such a convoy on May 9. He had worked *U-19* into a firing position that was well clear of the escort. All was ready for his first torpedo to burst from its tube. One last check through the periscope. Too late! The convoy was changing tack. After repositioning: 'Fire!' Spiess had no time to track his hastily despatched weapon. His boat shook as a depth charge exploded nearby. 'Submerge!' The torpedo ran under its target. The convoy passed on. And Spiess was left to contemplate the Allies' new terms of engagement.

Spiess also testified to one of the fundamental justifications for convoys: fewer targets. As he put it: 'not a sail, nor any smoke on the horizon'.[457] What he had witnessed was the point that Jellicoe never understood: convoys group ships into huddles. Huddles are hard to find in the immensity of the ocean. Spiess's own sinking figures bear this out. In May he sank five merchant ships. June saw four go to the bottom from his torpedoes. He had no success in July and had to wait until the last day of August to sink the 6400-ton *Miniota*. Two ships went down in September, none in the next two months. Then on December 28 he marked the end of the year with a final two sinkings.

By a fortunate coincidence for the Allies, convoys were introduced around the time that Britain's direction-finding stations were beginning to regularly locate U-boats through their careless radio transmissions to their bases. The timely reports of the code breakers in Room 40 enabled commanders to reroute convoys away from the path of the marauding boats. A typical daily report in July sent to Vice Admiral Bayly at Queenstown and to Beatty at Scapa Flow identified five U-boats operating off the south west of Ireland and three off the Scilly Isles, plus a minelaying boat around the Shetland area.

Despite these promising signs, at the end of May both optimists and pessimists could find reasons to sustain their predictions for the outcome of the war at sea. Only a reckless gambler would have bet on the outcome. The U-boat war was still in the balance.

23
The battle of the breakfast tables

Summer 1917

'The seriously inefficient state of the Admiralty'. – Haig, June 25, 1917.[458]

A FRIEND IN NEED

Fifty-two days after Ambassador Page and Admiral Sims had appealed to President Wilson to send vastly more ships across the water, and with around one million additional tons sunk, Sims still had only 28 destroyers. Writing from Admiralty House at Queenstown, he told Page: 'There are at least seventeen more destroyers employed on our Atlantic coast, where there is no war, not to mention numerous other very useful anti-submarine craft, including sea-going tugs, etc.'[459] It seemed as if the naval war would be over before large numbers of American warships were to cross the Atlantic.

Page and Sims realized that the American government did not believe their accounts of the perilous state of Britain's shipping. What more could they do, wondered Page. Suddenly, he saw the solution: they needed the help of someone whom the Americans trusted, someone who everyone knew would neither lie nor exaggerate: Arthur Balfour. As the Oxford Dictionary of National Biography remarks, Balfour had 'a reputation for sagacity' in defence matters both at home and abroad. No one was better placed to tell the truth to President Wilson. Balfour willingly played his part, writing to Wilson: 'it is absolutely necessary to add to our forces as a first step, pending the adoption or completion of measures which will, it is hoped, eventually lead to the destruction of enemy submarines at a rate sufficient to ensure safety of our sea communications. The United States is the only allied country in a position to help.'[460]

ONE MORE HEAVE?

There were anxieties in the Imperial Navy as well at this time. By June 1, when four months of unrestricted sinking had passed, there were still no signs of a British capitulation. Admirals, generals and civil servants met on June 2 in a melancholy mood. With no expectation of a victory on land, they once more agreed that the U-boats were the key to victory. They resolved to intensify the war at sea. Every boat that could be completed by January 1, 1919, was to be built. A further ninety-five U-boats were to be ordered (8 type U; 37 type UB-II; 39 type UC-II; and ten 2000-ton U-cruisers). There was, though, an element of delusion in this decision since every passing day left Germany weaker in manpower and materials. U-boat commissioning had peaked in 1916 at 108 new boats. The last two years of the war would see 87 boats commissioned in 1917 and 85 in 1918.

At the same time as commissioning large-scale boat production, the German Admiralty ordered the German Legation in Mexico in June to instruct the German agent-saboteur Kurt Jahnke to 'make every possible preparation' with 'close attention to all details' for establishing a U-boat base in Mexico. Since it was vital that the Allied Powers knew nothing of this plan, all supplies were to be shipped in sailing ships using auxiliary motors, crewed by 'well paid' Germans and Mexican-Germans. Jahnke was to select 'some unfrequented place' on the east side of the Yucatán Channel. Nothing seems to have come of this. Had work ever begun, it would have been quickly frustrated since Room 40 was reading the instructions to Jahnke, perhaps as fast as he was receiving them. (Jahnke had a record of sabotage in the United States, including a major explosion at the Mare Island Naval Shipyard in March 1917. He had moved to Mexico when the Americans entered the war.)

The introduction of convoys had coincided with the Imperial Navy's decision to resurrect the redundant cargo U-boats and convert them into raiders. With their long endurance they would be able to roam the distant seas off South America. The first to put to sea was the *Deutschland*, now reappearing as *U-155* under the command of Kapitänleutnant Karl Meusel. Beginning with the sinking of 1700-ton Norwegian *Hafursfjord* when south of Iceland on June 2, Meusel made his way far into the Atlantic Ocean. By August 7, he had sunk 19 ships totalling 54,000 tons of which only five were British. With no Allied anti-submarine forces in these remote waters, *U-155* voyaged over 10,000 unhindered miles. All but 620 miles were on the surface. Other U-boats joined in, enjoying the relative safety of these waters. In August, the British Admiralty responded by introducing new convoys for the South Atlantic trade routes. This speedy action, compared to the Admiralty's earlier lax record, showed that it was, at last, fully converted to convoys.

There was one U-boat action in June that was of little immediate consequence but was of longer term interest. On June 8 the 4000-ton *Isle Of Jura* was sunk by the U-boat ace Kapitänleutnant Walter Forstmann. For a man who would sink a total of 391,000 tons, the *Jura* was of little importance, but history takes an interest because Forstmann's Oberleutnant zur See was the 26-year-old Karl Dönitz, who would mastermind the Second World War U-boat campaign. Dönitz could not have had a better role model – Forstmann is still the second most successful submarine commander in terms of tonnage sunk. He certainly instilled into (the no doubt willing) Dönitz the ruthlessness needed for the job. When *U-39* sank a troopship, Dönitz said, 'I am not quite satisfied' since 'only 150 soldiers were lost out of 900'. This was 'a comparatively small loss to the enemy.' He continued: 'The object of war is to annihilate the armed forces of the enemy.'[461] In fact, Dönitz had less reason to be disappointed than he thought since the vessel concerned seems to have been the troopship *Minas*, which Forstmann sank on February 15, 1917. Nearly 900 people (mostly Italian, Serbian, and French soldiers) died in the sinking.

CONVOYS ASCENDENT

While the Imperial Navy searched for some means of delivering its promised victory, the British Admiralty had finally produced a plan for a full system of convoys – four months after the Imperial Navy had begun unrestricted sinking and with 2,600,000 tons sunk in that interval. The plan was quickly approved before being distributed on June 25. Progress would be slow, though. Taking May as the month when the convoys effectively began in earnest, the first four months under convoy resulted in average sinkings per month of 588,000 tons – near enough the same as the 596,000 tons for January to April.

In June the Admiralty tacitly admitted that convoys were the way forward when it established a Convoy Section under Fleet Paymaster H W E Manisty. His responsibilities included working with the Intelligence Division to ensure that convoy commodores always had the latest intelligence on U-boat activities. This required regular captures of ever-changing German code books, taken from sunken U-boats. A special team of divers was kept on standby, trained to recognize the relevant documents and to know their hiding places.

With convoys in rapid development, it would have been logical to end (or at least reduce) the manifestly pointless grand searches for U-boats, so releasing destroyers and cruisers for escorting. This was not how the Admiralty saw it in mid-June. Room 40 had reported that a large number of U-boats were to take the northerly route out of the North Sea around 15-24 June. Admiralty House ordered the Grand Fleet to undertake Operation BB, using all available destroyers and submarines to hunt down the U-boats. This action was to have 'priority over all other operations'. Beatty saw this as a splendid opportunity to sink U-boats before they had even begun their hunting. A force of four flotilla leaders, 49 destroyers and 17 submarines set out to catch the boats. Beatty had underestimated the skill of the German submariners, who were old hands at evading the clutches of surface craft. During the operation, Beatty's ships claimed to have sighted 37 U-boats and to have made attacks on ten boats. Even so, every single U-boat passed through the barrage of steel and powder, leaving in their trails eight merchant ships and one armed-trawler sunk. Two weeks later, Beatty's force claimed to have sunk a U-boat. He was not, though, triumphant, telling Ethel: 'these odd ones here and there are not sufficient. We must do much better than that or be defeated.'[462]

A few weeks later Beatty – despite his ardent support of convoys – was still showing a lingering faith in searches, writing to his wife: 'Our luck has been very bad. Every day we are within an ace of success, sometimes in two & even three places, but they can't quite pull it off ... It is a prodigious job, as it is like looking for a needle in a bundle of hay, and, when you have found it, trying to strike it with another needle. But we must stick to it ...'[463]

At the War Cabinet meeting of July 25, the Admiralty finally admitted the efficacy of convoys when Vice Admiral Henry Oliver, Deputy Chief of the Naval Staff, reported on sinkings for the previous 24 hours. The figures were too secret to be included in the minutes, but, said Oliver, the reports of 'the immunity of convoyed ships were most encouraging'.[464] Five days later the First Sea Lord reported that a convoy of 60 ships was approaching Home Waters without having lost a single ship.

Anti-submarine success: This year? Next year?

While convoys were showing encouraging results in reducing sinkings, finding and destroying U-boats remained problematic. From the start of the unrestricted sinking campaign, Germany had lost 21 U-boats but only 13 of those losses were due to British and French anti-submarine operations.

The battle of the breakfast tables

In search of an answer, the Admiralty arranged large-scale operational trials of the developing hydrophones, using four flotillas of six motor launches, based at Newhaven, Portsmouth, Portland and Dartmouth. It was painstaking work, listening for the faintest of sounds and trying to follow a trail without drawing attention to the tracking vessel. A few submarines were successfully followed for a few miles but they eventually eluded their pursuers. These results were all the more disappointing in that the trials had been carried out in ideal conditions: fine summer weather and with no other craft in the vicinity. These were laboratory conditions, not the conditions of war. At best, the results were good enough not to give up on the research on hydrophones, but not good enough to lay much of a bet on their imminent utility. Jellicoe's report to the War Cabinet was bluntly honest. The latest device, he told them on June 15, had been expected to detect U-boats up to a range of four miles, but 'was not proving satisfactory'.[465]

Depth charges were showing more promise, although their effective use was hindered by their trickle of a supply, plus a shortage of depth-charge throwers. In the last six months of the war, output would reach 2000 depth-charges per month, but in July 1917, the factories were turning out only 140 per month.

The Admiralty Board might have hoped for some ingenious new device from the Inventions Board, where Fisher had made anti-submarine warfare the Board's highest priority. The Board's work, though, was ill-supported by Admiralty House, as Fisher found in mid-1917. The Board hypothesized that much could be learnt from studying successful actions against U-boats, so Fisher asked the Admiralty for details of both successful and unsuccessful actions. His request, recalled Admiral Sir William Hall, caused great alarm in the Admiralty. The thought that top secret details of, for example, how a destroyer located a particular U-boat, being released outside the confines of Admiralty House was beyond imagining. The Inventions Board was cold-shouldered as the Admiralty chose obstruction rather than cooperation with its own research arm.

Air searches for U-boats were becoming increasingly common by mid-1917. Although only four U-boats are known to have been sunk by aeroplanes during the war, the presence of planes compelled U-boats to dive. Oberleutnant zur See Benno von Ditfurth in *UB-32* had sunk 11 ships in April. He blamed his sinking of only four boats in June on the ever-present air patrols. Oberleutnant zur See Karl Wacker also blamed strong air patrols, which repeatedly forced him to dive, for his failure to make any sinkings from June 17 to August 3. Kapitänleutnant Walter Remy reported an even closer encounter with the air patrols when planes dropped 20 bombs around his *U-90*. In the case of *U-34,* bombing by two float planes caused considerable damage to the boat even after it had crash dived.

As the Admiralty turned towards convoying in preference to search-and-destroy, one other anti-submarine tactic had not yet been attempted: the capture of the U-boat bases in Belgium. (The September 1916 proposal for the capture of the coastal strip had not been pursued.) The drive behind this new proposal came from Haig, who met Admiral Bacon at Calais on June 17 to discuss joint action. Haig wrote in his diary '[Bacon] is wholeheartedly with us, and has urged in writing to the Admiralty the absolute necessity for clearing the Belgium coast before winter.'[466] Nothing came of this, although the Admiralty bombed Belgian aerodromes and railway stations, leading the Imperial Navy to abandon the Ostend naval base in July. According to Bacon, 'after this date no vessel was ever seen inside Ostend harbour'.[467] By December, capture of the bases had become impossible since German troops from the Russian front were pouring through Belgium to reinforce the Western Front.

A GENERAL ON THE WARPATH

Field Marshal Douglas Haig was in England for the last two weeks of June for talks with the War Cabinet and the War Office. More informally, he went the rounds of the great and the good, including Colonel Repington at *The Times* and Queen Mary. His primary reason for such a long visit was his feeling, he told Lord Derby, that the War Cabinet had no confidence in 'my plan'. (This was not surprising since his plan was Passchendaele, which would add around 300,000 names to the casualty lists.)

Less officially, Haig had his eye on the ineffectual Admiralty. At separate meetings with Lord Curzon and the Prime Minister on June 25, he told them of his concern about 'the seriously inefficient state of the Admiralty'. On the following day, Haig was back for breakfast with the Prime Minister and Lord Milner. He listened to their proposals to replace 'Jellicoe and two or three other "numbskulls" now on the Board.'[468] The Prime Minister agreed that Jellicoe had to go, but made no commitment to act. Desperate to see changes made without delay, Haig rushed to the War Office to try to persuade Sir William Robertson, Chief of the

Imperial Staff, to take over as First Lord of the Admiralty. He refused, 'as that would mean becoming a politician!'[469]

On July 4 Ambassador Bertie recorded in his diary how Carson had described his work at the Admiralty as 'very strenuous' but 'all our men here and in the fleets work with great enthusiasm and loyalty'.[470] As Carson indulged in his complacent assessment of his work, Lloyd George was writing to King George to seek his approval for removing the First Lord from his post. Twelve days later, out went Carson and in came Geddes as the new First Lord of the Admiralty. Jellicoe survived the coup. As First Lord, Geddes needed a seat in the House of Commons. Mr Almeric Paget, the member for Cambridge, volunteered to resign his seat and Geddes was returned unopposed to Parliament one week later. (Paget's sacrifice was rewarded with a peerage in January 1918.)

Fantasy shipbuilding

In July, the continuing high losses of merchant shipping brought a new crisis: coal supplies. Both Italy and France depended heavily on British coal during the First World War. (France, in particular, had lost most of its coal fields to the German invasion in 1914, resulting in a fall in output from 22,000 million metric tons in 1913 to 2000 million metric tons in 1917.) In the winter of 1916-17, Italy had received only 60 per cent of its needs – in one week, the supply was 98 per cent below target. France, too, was in trouble, having received only 68 per cent of its requirements. Without more shipping, these deficiencies would only worsen. Yet, as the War Cabinet heard at the end of June, Britain had lost 2.1 m gross tons of shipping in the first six months of 1917 and world losses were 3.7 m tons. An emergency transfer of some of France's coal to Italy was ordered, although this did nothing to relieve the shipping crisis. There were three ways to alleviate this emergency: reduce imports, reduce sinkings and build more ships. The War Cabinet turned to this last, pie-in-the-sky, option at its meeting on July 10.

Building more ships was an attractive sounding policy, but the stark truth was that the June losses of 688,000 tons were *more than the entire output* of new shipping in 1916 at 630,000 tons. Even so, Geddes presented a proposal to build 'at least 3,100,000 tons' a year, which was an unthinkable figure compared to past performance. As if this far-fetched figure was not ridiculous enough, Sir Joseph Maclay protested that it was far too low. But the War Cabinet's discussion soon brought the fantasy shipbuilders back to reality: there was not enough labour to build Geddes' mammoth merchant fleet. The army was already below strength and agriculture was desperate for more workers. And, even if the men could be found, where was the steel to come from? As the Cabinet members grasped these truths, the Admiralty added one further demand: the men and steel would have to be found 'without delay' to take advantage of the good weather. Not surprisingly, the War Cabinet approved the report 'in principle' but took no steps to provide the men and the steel. As in Germany, the never-ending war was leading to ever-fewer options.

The shipping discussion had shown that the War Cabinet had still not accepted the futility of trying to beat the U-boats by out-building the sinkings. It was a fool's way of waging war. Geddes' proposed 3.1 m tons per year – had these ships been built – would have been wiped out in a year by sinkings of only 250,000 tons per month. Even before Germany had begun unrestricted sinking, the U-boats had sunk 367,000 tons in a single month: January 1917. Two days later, reality had returned to the War Cabinet as they discussed reinforcing convoying rather than trying to outbuild U-boat depredations. The members asked the Admiralty to review its distribution of anti-submarine craft with the aim of releasing 88 destroyers for convoy work. They were asked to report back in seven days' time. Once more it was those outside the Admiralty who were best able to see what needed to be done, and who best understood the urgency.

HARDENING HEARTS

After nearly three years of war, and with no sign of a German victory, the strains on human endurance were showing. Discontent on the German home front and mutinous insurrections in the German fleet were matched by hardened hearts in the U-boats, as the crew of the British steamer *Belgian Prince* found on the last day of July.

Kapitänleutnant Wilhelm Werner in *U-55* was cruising 175 miles north of Ireland when he encountered the 4700-ton cargo boat *Belgian Prince* in passage from Liverpool to Newport News in Virginia, carrying a full hold of blue clay. Just one of Werner's torpedoes was enough for the vessel to begin to fill with water. With no time to launch the boats, *Belgian Prince*'s crew jumped into the sea and were soon Werner's prisoners. He lined them up on the deck of *U-55* while his men destroyed the *Belgian Prince*'s lifeboats and took away the men's lifejackets, oars and spars. Having removed all means of the seamen's survival, Werner and his men disappeared down the conning tower and closed the hatch. Down went *U-55* along with Werner's one prisoner: Captain Harry Hassan.

Chief Engineer Thomas Bowman on the deck of the U-boat described that moment: 'Suddenly, I heard a rush of water and, shouting "look out, she's sinking," I jumped into the water ... Near me was an apprentice, aged 16, shouting for help, I held him up in darkness until about midnight when he became unconscious and died from exposure.'[471] Of the *Belgian Prince*'s crew of 41 men, just three survived to be picked up 11 hours later by a patrol vessel which took them to Londonderry, where the Sailors' Rest took care of them. By early August, news of the atrocity had reached London and was discussed by the War Cabinet on August 3. The First Sea Lord was asked 'to take steps to publish particulars of the outrage'.[472] The story, with accounts from Bowman and the second engineer, G Siliski, appeared in *The Times* on August 4. It was a shocking encounter but, fortunately, not typical of the war at sea. Perhaps Werner's action was one of despair as he contemplated the failure of the six months' unrestricted sinking to deliver the promised victory.

Digging for victory

For the British people, food stocks were proving resilient in mid-1917. There were shortages in different places at different times, mostly caused by distribution problems, but there was no absolute dearth. Britain was also fortunate in having thousands of acres of good fallow farmland. Lloyd George's *Corn Production Act* had set guaranteed prices for cereal crops, so providing an incentive for farmers to bring more land into cultivation. This resulted in an additional 2.2 m acres under the plough. Even royalty joined in, as the King's flowerbeds at Buckingham Palace burst forth with fresh vegetables.

More land under cultivation needed more workers in the fields. In June, the War Cabinet decided to send factory workers into the fields to bring in the harvest. Meanwhile, the army was to stop recruiting from the land and was ordered to supply 5000 men a week for ten weeks. The sight of the army compensating for the failures of the Admiralty set a new low for the navy.

It was at this time that Lloyd George ordered the building up of emergency food stocks as a precaution against the possible failure of the anti-submarine campaign. Also, he still feared the never-ending stalemate on the Western Front. Sugar stocks rose from 18,000 tons in May 1917 to

209,000 tons in January 1918 and reached 414,000 tons by the end of the war. This was an astonishing reserve of around 20 lb per person. There were similar reserves of meat, bacon, tea, cheese, butter and lard.

Women spreading manure as Britain brought more land into cultivation. (Illustrated War News, January 24, 1917.)

HUNGER, NOTHING BUT HUNGER

With unrestricted sinking having failed to drive Britain out of the war, the German people were faced with the prospect of a second Turnip Winter – one that was bound to be even worse than that of 1916-1917. Severe shortages made a nonsense of the official prices: in the south, black market prices were twice the official level; in Western Galicia (now part of Poland), illicit supplies were sold at six times the official figure. Ordinary people faced starvation by edict (rations of just 1100 calories per person per day) or starvation by poverty through being unable to afford black market prices. The meat ration was reduced to half-a-pound a week. Genuine coffee had disappeared from the shops and even the rationed ersatz version produced from barley was cut to 4 oz per month. Eggs were limited to one per week and butter to 1 oz per week. Nor were shortages confined to the civilian population. In the fleet, the men had 'miserable' rations while the officers ate well.[473] The working horses were treated no better. Before the war a working horse was fed 20 lb of oats a day. Their new ration was just 3 lb.

The battle of the breakfast tables

In July, the sailors in the light cruiser SMS *Pillau* refused to perform their duties as they gathered in the mess room and announced that they were on hunger strike. The next day, 140 men left the ship. This particular dispute fizzled out, but, a few days later, there were much more serious disturbances in the battleship SMS *Prinzregent Luitpold*. The arrest of 11 men escalated to a point where the army was called in. Other ships caught the atmosphere. One of the most protracted stand-offs was in the battleship *Friedrich der Grosse*. What started as a dispute over the quality of the soup, led to the next watch refusing to work. On this occasion the potential mutiny was brought to an end by the good sense of the officers, who listened to the complaints and acted on them. The ship returned to normality as the men were given more leave and better food, along with concerts and games to relieve the tedium of port-bound ship life. But this was just the beginning of what would become a full-blown fleet mutiny in the last days of the war. The submariners, though, had no time for mutinous thoughts as they continued to go out on patrol after patrol. Their war was not over. There were always more Allied ships to sink.

WHERE NEXT?

On June 28 another letter about the Admiralty's deficiencies landed on Lloyd George's desk. This came from the Shipping Controller, Joseph Maclay, who warned the Prime Minister of a new and potentially very serious problem: the Mercantile Marine were on the brink of refusing to put to sea: '[their] confidence in the Admiralty has pretty well gone'. The masters were protesting against the 'concentration areas': places where merchant ships gathered to form a convoy. While gathering, the ships lay without protection. The U-boats had discovered these easy pickings, which, Maclay told George, 'have become veritable death traps'. Fearing that the Prime Minister might not act, Maclay copied his letter to the Tory Party leader, Bonar Law, telling him, 'Changes are wanted right from the top downwards.'[474] The pressure was building on the Prime Minister to act over Jellicoe.

By July 31, Germany had waged six months of unrestricted sinking without the least sign of the promised British capitulation. Nothing suggested that the Imperial Navy could sink enough merchant ships, fast enough, to bring victory at sea before defeat came on land.

At the same time, the Allies had failed to sink enough U-boats to give any sense of victory at sea.

The battle of the breakfast tables

Could either side switch the balance in its favour?

24
Convoys on trial

Late 1917

'On the whole the convoy system had ... proved satisfactory.'
– Geddes' report to the War Cabinet, September 5, 1917.[475]

JELLICOE WAVERS

By August, the convoy system was developing rapidly, but the addition of incoming convoys was putting a huge strain on the navy's resources. The work was relentless: as soon as an escort had dropped off an incoming convoy it set off on two days of zigzagging to reach its next pick-up location.

Despite these difficulties, the speed with which the convoy system developed negated Jellicoe's repeated assertions that the navy did not have enough ships to provide escorts. The 238 ships convoyed in August was double the July figure and the system was still growing, with Mediterranean convoys beginning in September.

The U-boat commanders did their best to adapt to the convoys. In the early days of convoying they concentrated on the empty un-convoyed ships returning to America. Once convoys were running in both directions, the cruiser U-boats were dispatched to distant waters. Later, and until the end of the war, the U-boats favoured British coastal waters, where they tried to catch ships before joining and after leaving convoys. In one of his reports in 1917, Duff noted that, from April to August, 175 ships (35 per month) had been sunk over 50 miles from land. From September to December, only six had been sunk that far out. This shift to local hunting grounds ensured that merchant crews were much more likely to be rescued, and damaged anti-submarine craft were more likely to be recovered for repair.

By September convoys were routine, so they received little attention in the War Cabinet. That, coupled with Jellicoe's laconic reporting style, meant that their successes were never celebrated. A typical Jellicoe report was that of September 7: 'The First Sea Lord added that there were at present 224 ships at sea under convoy, excluding two convoys as to which the numbers comprised in the same were not yet known, but probably consisted of about eighteen ships in each.'[476] Jellicoe could also have mentioned the Admiralty's success in reducing sinkings. Only 1.43 per cent of homeward-bound ships had been lost. Outward-bound did even better with losses of under one per cent. Admiralty House's apparent continued hostility towards convoys meant that there was no sound of popping champagne corks as the good news came in. Instead, on at least one occasion, a staff officer's favourable remarks in a report on convoys were edited out.

A zigzagging merchant convoy.(Hurd 1917. 'The Merchant Navy', Vol. 3.)

By the end of September the convoys had proved their worth. Sinkings for the month had fallen to 352,000 tons against a mean for the preceding six months of 624,000 tons – a 48 per cent reduction in monthly tonnage sunk.

The convoys had also brought additional benefits. Rather than attack convoys, the U-boat commanders now preferred to hunt in the un-convoyed coastal waters. In these waters, small ships predominated, so commanders had to forego sinking the ocean giants. Even the small fry were increasingly hard to find. Kapitänleutnant Alfred Saalwächter in *U-93*, having sunk or damaged 12 vessels in June and July, found the seas deserted by August. His sinkings plummeted to three in August, two in September and two in December. Of his September to October patrol, he recalled: 'we saw only one steamer and one sailing vessel'. He was alerted to the presence of two nearby convoys but 'we failed to get close enough in to shoot'.[477] In September, the U-boats sank only 43 ships of over 500 tons. Added to the poor hunting, destroyers were never far away in coastal waters, causing commanders to be cautious about when and where they attacked. They did, though sink around ten per cent of the independent sailings. Meanwhile, in the convoys, sinkings plummeted to between one and two per cent.[478]

Further confirmation of the success of convoys came in mid-October when the Admiralty closed the Cape route to and from India in October. The shorter Mediterranean Sea route was safe once more.

With convoys established, it was time for the Admiralty to review the fundamental problem of the U-boat war: the need to find and destroy U-boats at a faster rate than Germany could build them. An Inter-Allied Naval Conference in September did little to illuminate this conundrum. The participants agreed that the best location for finding U-boats was at the exits from their bases but the best method of destroying the boats – mines – had nothing to do with locating them. Surface patrols using hydrophones, and spotters in kite balloons scoured the seas but rarely brought any sightings. And, when contact was made with a U-boat, destruction was rarer still. In the eight months prior to the conference there had been 216 contacts with U-boats but only one boat had been destroyed. Indeed, a sinking was a significant event as the commander of an American destroyer found in early September when he sank a U-boat. He signalled to Queenstown: 'Have sunk German submarine in position lat. 51° 30′ N., long. 8° 10 W′. Where am I?' to which Admiral Bayly replied: 'Top of the class!'[479] During three years of war, British anti-submarine methods had made little progress. In the month immediately preceding the September conference, the Imperial Navy lost five boats: three struck mines, one was rammed, and one sunk by its own mine. Meanwhile, 12 new U-boats went into commission in that month.

It was at the Inter-Allied Naval Conference that Admiral Sims – the newcomer who brought a fresh eye to the U-boat war – pointed out that convoys were not purely *defensive* as the British Admiralty seemed to think, but were also *offensive* since they 'compelled the enemy submarine to fight at a disadvantage'. (A point that Hankey had made in his February 'brainwave' paper on convoys.) This, Sims told the British admirals, was 'the one and only method of placing the U-boats on the chess-board of submarine warfare in a position of strategical and tactical checkmate'. The British commanders, he said, had missed the key question which was '[W]hat reply the enemy would make to the convoy system?'[480]

A LEAKY BARRAGE AND A DETERMINED COMMANDER

Although the Imperial Navy was now deploying an increasing number of inexperienced boat commanders, some of the longest serving men continued to confound Allied attempts to clear them from the seas. Success for the U-boat commanders was, though, becoming more elusive as autumn storms and hard-to-find convoys frustrated even the most experienced.

Spiess, who had returned to patrolling in May, had sunk five ships in that month and four in June. Then came two barren months. By the time that he was approaching the Dover Barrage at midnight on August 26 he was desperate to redeem his reputation as a successful commander. The strong wind whipped up the rain, smashing heavy drops into his eyes as he stood on the conning tower of *U-19*, peering into the unfriendly night. Hostile as it was, the weather was perfect for attempting to pass through the barrage since the patrols would be conveniently distracted by the heavy sea. Meanwhile, Spiess had other things than the waves to worry about. Ahead, were the buoy lights, bobbing vigorously in the swell. Beneath, were the nets and mines. But, to starboard, the masked lights of Calais provided a useful navigational aid. He ordered the engines stopped. He needed all the fine control of the electric motors to navigate the tangle of obstructions that lay ahead. *U-19* would soon be within inches of death by mine or capture by entanglement. For a moment, Spiess hesitated. He knew the risks. He had no idea what his chances of a safe passage were. Then, 'Slow ahead!'

Boldly ignoring the buoys that brushed the sides of his boat, Spiess edged ahead as his lookouts desperately sought clear patches in this sea of death. Fifteen minutes later, still unharmed, *U-19* was in a field of bobbing lights. There was not a sign of a patrol – only the darkness and the driving rain. Then Cap Gris-Nez on the French coast came into sight: *U-19* was through the barrage! Ahead, lay the Atlantic convoys. For now, though, the sea was the submariners' enemy. High, pounding waves threw the boat in every direction while the pummelling winds tore sheet metal off the conning tower. Slowly, *U-19* advanced, reaching Portsmouth after two days of desperate sailing. The tempest continued to rage around the small boat, forcing Spiess and his men to lie off the coast for two fruitless days, impotently watching targets moving to and fro.

Living conditions were especially bad since *U-19* was stuffed with extra torpedoes. For the sake both of the German war and of the men, the sooner their weapons were discharged, the better.

Spiess' chance came on September 1 when he found some ships in convoy at the western end of the Channel. One torpedo was enough to send the Norwegian SS *Akaroa* to the bottom, along with its cargo of grease and oil. At a mere 1350 tons it was a small reward for six days of gruelling sailing. Apart from sinking a 65-ton collier on 12 September, it would be 118 days before *U-19* next sank a merchant vessel. With one engine out of use, Spiess turned north to return to Wilhelmshaven via the west coast, Scotland and the North Sea, arriving on September 28. It had been a wretched patrol with just three vessels sunk, totalling 8000 tons. This was the new war. A war in which the U-boats would have to fight ever harder for ever diminishing returns. But the German people retained their faith in the boats as they rushed to subscribe to the issue of the seventh War Bond. Despite their poor rations, low morale and simmering insurrection five-and-a-half million people subscribed to raise just over 12½ m marks.

Twilight of the Q-ships

The U-boats were not the only vessels to find that the war was changing. The Q-ships, too, were struggling as the U-boat commanders grew more wary of seemingly disabled ships. The courage and skill of the Q-ship commanders were no longer sufficient to overcome the experience and circumspection of the U-boat commanders, as Commander Gordon Campbell found when he took on *UC-71* on August 8.

Campbell was on patrol in HMS *Dunraven* when he encountered *UC-71* under the command of Oberleutnant zur See Reinhold Saltzwedel in the Bay of Biscay. It was to be a battle of the giants of their trades. Saltzwedel had already sunk 111 ships and Campbell was the hero of the battle between HMS *Farnborough* and *U-83* in February. Saltzwedel began firing at a range of 5000 yards, to which Campbell replied with deliberately short-falling shots from a 2½ pound gun. At the same time, his wireless operator kept up the pretence of *Dunraven* being a harmless merchant ship as he sent out calls of 'Submarine chasing and shelling me' and 'Am abandoning ship'. Meanwhile, a panic party made the usual display of frantically taking to the boats. Below, Campbell's engineers feigned engine trouble. Clouds of black smoke and escaping steam enveloped the ship. Saltzwedel slowly approached *Dunraven* while still firing. Unconvinced of the ship's innocence, he sent a shell through *Dunraven*'s poop. One lieutenant lay dead and one depth charge exploded on the deck.

Campbell was now in serious trouble since the magazine was in the poop. Another well-aimed shell would bring a swift end to *Dunraven* and its men. The pretence had to end. A buzzer reverberated round the ship and the flaps came down to reveal *Dunraven*'s guns. Still, Campbell hesitated to order 'Open fire' since only the gun on the after bridge was able to bear on *UC-71*. His hesitation brought more shells, which caught two depth charges and some cordite on the deck. The 4-inch gun was carried away along with its crew. Saltzwedel realized that the shower of debris came from explosions. This was no helpless merchant ship: it was a Q-ship. He ordered *UC-71* to dive.

Campbell's next actions were in line with his disregard for personal safety and his determination to go down fighting, if that were necessary. He signalled to a warship that had answered his distress call, asking it to stand off. At the same time, Campbell put the wounded men below and prepared for the inevitable torpedo. Meanwhile, the fire hoses were out in a frantic attempt to protect the magazine from the perilous flaming deck.

The anticipated torpedo smashed into *Dunraven*'s engine room, leaving the ship a sitting target. Time was now short, but Campbell intended to fight to the end. He ordered the surplus crew to take to the boats, leaving just enough men for the remaining guns. He bade his time. At last, Saltzwedel re-surfaced and began a cautious reconnoitre of *Dunraven*, circling and nearing his prey. Still Campbell held back until the boat was just 150 yards away. *Dunraven*'s first torpedo passed close to the U-boat – but not close enough. The second was also a near miss. Saltzwedel had seen enough. *Dunraven* was a blazing wreck. *UC-71* dived and the battle was over.

For Campbell it was time to call for his stricken ship to be rescued. He and the rest of his men were taken on board the destroyer HMS *Christopher*. Under tow, *Dunraven* sank at 1.30 am. Only one man had died in the action. Jellicoe later said the action 'was perhaps the finest feat amongst the very many gallant deeds performed by decoy ships during the war'.[481] (It was somewhat typical of Jellicoe to single out for praise an unsuccessful action.) Saltzwedel would sink another 44 ships while in *U-71*. He would then sink one further ship in *UB-81* before dying when his boat struck a mine in December 1917.

August saw the end of two other Q-ships: HMS *Bracondale,* which was sunk by *U-44* on August 5; and HMS *Bergamot,* which was sunk by *U-84* on August 13. The U-boat commanders had learnt to be cautious when approaching apparently harmless or abandoned vessels. It seems likely that they had turned the Q-ship principle on its head: the more innocent a ship looked, the more likely that it was a Q-ship. The result was that the boats seem to have made a concerted attack on the Q-ships, sending 16 to the bottom in 1917.

The Q-ships had had their day, with their last U-boat sinking being in September 1917. Over 70 duels had been fought, resulting in around 14 U-boat sinkings at a cost of losing 27 Q-ships.

THE LEAKY BARRAGE

In August, a Lieutenant Commander Davis stood on the deck of a salvage vessel as he watched a tangled mass of metal and weeds rise from the depths of the English Channel. *UC-44* was wreathed in cables as it was slowly dragged out of the water. With the boat lying on Waterford beach, Davis and his men retrieved its papers before stripping the vessel of its secret equipment. The boat had been sunk by the explosion of one of its own mines, so it was extensively damaged, but its confidential papers revealed a secret that was to lead to Admiral Bacon's removal from the Dover Patrol. The astonishing document contained instructions to U-boat commanders on how to safely pass through the barrage: 'It is best to pass this on the surface; if forced to dive, go down to 40 metres', the notes advised. 'As far as possible, pass through the area between Hoofden and Cherbourg without being observed and without stopping; on the other hand, the boats which in exceptional cases pass round Scotland are to let themselves be seen as freely as possible, in order to mislead the English.'[482]

The most astonishing aspect of this revelation was that the Admiralty's own estimate was that 30 U-boats a month were passing through the barrage, yet no action had been taken. That Jellicoe knew how ineffective the barrier was, is just understandable. Yet, despite this knowledge, he still supported the idea of building a barrage from the Orkney Islands to Norway. He only failed in this because Britain did not have the necessary resources. Why, if Jellicoe knew that one barrage did not work, did he want to build another? (The Americans were to build the Northern Barrage in 1918.)

It would take another three months before action was taken over the Dover Barrage. Meanwhile, the convoys were about to confound all their naysayers.

25
Convoys vindicated

November 1917

'Losses in tonnage by submarine action had steadily declined since April last, while the destruction of enemy submarines had steadily increased.' – War Cabinet, October 4, 1917.[483]

ANTI-SUBMARINE SUCCESS

In October, the War Cabinet demonstrated its confidence in convoys by a move which would have seemed unimaginable a few months earlier: guns destined for merchant ships were to be diverted to the defence of London against the increasing air raids. Four guns which were waiting to be mounted in merchant ships were to be immediately diverted, to be followed by the whole of the next month's output of 3-inch guns. These guns would be used against the new Gotha GV plane which had gone into service in August. Its payload of fourteen 60 lb bombs seems nothing compared to what was to come in the next war, but it was enough to terrorize the London population. These resource diversions sounded like the War Cabinet's resounding tribute to the success of the convoys. Geddes, though, strongly objected to the diversions, telling the War Cabinet that they were being too optimistic about the U-boat campaign. He called for an increase in the rate of arming merchant vessels. In the winter, he told his colleagues, 'larger submarines' would be 'operating at greater distances'.[484] He concluded that merchant ships would be much more reliant on their own resources.

Events confounded Geddes' caution when, a week later, the War Cabinet received a welcome piece of news: not one British merchant ship had been sunk on November 7. (One foreign ship had been sunk.) When Wemyss reported this fillip to the War Cabinet, it went unremarked. Yet, only weeks before, that same Cabinet had been planning the most desperate curtailment of British imports in response to the tidal wave of sinkings. There was also success to report from the Northern Patrol. In 1915, the patrol had stopped 3098 vessels of which 1130 were neutrals – the ones most likely to break the blockade. By 1917 only 611 neutrals had arrived at the patrol line, showing that the mere presence of the patrol was deterring neutrals from entering the North Sea.

Changing anti-submarine warfare

Anti-submarine developments in late 1917 brought changes for both sides in the U-boat war. By August, 800 out of 3600 merchant vessels had been armed. The remainder were being armed at a rate of 37 per day. The increasing number of armed ships made attacking riskier for the U-boats. A U-boat commander in 1915 had been able to close on a merchant ship with impunity and sink it at his leisure. Now, if on the surface, he had to keep his distance and sink without warning, followed by a rapid dive. Sinkings without warning rose from 21 per cent in 1915 to 64 per cent in 1917.

The convoys, though, were also increasingly protected by that most subtle form of armament: intelligence. The output from the British listening posts to Room 40 resulted in many convoys being redirected away from U-boats. As a result, in October to December 1917, U-boats found only 39 of the 219 Atlantic convoys.

Alongside the success of the convoys in preventing the U-boats from finding the merchant ships, improved mines were now dispatching encouraging numbers of boats. Seven U-boats were lost to mines up to the end of August, and another eight would go in the rest of the year. The last year of the war would see 18 U-boats sunk by mines.

The Allies were assisted by the U-boat service failing to adapt to the new scenario. There were no attempts to coordinate U-boat attacks on convoys, despite the obvious advantage of forcing escort vessels to take on more than one attacker at the same time. (Fregattenkapitän Cäsar Bauer toyed with a change of tactics when he suggested turning *U-155* into an offshore command post to direct U-boats to coordinate what would have been the first wolf packs, but he could not persuade his masters to accept the idea.)

Convoys under fire

The main protection for ships in convoy came from the convoys being hard to find. Additionally, the presence of destroyers and other anti-submarine craft compelled the U-boats to stand off from the merchant vessels. Ultimately, though, a convoy could offer little protection from a determined an attack, particularly from an attack by a large surface vessel, as was the experience of a Norway-bound convoy in late 1917.

The convoy had left Lerwick at 6.00 pm on October 16. The 12 merchant ships were under the protection of the destroyers HMSs *Mary*

Rose and *Strongbow* and the armed trawlers *Elsie* and *P Fannon*. To the south, there were some light cruisers on patrol, but not with the convoy.

During the night, the rough seas scattered the convoy. When dawn broke, the destroyers began bringing the stragglers back into line. It was 6.00 am when a lookout in HMS *Strongbow* spotted two low shapes on the skyline. Lieutenant-Commander Edward Brooke quickly recognized the intruders as German light cruisers. The SMSs *Bremse* and *Brummer* were 4400-ton vessels with 6-inch guns – each was an overwhelming force compared to the 1000-ton destroyers with their 3-inch guns.

Brooke's instinct was to race towards the convoy to protect it, but he had barely given the order before shells from the cruisers were hitting *Strongbow*. At 4000 yards the first shell dealt a fatal blow as it plunged into *Strongbow*'s engine room. More shells found targets, destroying the forecastle and all but one of the guns. Already, many of the crew were dead or injured. With no reply coming from *Strongbow* the cruiser ceased firing and made for the convoy itself. Brooke went below to collect and destroy the confidential papers and returned to order 'Abandon ship'. Forty-six of his complement of 82 were dead.

Lieutenant Commander Charles Fox had ordered *Mary Rose* to make for the cruisers. Heading at full speed it came under fire at 3000 yards and almost immediately stopped. Shell after shell plunged into the vessel while the men fought back with their inadequate guns. With the battle lost, Fox ordered Isaac Handcock, the Master Gunner, to scuttle the ship. Then he went below to collect the confidential papers but never reappeared. Only ten of his complement of 80 men survived, clinging to life rafts in the freezing sea. They were rescued by a boat from an unknown merchant ship.

With no effective protection, all but two of the merchant ships were sunk. Tragic as this was, the disaster was of no significance in the convoy debate. Convoys were rarely attacked by such a massive force – indeed, Atlantic convoys were never at risk from cruisers since the Imperial Navy retained them near their North Sea bases.

Another ship which paid a high price for escorting was the armoured cruiser HMS *Drake*. On October 2, it had just brought Convoy *HH-24* safely across the Atlantic to Rathlin Island off the north coast of Ireland when Kapitänleutnant Otto Rohrbeck arrived in *U-79*. A well-aimed torpedo struck the ship in the boiler room, killing 18 seamen. The still-floating ship had a list and had lost its powered-steering. Even so, Captain Stephen Radcliffe was not ready to abandon ship: Church Bay on

Convoys vindicated

Rathlin Island was near enough, he thought. As he attempted to guide his barely manoeuvrable ship to safety, it collided with the cargo ship SS *Mendip Range*, forcing the latter to beach. Radcliffe decided that one collision was one too many and dropped anchor. His crew were taken off, leaving their ship to capsize in the bay, where a wreck buoy still marks its grave today. Jellicoe had been *Drake*'s captain in 1903-1904. His old ship had proved safe as long as it was in convoy. Only when separated from its convoy did it succumb to a U-boat. What an irony for the man who was so antagonistic towards convoys!

A German picutre-postcard celebration of the attack on the Norway convoy in October 1917.

A NEW FORCE

It was in October that the American ships working out of Queenstown began to augment Bayly's seriously over-worked anti-submarine force. One of the earliest American arrivals was the Mahan-class destroyer USS *Cassin*. Lieutenant Commander Walter N Vernou soon discovered how dangerous the work was.

Cassin was on patrol off the Irish coast in mid-October near Minehead on the Somerset coast when a lookout spotted a U-boat. Almost at that moment Kapitänleutnant Victor Dieckmann ordered *U-61* to dive, leaving *Cassin* in a vulnerable position. Half-an-hour later, Vernou, who had first seen action in the 1898 naval blockade of Cuba, saw the white streak of a torpedo heading for his ship. He put the helm over and called for full speed. Simultaneously, Gunner's Mate First Class Osmond Ingram also saw the torpedo and realized that it was heading for the depth charges stored on deck. He raced across the deck and switched the charges to 'safe'. Moments later the torpedo struck *Cassin*. Ingram was caught by the full blast of the torpedo's charge and the 850 tons of TNT that were in the hold. *Cassin*'s aft was left severely damaged and with its rudder unusable. All it could do was circle. And then its dynamo failed.

American subchasers at Queenstown.

Cassin now sat helplessly becalmed with no power and its wireless wrecked. The wireless operator rigged up a temporary aerial and used the auxiliary wireless to send out a distress call. But, before help could arrive, *U-61* surfaced. *Cassin* opened fire. The boat withdrew, leaving the vulnerable destroyer to await help. The first ship to arrive was the American Tucker-class destroyer *Porter*, followed by the British sloops HMSs *Jessamine* and *Tamarisk*. The initial attempt at towing *Cassin* to safety failed at 3.30 am when the tow broke. Nearly 24 hours after *Cassin* had been torpedoed, the sloop *Snowdrop* finally brought it into harbour. It was six months before *Cassin* was ready to return to sea. As to Dieckmann, he disappeared in March 1918 when *U-61* went missing. He had sunk 92,000 tons of shipping.

Cassin was particularly unfortunate since it came across *U-61* towards the end of the U-boat's useful life. The boat had sunk 36 ships since March 2 – just about one ship per week. After the attack on *Cassin, U-61* would sink only one more ship in 1917. U-boat productivity was declining. This was apparent in Duff's report for October merchant sinkings. There had been 99 homeward-bound convoys totalling 1502 steamers of which only ten had been lost to torpedoes – a sinking rate of 0.6 per cent.

For the more senior Americans now in the war, life was not confined to dull patrolling and dangerous actions. By October, soldiers and sailors were being welcomed into the great society houses in London: 'Everybody's thrilled to see them,' Walter Page told Doubleday. 'Our two admirals are most popular with all classes, from royalty down. English soldiers salute our officers in the street and old gentlemen take off their hats when they meet nurses with the American Red Cross uniform.'[485] It was a welcome change from the days when the appearance of the American flag on cinemas screens had caused near riots.

MAINTAINING THE CORDON

In November, British forces were involved in a minor action in the Admiralty's attempts to stop the U-boats from reaching the convoys. The Royal Navy maintained a minefield in the Heligoland Bight, designed to obstruct the passage of German vessels into the North Sea. Night after night, British ships laid mines. Day after day, the Imperial Navy sent out minesweepers to clear the devices as best they could. These sweepers were accompanied by a significant warship presence. To the British Admiralty the sweepers seemed vulnerable to a surprise dawn raid before the German ships withdrew.

Around 7.30 am on November 17 the battlecruiser *Courageous* accompanied by two large cruisers, eight light cruisers and ten destroyers, approached the German ships in the growing dawn. They faced two battleships, four light cruisers and eight destroyers, which were protecting 14 German minesweepers. Despite the size of the German force, Admiral Hans von Reuter made no attempt to mount a great big-ship battle. His priority was to protect the minesweepers. As soon as he sighted the British warships, he ordered a fighting retreat. It was an inglorious engagement. When the forces parted at around 10.00 am the losses were limited to one minesweeper. The ships of both forces had suffered minor damage, but it was nothing compared to the firepower amassed in the Bight that day.

Beatty, who was not involved in the action, thought that the engagement had 'a demoralizing effect on the enemy ... [who] realized that systematic minesweeping so far afield could no longer be carried out with impunity'.[486] Certainly, it was one more demonstration to the Imperial Navy that its massive fleet served little purpose. It had strutted before the British forces in that dawn, and then withdrawn – a replica of Scheer's behaviour at Jutland a year and a half earlier.

Three days after the Bight episode, 476 British tanks went into action at the Battle of Cambrai – the first large-scale use of tanks in battle. While the Bight action underlined the decline of the big ship, Cambrai foretold the rise of mechanised land warfare.

Belt-tightening

The toll on Britain's merchant tonnage seemed to ease in the summer with decreases month on month from 688,000 tons sunk in June to 352,000 tons sunk in September. Then came the shock of 459,000 tons lost in October. At the War Cabinet, Balfour told the members that even on 'the most optimistic estimate', 1918 imports would need to be cut by 8 m tons. Worse, if munitions and foodstuffs were to be kept at their present levels of 15 m and 14 m tons 'we should not be able to import in 1918 a single ton of anything else'. The War Cabinet declined to consider any new reductions on the grounds that they had already exceeded their 1917 reductions target by 2 m tons. The minute concluded: 'No decision was reached.'[487]

Perhaps the War Cabinet members had a premonition that October was in some way exceptional – Jellicoe seems to have thought so when he said on November 7, 'It is evident that the Germans, for political purposes, had made an exceptional effort in October.'[488] And he was right. The October sinkings of 459,000 tons would never be matched again. Even so, the War Cabinet had to take some harsh decisions on reducing imports. For over three years, the government had sought every possible device to avoid food rationing. Total imports in 1917 were 35 per cent below their 1914 level. The largest reductions had been in timber and manufactured goods which had been cut by 74 per cent, while cereals for human consumption had been reduced by only 13 per cent. The catastrophic sinkings of 1917 and the slow rate of new shipbuilding meant that the government could no longer shield the people's shopping baskets from the ravages of the U-boats. The British were to join the German households in rationing.

Coal was the first commodity to be restricted. Londoners faced its rationing for the first time in October. Each household had to register with a coal merchant to receive a supply of two cwt a week for a house of up to four rooms and three cwt a week for a house of five or six rooms. Students at Newnham College Cambridge were each allocated half a scuttle of coal a day, which was far from enough to heat a room. They took to sharing fires lit on alternate days. The students showed similar enterprise in livening up their dull food by foraging in derelict orchards to make jams from windfalls.

Coal on the front line at home.

In Germany, the food situation continued to worsen. Princess Blücher, then living in the countryside, 'begged in vain' at peasants' homes when in search of 'a miserable quarter pound' of butter. 'Coffee and tea have entirely run out,' she noted. She envied those peasants who could make 'a most delicious syrup' from homegrown sugar beet.[489] In her local town her gardener watched people queueing for an hour just to buy a pound of onions or cabbage. At least, though, the imposition of maximum prices ensured that the poor people were better able to afford something to eat if they could find it.

Alongside the scrounging and foraging for food in Germany, the collection of metals became ever more urgent. Nothing was too sacred to escape the rapacious carts and trucks that toured towns and villages – even organ pipes were stripped from churches. In one small town, the departure of their bell was so deeply felt that the townspeople gathered in a long funeral procession to escort it to the authorities. The wake was headed by a priest in his robes, accompanied by his assistants, swinging their incense burners. The bell itself was smothered in sad wreaths. Oil was so short that even the small altar lights in Catholic churches were extinguished. Germany was a nation at the extremities of endurance. And all the while, telegrams of 'killed in action' came with relentless intensity.

Down, but not out

On both sides, the endurance of the soldiers was astonishing. Equally, if not more astonishing, was the endurance of the merchant seamen who were under no obligation to venture onto the ocean battleground. These men who brought food to British tables were just as much on the front line as the men in the trenches – nearly 15,000 of them lost their lives at sea. They were not conscripted and could freely chose to abandon the fearsome prospect of sailing through U-boat-infested waters. Day and night, on watch, at rest or asleep, they were never free from the fear of the sickening, shattering crash on a steamer's hull, followed by taking to boats and rafts in which to float helplessly on an icy-cold sea. Yet many seamen who survived such experiences went straight back to sea. Lloyd George met such a man when he was returning from an Inter-Allied Conference in France. The 'old sea-captain' told him of his six sinkings, but he was not journeying to a warm hearth and a safe bed. Rather he was on his way to Liverpool to take charge of another steamer. Nor was this dauntless old salt exceptional. At the end of October 1917 Havelock Wilson, founder in 1887 of the National Sailors' & Firemen's Union, told Lloyd George that his union had 'a very large number' of sailors who had been 'in as many as five or six ships that have been torpedoed'. All of them, Wilson said, 'immediately sought employment on other ships'. Some went back to sea without even stopping to claim the £4-£5 union shipwreck payment. He put this into perspective as he recalled the many men whom he had visited in hospital who were recovering from limb amputations – their one complaint being 'not able to render further assistance to their King and Country'.[490]

A BROKEN ADMIRAL

By October, Rear Admiral Roger Keyes, Director of Plans at the Admiralty, was ready to act on the harvest recovered from *UC-44*. He had not forgotten that, in April 1915, Bacon had declared that he would stop the passage of the U-boats through the Strait. Now having clear evidence that Bacon's barrier and patrols were no impediment to intrepid U-boat commanders, Keyes was determined that Bacon must go – except that he gave Bacon one last chance. He drew up a detailed plan for the defence of the barrage, involving the use of patrols and mined nets, with particular emphasis on preventing the U-boats from passing through under cover of darkness. Keyes dispatched Captain Dudley Pound (later, Admiral of the Fleet) to Dover, where he was to explain the plan to Bacon. Bacon listened and said that he 'did not approve of it'.[491]

Keyes bade his time but, for him, Bacon had no future at Dover.

26
Old men depart

Year's end 1917

'We gave Jellicoe 13 months' time and the d–d German menace is really worse than ever.' – Admiral Fisher, January 1918.[492]

THE OLD GUARD

Since 1914 Britain had called on its old men to run the war. In 1914 Asquith was 62, Jellicoe was 55, Field Marshal Sir John French was 62, Arthur Balfour was 66 and Admiral Fisher was 76. Fisher's replacement, Jackson, was 59, while Carson was 61 when he replaced Balfour. But war is a young man's game (and a young woman's game nowadays). Nelson was 47 at the Battle of Trafalgar, Wellington was 46 at Waterloo and Caesar was 42 when he set out to conquer Gaul. The Admiralty had been slow to recognize that it was running the war with men who lacked the passion and vigour to win. A start had been made with 63-year-old Carson being replaced by the 41-year-old Geddes. Now a turnout of the remaining older men was to unleash the courage, energy and ideas of the next generation. By the end of the year Admiralty House was to merit the placard 'Under new management.'

JELLICOE'S DEPARTURE

On December 22, Vice Admiral Wester Wemyss was enjoying dinner with his wife at home in Cumberland Place when a message arrived asking him to call on Geddes that evening. On meeting Geddes, Wemyss was stunned to hear that the First Lord had decided to dismiss Jellicoe. Would Wemyss take his place? Wemyss protested that he did not feel up to the post but, after a good deal of flattery from Geddes, he agreed. (Oddly, there was no promotion in rank. Wemyss did not become a full admiral until 1919.)

Two days later – Christmas Eve – with festive lights strung along the Mall and carol singers in Trafalgar Square, Jellicoe was still in his office when a messenger arrived and handed him a blue envelope marked 'Personal and strictly private'. The letter from Geddes was as blunt as could be: 'After very careful consideration I have come to the conclusion that a change is desirable in the post of First Sea Lord.'[493] Much has been written about the manner of Jellicoe's dismissal and the fact that Geddes never gave any explanation for his action. That aside, Jellicoe's removal was no surprise to those people who had watched him over the last year or so. Haig, as we have seen, called him 'feeble to a degree and vacillating'.[494] Keyes had remarked, 'I thought he looked tired and harassed'.[495] And, as the historian Stephen Roskill later said, 'he was not a success as First Sea Lord' and 'cannot be acquitted' for his 'very tardy introduction of the convoy' … 'a very tired man'.[496] Fisher was also disappointed in the man who, long before the war, had been his protégé, telling Hankey: 'We gave Jellicoe 13 months' time, and the d–d German menace is really worse than ever.'[497]

A tank in Trafalgar Square helping to sell war bonds.

Geddes left no memoirs, so we can only guess as to his reasons for losing confidence in Jellicoe. The answer almost certainly lies in Jellicoe's lack of energetic leadership. Both his resistance to convoys and his reports to the War Cabinet had an air of defeat about them. The

Admiralty needed a 'can do' personality; in Jellicoe it had a man who appeared defeated by three years of gruelling war.

BACON'S DEPARTURE

The final days of Bacon's command of the Dover Patrol had begun in early December when Jellicoe and Keyes had discussed ways of strengthening the barrage. They agreed to send a telegram to Bacon asking him to report on his plans for day and night patrols of the barrier. Keyes recalled that Bacon's reply was 'very unsatisfactory' and showed that 'Admiral Bacon had no intention of exposing any vessels under his command to possible attack'.[498]

Bacon was outraged by this intervention. Rather than cooperate with his superiors, he turned to his diary to confide his distress. On December 7 he wrote: 'If the Admiralty are going to try and run operations in this area there will be no room for me.' Two days later he declared: 'I must have a clear understanding whether I run the Patrol, or an irresponsible committee.' And a week later, after 'answering the Admiralty letter *re* mine-barrage' he complained that their interference was 'getting beyond a joke'.[499]

In that same week, Jellicoe reported to the War Cabinet that 'nearly all the German submarines were passing out to the open sea' via the Dover Barrage.[500] Weymss in his memoirs recalled: 'The Intelligence Department satisfactorily proved to me that the enemy did pass the Straits successfully and almost unchallenged.'[501] Rather than take action over these reports, Bacon simply denied their veracity. (Later research would reveal that 51 boats had passed through the Straits between 21 November and 5 December.)

Bacon was removed from the Dover Patrol on January 1, 1918, but his dismissal was not made public until January 12 when *The Times* reported his appointment as Controller of the Munitions Inventions Department at the Admiralty. Only one person recorded his regret at this change: Haig, who wrote in his diary 'I was sorry to hear this because Bacon had worked whole-heartedly with me and the soldiers and no sort of difficulty had arisen.'[502]

Bacon was mortified by his removal from the patrol, but there is abundant evidence that he had long ceased to think imaginatively and act expeditiously. The concept of delegation was alien to him. When he handed over the patrol to Keyes, he explained that he had no documents that he could pass on since the work was 'all a question of experience' and existed only in his head.[503] Not only did Bacon try to do everything himself, but he kept vital knowledge to himself as well. When Keyes opened Bacon's personal safe at the patrol headquarters in Marine Parade, Dover, he was astonished to find a cache of key naval intelligence documents. Amongst these was the admiralty's report on *UC-44*, with its crucial evidence of the passage of U-boats through the barrage. Instead of sharing this vital intelligence with his staff, Bacon had simply put it beyond their reach and ken.

WAS VICTORY POSSIBLE?

On the wider naval front, the year ended with two belated successes in the North Sea. First, the Northern Patrol, which had operated from the outbreak of war, was no longer needed. In the early years of the war, vessels from the four corners of the globe tried their luck in passing through the northern blockade in order to trade with Germany. The success of the patrol in turning back blockade runners, combined with the fear of U-boat attacks, brought a huge drop in the number of vessels attempting to enter the North Sea. In the April to May quarter of 1917, 611 neutral ships had tried to enter the area. By the October to December quarter that number had dwindled to just 162 neutral vessels. From being a key part of the front line in the early years of the war, the Northern Patrol had become a side show. The patrol was withdrawn, and its vessels switched to the now more vital task of convoy protection.

A second success was the performance of the Dutch convoys. After running 520 eastbound and 511 westbound convoys only six merchant ships had been lost along with five destroyers. These convoys had the double benefit of bringing continental food to Britain and, thereby, ensuring that it did not find its way into German kitchens.

Successes like these, though, did not amount to the ever elusive victory. When the War Cabinet met on November 6, it was to receive the news that, despite the fall in merchant sinkings, the tonnage shortage remained at crisis levels. Balfour described the shortage as 'the most important thing in the war'. (In Germany, Hindenburg shared this view, having recently said that 'the hope of Germany lay not in their Army but in their submarines'.[504]) Sir Joseph Maclay declared that the continuing sinkings necessitated a further cut in imports of 6 million tons in 1918. Britain was finally facing the sort of blockade that it had forced on Germany for the last three years. Not one voice in the War Cabinet offered any hope of avoiding the looming defeat at sea while the British armies remained undefeated in the field.

The prospects for the Imperial Navy were uncertain as 1918 approached. Merchant sinkings in December (399,000 tons) were higher than for November (289,000 tons) but the average U-boat survived only six patrols. The boats faced a better-armed, better-trained and better-organized foe. During 1917, the number of armed merchant ships had risen from 1420 in January to around 4400 in December. Thousands of masters, officers and men had passed through the Admiralty's anti-submarine courses at Portsmouth, Chatham and Devonport. Naval officers had also visited ships to provide on-board instruction and had trained the men in nearly 7000 ships in this way. Attacking a merchant vessel on the surface had become a risky undertaking.

Despite the all-out efforts of the Imperial Navy to intensify the undersea war, the U-boats were flagging. The tonnage sunk per boat per day had fallen from 775 tons in January to 284 tons in December. The primary reason for this fall was that convoys made it harder for the U-boats to find targets. And, when they did approach Allied vessels, the U-boats faced more effective anti-submarine devices, including depth charges, hydrophones and better mines.

Additionally, many U-boats now went to sea with inexperienced crews, rendering them vulnerable to sinking. From an average of six boat losses per month in July and August, the September figure leapt to eleven boats lost. Not that the anti-submarine craft could boast about their contribution. Five of the boats were lost when not in contact with Allied vessels. Of the others, two were mined, two were rammed, one bombed and one torpedoed. With five boats commissioned in November and six in December, these boat losses were just acceptable to the U-boat service. Each sinking, though, meant the loss of a trained crew.

Too late

In early 1917 Grand Admiral Holtzendorff had promised that the U-boats would defeat Britain in six months. The staggering sinking of 881,000 tons of shipping in April of that year had endorsed his confident assumption, with the result that, in the second half of the year, orders for new U-boats had been cut back. By December, with sinkings declining and a stalemate land war, there was an urgent need for new U-boats. Orders for 120 boats were placed in that month, followed by an order for a further 220 boats being placed in January.

But it was all too late. These boats would never appear. New commissions trickled out in 1918 at three in January, six in February and eight in March. The 1917 reduction in U-boat construction had proved to be a disastrous decision now that Germany was staking all on wining the U-boat war. Richard von Kühlmann, Germany's Secretary of State for Foreign Affairs, seemed to have appreciated this. He was, noted Princess Blücher in her diary 'on the verge of a breakdown' as he raged in January about 'the fatal mistakes of the U-boat war'.[505]

HAVING FAITH

As the clocks struck 12.00 midnight on December 31, Britain entered the New Year in a perilous position. The land war was an unending stalemate, as Prime Minister Clemenceau recognized when he told General Pétain, 'I am not in favour of the offensive, because we have not the means. We must hold on. We must endure.'[506] But, at sea, Britain had no choice: 'holding on' was an unthinkable strategy as shipping losses for the month reached 399,000 tons. Massive cuts to imports were scheduled; rationing was on the way; the people were tired; the National Debt was rising by over £4 m per day; and the U-boats kept coming. The War Cabinet could see no way out of the impending defeat at sea.

Just one man seemed to have faith: Eric Geddes, as Lord Riddell recorded in his diary in mid-December: 'He said he was convinced that during the next year the menace would be overcome, and that we should make it so hot for the submarines that they would practically be driven out of the sea.'[507]

27

The darkest hour

January - March 1918

'We always used to be able to count on Sundays. But all that changed as soon as Sir Roger came!' – Dover Patrol bluejacket.[508]

UNDER NEW MANAGEMENT

Rear Admiral Roger Keyes took charge of the Dover Patrol and Barrage in the New Year. As Director of Plans at the Admiralty he was already well-briefed about the deficiencies of Britain's first line of defence against the ocean-going U-boats. Every U-boat that was sunk at the barrage was one boat fewer prowling the sea lanes. Every U-boat that baulked at the barrage faced a week or so of additional fruitless cruising to pass round the north of Scotland to its hunting grounds. Under Bacon, the U-boat commanders had mocked the barrage. Now, Keyes, who had been so critical of his predecessor's complacency, had the chance to put his own ideas into effect. His welcome on arrival was muted. One bluejacket recalled: 'We always used to be able to count on Sundays. But all that changed as soon as Sir Roger came!'

Keyes' force consisted of over 300 patrol vessels (mostly drifters, trawlers and similar small ships) engaged in hunting for U-boats, and in destroying the mines that German boats laid in the swept channels through the barrage. The patrol also provided destroyer escorts for the troop and hospital transports between England and Flanders.

On his arrival, Keyes issued new orders which revolutionized the patrol's operations. No longer would the patrol craft vainly wander in the Channel waters and approaches, advertising their presence so that the U-boats could evade them. No more were the U-boats to have a safe surface passage through the Strait. Instead, Keyes removed all the shallow mines from the barrage so that the small craft could patrol over the minefield itself. The U-boats attempting the passage were to be forced down, where the deadly embrace of the nets awaited them.

Keyes' immediate task was to improve the lighting of the minefield so that the U-boats would be compelled to submerge even at night. Over 100 patrol craft were fitted with magnesium flares so that, Geddes told the

House of Commons in March, 'any submarine attempting the passage on the surface has a reasonable chance of being engaged.'[509]

Putting Keyes' plan into action would take time, so Admiral Sir William Hall in Room 40 concocted a deception operation to make the U-boat service think that the barrage was impenetrable. He prepared a false plan for a barrage that included electrical devices to detect and destroy approaching submarines. A German agent happily paid £2000 for a copy of the plan, which he forwarded to Berlin. Whether the U-boat service fell for the deceit is not known, but it is easy to imagine that U-boat commanders might have thought twice about attempting to penetrate such a barrage.

Other forces were at work to keep the U-boats away from the barrage. By a fortuitous coincidence, three U-boats were lost in quick succession on January 15 and 16. The U-boat service assumed that these boats had been caught in the barrage. In fact, not one had fallen victim to it. *U-84* had passed through and was hunting off the Atlantic coast of France when it foundered. *U-95* had also passed through the barrage before sinking in the Channel a short while later. Nothing is known about the fate of the third missing boat, *U-93*, except that it was not caught in the barrage. Under the belief that these boats had failed to pass Dover, the U-boat service ordered the ocean-going boats to take the northerly route, thereby greatly reducing their productivity. This may explain why Wemyss was able to tell the War Cabinet on January 15 that 'at present there was only one German submarine operating in the English Channel'.[510]

By March, a combination of faulty German intelligence and Keyes' improvements to the barrage had effectively closed the Dover Strait route to the U-boats. From 38 passages in December under Bacon, 17 boats passed through in January and 12 in February. *U-55* is thought to have been the last boat to pass through, which it did on April 22. One other boat may have attempted the passage in September – *UB-103* – but was sunk by a mine.

The presence of the Dover Barrage so near to the German ports made it a tempting target for tip and run raids by German destroyers. One of these occurred when, at 1.00 am on February 15, five German destroyers came roaring out of the black night and fell upon the 13 drifters and one paddle minesweeper that were on patrol. The drifters were in a line, creating an easy target as the destroyers ran up one side of the line and down the other, their guns tearing into the fragile craft. Nor was the firing casual: the German gunners took careful aim at vital areas such as engines. Nine vessels foundered in minutes.

In one drifter, two men survived down below, coming up on deck only when the firing had ceased. Fearing for their lives, they escaped in the still undamaged lifeboat. Later, when the German ships left, they reboarded their damaged vessel and brought it into harbour. Others had lucky escapes, too. In one boat, the gunners lay dead alongside their silent gun. The master switched off the ship's searchlight, and the German ships ceased attacking it.

For some of the defenders, the battle was a matter of seconds. In one drifter, a man coming up from below saw a shell strike another boat: it rose into the air, enveloped in a great sheet of flame. He recalled, 'I distinctly saw her two masts and funnel fall with a splash into the water, sending up spray in all directions ... The noise of the fight was terrible. Shells were falling in all directions.'

The action was one of the most closely fought of the sea war, with the destroyers standing off at only 50 yards. Salvo after salvo shredded boats which were never designed for war: 'They had no time for fancy shooting and there were few misses,' said a survivor.

There was still room for heroism. When the drifter *Clover Bank* was hit, the ship collapsed into a mass of fragmented wood. Only the deckhand, Plane, survived. He dashed along the flaming boat to reach the forward gun and, says the Admiralty record, 'returned the fire at point-blank range, single-handed, half-blinded, stupefied by smoke and din'.

In the *Violet May* there were just two unwounded men: Engineman Ewing and Engineman Noble. They launched the ship's boat and lowered a mortally-ill man and a wounded deckhand into it. 'The remainder of the crew lay inextricably entangled in the blazing wreckage, dead.'

As one survivor said, the raid was 'Just slaughter'. In addition to the 22 dead and 13 wounded, 54 men were listed as 'missing in action'.[511] Seven drifters and one trawler were lost, along with the paddle minesweeper. Later that day, the dead were laid out in the Market Hall at Dover, watched by crowds of onlookers. The commanders of the *M-26* monitor and those of the destroyers *Amazon* and *Termagant* were all relieved of their posts for having failed to adequately challenge what turned out to be enemy vessels.

Superficially, the raid was a spectacular success for the Imperial Navy, but closer inspection suggests that its value lay solely in morale-raising. The barrier was left unscathed and as unpassable as before. As

Scheer said in his memoirs when writing about the raid, Keyes's improved barrier 'made it very much more difficult for our U-boats to get through unmolested, and the Straits were actually almost impassable'.[512] The raid did, though, show that, after over three years of war, the Imperial Navy was still eager to fight. Both sides knew that 1918 had to be the decisive year.

THE ROAD TO RATIONING

With no sign of victory on land or at sea, the British people prepared for yet another year of war. No service was more over-stretched than the mercantile marine as it struggled to bring food to British dining tables. There was only one answer: rationing.

For nearly two years, the government had promulgated various stratagems to reduce the consumption of grains, sugar and other foods, without resorting to formal rationing schemes. All depended on voluntary constraint although, in practice, local shortages ensured that informal rationing took place at the grocers' counters. Now, there were to be formal rations for civilians. The sugar ration was to be 8 oz per week. Bread rations were to range from 8 lb a week for men doing heavy industrial work down to 3½ lb per week for women in sedentary jobs. The meat ration was to be 2 lb per week.

Further shipping losses forced yet another round of cuts to imports. Paper and pulp imports were cut from the 1917 figure of 600,000 tons to 350,000 tons for 1918. (This would necessitate newspapers and magazines being halved in size.) Cotton imports were to be reduced by 200,000 tons, which would put 75,000 factory workers out of work. Both those in and out of work were to have their recently allocated sugar ration of 8 oz per week reduced to 6 oz from mid-February.

Army allocations were to be reduced, as well. Their meat ration was to be cut from 12 oz per day to 8 oz; sugar and butter rations went from 2 oz per day to 1 oz. One group, though, escaped a proposed reduction in their existing rations: the 414,000 horses in the British and French armies. The War Cabinet had proposed to reduce their daily oat ration by 2 lb to 10 lb, but were told that the animals would not be able to do their heavy work at that level.

In addition to cutting imports, the British government continued to promote the cultivation of land for food. This was the work of the County War Agriculture Committees which had been established in 1915. No landowner was too small to be over-looked nor was any too mighty to escape their obligations, as Winston Churchill found in March 1918. Now Minister of Munitions and living in the rented Hoe Farm in Surrey, he had inadvertently become a landowner. His visit from a Mr H E Cooke of the Surrey Agricultural Committee in March did not go well. Cooke surveyed Churchill's fallow acres and issued a notice ordering him to plough and sow. Churchill protested that he was willing to extend his cultivation, but the German prisoners whom he had been offered had not been satisfactory. He had not been able to get the hay in before it rotted and the only labour that he now had was 'one gardener, one very old and crippled man and two boys'.[513]

Hoe Farm in Surrey, where Churchill was pressurised to sow cearals in 1917. (Illustrated War News, September 1, 1915.)

In July, Cooke was still badgering the reluctant farmer. Why had Churchill not ploughed the land? Churchill pointed out that he had spent £100 (c £6000 today) in wages on clearing the fields of trees, but he was reluctant to spend more, telling Cooke: 'I hope I shall not be called upon to embark on the absolutely unremunerative task of ploughing up the two fields.'[514] (The Churchill archives fail to tell us how this story ended, which suggests that Cooke left the War Minister to his greater responsibilities.)

A COMMANDER'S ERROR

It was at this time that Oberleutnant zur See Karl Dönitz received his first command with his appointment to *UC-25,* a type UC-II boat being used as a minelayer in the Mediterranean. Small as his boat was, Dönitz said, 'I felt as mighty as a King.'[515] His first assignment was at Port Augusta in Sicily in mid-March, where intelligence suggested that the British repair ship *Cyclops* was moored. Reaching the target was a perilous task, given the shallow water in the mooring. Capture was more than probable. With his men in life jackets Dönitz placed the confidential papers in a sack together with an explosive charge. Then he turned his boat towards the narrow fairway and crept forward at three knots. No one had spotted his periscope. He moved into a firing position and at 10.49 am ordered 'First tube away!' A second torpedo followed, which resulted in a loud explosion. Not content, Dönitz turned his boat around and fired from a stern tube. By now, the target ship was listing. Fifteen minutes later it lay on its side. Dönitz had seen enough. Boats were moving in the harbour. It was time to go. At 11.35 am *UC-25* was safely in the open sea.

It had been a perfect operation – except for the target. Dönitz had actually sunk the *Massilia*, a 5000-ton empty coal hulk. Not that he or the Imperial Navy knew of his erroneous identification. He was awarded a Knight's Cross for the supposed sinking of the 11,000-ton *Cyclops*. (German intelligence was badly wrong about *Cyclops* since it spent the whole war at Scapa Flow. It would also survive the Second World War, when Dönitz would make a much better job of hitting the targets that mattered.)

LAST OF THE RAIDERS

Germany's fleet of ocean commerce raiders had been retired in March 1917, except for one last ship. The SMS *Wolf* did not return to Germany until February 1918 after 451 days at sea and with a cargo of 467 civilian prisoners. It had sunk 110,000 tons of shipping. One of the passengers, Frederic Trayes, later wrote a book about his life as a prisoner on the raider.

Trayes, who was Principal of the Royal Normal [teacher training] College of Bangkok, was a passenger on the Japanese SS *Hitachi Maru* when it left Colombo on September 24, 1917. Two days later, the German raider *Wolf* was seen approaching. Despite several orders from the *Wolf* to stop, the *Hitachi Maru* kept on course until *Wolf* 'opened fire on us in dead earnest', recalled Trayes. The passengers, having anticipated the outcome of the challenge, were standing on the deck, wearing their life belts while fearing the worst. When the *Hitachi Maru* finally stopped, men from the *Wolf* put the passengers into the lifeboats for the short passage from freedom to being prisoners of war in the *Wolf*.

HMS Cyclops – the ship that Dönitz didn't sink, so demonstrating the hazards of identifying ships through periscopes. (R. J. Mundy.)

At first acquaintance, the *Wolf* seemed quite civilized. The crew busied themselves finding chairs for the ladies, before handing round tea and cigarettes. As darkness fell, a lieutenant informed the *Hitachi Maru* passengers that they would be held for just a few days. Meanwhile, he would ensure they were comfortable – 'the first of a countless number of lies', recalled Trayes.

A few days later, when the *Hitachi Maru* had been repaired, Trayes and his fellow passengers were transferred back to their ship and allocated cabins. Conditions for the 29 passengers were raw. The death of the washerwoman was a particular hardship for those who had never had to wash their own clothes. A month passed as *Hitachi Maru* followed

Wolf around the ocean. Food became short. The supplies of fruit, cheese and vegetables, coffee and jam were all exhausted. The eggs had gone bad and the meat 'became more and more unpleasant'. Cases of beriberi broke out, followed by typhoid.

Prisoners on the deck of the raider Wolf.

Meanwhile, German workers were busy stripping the *Hitachi Maru* of anything moveable. First went the coal and *Hitachi*'s valuable cargo of tea, tin, copper, antimony, hides and coconut. Then the bunks and cabin fittings disappeared, followed by the lighting, heating, clocks and fans. Even the books and the piano were hoisted up onto the *Wolf*. With the *Hitachi* gutted, Trayes and his fellow passengers were transferred back to the *Wolf* before their ship was sunk with bombs.

Wolf had been raiding before meeting the *Hitachi Maru* and now had over 400 prisoners from its various sinkings on board. At least the food was marginally better, including horsemeat taken from a previous capture. Christmas saw the killing of a cow and three pigs 'but they did not go far between eight hundred people'.

In late January, the Kaiser's birthday was celebrated with the killing of the last calf, while the ship was thrown about by hurricane winds. A few weeks later, the *Wolf* was in the Arctic Circle as it neared home. The prisoners froze in their unheated cabins. They longed for a British patrol to appear, but the sea was inhospitably empty. Rescue seemed unimaginable. And then, a mere accident brought deliverance: the *Wolf* ran aground off the Danish coast. A Danish lifeboat took off all the passengers. 'It was a miraculous escape,' said Trayes. A few more miles and the *Wolf* would have been in German waters. Trayes reached London on March 10 having travelled via Copenhagen, Helsingborg, Oslo, the Shetland Islands and Aberdeen. His first task was to report all that he had seen to the British Admiralty. And so ended the Imperial Navy's dabbling in piracy.[516]

Admiral Scheer congratuating Captain Nerger of the raider Wolf in Febuary 1918.

MINELAYING AT HELIGOLAND BIGHT

In home waters, the Admiralty was keeping up its mining operations off the exits from the U-boat bases. Commander Taprell Dorling in the destroyer *Telemachus* joined ten other vessels in a typical minelaying operation of this type in the Heligoland Bight towards the end of March. To reach the area the ships had to navigate at night through the invisible mass of the existing Allied minefield, marked simply by red lines on their charts. A few yards of error would be fatal for both the men and the ships. Additionally, uncharted German mines heightened the danger of the mission. At times, Dorling had 'an attack of cold shivering' at the sight of the German mines.

The operation was one of great secrecy. The ships had new numbers painted on their sides and the mines were hidden on deck under canvas screens, painted with images of guns and other devices. As the flotilla passed the North and South Dogger Bank lightships the men knew that those were the last navigational aids that they would see until their return. With their own navigation lights switched off, and signalling lamps being out of the question, everything now depended on dead reckoning and stopwatch-precision timing. Every so often, Dorling recalled, 'yellow painted monstrosities' would pop up in the wake of his ship: one more grateful prayer was said. 'We simply had to take our chance.'[517]

Captain Berwick Curtis in HMS *Abdiel* flashed a zero-hour signal. One by one, each ship then laid its mines in a field of V-shaped lines. The least delay or an incorrect turn would be hard to remedy in the darkness. (Captain Curtis would retire with the rank of vice admiral and return to sea as a convoy commodore in the Second World War.)

There were the inevitable accidents in these operations, as on the occasion when a flotilla was laying mines on a foggy night. The *Sandfly* missed a turning and later broke out of the fog to find itself heading for *Telemachus*' bow. Helms were thrown over, but to no avail, as *Telemachus* thrust itself into *Sandfly*'s boiler room. *Sandfly* was disabled and only fit for a tow. *Telemachus* made the first attempt but the tow broke. Another ship succeeded in securing a tow and *Sandfly* came home at 8 knots under the cover of the continuing fog. Despite such incidents, the Bight minefield caused the Imperial Navy a great deal of trouble, as German minesweepers endlessly sought to clear it, only for the British minelayers to replenish the swept mines. In the process, Germany lost 28 destroyers and around 70 minesweepers.

WITHOUT MERCY

In early 1918, with the combination of more boats at sea, inexperienced commanders, and the desperation from failing to sink Britain into surrender, U-boat commanders were increasingly willing to take risks. Kapitänleutnant der Reserve Wilhelm Kieswetter was the greenest of commanders when he put to sea in *UC-56*. He was on the twenty-fifth day of his first and only command when he came across a large steamer in the Channel on February 26. The ship had a prominent white band along the full length of its hull and three conspicuous red crosses on each beam. It also had many lights burning – a clear sign that it was a hospital ship with nothing to hide.

It was 4.00 am when Kieswetter's torpedo slammed into *Glenart Castle*'s N° 3 hold, simultaneously wreaking almost all the lifeboats. All power was lost, leaving the ship in darkness. Eight minutes later it sank stern-first, taking down many of the patients. Those in the water had little chance of being seen, let alone saved, as they were cruelly tossed around by the rough waves. Just 32 people were rescued while 162 died at the scene. These included Captain Bernard Burt and Matron Miss Kate Beaufoy.

Kieswetter was reported as having left people in the water, crying for help. Others accused him of having shot people in the water. After the war he was arrested and placed in the Tower of London, but he was released since the arrest was in breach of the Armistice terms.

The luckiest person that day was *Glenart Castle*'s navigating officer who was found in the water 15 hours later by the desroyer USS *Parker*. The destroyer could not risk stopping to pick him up, so he was rescued by two of *Parker*'s men, who jumped into the rough sea and swam to his raft.

A THREATENING TURN IN THE LAND WAR

In early March, Germany had signed the Treaty of Brest-Litovsk with the new Bolshevik government of Russia, so bringing an end to war on the Eastern Front. Almost all Germany's land forces in the east could now move to the Western Front. The result was to be the massive 1918 spring offensive.

Churchill, by chance, witnessed the opening of the great onslaught when he was at the front as a guest of General Sir Henry Wilson. At 4.00 am on March 21, he woke to an earie silence. Nothing moved. No stray rifle shots. No distant rumble of artillery. The silence seemed absolute. Forty minutes later: 'there rose in less than one minute the most tremendous cannonade I shall ever hear ... Far away to the north and to the south, the intense roar and reverberation rolled upwards to us.'[518] The British lines were the target of 6000 guns and 3000 mortars. Over 1,100,000 shells were fired in five hours. At the end of the day, German forces had advanced four and half miles.

Unrestricted sinking had failed. For one last time, Germany was putting its faith in the army. The following day, Walter Page cabled President Wilson: 'Send the men and send them at once ... I pray God that you will not be too late!'[519] On the next evening Page was hosting an embassy dinner in London at which Lloyd George was present. Throughout the dinner Lloyd George kept sending his secretary out for news of the war. Each time that the secretary returned he whispered the latest news from the Front in Lloyd George's ear; Lloyd George shook his head in disbelief but said nothing. It was less than a year since Page had pleaded with Wilson to send more destroyers. Suddenly the clarity of defeating Germany through convoys and anti-submarine warfare had gone. Was Germany, after all, to smash the Allies on land, leaving the failing U-boats to their fate?

28
The taming of the U-boats

April to June 1918

'The Imperial Ministry of Marine has demanded the immediate supply of 2,200 skilled workmen for the Imperial shipyards at Danzig, Wilhelmshaven, and their Reiherstieg shipyard in Hamburg,' – Scheer, June 1918.

ZEEBRUGGE

Although the U-boats were faltering, Keyes was by no means ready to rely on their inexorable failure. Instead, he was to launch a raid on part of their home territory: Zeebrugge. His raid addressed the fundamental problem that the Allied forces had in the U-boat war: the difficulty of finding the U-boats once they had put to sea. Keyes' solution was to trap the U-boats inside their bases by using blockships to close the entrance to the Bruges-Zeebrugge canal. After months of Admiralty hesitation, the action was set for the night of April 22-23.

The proposed blocking of the massively defended approach to the canal was a formidable task. The immediate coastline was protected by 40 guns. Also, the huge mole at the entrance to Zeebrugge was heavily fortified, bristling with guns with a 360-degree arc of fire. Only darkness and surprise could mitigate these factors.

Just before midnight on April 22, the expedition's flotilla crossed the Channel. In the lead were motorboats, tasked with setting a smokescreen over the mole before the larger vessels arrived. As the motorboats approached the mole, their roaring engines alerted the mole's defenders. Star shells soared into the rainy sky and the mole's defending guns fired into the brightly illuminated battle area. Next came the cruiser HMS *Vindictive*, carrying the troops who were to take possession of the mole. It was just 300 yards from the mole lighthouse when the wind rose and blew away the smokescreen. *Vindictive* now stood out against the black sky – a perfect target for the shore-based guns. The troops on the deck came under murderous fire. The two leading task force officers – Lieutenant Colonel Bertram Elliott and Major Alexander Cordner lay dead – and Captain Henry Halahan, who was to command the landing parties, had been shot in both legs. In this chaos, *Vindictive* overran its landing location. The assault party had been carried far beyond its target of the mole gun emplacements.

While the mole landing party was in disarray, submarine *C-3*, tasked with blowing up the viaduct joining the mole to the mainland, had better fortune. Lieutenant Richard Sanford successfully rammed his boat into some girders under the viaduct and set the timer for the boat's heavy charge. He and his men made their escape in a motorboat while *C-3* successfully blasted a huge gap in the viaduct.

The state of 'Vindictive' testified to the futility of attempting to storm heavily fortified positions.

It was now the turn of the blockships to move into position. The ancient protected cruiser HMS *Thetis* was the first to turn into the channel that led to the Bruges canal. It came under heavy fire at 200 yards from the guns on the pillars at the canal entrance. Then its propellors fouled. In the wrong position for blocking the waterway, the lifeless *Thetis* was still under heavy fire when Lieutenant Stuart Bonham Carter swung out the stern and blew the charges. *Thetis* settled into the mud, so obstructing rather than blocking the entrance. It was now up to the cruisers HMSs *Iphigenia* and *Intrepid* to close off the entrance. *Intrepid* went in first and Captain Edward Billyard-Leake placed it across the canal entrance. He blew the charges; then he and his men dropped over the side to the waiting motorboat. In turn, Lieutenant Edward Billyard-Leake sank *Iphigenia* alongside.

Over 200 men died in the raid and nearly 350 were wounded. Yet it had all been in vain. With the blockships ill-positioned the U-boats were moving in and out at high tide within a few days. Similar later raids on Ostend were equally unsuccessful. These actions were in line with the futility of trench warfare. Attacking an enemy face-to-face at short range had been made suicidal with the development of the machine gun. Without initial air support to severely disrupt a defending force, ground attack was futile. Attacking a heavily fortified harbour entrance was equally problematic.

Barrage success

The failure of the Zeebrugge raid mattered little since, by now, the Dover Barrage was seriously impeding the capacity of the U-boats to reach the shipping lanes. In April alone three boats struck mines in the Strait. *UC-79* had only sunk two ships in 1918, both under 300 tons, so was not a significant loss to the U-boat fleet. In the case of *UB-55* the capture of Kapitänleutnant Ralph Wenninger deprived Germany of a highly successful commander – he had sunk 103,000 tons of shipping. Oberleutnant zur See Fritz Gregor's death in the sunk *UB-33* was less significant since his total sinkings since August 1917 amounted to only 9100 tons.

Back to the USA

The commerce U-boats had not proved much of a success since *U-151*'s first triumphant visit to the United States in May 1916. With the need for more U-boats on patrol, these giants of underwater blockade-busting were converted to patrol work. Too big and cumbersome for the waters around the British Isles, they were despatched to the other side of the Atlantic where they could roam more freely.

The Americans were formidably well-prepared for their visitors, having, since they entered the war, carefully studied British experience and avoided British mistakes, plus having benefitted from the advice of Admiral Sims. Convoy routes were established for eastbound shipping, while local traffic was to hug the coastline. Nets and minefields were ready to greet the U-boats. Listening stations were alert to warn of the approaching enemy. Patrol craft were on stand-by to sweep the navigation channels; and the intelligence services were listening for every scrap of careless radio traffic.

News of the first boat to set out for the American coast came on May 1 in a cable from the British Admiralty, advising the Americans that a Deutschland type U-boat had set sail to attack either American troop transports or other American shipping. The British warning advised that these boats avoided shallow waters and rarely attacked when submerged. They almost exclusively used gun fire to sink ships. Their single hulls made them particularly vulnerable to depth charges.

U-151 announced its arrival across the water by attacking the 325-ton American *Edna* on May 24. Its attempt to scuttle the vessel failed and the *Edna* was later towed into harbour. In just over four weeks *U-151* sank or damaged 24 vessels totalling 60,000 tons. Of these, 13 were American and seven Norwegian. Curiously, the boat was withdrawn from service after this successful raid, only to surrender to France in November.

Just under 100 ships were sunk in these waters before the last – the 6700-ton American *Lucia* – was sent to bottom on October 17 by *U-155*. Many of these vessels were of no strategic value: they were mostly tugs, barges and motor boats. An American survey of this campaign concluded that 'so far as concerned the major operations of the war, [it] was a failure'.[520] The attacks never interrupted regular sailings, either coastal or Europe-bound. The operation was also a foolish diversion of resources. The Imperial Navy knew how near Britain was to defeat through merchant sinkings. For Britain, every sinking was a step nearer to collapse. In America's case, Germany could never have sunk enough shipping to have any perceptible effect on the war's outcome. (America owned only two per cent of the world's merchant tonnage while Britain owned about half the world's tonnage.)

One of these large boats – *U-156* – strayed further north and sank ten Canadian ships in a week. The largest of these was a steamer of 583 tons, while most of the other vessels were under 150 tons. This suggests that *U-156* was desperate to avoid the American anti-submarine forces, to the point of operating in an area with no targets of strategic significance.

At the enemy's table

Despite the near apocalyptic conditions under which the German people lived in early 1918, the U-boats still put to sea with well-stocked larders. M H Saunders, mate of the American cargo ship *Hauppauge*, was one of

21 men held captive for a few days on *U-151* in May 1918 after his ship was damaged. The food, he said, 'was good' and included fresh rolls and butter. Cognac was handed round in plentiful quantities. There were three gramophones on board and the crew entertained their prisoners in style. Perhaps one reason for the jolly atmosphere was the submariners' initial ignorance of the state of the war. This was shattered when Saunders and his mates told their captors that America had already shipped two million men to Europe (a considerable exaggeration). This unwelcome news brought a sudden change of attitude in the submariners. So much so, that Saunders was relieved when two ships arrived, and he and his fellows were ordered to the deck. But, instead of being transferred to one of the arrivals, they stood on the U-boat's deck to watch the sinking of the vessels and their seaman being put into the lifeboats. That day, June 2, *U-151* sank seven ships, including the 5000-ton American passenger ship *Carolina*.

A GRUESOME AFFAIR

The US Navy Department's history of the U-boat operations on the Atlantic coast provides considerable details of the individual sinkings. In most cases, the seamen were given time to get into their boats, but the sinking of the 5000-ton steamship *Ticonderoga* on September 30 was a gruesome affair. At Norfolk, Virginia, it had taken on supplies for the American army in France and had departed from New York on September 22. Eight days later, engine trouble had compelled the ship to drop behind its convoy.

Ensign Gustav Bingelman on *Ticonderoga* was the first to sight *U-152*, 200 yards off the port bow and fully surfaced. Lieutenant Commander James Madison, thrust the helm hard over in an attempt to ram the U-boat, while others rushed to the forward gun. Just at that time, an incendiary shell tore into the bridge. The helmsman lay dead and all the navigation instruments were destroyed. The ship was not steerable; the commander was severely wounded; and midships was ablaze. Then, as the forward gun crew prepared to fire, the gunners and their gun were felled by six shells from the U-boat's aft gun.

Kapitänleutnant Adolf Franz pulled away from the stricken ship until *U-152* was standing off at about four miles while still firing its guns. After two hours of battle, Ensign Bingelman recalled, 'most everybody ... was either killed or wounded'.[521] He thought that about 50 out of the 237 men on board were still alive. With all the davits shot away, the lowered boats had been swamped as soon as they hit the waves. All the while, the U-boat kept firing, now at about 10,000 yards. Three men – Bingelman, a chief boatswain mate, and a gunner's mate – were at the 6-inch gun. Then it too was hit. Still, *U-152* had not finished with its foe. Franz neared the ship and fired a torpedo into the engine room.

The ship had only minutes of life left. A few of the remaining able-bodied men lashed the wounded to a raft and shoved it overboard. Three minutes later the *Ticonderoga* slid into the sea. Now clear of any danger, *U-152* approached the scene to take the executive officer from the sea and the first assistant engineer from the raft. With the two men on board, Franz took the only functioning lifeboat in tow and moved off. The tow soon broke. Twenty-two men, including the badly wounded captain, were alone on the ocean in an open boat. With the radio having been shot away by one of the first shells to strike the ship, there had been no opportunity to send a distress call. The men had just eight gallons of water, two cans of hardtack, one case of apricots and one of pineapples to sustain life until someone chanced to find them. They rigged a sail, pointed for Newfoundland, and hoped. It was four days and three nights before the survivors were found by the British steamer *Moorish Prince*.

The commander of *U-152* had only taken charge of the boat on August 25. The *Ticonderoga* was his first sinking. He went on to sink one more ship: the 1700-ton sailing ship *Stifinder* on October 18.

THE TURNING TIDE

The last few days of April and the month of May had seen an increasing number of U-boats being frustrated by anti-submarine forces. Fifteen boats had been sunk in May, against the commissioning of ten new boats. One factor in the increased U-boat sinkings was the American invention of the depth charge rack, which enabled sequential, timed drops to be made in quick succession, so covering a larger area of sea. Added to this, was the decline in U-boat productivity. In 1917 one merchant ship had been sunk for every two days that a boat was on patrol. By the summer of 1918 fourteen days of patrolling were needed to sink one ship.

With the war in its fourth year, the U-boat service was manned by an increasing number of inexperienced men, who served alongside others worn down by the struggle that seemed without end. Oberleutnant zur See Friedrich Traeger was a typical newcomer who failed to make the grade. The fate of his *UB-72* can be attributed to these factors.

The taming of the U-boats

Traeger found his first target – the 3500-ton armed boarding steamer *Tithonus* – off Aberdeen on March 28. He promptly sank it, leaving four dead. The 1300-ton Norwegian steamer *Vafos* went to the bottom two days later. Traeger rounded Scotland and sank the 3000-ton steamer *Sandhurst* and its cargo of iron ore in the North Channel between Ireland and the south-west of Scotland. He then turned south and damaged the 3400-ton *Quito* off Barrow and, on May 9, sank the 1800-ton *Baron Ailsa* off the Pembrokeshire coast.

By now *UB-72* was in heavily patrolled waters. In every direction, Traeger found destroyers and other patrol craft. A two-hour depth-charging left his boat with an oil leak. Then came another attack with 23 charges, resulting in minor damage to the lights, plus a new oil leak. Despite the clear signs that the west coast was a treacherous place, Traeger kept moving forward. Nevertheless, he patrolled off Brest without finding any targets before returning to the Channel in the second week of May.

At 4.30 am on May 12, Lieutenant Claud Barry in *D-4* sighted *UB-72* at a distance of two miles. Barry submerged and, over the next 20 minutes, raised his periscope for brief observations of the enemy boat. It was clear that Traeger was unaware of *D-4*'s presence. At 600 yards Barry fired a torpedo at the still surfaced U-boat. A second torpedo soon followed. The explosion that ensued was so close to *D-4* that Barry's men felt its violence. It was time to surface. Just three men were swimming round in the filthy patch of oil that was all the visible remains of *UB-72*. At the moment of impact, Petty Officer Heroch and lookouts, Laabs and Diers had been on deck. Another seaman, Gabriel, who had just come on deck, jumped straight into the sea. The three men on the bridge were washed down the conning tower by the rush of water into the boat, only to be shot out a moment later as the air was expelled. Heroch was never seen again, but Laabs, Diers and Gabriel were rescued by *D-4* to become prisoners of war. All three men were on their first patrol. *UB-72*'s fate was as much a product of an inexperienced commander and crew as it was a victim of Barry's prowess.

The inexperienced Kapitänleutnant Günther Kretch was another example of the reduced state of the U-boat service at this time. His *UB-85* was one of the few boats commissioned in late 1917 when new boats had been out of favour. Kretch was 32 years old and in his first command when he took the boat out on its first patrol in February 1918. He returned without having sunk or damaged a single ship. Now on his second patrol, Kretch found a target off the Irish coast near Belfast on April 30. As he manoeuvred into a firing position, a patrol ship appeared. He ordered a dive. For some reason, the hatch failed to close fully. That, and a watertight door jammed by a loose cable, left the boat fast filling with water. Surrender was the only option. Kretch and his crew were picked up by the drifter *Coreopsis II*. A new boat had gone to the bottom; a new commander was a prisoner of war; and not one ton had been sunk. (The jammed door was Kretch's fault since he had asked for the offending cable to be laid for a heater in the officers' compartment.) Later, tales began to circulate about a sea monster that had attacked and damaged the boat on the night before its sinking. Kretch is reported to have described 'a monster with large eyes, set in a horny sort of skull'.[522] The men had attacked the monster with their side arms but, claimed Kretch, the boat was left too damaged to submerge. This sounds like an inglorious excuse for the poor seamanship that now blighted the U-boat service.

Kapitänleutnant Rudolf Andler also found his patrolling disrupted by the presence of overwhelming anti-submarine forces when he put to sea on May 14 for his second patrol. Ten days later, Andler was in the St George's Channel, where he encountered British submarines and was forced to lie low. Later, he spotted a large cargo ship with an escort of three destroyers. Andler had no intention of doing battle with such a force so he contented himself with firing a torpedo at long-range. His miss brought the wrath of the destroyers. *U-98* was duly depth-charged, but escaped unharmed.

On May 26 Andler at last found a modest target: the 1400-ton Norwegian steamer *Janvold*, carrying iron ore from Bilbao to Glasgow. Having sunk the *Janvold* he soon found another small ship, but the arrival of an airship forced him to crash dive. The next day found Andler in Cardigan Bay on the surface when he heard depth charges exploding not far away. He dived as more depth charges followed. But Andler escaped once more and spent the night submerged. On surfacing, the presence of a hostile submarine sent *U-98* straight back down. Later that day Andler had a convoy in his sights, but the convoy's destroyers had already seen his boat and were detaching themselves for an attack. Yet again, he was compelled to hide below the waves. When *U-98* tied up at Emden on May 30 all that Andler could report was one small ship sunk.

Korvettenkapitän Hermann Gercke's fate followed the same pattern. He had sunk five ships totalling 8100 tons before his *U-154* was found by

The taming of the U-boats

the submarine *E-35* off the Portuguese coast on May 11. Lieutenant Commander D'Oyly-Hughes first saw the boat just after 4.00 pm. There was a high sea running, but *E-35* had an extra-long periscope so D'Oyly-Hughes was able to keep the boat in sight. For two hours he tracked the boat as it moved away from *E-35*. Then the U-boat turned to come towards D'Oyly-Hughes. There was no time for fine-tuning *E-35*'s position. D'Oyly-Hughes risked a single torpedo. The sea took over as it lifted *U-154* clear of the weapon. Two more torpedoes went off in the trough between two waves. Both warheads detonated, followed by a massive explosion from the U-boat's munitions. A spreading patch of oil was the sole witness to the sudden death of *U-154*'s complement of 77 men. Gercke had been on his first patrol, as had been his boat. Neither he nor the boat had proved to be much of an asset in the U-boat war. (D'Oyly-Hughes was to lose his own life through carelessness when he was in command of the aircraft carrier HMS *Glorious* at the time of the Norwegian Campaign in May 1940. Sailing without air cover, he was taken by surprise by *Scharnhorst* and *Gneisenau*. He was one of the over 1500 men who died that day.)

By late May, even experienced commanders were victims of the improved anti-submarine technology. Oberleutnant zur See Ernst Steindorff had sunk 30 ships and damaged six others as May drew to a close. Now tracking a convoy in *UB-74* he failed to notice that he was dangerously close to one of the escorts: the armed yacht HMS *Lorna*. A lookout on *Lorna* sighted the boat's periscope at 30 yards. Its commander closed the gap to ten yards. Still Steindorff gave no indication that he sensed danger. Two depth charges shot into the air. As the boiling sea settled after their explosion, the surface was littered with debris. The calls for help from four bobbing objects came too late to stop the third depth charge from detonating. When the sea finally subsided, only one man remained to be rescued but he died from his injuries shortly afterwards. Another U-boat commander had gone, depriving the Imperial Navy of over a year's experience in three different boats.

A further indicator of the declining expertise in the U-boats was the loss of 14 boats in May. Twelve were lost to anti-submarine tactics: four were rammed; three were torpedoed; and two were depth-charged. Mines, air attack and gunfire each accounted for one boat. The remaining two were captured when they experienced mechanical problems.

The fate of Kapitänleutnant Robert Moraht in June showed that even the best performers were constrained by the new ferocity of the anti-submarine forces in mid-1918. In 1917 Moraht had sunk or damaged 37 ships. In 1918, he had sunk or damaged only eight vessels and his tons sunk per month had declined from 9160 in 1917 to 5380 in 1918. Ahead of him now lay his boat's fatal encounter with the depth charges from HMS *Lychnis*.

Moraht's loss of *U-64* was through an error on his part, when he mistakenly attacked a convoy from the inside. He had just fired a torpedo and turned his boat, as he thought, to run alongside the convoy. Instead, he found himself heading straight towards an escort ship. As he crash-dived, the first depth charges followed him down. *U-64* rocked under the explosions and the lights went out. With the emergency lights on, a leak in the stern was soon fixed, but the steering gear was damaged beyond use. Meanwhile, the boat was rising on its own accord. Moraht's next glance through the periscope revealed that his boat was surrounded by ships. Fire from the destroyers brought an abrupt command to dive. *U-64* plunged to a depth of 60 feet, where the hydroplanes failed. In a desperate move to get outside the convoy, Moraht ordered full ahead. But the boat had a mind of its own and came to the surface. Fearing the worst, he opened the hatch. He found the inevitable: a destroyer coming straight towards him. 'Dive!' No response. The destroyer's 1250 tons of steel rammed into *U-64,* which reeled under the blow and began to sink. Once more, the boat took charge as if it intended to go all the way in its descent. Die on the bottom or take his chances on the surface? Moraht knew the answer. With the tanks blowing, *U-64* was on the way up again. Standing ready to open the hatch, he cried, 'Man the guns! His men obeyed without a moment's hesitation. Thirty-eight men died on the deck and in the sea, leaving just five submariners to go into captivity.

During this period of the rapid decline of the U-boats, one attempt was made to take a different approach. Kapitänleutnant Claus Rücker had sunk or damaged 31 ships since March 1915. But he could see that the terms of engagement in the new age of the convoy demanded a changed approach. With some fellow commanders he decided to develop coordinated attacks on convoy escorts.

The eight or so boats (accounts vary) were operating off the Scillies in a channel through which several convoys were passing. This might have led to a massacre, but Rücker in *U-103* found that it was impossible to coordinate the boats in the area. The boats had to content themselves with sinking three stragglers at a cost of two boats lost to the destroyers. These losses were disproportionate compared to the small tonnage sunk. No further attempts were made to coordinate attacks on merchant shipping.

This first attempt at what would become wolf packs in the Second World War had failed because a single U-boat commander has no overall view of the battle area and the locations of his accompanying boats. (Karl Dönitz was to solve this problem in 1939 by coordinating attacks by radio from the U-boat service headquarters, based on reported sightings of convoys and the coordinates of each boat's position.)

This catalogue of U-boat failings rightly foretold the unstoppable decline in the performance of the boats, yet that is not how Scheer saw it in June 1918. To him, the Western Front was a cess pit of indecisive battlefields. At Wilhelmshaven and Kiel the great battlefleet lay despised and becalmed. It was time, once again, to seek victory through the neglected U-boats. He resurrected the cancelled building plans of 1917 and ordered yet more boats. Not one of these was ever delivered. Indeed, the construction schedule had been so badly managed that 200 of these boats never got as far as being laid down. The U-boat war was all but over.

Nothing so revealed the failure of the U-boats to break the British blockade as did the crippling shortages in the German economy. There was virtually no item that was not either totally unavailable or in desperately short supply by mid-1918. Doctors lacked bandages, gloves and disinfectants. Bicycles and cars had improvised tyres made with hinged metal flaps. Metal door-furniture had long been replaced by wooden fittings. Makeshift babies' nappies were made from newspapers. Much clothing was also made from paper. Real soap was a memory, replaced by a pumice-based concoction. Smokers imbibed the aromas of trees and shrubs. In summary, the conditions of daily life bordered on destitution.

A RETURN TO EASY TARGETS

Despite the poor performance of many of the U-boats at this stage of the war, several of the more experienced commanders were sustaining the tonnage sunk by targeting large vessels – especially troop and hospital ships.

On May 27 Kapitänleutnant Ernst Krafft in *UB-51* had his thirty-seventh hit of the war when he torpedoed the 9700-ton troopship *Leasowe Castle* in passage from Alexandria to Marseilles. The ship was carrying 2900 troops and was being protected by six destroyers. (It had

The taming of the U-boats

been hit, but not sunk, by Kapitänleutnant von Arnauld de la Perière in April 1917.)

'Nearly all of us were asleep in bed,' recalled a Captain Sutton. 'I was subconsciously aware of a sudden jar.' Sutton was not over anxious about the situation since he knew how well the ship was prepared for a potential sinking. Its master, Captain E J Holl, was renowned for his insistence on boat drills. (Holl had his reasons for his life-drill obsession. In 1886, when he was an apprentice in the *Dunnottar Castle*, the ship had grounded on a deserted island in the Pacific. He volunteered to help man a lifeboat to row for help, which was 1200 miles away in Hawaii. It took the men 50 days to cross the ocean and so save themselves and those left on the island. No wonder that every man on the *Leasowe Castle* knew his boat drill and had practised the procedures.)

UB-51's torpedo had blasted into *Leasowe Castle*'s starboard stokehole, killing some firemen and destroying two lifeboats. The ship immediately began to take on water at an alarming rate. Sutton was aware of his unconventional dress as he stepped through the flooded aft well deck, clad in pyjamas and a pair of canvas shoes. He climbed down a ladder over the side of the ship and then jumped: 'I had a life belt on, a splendid thing.'

The 38 lifeboats which were still functioning had already been filled with 2000 men and were pulling away from the ship to avoid being caught in the down-rush. Another 400 men were taken off directly by a destroyer.

A few men turned to their own resources, as did an army officer called Lawson. When the ship's end seemed perilously close, he organized some volunteers to launch the rafts. As the deck flooded beneath them, Lawson shouted, 'Come on men.' Fred Marshall recalled, 'We scrambled over the side and the ship stood up.'[523]

Those who looked back to watch the ship's last moments could see the white-haired captain with his Union Castle beard standing alongside his first officer, Mr Rae; the radio officer; and the colonel. The ship gave a sudden lurch and began to upend. Only Mr Rae survived these final moments.

Ten hours later, the survivors – all but 102 of those on board – were disembarking in Alexandria, where they were given new uniforms and, from the Red Cross, tea and biscuits.

At this stage of the war, the American troopships which were bringing soldiers to the Western Front should have been a priority target for the U-

The taming of the U-boats

boats. In fact the few U-boat attacks on these transports had no material effect on the steady flow of fresh troops into Europe, even when they scored a hit.

Just four days after *UB-51*'s attack on *Leasowe Castle*, Kapitänleutnant Walter Remy in *U-90* attacked the troopship USS *President Lincoln*, which was returning to the United States. At 18,000 tons it was to be one of the largest sinkings of the war, but there were only 715 men on board. The ship was sailing alone on May 31, having dropped its destroyer escort on leaving the perceived U-boat danger zone. The under-age Samuel Hart had just finished his breakfast after his 6.00 am to 8.00 am stint in the crow's nest and had gone to his quarters when he heard what he thought to be firing practice. Then came two loud explosions followed by the battle alarm. He grabbed his life jacket to rush to his battle station, but he never reached it. After three torpedo hits the ship was taking on water like a paper boat caught in a waterfall. The cry of 'Abandon ship!' rang through the vessel. Hart helped push some life rafts into the sea and took off his heavy hobnail boots. He jumped into the water and swam to a raft before being heaved into a boat.

U-90 was still on the surface, moving between the boats, in search of the captain. With their insignia removed so as to avoid capture, the officers were hard to identify. One though – Lieutenant Edouard Izac – was still displaying part of a flash. In the hope that he would lead them to the captain, the submariners took Izac prisoner. They never found the captain, so Izac ended up in a prisoner of war camp. His determined attempts at escape triumphed in October when he reached Switzerland. Later, his courage was recognized with a Medal of Honour. Twenty-six of the 715 men on board died in the sinking. Izac was the sole person to go into captivity.

The hospital ship *Llandovery Castle* was another victim of this phase of rearguard U-boat activity. Oberleutnant zur See Helmut Patzig in *U-86* had averaged sinkings of 16 tons per day from 14 ships hit in 1918. He was eager for something bigger as June drew to a close. This he found when, in just six days, he sank the passenger ship *Atlantian*, the troopship *Covington* and the hospital ship *Llandovery Castle*. Between them they totalled 37,000 tons of shipping. With the sinking of the last of these vessels, Patzig demonstrated the desperate state of the U-boat war and committed a war crime at the same time.

Llandovery Castle was in passage from Halifax, Nova Scotia, to Liverpool and was about 116 miles west of Fastnet when Patzig found it on June 27. His torpedo blasted into the ship's starboard side, killing some men in the engine room, destroying the wireless and extinguishing the lights. There were no patients on board, so the prospects of the medical staff and crew reaching the safety of the boats should have been good. But, with the engine room inaccessible, the ship could not be stopped. The boats were lowered into the churning sea. One was immediately swamped. Another was torn to pieces by the pounding screws. Many people were still on deck and trying to get into lifeboats when the boilers exploded, and the ship sank beneath them.

Patzig, knowing that he had committed a war crime, sought to excuse and cover up his action. First, he began a search for evidence of military personnel or weapons on board the *Llandovery Castle* to justify his attack on the ship. The best he could do was to accuse Major Thomas Lyon MD of the Canadian Army Medical Corps of being an airman. Lyon returned to his boat with a broken ankle. Not finding any further 'evidence', Patzig turned to massacring the witnesses to his actions. He used *U-86* to repeatedly ram the lifeboats and he turned its 3½ inch gun onto both the survivors in the boats and those in the water.

When Captain Kenneth Cummins of the armed merchant cruiser HMS *Morea* arrived on the scene, he found that he was sailing through 'bodies of women and nurses, floating in the ocean ... Huge aprons and skirts in billows, which looked almost like sails because they dried in the hot sun.'[524]

Accounts vary as to the number of survivors, but the probable figure is 24 out of an original 258 crew and medical staff.

After the war, Patzig escaped trial by fleeing to Danzig, which was not then part of Germany. Two of his men, who had stood on the U-boat deck at the time of the shootings, were sentenced to four years imprisonment, but were acquitted on appeal on the grounds that they were obeying orders.

A LATE BARRAGE

The entry of the Americans into the war had brought vast resources to the Allied cause, including the capacity to build the Northern Barrage which Jellicoe had hoped to see constructed in late 1917. The barrage would stretch from the Orkney Islands in the west to Norway in the east and was to be built in America under the direction of Captain Reginald Belknap before being shipped over for installation. The scale was astounding. It was to cost $40 m ($720 m today) and involved the production of

100,000 mines by 500 contractors. The mines were shipped by train to Norfolk, Virginia, where 24 cargo ships made two or three sailings every eight days to Scotland. With the barrage came 3000 American officers and men, to be stationed in Inverness and Invergordon. They soon ingratiated themselves with the locals, and the young women delighted in learning the steps of American dances. With this force came six specially constructed minelayers. Each made ten excursions to lay the 56,571 mines. British minelayers laid an additional 13,546 mines.

Even before its completion on October 26, this mighty barrage was a challenge to the U-boats. A surface crossing took three hours; when submerged, it could take up to six hours. Admiral Sims reported that 'Submarine prisoners constantly told us how they dreaded the mines.'[525]

American mines being laid to create the Northern Barrage.

Right at the end of the war a letter reached 'My Little Girl' somewhere in America from her proud sweetheart, Frank, telling her of his part in the minelaying. His ship had laid 6049 mines in one of its sorties. 'We completely enclosed the North Sea,' he breathlessly told her. He continued, 'The English were greatly pleased with our work, as they had pronounced the task impossible.'[526]

How successful the barrage was is hard to determine. Boats lost in the barrage simply disappeared and were not countable. Admiral Sims thought that four boats were 'certainly destroyed' but the figure could have been six to eight. However, the naval historian Stephen Roskill was of the opinion that 'the whole idea of the Northern barrage underlines the lack of the Admiralty's faith in the strategy of convoy and escort'.[527]

A HINT OF VICTORY

On the Allied side, good news came when Geddes stood up in the House of Commons at the end of June to report on the shipping situation. In the last quarter, he told the members, world shipbuilding had exceeded shipping losses. For the quarter ending June 30, the excess had run at 100,000 tons a month. In terms of British shipping, losses for June at 256,000 tons were the lowest loss since the 230,000 tons lost in September 1916. Shipbuilding was also benefitting from a strange side-effect of the introduction of convoys. U-boats generally avoided convoys, preferring to attack independent sailings. These ships now tended to hug the coast where, if sunk, were more easily salvaged. This, Geddes told the Commons in July, 'enormously increased' the supply of steel from salvaged vessels.

It had taken a full year of convoying to move from net shipping losses to net shipping gains. With shipping being Britain's lifeline, this was one of the most important victories of the war. The U-boats had been tamed.

29
Downfall of the U-boats

July – September 1918

'Surface craft operating from Bruges, Zeebrugge, and Ostend had suffered enormous losses since last March. Their Flanders Flotilla showed a 50 per cent net loss since that date.' – War Cabinet report, September 3, 1918.[528]

Sub-chasers

In July there were further additions to the American naval forces with the arrival of the subchasers: small, mass-produced vessels 110 feet long and designed to operate in restricted waters. Two squadrons under Captain Lyman Cotton were stationed at Queenstown, along with their support ship USS *Parker* under Commander Wilson Brown.

The subchasers had an early success when Ensign Ashley Adams detected the sound of a U-boat about 150 miles off Land's End on September 6. A barrage of depth charges 'so generously sowed ... that it seemed an impossibility that the Germans could have escaped' soon followed. As the noise and waves subsided, the men in the chasers listened once more. Sounds of a boat trying to get under way could clearly be heard. Then came the 'sharp metallic sounds' of hammering. With their supply of depth charges exhausted the subchasers could not take advantage of the boat's stranding. Two chasers were sent off to Plymouth for resupply. On their return, they found that the U-boat was still motionless on the seabed. A fresh round of depth charges was soon blasting the cornered boat. At 5.00 pm 'a sharp piercing noise came ringing over the wires'.[529] The listeners froze. They knew the sound: pistols. Down below, the U-boat's crew was committing suicide.

The destroyer USS *Parker*, patrolling with USS *Wilkes* and 12 subchasers, had less success when it encountered *U-53* at 250 miles off Brest in early September. It was in this boat that Hans Rose had provocatively sunk ships off the American west coast in 1916. The boat's new commander, Kapitänleutnant Otto von Schrader, who had already damaged or sunk over 100,000 tons of shipping, was bound to prove a challenging adversary for the subchasers.

A 'suspicious sound,' says Sims, was heard on *Parker*. Then a mast and sail appeared – *U-53*'s usual attempt at a disguise. The boat dived as Commander Wilson Brown raced *Parker* at full speed towards the enemy. Down went 16 depth charges, but neither debris nor oil rose to the surface. Brown detached three chasers to remain at the scene to hover and listen. Meanwhile, Schrader had chosen to stay and fight. For two-and-a-half hours he circled in the vicinity before Brown found him just 300 yards north of where he had submerged. Four more depth charges tumbled down onto the boat. Once more the subchasers moved in to listen. Nothing. Days later, a listening station picked up Schrader's signal reporting his position as being North of Scotland and homeward bound. On the way, Schrader had sunk the 3100-ton *War Firth* off the Clyde and damaged the 730-ton sailing ship *Rio Mondego* off Land's End. Once beached in the Isles of Scilly, the *Mondego*'s cargo of port wine was soon liberated by the locals, despite the presence of a guard. After the war, the Americans tried to find out more about their encounter with the elusive *U-53*, but the relevant pages of the logbook had mysteriously disappeared.

In addition to the subchasers stationed with the Coast of Ireland Command, there were two squadrons at Corfu, strategically placed for attacking traffic in and out of the Adriatic. Sims described the location as 'ideal' because the Mediterranean waters were too shallow for the U-boats to hide on the seabed. In these waters, acoustic detection resulted in frequent contacts with Austrian submarines. 'Two weeks after their arrival it was impossible to compel an Austrian crew to take a vessel through the straits, and from that time not a single Austrian submarine ventured upon such a voyage,' wrote Sims.[530]

As the American contribution to the anti-submarine forces grew in mid-summer, an American friend of the British Admiralty departed. Ambassador Walter Page, who was seriously ill, sent in his resignation to President Wilson. (Page would die in December.) On hearing this news, Lloyd George wrote to express his regret at Page's departure: 'We are sorry that you are leaving us, all the more because your tenure of office has coincided with one of the greatest epochs in the history of our two countries and of the world, and because your influence and counsel throughout this difficult time have been of the utmost value to us all.'[531] Page had been critical to supporting Sims in getting the first American destroyers sent over in mid-1917. Without those ships Britain might have been forced out of the war within months.

Last Gasps

In August, Holtzendorff was eased out of his post of Chief of the Imperial Admiralty Staff after disagreements with the Supreme Army Command over war aims. Admiral Scheer became Chief of the Naval Staff while Admiral Hipper took up the post of Commander-in-Chief. Neither Scheer nor Hipper took the same interest in the political aspects of the war as Holtzendorff had done, so the change had little observable effect.

A few U-boat commanders continued to sink ships with regularity. Even some newcomers could still prove deadly foes. Kapitänleutnant Heinrich Middendorff, who had only been a commander since April, made two major sinkings in the last days of the war when in *U-82*. First came the American troopship USS *Mount Vernon* on September 5.

Men from the first toopship (USS Mount Vernon) being transferred to the lighter Knickebocker. (US Department Of The Navy.)

The force of the explosion from Middendorff's single torpedo sent a huge column of water and debris into the air. One crewman thought the ship had even been lifted out of the water. Men had been thrown violently across the deck and one of the 5-inch guns lay on the deck, torn from its mountings. The dead in the engine room included the young Robert

Orville Carver, who was due to be relieved ten minutes later. Chief Water Tender Charles O'Conner, one of the two engine room men to survive, recoiled as an eight-foot wall of water thundered into the engine room: 'Boxes, shovels, and anything not tied down, was sucked into the vortex.' He made for the ventilator shaft and managed to climb up eight feet before hands grabbed him and pulled him to safety. Fireman Harry S Smith was thrown across the engine room by the force of the explosion and then carried by the torrent of water into the coal bunker. His screams for help brought rescuers, who used chisels to hack open the bunker and release him. The other engine room men died when the area was sealed off to prevent the ship from sinking. This painful act limited the deaths to just 36 of the 1450 on board and enabled *Mount Vernon* to limp to the safety of Brest.

Seven days later, *U-82* torpedoed the passenger steamer *Galway Castle* in the Atlantic, leaving the ship severely damaged with its back broken. On board were around 400 walking wounded, 346 passengers and a crew of 204. The rough seas resulted in swamped lifeboats. Destroyers from Britain retrieved many survivors, but 143 lives were lost. This was near enough the end of *U-82*'s slaughter. Since December 1916, it had sunk or damaged 35 vessels, totalling 131,000 tons. *Galway Castle* added 8000 tons to that total. The steamer 2244-ton *Madryn* was to be its last sinking four days later.

An unforeseen decline

August merchant sinkings of 284,000 tons were up compared to the 261,000 tons sunk in July. At the War Cabinet meeting on September 17, Wemyss forecast September sinkings of 270,000 tons. Geddes was even more cautious, telling his colleagues that they 'must not look for reduced shipping losses, as the situation was likely to get worse' since the Allies were sinking fewer U-boats. In fact, the U-boat collapse had begun. September sinkings would turn out to be 188,000 tons. – a 34 per cent reduction on the August figure. After 50 months of dominating the seas, the U-boats were in rapid retreat.

A deluded Kaiser

The members of the British War Cabinet were not alone in failing to see the U-boats' fast-approaching end. While Geddes and the British Admiralty were sunk in gloom, the Imperial Navy was engaging in a final act of delusion as the Kaiser visited the U-boat School at Kiel. He reviewed the more than 200 new officers in training; he inspected a torpedo workshop; and he visited the newly-enlarged Imperial shipyards to see the work on new boats. The atmosphere was that of a service at its peak, ready to release hundreds of brilliant officers in masses of new boats, eager to sink merchant ships with nonchalant ease. It was no more than a foolish fancy. As the Kaiser and his party returned to General Headquarters, news reached them that the Bulgarian front had collapsed. In the urgent discussions that followed, Scheer nonsensically both authorized the evacuation of the Flanders U-boat base and obtained the Kaiser's permission to continue building more U-boats. For this, he would need an additional 60,000 shipyard workers. No one asked him from where these men could be found. In Kiel, make-believe ruled the day, while at sea and on the battlefields the war was beginning its now inexorable collapse.

30
Surrender

1 October – 11 November 1918

'Brutes they were and brutes they remain.' – Balfour.[532]

THE ARMISTICE WRECKER

At 9.00 am on October 12, the packet steamer RMS *Leinster* left the Carlisle Pier in Kingstown (now Dun Laoghaire), bound for Holyhead in Anglesey. In command was the 61-year-old Captain William Birch, who had been crossing the Irish Sea since 1902 and was now the City of Dublin Steam Packet Company's senior captain. Birch was a steady man who could be trusted with a 2600-ton steamer and a crew of 78, together with about 100 passengers and 500 military personnel. Also, busily working below as the ship pulled away, were 22 postal workers in the on-board sorting office.

The weather was fine, but the sea was still rough from storms. Lurking in the depths below was *UB-123*, commanded by Oberleutnant zur See Robert Ramm. His boat had been commissioned in April, but he had yet to sink anything. (Ramm had captured and released three small steamers.) There could be no better example of a failing U-boat and a failing commander who needed to prove himself worthy of his command before the war's end.

Just before 10.00 am, when the *Leinster* was 16 miles out, several passengers on deck saw the streak of a torpedo. Their instant terror subsided as the weapon harmlessly passed ahead of the ship. Their relief was short-lived: a second torpedo smashed into the ship's side, tearing its way into the postal sorting room. Then came the third torpedo. It pierced the ship's starboard side, drove deep into the ship, and exploded with a ferocity that seemed to tear the vessel in two. Within minutes, the *Leinster* had sunk.

When the ship sank, some of the lifeboats were reasonably full as they tossed around in the heavy swell. Many survivors were clinging to the sides of the boats. Others were bobbing up and down in the sea while some were slipping below.

Surrender

Final delivery, bearing the words 'Recovered from the Leinster'.

Around 500 people lost their lives in the sinking, including all but one of the postal workers. Higgins was working with two others in the Registered Letters enclosure when the third torpedo struck. He called to his co-workers, Murphy and Attwooll, to get out, but they ignored his cry. As soon as Higgins stepped out of the room, he found himself waist-deep in water. Above and around him, the ship was a mass of twisted metal. He swam through a letter-strewn sea inside the ship before finding a damaged stairway. With the aid of some cabling Higgins pulled himself up to reach the mail shed. There, he grabbed two lifebelts and made for the deck. Over the side he could see a partly-filled boat. A dangling rope sufficed for him to slide down to safety. Two hours later, a destroyer rescued the passengers from the boats and the sea. When Higgins reached home that afternoon, he found his distraught wife praying for his safe return. She had heard of the sinking on the radio and had feared the worst.

Amongst the over 500 dead was the 19-year-old Josephine Carr, who became the first Wren to die on active service. The other notable casualty was Captain William Birch, a father of ten children.

Arthur Balfour called the sinking 'an act of pure barbarism' adding, 'Brutes they were and brutes they remain' – strong language from such a mild man.[533]

The sinking of the *Leinster* was a disaster for Germany. At that time, negotiations for an armistice were well-advanced. The United States government had already warned Germany that 'Nations associated against Germany cannot be expected to agree to cessation of arms while acts of inhumanity, spoliation, and desolation are being continued which they justly look upon with horror and with burning hearts.'[534] President Wilson cancelled his peace talks and declared that he would now only negotiate with a democratic Germany. In the view of *The Times*, Wilson's rebuff 'makes an end of all idea of a bargained peace ... [it] tells the Germans that the terms of the armistice must be settled by the generals in the field'.[535] In reality, there was no fight left in the German army, but the U-boats kept sailing. *They* were not ready for surrender.

Defeat in the Air

By October, suffering both at the German front line and on the home front had reached unimaginable levels. Prince Max of Baden recalled that, in the towns and cities, 'the middle of October was indescribable' with 'No coal, no adequate clothing'.[536] There was never a waking moment that was free from unbearable hunger. Grain and fodder imports for 1918 were 96 per cent below those for 1917. Legumes were down by 99 per cent and butter by 84 per cent. Philipp Scheidemann, a social democratic politician who had just joined the government, was horrified when he discovered that there was no meat to be had, while a shortage of 4000 lorries prevented the distribution of potatoes. Added to that, fat was completely unobtainable. Society was on the verge of collapse.

And then came influenza, which was to bring 174,000 German deaths in 1918, to be followed by 42,000 and 57,000 deaths in 1919 and 1920 respectively.

On October 1, Ludendorff gathered together some of the army staff to tell them that he had just informed the Kaiser that the German front could hold no longer. The war could not be won, he said, because the army had been 'heavily contaminated with the poison of Spartacus-socialist ideas'. (The Spartacus League was a Marxist revolutionary movement in

Germany.) He added, 'some troops had proven themselves so unreliable that they had had to be quickly pulled from the front'. General Albrecht von Thaer recalled that Ludendorff's address was accompanied by 'quiet sobbing and moaning'.[537] Meanwhile, Chancellor Count Georg von Hertling had resigned. (Ludendorff made no mention of the state of the navy.)

LATE DELUSIONS

While the German front was collapsing and the U-boats had long passed being a critical threat to Britain, a bizarre meeting took place in Cologne. Ernst Ritter von Mann, the Minister of Marine, and Colonel Max Bauer from the Supreme High Command, along with Scheer, met to discuss the need to increase U-boat production. Scheer asked the army to provide him with 15-20,000 men in 1918 for U-production, with more being needed in 1919. Bauer readily agreed to provide the men. The picture of an army, with men deserting in vast numbers, handing over men to a navy that was itself only days from mutiny is hard to credit. There was an utter refusal to recognize that the war was irredeemably lost.

Alongside the plans for more U-boats in general, there were grandiose schemes for a new and larger boat – the Type 139. This was to be a pure war machine and a successor to the abandoned merchant cruising boats. Three of these 1900-ton monsters reached commissioning. They came too late to significantly affect the declining power of the U-boats. *U-141* never went on patrol. *U-140*, which had been commissioned in March, had only sunk 31,000 tons by the end of the war – a rate of 221 tons per day.

LAST PATROLS

U-139 was under the command of the ace submariner von Arnauld de la Perière, who had sunk or damaged 198 vessels when in *U-35*. Now, success was harder to come by. In *U-139*'s sole patrol, de la Perière sank five ships in the first two weeks of October. His first sinking was the 3300-ton steamer *Bylands* on October 1. Two other small steamers were sunk on the same day. Ignominiously, *U-139* ended its career with the sinking of the 300-ton sailing ship *Rio Cavado*, packed with wine from Oporto and bound for Cardiff; and the 490-ton Portuguese naval trawler *Augusto De Castilho*. Unable to rejoice in any war-changing sinkings, the lack-lustre crew of *U-139* comforted themselves with the *Rio Cavado*'s wine. This was not enough, though, to lift the spirits of the men whose massive U-boat had achieved less than the obsolete boats such as *U-9*, which had served from the start of the war. As the hapless boat made its homeward run, news of the army's collapse on the Western Front came over the radio. There would be no fêted welcome from wives and girlfriends, standing on the quay. Instead, as *U-139* ran into Kiel on November 14, the 62 weary sailors saw the fluttering red flags of the November revolution. The Germany they had fought to defend was no more.

On October 21, the U-boats at sea were recalled as a condition of the Armistice negotiations. Given the vulnerability of the outlying Flanders base, Scheer closed down its operations. The Naval Corps protecting it was withdrawn, but the massive guns on the seafront continued to be manned by men of the marine artillery.

The detritus of defeat in Bruges harbour. (Contemporary postcard.)

The Bruges shipyard and the facilities at Zeebrugge were evacuated too. As the sea-worthy boats and ships departed, they were followed by four torpedo boats a few days later. All that remained were four U-boats and three large torpedo boats. Unfit to go to sea, these were destroyed at their moorings. Other craft in the area made their way to Antwerp, while the local aircraft were transferred to Army Command IV. Those large guns which could be moved were put onto trains; the remaining guns were destroyed by explosive charges. Within a few days the great Belgian-based U-boat facilities stood empty, apart from the detritus of the hurried destructions. The abandoned bases symbolized Germany's defeat. Before the war, annexionist politicians such as Gustav Stresemann had dreamed of Germany retaining the Belgium coast as a launchpad for a great empire. Now, that coast, so briefly possessed, had slid from German hands.

The abandoned bases were the final proof that Germany had gained nothing from the over 1.7 m dead and 4.2 m wounded during the last four years.

At the start of the war, the U-boats had attempted to attack the Grand Fleet in Scapa Flow. The U-boat war was to end in exactly the same way. *UB-116* had been commissioned in May and had begun patrolling in August. By late October it was on its fourth patrol. Oberleutnant zur See Hans Joachim Emsmann had previously served in *UB-10* and *UB-40,* and had sunk 23 ships totalling 11,600 tons. *UB-116* itself had no sinkings to its name. Emsmann's mission was to strike at the Grand Fleet in Scapa Flow. Gone were the triumphant days of 1914 when von Hennig entered the flow and cruised at ease. Now Scapa was defended by a war's worth of anti-submarine developments. Not that there was anything there to interest a U-boat since the fleet had not been at the Flow since April. As Emsmann entered the Flow on October 28, hydrophones picked up the sound of *UB-116*'s engines. The time was 9.21 pm when an operator flicked a switch to activate an electric detonator. A string of mines exploded in unison. After, there was not a sound from the hydrophones. When daylight came, patrol boats found the surface strewn with debris. The only sign of *UB-116*'s occupants was a single jacket. Later, divers went down and recovered the boat's logbook. *UB-116,* was the last U-boat to be sunk during the war, other than the boats that were scuttled to prevent them from falling into Allied hands.

Mutinies

On October 29, the crews of the Imperial Navy warships began damaging their ships in port. When news of a proposed last sortie of the High Seas Fleet reached them on the following day, the men refused to obey. It was mutiny. There was to be no honour-redeeming last battle as Scheer had imagined. All that remained was the humiliation of a navy that refused to fight.

Otto, a sailor in the High Seas Fleet, told his father: 'if the armistice isn't signed soon ... the most awesome military revolt will break out here'.[538] By November 2, the commanders on his and other ships feared giving the order to raise steam. The sortie's departure time was extended again and again. When it was eventually cancelled (using the excuse of bad weather) the men felt their own power. On the following day, the sailors and dockworkers declared the ships to be in revolutionary hands. Men marched in their tens of thousands through the streets of Kiel as the Social Democratic Party moved in to turn protest into revolution. By November 5, the Red Flag was flying over Kiel. On the following day, the sailors issued an ultimatum with 14 demands of which the last was: 'All future orders must be countersigned by the Council.'[539] It was not just the end of the navy: it was the end of the German state. Hipper, whose whole life had been the navy, and who had so recently crowned his career with the command of a fleet that would never sail, railed at the mutineers: 'whoever abandons the struggle now ... stamps himself as a coward', he told the mutineers. All that he received in response was 'coarse laughter'.[540]

In this atmosphere of mutiny, Commodore Andreas Michelson, who had become commander of the U-boats in June 1917, ordered Spiess to report to him on the *Hamburg*. There, Michelson asked him: 'Are you absolutely sure of your crew?'[541] On Spiess replying that he had total faith in his men, Michelson told him of the gathering mutiny in the warships. What came next, horrified Spiess: he was to proceed to Admiral Hipper's flagship, SMS *Baden*, for further orders. 'I would have wished for any mission but that,' he recalled. 'I took my leave with orders to take my new submarine [*U-135*] to attack warships of the German navy.'[542] From the glamour of sinking enemy vessels, Spiess was to be demoted to the abhorrent task of suppressing mutiny.

Spiess found the commander, who had by now transferred to the nearby *Kaiser Wilhelm II*. Once more he was solemnly asked, 'Are you sure of your men?' He replied that he was, and received orders to accompany a Lieutenant Grimm to assist in arresting the crews of the *Thüringen* and the *Helgoland*. He asked for the order in writing, but the commander refused. Next came Spiess's first (and probably only) meeting with the new Commander-in-Chief of the High Seas Fleet. The encounter with Hipper was brief: a few words of command, a slight bow, and Spiess was off yet again in search of the disappearing war.

U-135 put to sea, passing out of the lock to be rocked by the wake of steamers carrying troops to suppress the naval mutiny. As it proceeded towards the rogue ships, Spiess' men heard about the mutiny for the first time: 'they could not believe their ears.' Loyal to the end, his crew loaded the torpedo tubes and readied the gun. By the time that *U-135* reached the *Thüringen*, soldiers were aboard the ship. The mutinous men had been herded towards the prow and had been given five minutes to surrender. There was no surrender. *U-135* was ordered to a new position 'with all possible speed' while a destroyer received similar orders. 'The mutineers' hour of punishment had arrived,' wrote Spiess later.[543] While these final preparations for attack were being made, the mutineers relented. Only after these events did Spiess notice that two of *Helgoland*'s guns had been trained on *U-135*.

Some of the U-boats made a tentative attempt to outflank the revolution. As the crews were deserting their warships, whispered voices spread through the U-boats for a rendezvous at Heligoland to make a last stand for the Kaiser's war. Spiess leapt at the chance, even though his boat was in for repairs and lacked a working periscope. He discarded the periscope, covered the hatch with a piece of sheet metal and put to sea once more: 'I wanted to be there for the last battle.'[544]

LAST DAYS

As the last hours of the U-boat war were played out in mutiny-filled home waters, there was just time for one last major sinking. Oberleutnant zur See Heinrich Kukat in *UB-50* had only begun his submarine career in April and had already sunk or damaged 13 vessels. He had specialized in seeking out large targets, including two tankers totalling 11,100 tons, plus five steamers of over 3000 tons.

On November 9 the 16,000-ton pre-dreadnought battleship *Britannia* was off the Spanish coast at Cape Trafalgar when it was struck by one of Kukat's torpedoes. The ship soon began to list to port. A second torpedo drove into the ship's magazine, causing an explosion. With all lights gone the crew could not locate the flooding valves for the magazine. The ship's fate was inevitable, although it took two hours to sink. Fifty of her complement of nearly 800 men died.

Kukat would have been a dangerous menace had the war allowed him a longer time at sea. He was to die in the chaos following the Kapp

Putsch in March 1920. (The failed Kapp Putsch was a right wing coup which aimed to bring down the newly established Weimar Republic.)

Mutinous sailors storming through Kiel in November 1918.[545]

On the same day as *Britannia*'s sinking, the Kaiser told Scheer of his intention to abdicate. Scheer, loyal to the humiliating end, objected, saying that the navy would be left without a leader. The Kaiser – for once, clear-headed – retorted: 'I no longer have a navy.'[546] They parted. It was Scheer's last encounter with his emperor. On November 10, a train carried Wilhelm over the border into the Netherlands and exile, never to set foot in Germany again.

By coincidence, Admiral Beatty, one of the victors, mirrored the Kaiser's despondent lament, telling his mistress: 'The Fleet, my Fleet, is broken-hearted, but [the men] are still wonderful, the most wonderful thing in Creation ...'[547]

At Kiel, Admiral Hipper surveyed the empty decks of his redundant flagship. A large number of his seamen were now behind bars. The Kaiser had no navy; Hipper had no one to command. He walked to the foot of the mainmast and, in humiliation, hauled down his own flag. The fleet-less admiral left the ship and disappeared into post-war obscurity (he left no memoirs). Two days later, the Armistice came into force at

Surrender

11.00 am on November 11. Hipper called the terms 'simply crushing'.[548] At the Western Front near Sedan a *Times*' correspondent told the paper's readers: 'There was nothing to do, except to be glad.'[549]

One of the clear victors of the naval war was the Grand Fleet. Despite all the Kaiser's ambitions, neither the High Seas Fleet nor his U-boats ever significantly weakened the ships that stood between Britain and invasion. The men in Beatty's ships knew this, as they celebrated their victory on November 11. Two tots of rum were served all round and, as dusk fell, beams from the fleet's searchlights lit up the sky. Midshipman Basil Jones recalled that 'every ship's siren was sounded continuously and made an unholy din until midnight'. Rockets and fireworks were fired and the men 'danced and jazzed round the upper deck furiously'. After an uproarious dinner, Jones concluded: 'It's been the most wonderful day since the world cooled down.'[550] (Jones became Captain Jones, DSO, DSC in the Second World War, and a zealous destroyer commander.)

The last U-boats to return to port found a changed world. On reaching Kiel, de la Perière and his men in *U-139* saw the Red Flag flying over the city. He and his first lieutenant took the precaution of donning civilian dress before venturing ashore. It was, he said, 'a queer finale for the most successful submarine commander in history whose sinkings totalled over 400,000 tons'.[551]

Around two-thirds of the U-boats which surrendered were scuttled by the British in the Atlantic in Operation Deadlight over the next four months, while the remaining third were claimed by other Allies, including Japan and the Soviet Union.

BATTLE SUMMARY

Germany had built 373 U-boats of which 178 – nearly 50 per cent – were lost in action. Allied mines destroyed 40 boats and the anti-submarine ships dispatched 30 boats by depth charges and 13 through Q-ship attack. Many were lost in accidents and unaccounted sinkings. Over 500 officers and nearly 5000 men died in the boats.

After the first few months of the war, the boats' main target was merchant shipping. Nearly 6000 vessels totalling just over 11 million tons were sunk.

The work of the U-boats was supported by numerous patrol craft of which Germany lost 68 destroyers and 55 torpedo boats.

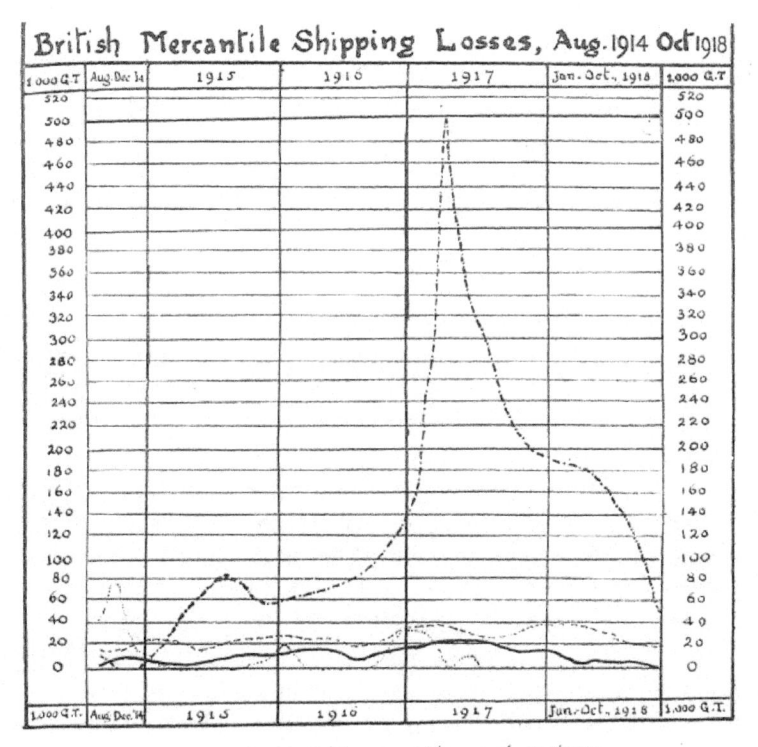

Merchant shipping losses 1914-1918. (Contemporary record.)

By the end of the war Britain was deploying 215 destroyers, 106 torpedo boats, 76 submarines and 3727 auxiliary craft in anti-submarine work. During the war, 64 destroyers, 22 torpedo boats, 54 submarines were lost. The United States anti-submarine forces included 24 destroyers at Queenstown and a large number of subchasers.

The impressive number of British auxiliary craft had little to do with effectiveness. On average, it took 98 auxiliary craft to sink one U-boat, whereas it took only 15 destroyers to achieve the same result. But both types of craft were spectacularly overshadowed by submarines. Only five submarines were needed to sink one U-boat. To put these figures more starkly: if Britain had had 100 more auxiliary craft, there would have been one more sinking; with 100 more destroyers, six more boats would have been sunk; and, with 100 more submarines, then 20 more boats would have been sunk.

The convoys had escorted 9250 ships in Atlantic homeward-bound convoys, of which 104 had been sunk a – loss rate of 1.1 per cent. 7289 ships had been convoyed outward-bound with a loss of 50 ships – a loss rate of 0.68 per cent. The combined loss rate was 0.92 per cent.

Conclusions

For such a devastating war, neither side treated the U-boats as being a matter of priority. The German generals in the west launched new offensive after new offensive, none of which brought any strategic benefit. They only supported U-boat warfare in the dark moments when the land war was seen to be failing. As to the British Admiralty, Jellicoe did not mention the U-boat threat until the War Cabinet meeting of March 2, 1917 and, even then, he did not see the U-boats for what they were: an existential threat. With both sides convinced that the war would be decided on the Western Front, both were dilatory in pursing the U-boat war. The Imperial Navy delayed building U-boats and the British Admiralty delayed introducing convoys. Each came perilously close to defeat more through its own indolence than its lack of prowess. That the Allies finally tamed (but never defeated) the U-boats was far from inevitable.

Memorials

In Germany, war weariness, the appalling hardships of daily life and the post-war revolution, deprived the returning U-boat men of any grand homecomings. Their U-boat war is remembered with a simple recording of the names of the dead at the Möltenort U-Boat Memorial, which was opened in 1930. (It now records the submariners of both wars.) The plaque for the First World War simply reads:

> 1914-1918
> 4,744 dead
> 200 U-Boats lost.

The British memorial to the merchant seamen who died in the war stands in Trinity Square Gardens at Tower Hill. The inscription reads:

> 1914-1918
> To the glory of God

and to the honour of
twelve thousand
of the merchant navy
who have no grave but the sea.

There is no specific memorial to those who died in anti-submarine patrols since those men are included in the overall naval memorials at Plymouth, Chatham, and Portsmouth which together commemorate the 7251 naval men who died at sea.

Appendix 1
Strategic errors and successes

GERMANY'S STRATEGIC ERRORS

1. Constructing a High Seas Fleet which had no strategic purpose.
2. Failing to attack the early troop transports.
3. Relying on a policy of attrition of the Grand Fleet as a prelude to destroying it in a major action.
4. Failing to prioritize building U-boats over all other naval activity.
5. Failing to recognize that unrestricted sinking was not a politically feasible option if America was to be kept out of the war.
6. Failing to develop pack attacks in response to the introduction of convoys.

BRITAIN'S STRATEGIC ERRORS

1. Britain had prepared for the wrong naval war by failing to anticipate U-boat attacks on merchant shipping, and hence had no means of defending that shipping.
2. Failure of the War Council (1914-1916) and the War Cabinet (1916-1918) to recognize the existential threat posed by the U-boats until the last possible moment.
3. Failure to use convoys as the prime means of defence against U-boat attacks.
4. Failure to make anti-submarine research the Admiralty's highest priority.
5. Failure to recognize the waste of resources tied up in the ineffective search patrols.
6. Failure to recognize that sinkings by Q-ships were negligible compared to the forces involved.

BRITAIN'S STRATEGIC SUCCESSES

1. The blockade, which seriously weakened Germany's capacity to wage war.
2. The Northern Patrol, which was particularly effective in disrupting the passage of vessels bound, directly and indirectly, for German ports.

3. The listening stations and Room 40, which together ensured that the Admiralty had regular and timely intelligence on the general locations of the U-boats at sea.
4. The introduction of convoys, which brought huge reductions in sinkings.
5. The close collaboration of American and British anti-submarine forces from late 1917 onwards, which brought a density of anti-submarine activity that seriously frustrated even experienced U-boat commanders.

Appendix 2
People

Asquith, Herbert Henry MP (1852-1938). Prime Minister and Leader of the Liberal Party 1908-1916; remained party leader until the party split at the end of 1918.
Bachmann, Admiral Gustav (1860-1943). Chief of the German Naval Staff Feb to Sept 1915.
Balfour, Arthur (1st Earl of Balfour) MP (1848-1930). An ex-Prime Minister; First Lord of the Admiralty 1915-1916.
Battenberg, Admiral Prince Louis Alexander (1854-1921). First Sea Lord Dec 1912 to Oct 1914.
Bauer, Fregattenkapitän Hermann (1875-1958). Commander of the German submarines Apr 1914 to June 1917.
Bayly, Admiral Sir Lewis (1857-1938). Commander of the Channel Fleet 1914-1915; Commander-in-Chief, Coast of Ireland, 1915-1919.
Beatty, Vice Admiral David (1871-1936). Commander of First Battlecruiser Squadron 1913-1916; Commander-in-Chief, Grand Fleet, 1916-1919.
Bernstorff, Johann Heinrich Graf von (1862-1939). German Ambassador to the United States of America 1908-1917.
Blücher, Princess (1876-1950). English aristocrat Evelyn Stapleton-Bretherton who married the German Gebhard Blücher von Wahlstatt. Diarist.
Bertie, Francis, 1st Viscount Bertie of Thame (1844-1919). British Ambassador to France 1905-1918. Diarist.
Bethmann-Hollweg, Theobald von (1856-1921). German Chancellor July 1909 to July 1917.
Bryan, William Jennings (1860-1925). US Secretary of State 1913-1915.
Callaghan, Admiral Sir George (1852-1920). Commander-in-Chief, Home Fleet, 1911-1914; Commander-in-Chief, The Nore, 1914-1918.
Capelle, Eduard von (1855-1931). Secretary of State to the German Naval Dept. from Mar 1916 to Oct 1918.
Carson, Sir Edward MP (1854-1935). Leader of the Ulster Unionist Party 1910-1921; Attorney General 1915-1916; First Lord of the Admiralty 1916-1917; Minister without Portfolio 1917-1918.
Churchill, Winston (1874-1965). First Lord of the Admiralty 1911-1915; Munitions Minister 1917-1919.
Curzon, George, First Marquess Curzon of Kedleston (1859-1925). Viceroy of India 1899-1905; President of the Air Board 1916-1917; Lord President of the Council 1916-1919.
Duff, Rear Admiral Alexander (1862-1933). Second-in-Command of the Fourth Battle Squadron 1912-1917; Director of the Anti-Submarine Division 1917-1919.

Appendix 2: People

Falkenhayn, General Eric (1861-1922). Chief of the German General Staff 1914-1916. Various commands in the field 1916-1919.
Fisher, Admiral of the Fleet Lord John (1841-1920). First Sea Lord 1904-1910 and 1914-1915; Chairman of the Board of Invention and Research 1915-1918.
French, John, 1st Earl of Ypres (1852-1925). Commander of the BEF 1914-1915; Commander-in-Chief of the British Home Forces 1915-1918; Lord Lieutenant of Ireland 1918-1921.
George, David Lloyd MP (1863-1945). Chancellor of the Exchequer 1908-1915; Munitions Minister 1915-1916; Prime Minister 1916-1922.
Gerard, James (1867-1951). US ambassador to Germany 1913 to 1917.
Grey, Edward, 1st Viscount Grey of Fallodon (1862-1933). Foreign Secretary 1905-1918.
Hall, Admiral William (1870-1933). Director of Naval Intelligence (DNI) 1914-1919.
Haig, Douglas, Field Marshal 1st Earl Haig (1861-1928). Commander of First Army Corps 1914-1915; Commander of the BEF 1915-1918.
Hamilton, General Sir Ian (1853-1947). Commander of Home Defence 1914-1915; Commander of the Mediterranean Expeditionary Force 1915.
Hankey, Maurice, 1st Baron Hankey (1877-1963). Soldier. Secretary of the Committee of Imperial Defence (1912-1938).
Hertling, Georg von (1843-1919). German Chancellor (1917-1918).
Hindenburg, Field Marshal Paul von (1847-1934). Commander of East Prussia Aug 1914; Commander-in-Chief of the German armies in the East Sept 1914 to Aug 1916; Army Chief of Staff Aug 1916 to June 1919.
Hipper, Admiral Franz Ritter von (1863-1932). Commander 1st Scouting Group 1913-1918; Commander-in-Chief of the High Seas Fleet Aug to Nov 1918.
Hobhouse, Charles MP (1862-1941). Postmaster General 1914-1915. Diarist.
Holtzendorff, Grand Admiral Henning von (1853-1919). Chief of the Naval Staff Sept 1915 to Aug 1918.
Hötzendorf, Franz Conrad von (1852-1925). Austrian Chief of Staff Nov 1906 to March 1917.
Ingenohl, Admiral Friedrich von (1857-1933). Commander-in-Chief of the High Seas Fleet Jan 1913 to Jan 1915.
Jackson, Admiral Henry (1855-1929). Chief of the Admiralty War Staff 1913 to May 1915; First Sea Lord May 1915 to Dec 1916.
Jagow, Gottlieb von (1863-1935). State Secretary of the German Foreign Office 1913-1916.
Jellicoe, (1859-1935). Commander-in-Chief of the Grand Fleet 1914 to 1916; First Sea Lord Nov 1916 to Dec 1917.

Appendix 2: People

Keyes, Admiral of the Fleet Roger (1872-1945). Commander of the battleship *Centurion* 1914-1917; Commander of Fourth Battle Squadron 1917-1918; Commander of the Dover Patrol 1918.
King-Hall, Lieutenant Stephen (1893-1966). Writer and politician. Served in HMS *Southampton* and the 11th Submarine Flotilla during the First World War.
Kitchener, Lord (1850-1916). War Minister 1914-1916. Drowned June 5, 1916.
Kühlmann, Richard von (1873-1948). Diplomat. German Foreign Secretary Aug 1917 to July 1918.
Lansing, Robert (1864-1928). US Secretary of State June 1915 to Feb 1920.
Ludendorff, General Erich (1865-1937). Quartermaster General to von Bulow's Second Army 1914-1916; Chief of Staff of German army 1916-1918.
Maclay, Joseph (1857-1951). Businessman. Minister of Shipping 1916-1921.
Millerand, Alexandre (1859-1943). French War Minister Aug 1914 to Oct 1915.
Müller, Admiral Georg von (1854-1940). Chief of the German Naval Cabinet 1906-1918.
Oliver, Rear Admiral Sir Henry (1865-1965). Naval Secretary 1914-1916; Deputy Chief of the Naval Staff 1916-1919.
Pohl, Admiral Hugo von (1855-1916). Chief of the German Naval Staff Apr 1913 to Feb 1915; Commander-in-Chief of the High Seas Fleet Jan 1915 to Jan 1916.
Repington, Charles à Court (1858-1925). Soldier and journalist.
Riddell George, 1st Baron Riddell (1865-1934). Solicitor and newspaper proprietor.
Scheer, Admiral Reinhard (1863-1928). Commander of Second Battle Squadron 1914; Commander of Third Battle Squadron 1915; Commander-in-Chief of the High Seas Fleet Jan 1916 to Aug 1918; Chief of the Naval Staff Aug 1918 to Nov 1918.
Scrimgeour, Alexander (-1916). Diarist and midshipman. Died at the Battle of Jutland.
Sims, Rear Admiral William (1858-1936). US senior naval representative in Europe 1917-1918.
Stanley, Venetia (1887-1947). Aristocrat and socialite with whom Herbert Asquith had a prolific correspondence.
Stresemann, Gustav (1878-1929). German politician who was a leading proponent of unrestricted submarine warfare and the annexation of the Belgian coastline.
Sturdee, Doveton, Admiral of the Fleet (1859-1925). Chief of the War Staff at the Admiralty July 1914; Squadron Commander at the Battle of the Falklands 1914; Commander Fourth Battle Squadron 1915-1918; Commander-in-Chief Nore 1918-1921.
Tirpitz, Grand-Admiral von (1849-1930). Secretary of State to the German Naval Department 1897 to Mar 1916.

Appendix 2: People

Tyrwhitt, Admiral of the Fleet Sir Reginald (1870-1951). Harwich Force commander 1914-1919.
Wemyss, Admiral Rosslyn (1864-1933). Commander of the Twelfth Cruiser Squadron in the Channel Fleet 1914; Various duties at Dardanelles and Gallipoli 1915; Commander of the East Indies & Egyptian Squadron 1916; Second Sea Lord 1917; First Sea Lord Jan 1918 to Nov 1919.
Wilhelm II (1859-1941). German Emperor. Reigned 1888 to 1918.
Zimmermann, Arthur (1864-1930). Germany Secretary of State for Foreign Affairs 1916-1917.

Sources

USEFUL WEBSITES

Naval-History website, WW1 section: http://www.naval-history.net/Index0-1914.htm
Sinkings of ships of all kinds: https://www.wrecksite.eu/
The World War I Document Archive: http://www.gwpda.org/index.html
U-boat patrols and their commanders: Uboat.net https://uboat.net/

OTHER SOURCES

– *German prisoners in Great Britain 1916.* Bolton and London: Tillotson.
– 'Submarine Warfare - Austria' *The American Journal of International Law*, Vol. 11, N° 4, 1917, pp 155-221. JSTOR, www.jstor.org/stable/2212351. Accessed 4 Mar. 2021.
– *Memoirs & Diaries - War at Sea.* https://www.firstworldwar.com/diaries/waratsea.htm
– *Proceedings of the Twenty-Fourth Annual Historical Diving Conference, Poole 2014.* https://www.thehds.com/product/proceedings-of-the-24th-annual-conference-2014/
– 1917. *The War On Hospital Ships, From The Narratives Of Eye-Witnesses.* T Fisher Unwin Ltd.
– 1919. *The Northern Mine Barrage: Mine Force United States Atlantic Fleet.* Annapolis: US Naval Institute.
– 2018. *Diplomatic Correspondence with Belligerent Governments Relating to Neutral Rights and Commerce.* Palala Press.
Andrew, C. *The Defence of the Realm.* London: Allen Lane, 2009.
Aspinall-Oglander, C F. *Roger Keyes Being the Biography of Admiral of the Fleet Lord Keyes of Zeebrugge and Dover.* London: Hogarth Press, 1951.
Asprey, R B. *The German High Command at War: Hindenburg and Ludendorff Conduct World War I.* New York: W. Morrow, 1991.
Asquith, H H (ed Brock). *Letters to Venetia Stanley.* Oxford: Oxford University Press, 1982.
Asquith, Lady Cynthia. *Diaries 1915-1918.* London: Hutchinson, 1968.
Bacon, R. *The Dover patrol 1915-1917.* London: Hutchinson, 1919.
Barnett, C. *Hitler's Generals.* London: Phoenix, 1995.
Barnett, C. *The Swordbearers.* London: Cassell, 2000.
Barnett, L M. *British Food Policy During the First World War.* London: Allen & Unwin, 1985.
Bayly, L. *Pull Together! The memoirs of Admiral Sir Lewis Bayly.* London: George G Harrap & Co. Ltd. 1939.

Sources

Beaverbrook, Lord. *Politicians and the War 1914-1916*. London: Thornton Butterworth Ltd. 1928.
Beaverbrook, Lord. *Men and Power 1917-1918*. London: Hutchinson, 1956.
Beckett, I. *Home Front 1914-1918: How Britain Survived the Great War*. London: The National Archives, 2006.
Beesly, P. *Room 40: British Intelligence 1914-18*. London: Hamish Hamilton.
Berg, A C. 2013. *Wilson*. New York: Berkely Books, 1982.
Bernstorff. *My Three Years in America*. London: Skeffington & Son Ltd., 1920.
Bertie, Lord (Ed Lennox). *The Diary of Lord Bertie of Thame 1914-1918*. London: Hodder & Stoughton, 1924.
Bilbrough, E M. *My War Diary*. London: Ebury Press, 2014.
Black, N D. 2005. *The Admiralty War Staff And Its Influence On The Conduct Of The Naval War Between 1914 and 1918*. PhD Thesis. University College: University of London. https://discovery.ucl.ac.uk/id/eprint/1445317/1/U592637.pdf
Blake, R (ed). *The Private Papers of Douglas Haig*. London: Eyre & Spottiswoode, 1952.
Blake, R. *The Unknown Prime Minister*. London: Eyre & Spottiswoode, 1955.
Blickle, K. *Pandemics Change Cities: Municipal Spending and Voter Extremism in Germany, 1918-1933*. Federal Reserve Bank of New York Staff Reports, 2020.
Blücher, E. *An English Wife in Berlin*. Alpha Editions, 2019.
Breemer, J S. *Defeating the U-boat: Inventing Anti-submarine Warfare*. Newport, Rhode Island: Naval War College Press, 2010.
Breitung, E N. *Purchase of Steamship 'Dacia': Statement of the Motives and Facts Concerning The Purchase Of The Steamship 'Dacia'*. Charleston, South Carolina: Nabu Press, 2011.
Brett, M V (ed.). *Journals and Letters of Reginald Viscount Esher*, Vol 3 1910-1915. London: Ivor Nicholson & Watson Ltd, 1938.
Brittain, V. *Testament of Youth*. London: Virago Press, 1978.
Broadberry, S & Howlett, P. *The United Kingdom During World War I: Business as usual?* https://www.researchgate.net, 2005. Accessed 22 Jan 2021.
Brock, M G & Brock, E. *Margot Asquith's Great War Diary 1914-1916: the view from Downing Street*. Oxford: Oxford University Press, 2014.
Bull, R. *History of Lyme in Objects: 16. c.1914 - Boot from HMS Formidable*. Lyme Regis Museum, 2013.
Campbell, G. *My Mystery Ships*. London: Hodder and Stoughton, 1937.
Carlisle, R. 'The Attacks on US Shipping that Precipitated American Entry into World War I'. *The Northern Mariner/Le marin du nord*, XVII N°· 3 (July 2007), pp. 41-66.
Chalmers, W S. *The Life And Letters of David, Earl Beatty*. London: Hodder & Stoughton, 1951.
Chatterton, E K. *Q-Ships and Their Story*. London: Sidgwick & Jackson, 1922.
Chatterton, E K. *The Big Blockade*. London: Hurst & Blackett, 1932.

Sources

Churchill, W S. *The World Crisis*, Vols I & II. London: Oldham Press Ltd, 1938.
Churchill, W S. *The World Crisis 1914-1918*, Abridged ed. London: Macmillan, 1941.
Coder, B J. *Q-Ships of The Great War*. Alabama: Air University Press, 2012.
Compton Hall, R. *Submarines and the War at Sea, 1914-18*. London: Macmillan, 1991.
Consett, M W W P. *The Triumph of Unarmed Forces*. London: Williams and Norgate, 1928.
Corbett, J S. *Naval Operations*, Vols 1-3. London: Longmans Green, 1920-1.
Curtis, J. *'To The Last Man' - Australia's Entry To War In 1914*. Australian Parliamentary Paper (aph.gov.au), 2014.
David, E (ed). *Inside Asquith's Cabinet*. London: John Murray, 1977.
De Chair, Sir Dudley. 1961. *The Sea Is Strong*. London: George G. Harrap & Co.
Deayton, A & Quinn, I. *Turbine Excursion Steamers: A History*. Stroud: Amberley Publishing, 2012.
Dewar, K. *The Navy From Within*. London: Gollancz, 1939.
Domville, C W. *Submarines, Mines, and Torpedoes in the War*. London; The Daily Telegraph War Books, 1914.
Edwards, M L. *Stresemann and the Greater Germany*. New York: Bookman Associates, 1963.
English Heritage. 2015. *First World War Wireless Stations in England*. Oxford Archaeology, 2015.
Falkenhayan, E. *General Headquarters 1914-1916 and its Critical Decisions*. Nashville: The Battery Press, 1919.
Field, C. *The British Navy Book*. London: Blackie & Son Ltd. 1915.
Fitch, T & Poirier, M. *Into the Danger Zone*. The History Press, 2015.
Forstner, F. *The Journal of Submarine Commander Von Forstner*. Boston & New York: Houghton Mifflin Company, 1917.
Freeman, R. *Atlantic Nightmare*. London: Lume Books, 2019.
Freeman, R. *Tempestuous Genius*. CreateSpace edition, 2020.
Gazeley, I & Newell, A. 'The First World War and Working-class Food Consumption in Britain'. *European Review of Economic History*. Jan 2013. 17(1):71-94.
George, D Lloyd. War Memoirs of David Lloyd George, Vol II. London: Ivor Nicholson & Watson, 1933.
George, D Lloyd. *War Memoirs of David Lloyd George*, Vol III. London: Ivor Nicholson & Watson, 1934.
Gerard, J W. *My Four Years in Germany*. London: Hodder & Stoughton, 1917.
Gibson, R H & Prendergast, MP. *The German Submarine War 1914-1918*. London: Imperial War Museum, 1931 (reprint).
Gilbert, M. *Winston S Churchill*, Vol III. London: Heinemann, 1971.
Gilbert, M. Winston S Churchill, Vol. IV. London: Heineman, 1972.

Grant, R M. *U-boats Destroyed: The effect of anti-submarine warfare 1914-1918*. London: Putnam, 1964.
Grant, R M. *U-boat Intelligence 1914-1918*. Archon Books, 1969.
Grattan, C H. 1969. *Why We Fought*. Indianapolis: Bobs-Merril Co.
Gray, E. *The Devil's Device: the story of Robert Whitehead, inventor of the torpedo*. London: Seeley, 1975.
Gray, E. *The U-Boat War 1914-1918*. London: Leo Cooper, 1994.
Gregory, R. A. 1958. 'New Look at the Case of the Dacia'. *The Journal of American History*, Sept 1968, Vol. 55, No. 2.
Gretton, P. *Former Naval Person: Winston Churchill and the Royal Navy*. London: Cassell, 1968.
Hallam, R & Benyon, M. *Scrimgeour's Small Scribbling Diary 1914-1916*. London: Conway, 2008.
Halpern, P G. *A Naval History of World War I*. London: UCL Press, 1994.
Halpern, P G. *The Battle of the Otranto Straits*. Bloomington: Indiana University Press, 2004.
Ham, P. *Young Hitler: the making of the Führer*. New York: Doubleday, 2017.
Hankey, Lord. *The Supreme Command 1914-1918*, 2 vols. London: George Allen & Unwin Ltd., 1961.
Hardinge, C. *Old Diplomacy: the reminiscences of Lord Hardinge of Penshurst*. London: Murray, 1947.
Hart, P. *Voices From the Front*. London: Profile Books, 2015.
Healy, T M. *Letters and Leaders of My Day* Vol II. New York: Frederick A Stokes Co., 1929.
Hendrick, B J. 1923. *The Life and Letters of Walter H Page*, 2 vols. London: Heinemann.
Hodgson, G R. 'Causing Unnecessary Anxiety?: British Newspapers and the Battle of Jutland'. In: Hart, C, (ed.) *World War I Media, Entertainments & Popular Culture*. Midrash, Chester, 2018.
Hough, R. *The First Mountbattens*. London: Hutchinson, 1974.
House, Colonel. *The Intimate Papers of Colonel House*, 2 vols. London: Ernest Benn Ltd., 1926.
Hurd, A & Bashford H H. *A Short History of the Naval War 1914-1918*. New York: Doubleday, Page and Company, 1919.
Hurd, A. *The Merchant Navy*. London: John Murray, 1921.
Hurd, A. *Who Goes There?* London: Hutchinson, 1941.
Hurd, A. *History of the Great War. the Merchant Navy*: Vol I. London: Naval & Military Press, 2006.
James, W J. *The Eyes of the Navy*. London: Methuen, 1955.
Jameson, W S. *The Most Formidable Thing*. London: Rupert Hart-Davis, 1965.
Jarausch, K H. *The Enigmatic Chancellor*. London: Yale University Press, 1973.
Jellicoe, J R. *The Crisis of the Naval War*. London: Cassell, 1920.

Sources

Jellicoe, J R. *The Submarine Peril: the Admiralty policy in 1917*. London: Cassell. 1934.
Jellicoe, J R. *The Grand Fleet 1914-1916: its creation, development and work*. Ringshall: Ad Hoc Publications, 2006 [1920].
Jones, T. *Whitehall Diary Vol I: 1916-1925*. London: Oxford University Press, 1969.
Keegan, J. *The Price of Admiralty*. New York: Penguin Books, 1988.
Keyes, R. *Naval Memoirs 1916-1918*. London: Thornton Butterworth Ltd., 1935.
King-Hall, L. *Sea Saga*. London: Victor Gollancz Ltd., 1935.
King-Hall, S. *A North Sea Diary 1914-1918*. London: Newnes, 1936.
King-Hall, S. *My Naval Life 1906-1929*. London: Faber, 1952.
Knight, E F. *The Harwich Naval Forces*. London: Hodder & Stoughton.
Lilley, T N. *Operations of the Tenth Cruiser Squadron*. PhD thesis, University of Greenwich, 2012.
Lowell T. *Raiders of the Deep*. New York: Doubleday, Doran & Co., 1928.
Macfarlane, J A C. *Naval Travesty: the dismissal of Admiral Sir John Jellicoe, 1917*. University of St Andrews PhD thesis, 2014.
MacLeod, R M & Andrews, E. Kay. 'Scientific Advice in the War at Sea, 1915-1917: The Board of Invention and Research' *Journal of Contemporary History*, Vol. 6, N⁰· 2 (1971), pp. 3-40.
Mansergh, R. *Barrow-in-Furness in the Great War*. Barnsley: Pen & Sword Military, 2015.
Marder, A J. (Ed). *Fear God and Dread Nought*, Vol I 1854-1904. London: Jonathan Cape, 1952`.
Marder, A J. (Ed). *Fear God and Dread Nought*, Vol III 1914-1920. London: Jonathan Cape, 1959.
Marder, A J. *From the Dreadnought to Scapa Flow'* Vol I 1904-1914 & Vol II 1914-1916. Barnsley: Seaforth Publishing, 2013.
Marder, A J. *From the Dreadnought to Scapa Flow'* Vol III May-Dec 1916; Vol IV 1917; & Vol V 1918-1919. Barnsley: Seaforth Publishing, 2014.
Massie, R K. *Castles of Steel*. New York: Random House, 2003.
Max. *The Memoirs of Prince Max of Baden*. London: Constable & Co. Ltd., 1928.
Maxwell, D. *Listen Up*. Aberdour: Aberdour Cultural Association, 2014.
McEwen, J M. *The Riddell Diaries*. London: The Athlone Press, 1986.
Messimer, D R. *Find and Destroy: Antisubmarine warfare in World War I*. Annapolis: Naval Institute Press, 2001.
Morgan, J V. *Life of Viscount Rhondda*. London: H R Allenson, 1918.
Moyer, L V. *Victory Must Be Ours*. London: Leo Cooper, 1995.
Navy Department. *German Submarine Activities on the Atlantic Coast of the United States and Canada*. Washington: Navy Department Office of Naval Records and Library. 1920.
Newbolt, H. *Submarine and Anti-submarine*. London: Longmans, Green & Co., 1919.

Newbolt, H. Various dates. *Naval Operations*. Vols III & IV. London: Longmans Green.
Oram, H P K. *Ready For Sea*. London: Seeley, 1974.
Padfield, P. *Dönitz, The Last Führer: portrait of a Nazi war leader*. London: Gollancz, 1984.
Patterson, A T. *The Jellicoe papers: selections from the private and official correspondence of Admiral of the Fleet Earl Jellicoe of Scapa*. Shortlands Kent: Navy Records Society, 1966.
Patterson, A T. *Tyrwhitt of the Harwich force: the life of Admiral of the Fleet Sir Reginald Tyrwhitt*. London: Macdonald & Jane's, 1973.
Peck, G. *The Great War in America*. New York: Pegasus Books, 2018.
Perren, R. 'Farmers and consumers under strain: allied meat supplies in the First World War'. *The Agricultural History Review* Vol. 53, No. 2 (2005), pp. 212-228. British Agricultural History Society.
Philbin, T. *Admiral von Hipper. The inconvenient hero*. Amsterdam: B R Gruner Publishing Co., 1982.
Phillips, A. *A Newnham Anthology*. Cambridge University Press, 2010.
Phimester, J. *First World War Wireless Stations in England*. Swindon: English Heritage, 2015.
Pirzio-Biroli, C. *My Great-Grandfather Grand-Admiral Von Tirpitz*. Archway Publishing, 2016.
Repington, à Court. *New Wars for Old – The submarine menace* –Blackwood's Magazine CLXXXVII Jan-June 1910. 'New Worlds for Old' *Blackwood's Magazine*.
Reynolds, F J, Churchill, A L & Miller, F T. *The Story of the Great War* Vols 1-8. New York: Collier & Son., Various dates.
Riddell, Lord. *Lord Riddell's War Diary 1914-1918*. London: Ivor Nicholson & Watson Ltd., 1933.
Ring, J. *How the Navy Won the War: The real instrument of victory 1914-1918*. Barnsley: Seaforth Publishing, 2018.
Ritschl, A. *Germany's Economy at War 1914-1918 and Beyond*. Berlin: Humboldt University, 2003.
Robinson M F & Robinson G J. *Der Kapitan: U-Boat Ace Hans Rose*. Stroud: Amberley Publishing, 2019.
Roskill, S W. *Hankey: Man of Secrets*. London: Collins, 1970.
Roskill, S W. *Admiral of the Fleet Earl Beatty*. London: Collins.
Rumbold, Sir H. 1940. *The War Crisis in Berlin July-August 1914*. London: Constable & Co Ltd., 1980.
Russell, B. *International Law at Sea, Economic Warfare, and Britain's Response to the German U-boat Campaign during the First World War*. PhD thesis. The Open University, 2008.
Salter, J. A. *Allied Shipping Control: an experiment in international administration*. Oxford: Clarendon Press, 1921.

Sources

Sassoon, S. *Siegfried Sassoon Diaries, 1915-1918*. London: Faber & Faber. Reprint edition, 1983.
Scheer, R. *Germany's High Sea Fleet in the World War*. London: Cassell and Company, Ltd., 1920.
Seeger, A. *Letters and Diary of Alan Seeger*. New York. Charles Scribner's Sons, 1917.
Sims, W S. *The Victory at Sea*. London: John Murray, 1920.
Smith, P C. *Hard Lying*. London: Kimber, 1971.
Spiegel, F von. *U-Boat 202: the war diary of a German submarine*. Connecticut: Mews Books, 1976.
Spiess, J. *Six Ans de Croisières en Sous-Marin*. Paris: Payot, 1927.
Stevenson, D. *1917 War, Peace, and Revolution*. Oxford: OUP.
Taffrail, D H (Captain Taprell Dorling) 1931. *Endless Story*. London: Hodder and Stoughton, 2017.
Taussig, K J. (ed William N. Still, Jr.) *The Queenstown Patrol, 1917. The Diary of Commander Joseph Knefler Taussig*, Newport, Rhode Island: US Navy. Naval War College Press, 1996.
Taylor, A J P. *English History, 1914-1945*. Oxford: Clarendon Press, 1965.
Taylor, A J P. *The Origins of the Second World War*. London: Penguin Books, 1991.
Thaer, Colonel von. *Diary Notes of Oberst von Thaer*, 1918. http://www.gwpda.org/1918/thaereng.html
Tirpitz, A von. *My Memoirs* Vols I & II. New York: Dodd, Mead and Co., 1919.
Toye, F. *For What We Have Received*. London: William Heinemann Ltd., 1950.
Trayes, F G. *Five Months on a German Raider*. London: Headley Bros., 1919.
Tupper, R. *Reminiscences*. London: Jarrolds, 1929.
US Govt. *Diplomatic Correspondence with Belligerent Governments Relating to Neutral Rights and Duties*. Washington: US Government Printing Office, 1915.
US Govt. *Papers Relating to the Torpedoing of the SS Sussex*. Washington: United States. Department of State, 1916.
US Govt. *Papers Relating to The Foreign Relations of the United States 1916 Supplement*. Washington: US Govt Printing Office, 1929.
Waldeyer-Hartz, H. *Admiral von Hipper*. London: Rich & Cowan, 1933.
Watson, A. *Ring of Steel: Germany and Austria-Hungary at War, 1914-1918*. London: Penguin Books, 2015.
Wemyss, L. *The Life & Letters of Lord Wester Wemyss*. London: Eyre and Spottiswoode, 1935.
Wiegand, K H von. *Current Misconceptions About The War*. New York: The Fatherland Corporation, 1915.
Williams, G H. *The United States Merchant Marine in World War I: Ships, Crews, Shipbuilders*. Jefferson (USA): McFarland & Co Inc., 2017.
Winton, J. *Jellicoe*. London: Joseph, 1981.

Sources

Wrench, E. *Alfred, Lord Milner, the man of no illusions, 1854-1925*. London: Eyre & Spottiswoode, 1958.

Index

Adams, Ensign Ashley, 323
Airships, 109, 252
Anderson - boatswain, 116
Andler, Kaptl. Rudolf, 9, 314
Anti-Submarine Division, 232, 343
Anti-Submarine Warfare Department, 230
Arnauld, Kaptl. Lothar von, 10, 166, 317, 331
Asquith, Cynthia, 141
Asquith, H H, 15, 51, 55, 72, 81, 84, 101, 102, 204, 289
Asquith, Margot, 98
Astor, Viscountess Nancy, 224
Attwooll - Postal worker, 329
Bachmann, Adm. Gustav, 134, 150, 343
Bacon, Rear Adm. Reginald, 119, 191, 195, 264, 277, 288, 291, 295
Balfour, Arthur, 26, 135, 136, 137, 150, 173, 201, 202, 218, 259, 285, 289, 292, 328, 330, 343
Ballard, Cmdr. Charles, 87
Bannerman, Cpt. Thomas, 116
Barry, Lieut. Claud, 313
Bartlett, Cpt. Charles, 199
Battenberg, Admiral Prince Louis of, 17, 74, 343
Battle of Dogger Bank, 89, 96
Battle of Heligoland Bight, 37, 44
Battle of Jutland 1916, 41, 119
Bauer, Fgt Cäsar, 280
Bauer, Colonel Max, 331
Bauer, Hermann, 208, 211
Baxter, Mr - a Chief Officer, 116
Bayly,Vice Adm. Lewis, 72, 86, 87, 88, 140, 141, 146, 247, 258, 273, 282
Beatty, Adm Beatty, 28, 37, 38, 39, 40, 41, 45, 54, 62, 70, 75, 89, 90, 187, 188, 231, 232, 234, 235, 248, 249, 258, 262, 285, 336, 337, 343, 348, 352
Beaufoy, Matron Kate, 305
Beaverbrook, Lord, 22, 348
Belgian Relief Mission, 99
Belknap, Cpt. Reginald, 320
Bell, Cpt. John, 103, 104
Benckendorff, Count Constantine, 59
Beresford, Adm. Lord Charles, 74, 89
Berger, Kapt Gerhard, 216
Bernstorff, Johann, 128, 132, 148, 195, 213, 214, 225, 343
Bertie, Lord, 265
Bilbrough, Ethel - housewife, 227
Billyard-Leake, Cpt. Edward, 308
Bingelman, Ensign Gustav, 311, 312
Birch, Cpt.William, 328, 330
Bircham, Cmdr. F R S, 106
Birkenhead, Lord, 22
Blair, Sergeant Hubert, 117
Blücher, Princess, 21, 90, 130, 149, 159, 160, 176, 184, 209, 245, 286, 294
Board of Invention and Research, 135, 136, 174, 251, 263, 344, 351
Bone, James, 11
Bothmer, Kaptl. Thorwald von, 188
Bowman, Thomas, 267
Bowring, Charles W, 126
Breemer, Jan S, 200
Breitung, E N, 102, 348
Brooke, Lieut. Cmdr. Edward, 281
Brown, Cmdr. Wilson, 323, 324
Bryan, Sec. of State William, 31, 81, 82, 93, 132
Buckley - ship's steward, 221
Burney, Adm. Cecil, 187
Burt, Cpt. Bernard, 305
Caesar, Julius, 289

Index

Callaghan, Adm. Sir George, 17, 22, 343
Cambon, Paul, 14
Campbell, Cmdr. Gordon, 211, 212, 275, 276
Capelle, Adm. Eduard von, 3, 167, 343
Carey, Cpt., 68
Carnaby, Mr. - Radio officer, 221
Carr, Josephine, 330
Carson, Edward, 226, 289
Carver, Robert Orville, 326
Cattaro naval base, 122, 151, 153
Chatterton, Cpt. Herbert, 39
Chave, Cpt. Benjamin, 220, 221, 222
Churchill, Winston, 1, 16, 18, 19, 21, 22, 28, 30, 36, 37, 39, 48, 54, 55, 59, 62, 67, 72, 73, 74, 78, 84, 88, 89, 90, 106, 119, 134, 135, 149, 191, 299, 305
Clemenceau, Georges, 294
Coleman, Frank, 162
Committee of Imperial Defence, 12, 16, 24, 80, 84, 136, 344
Convoys
  HH24, 281
Cooke, H E, 299
Coombes, Frank, 164
Cordner, Major Alexander, 307
Cormack, Cpt. John, 56
Cornwallis-West, Mrs, 74
Cotton, Cpt. Lyman, 323
County War Agriculture Committees, 298
Creagh, Cmdr. James, 107
Crocker, George, 168
Cromie, Lieut. Cmdr. Francis, 158
Crowe, Sir Eyre, 31, 231
Cummins, Cpt. Kenneth, 320
Cunard, Lady, 141
Curtis, Cpt Berwick, 304, 349
Curzon, Lord, 204, 228, 264
Custance, Adm. Sir Reginald, 24
D'Oyly-Hughes, Cmdr., 315
Dampier, Cpt. Frederick, 70, 71, 72
Davies - Captain of *Falaba*, 116

Davis, Lieut. Cmdr., 277
Day, Cmdr. Selwyn, 220
de Chair, Rear Adm. Dudley, 161
de Robeck, Rear Adm. John, 123
Declaration of London 1909, 29, 31
Depth-charges, 263
Derby, Lord, 130, 198, 264
Dernberg, Dr. Bernhard, 128
Devonport, Lord, 238, 255
Dewar, Cmdr. Kenneth, 21, 22, 235
Dieckmann, Kaptl. Victor, 283
Diers - Seaman, 313
Ditfurth, Kapt. Benno von, 263
Donaldson, Sir Hay Frederick, 181
Dönitz, Oberl. Karl, 261, 300, 317
Donnington Hall Camp, 253
Dorling, Cmdr. Taprell, 303, 304
Doubleday, Frank N - publisher, 256, 257, 284
Dover Barrage, 92, 105, 115, 119, 195, 211, 274, 278, 291, 296
Dover Patrol, 119, 277, 291, 295, 345
Drury, Alice, 127
Duff, Douglas, 219
Duff, Vice Adm Arthur, 33, 67, 229, 230, 232, 233, 234, 235, 236, 237, 271, 284
Dyffryn Aled Hall prison camp, 79
Eastaway, Cpt., 244
Edward VII, King, 14, 172
Edwards, ship's engineer, 116
Eighth Submarine Flotilla, 20, 30
Ellershaw, Brig. Gen. Arthur, 181
Elliott, Lieut. General Bertram, 307
Emsmann, Oberl. Hans Joachim, 333
Ewing - Engineman, 297
Exeter Maryoress, 143
Falkenhayn, General von Erich, 20, 46, 77, 132, 177, 179, 205
Favell, Lieut. Cmdr. Ernest, 42, 43
Feldkirchner, Kapt. Johannes, 64, 65, 76
Fifth Battle Squadron, 41, 86
Finch, Cpt. William, 146, 147

Index

Fisher, Adm. of the Fleet Lord, 36, 51, 70, 74, 75, 89, 119, 134, 135, 137, 138, 167, 197, 198, 251, 263, 289, 290, 344
Fisher, Andrew, 57
Fitzgerald, Lieut. Col. Oswald, 181
Fleet Reviews, 17
Fleming, Prof. J A, 135
Flour and Bread Order 1917, 238
Forstmann, Kaptl. Walter, 152, 261
Forstner, Korv-Kapt. Georg-Günther von, 100, 116, 117
Fox, Cpt. Cecil H, 26, 27, 28
Fox, Lieut. Cmdr. Charles, 281
Frank – a minelayer, 321
Franz, Kaptl. Adolf, 89, 311, 312, 344
Frederick III, 12
Fremantle, Cmdr. C A, 66
Fryatt, Cpt. Charles, 185, 186
Fürbringer, Kaptl. Gerhardt, 138, 139
Gabriel - Seaman, 313
Galbraith, Lieut. Thomas, 71, 72
Galibin, Lieut., 59
Gansser, Kapt. Konrad, 152, 165, 186
Gaunt, Cpt Guy, 214
Geddes, Sir Eric, 250, 265, 266, 271, 279, 289, 290, 294, 295, 322, 326
George V, King, 22, 140, 227
Gerard, Ambassador James, 131, 344
Gercke, Kvtk. Hermann, 314, 315
German War Zone, 96, 97, 98, 99, 100, 101
Godfrey-Faussett, Eugénie, 248
Goodenough, Cpt. William, 37, 38, 39
Gorman, Mary, 56, 152
Goschen, Sir Edward, 17
Graeff, Kaptl. Ernst, 140
Granados, Enrique, 169
Grand Fleet, 15, 19, 22, 25, 32, 34, 37, 38, 48, 61, 62, 64, 67, 70, 74, 75, 77, 84, 86, 90, 117, 119, 121, 149, 167, 171, 177, 178, 179, 187, 188, 191, 202, 262, 333, 337, 343, 344, 351
Grave, Karl, 112
Green, Dr Clayton, 168
Greil, Cecile, 155
Grey, Sir Edward, 82, 93, 102, 131, 146, 148, 157, 189, 195
Gross, Oberl. Karl, 2, 61, 119, 120
Gruetz, Mayor, 215
Guttmann, Bernhard, 246
Habenicht, Lt Cmdr Richard, 59
Haddock, Cpt. Herbert, 71
Haig, Field Marshal Douglas, 191, 202, 205, 226, 249, 259, 264, 290, 291
Halahan, Cpt. Henry, 307
Hall, Adm. Sir William, 79, 80, 81, 129, 186, 214, 216, 263, 296, 344
Hall, Cpt. Reginald, 59
Hamilton, Duke & Duchess of, 137
Handcock, Isaac, 281
Hankey, Sir Maurice, 24, 29, 52, 84, 204, 228, 229, 231, 232, 234, 235, 290
Hardinge, Lord, 246
Hart, Samuel, 319
Harwich Force, 7, 30, 187
Hashagen, Kpt Ernst, 216
Hassan, Cpt. Harry, 267
Hawkcraig Experimental Station (HMS *Tarlair*), 174
Hearley, John, 167, 170
Heimburg, Kaptl. Heini von, 145
Heinecken, Dr Philipp, 21
Helfferich, Karl, 192, 207
Henderson, Cmdr. Reginald, 230, 231
Henderson, MP, Arthur, 204, 228
Hennig, Kapt von, 78, 79, 80, 333
Herbert, Ltn-Cmdr Godfrey, 146
Heroch, Petty Officer, 313
Hersing, Oberl. Otto, 42, 91, 92, 122, 123

358

Index

Hertling, Chancellor Georg von, 331, 344
Higgins - Postal worker, 329
High Seas Fleet, 19, 34, 39, 41, 51, 74, 76, 84, 90, 96, 149, 171, 172, 176, 177, 178, 179, 187, 188, 201, 333, 334, 337, 341, 344, 345
Hildyard, Nona, 152
Hipper, Adm. Franz von, 75, 76, 89, 90, 325, 334, 335, 336, 337, 344
Hobhouse, Charles, 55, 57, 73, 102, 159, 344
Holl, Cpt. E J, 318
Hollweg, Chancellor Bethmann, 20, 42, 132, 134, 192, 208, 343
Holtzendorff, Vice Adm. von, 150, 192, 206, 207, 220, 226, 293, 325, 344
Hood, Adm. Horace, 21, 119
Horton, Lieut. Cmdr. Max, 44, 45, 53, 54
Horwood, Henry, 120
House, Colonel Edward, 129, 148, 154, 157, 213
Houston, Mr A, 118
Howaldt, Kaptl. Hans, 245
Hoy, Mrs, 216
Huggins, Tooper Reginald, 243, 244
Huxley, Aldous, 44
Huyshe, Wentworth, 68
Hydrophones, 174, 190, 252, 263, 273, 293, 333
Ingenohl, Adm. Friedrich von, 19, 34, 89, 96, 344
Ingram, Osman, 283
Izac, Lieut. Edouard, 319
Jackson, Adm Sir Henry, 135, 150, 201, 289, 344, 348
Jagow, Gottlieb von, 131, 192, 208, 344
Jahnke, Kurt - sabateur, 260
James, Henry, 132
Jellicoe, Adm. Sir John, 22, 30, 37, 38, 62, 71, 72, 73, 74, 75, 77, 78, 81, 94, 95, 164, 171, 172, 178, 179, 180, 181, 187, 188, 191, 198, 201, 202, 205, 206, 218, 226, 227, 228, 229, 230, 232, 233, 234, 235, 236, 237, 241, 248, 249, 252, 257, 263, 264, 269, 271, 276, 277, 282,285, 289, 290, 291, 320, 339, 344
Joffre, General Joseph, 191, 205
Johansson, Anders, 120
Johnson, Cpt. Robert, 49, 64
Jones, Midshipman Basil, 203, 337
Joynson-Hicks MP, William, 89
Kelk, Dorothy, 147
Kenrick, RNVR, Cmdr. Henry, 230
Keyes, Rear Adm. Roger, 8, 20, 30, 36, 37, 38, 39, 40, 54, 180, 185, 202, 288, 290, 291, 295, 296, 298, 307, 345
Kiehnert - Radio operator, 59
Kiel Regatta, 14, 15
Kieswetter, Kaptl. Wilhelm, 304, 305
King-Hall, Lieut. Stephen, 9, 11, 57, 62, 67, 113, 176, 178, 345, 351
Kitchener, Lord, 73, 75, 181, 182, 345
Kohnstern, Anna, 184
Kolbe, Kapt. Constantin, 66
Kophamel, Korvetk. Waldemar, 152
Krafft, Kaptl. Ernst, 317
Kratzsch, Kapt. Hans, 107
Kretch, Kaptl. Günther, 313, 314
Kuhlken, Cpt., 57
Kühlmann, Richard von, 120, 294
Kukat, Oberl. Heinrich, 335
Laabs - Seaman, 313
Lamura, Mrs Frances, 156
Lancashire and Cheshire Royal Garrison Artillery, 92
Lansdowne, Lord, 14
Lansing, Robert, 132, 162, 166, 171, 213, 217, 345
Laughlin, Ian B, 189
Law, Bonar, 22, 198, 204, 228, 269

Index

Lawson - Army offier in *Leasowe Castle*, 318
Lawson, Lieut. Frederick, 220
Lee MP, Arthur, 74
Lepsius, Oblt. Reinhold, 103, 104
Liners - German
  Kronprinzessin Cecilie, 23
Listening stations, 41, 53, 58, 60, 89
Lloyd George, David, 264
Lloyd George, David, 22, 28, 73, 173, 191, 198, 201, 203, 204, 224, 229, 230, 231, 232, 234, 235, 236
Lowestoft and Yarmouth raid, 171
Loxley, Cpt., 87, 88
Ludendorff, General Erich, 192, 207, 330, 331
Lyon, Major Thomas, 320
Maclay, Sir Joseph, 265, 269, 292
Madison, Lieut. Cmdr. James, 311
Mahan, Alfred, 12
Manisty, Flt. Paymaster H W E, 261
Mann, Ernst Ritter von, 331
Marlborough, Duke of, 159
Marshal, Cpt George, 143
Marshall, Edward, 168, 318
Martin-Peake, Cpt. Francis, 43
Mary, Queen, 256, 264
Max of Baden, Prince, 330
Maxwell, Frank, 139
McHarg, Mr, 168, 169
McKenna, Reginald, 81
McKirkman - donkeyman, 116
McNeely, Robert, 162
Merchant ships & liners
  Aguila, 116, 117
  Akaroa, 275
  Algonquin, 216
  Algonquin, 217
  Alnwick Castle, 220, 221, 222
  Amiral Ganteaume, 68, 69, 70, 86, 197
  Ancona, 155, 156, 157
  Arabic, 146, 147, 148
  Ascaro, 252
  Atalanta, 115

Aztec, 222
Baron Ailsa, 313
Batavier IV, 100
Belgian Prince, 266, 267
Belridge, 98, 99
Bergensfjord, 112, 113
Brussels - ferry, 186
Bylands, 331
Californian, 152
Canadia, 111, 112
Carolina, 311
Carthage, 123
Dacia, 102, 103
Dirigo, 109, 110
Dunnottar Castle, 318
Edna, 310
Elizabeth, 120
Englishman - liner, 170, 219
Falaba, 116, 117, 118
Fenay Bridge, 170
Fingal, 118
Folke, 104
France IV, 155
Frinton, 221
Galway Castle, 326
Glitra, 64, 65, 76
Gulflight, 123, 124
Gyller - collier, 99, 100
H C Henry, 152
Hafursfjord, 260
Hanna, 99, 100
Harpalyce, 120
Hawppauge, 310
Hitachi Maru - Japanese, 301, 302
Hobart, 57
Horsa, 252
Housatonic, 222
Isle Of Jura, 261
Janvold, 314
Laertes, 90, 91
Leinster, 328, 330
Lucia, 310
Lusitania, 124, 125, 126, 127, 128, 129, 130, 131, 132, 142, 146, 163, 170
Madryn, 326

360

Index

Marie Thérèse, 169
Massilia, 300
Medea, 100
Mendip Range, 282
Miniota, 258
Moorish Prince, 312
Navahoe, 112
Nicosian, 145, 146
Olympic, 71, 73
Oscar II, 103
Parthenon, 252
Persia, 162
Pfalz, 57
Pioneer, 110
Provincia, 152
Quito, 313
Rio Cavado, 331
Rio Mondego, 324
Rizal, 189
Saint Paul, 132, 147
Salybia, 170
Sandhurst, 313
Sea Connet, 109
St Cecilia, 170
St Stephen, 116
Stralsund, 110
Sussex, 167, 168, 169, 170, 172
The Queen, 68, 69, 197
Thordis, 103
Thornhill, 72
Ticonderoga, 311, 312
Tithonus, 313
Tobia, 152
Trondhjemsfjord, 103
Vafos, 313
Venezia, 221
Vigilancia, 217
War Firth, 324
Zaanstroom, 100
Meurer, Vice Admiral Hugo, 7
Meusel, Kapt. Karl, 260
Michelson, Commodr. Andreas, 334
Middendorff, Kaptl. Heinrich, 325
Millman, Cpt. Peter, 143
Milner, Lord, 146, 204, 235, 264
Moltke, FM. Helmuth von, 46, 89

Money, MP, Leo, 234
Montague, MP, Edwin, 142, 197
Moraht, Kaptl. Robert, 315, 316
Muller, Admiral Georg von, 2
Murphy - Postal worker, 329
Musgrave, Kit, 50
National Kitchens, 256
National Sailors' & Firemen's Union, 287
Naval Estimates, 61
Nebeker, Acel, 147
Needs of the Navy Campaign 1893-4, 61
Nelson, Admiral Lord, 289
Nicholas II, Tsar, 12
Niemer, Ober. Lt. Hans, 110
Nikolaevitch, Nikokai (Red Cross), 165
Noble - Engineman, 297
Nordberg, Cpt, 217
Northern Barrage, 277, 320
Northern Patrol, 62, 77, 92, 101, 108, 112, 122, 161, 279, 292, 341
O'Beirne, Hugh - diplomat, 181
O'Conner, Charles, 326
Oliver, Rear Adm. Henry, 59, 233, 262, 345
Operation BB, 262
Operation Deadlight 1918-1919, 337
Oram, Sub Lieut. Harry, 19, 31, 179
Otranto Barrage, 153, 255
Otranto Strait, 153, 255, 350
Ouvry, Midshipman John, 90
Page, T N, 155
Page, Walter, 31, 93, 102, 103, 142, 146, 148, 154, 155, 160, 163, 189, 213, 218, 223, 224, 238, 241, 242, 245, 256, 257, 259, 284, 305, 306, 324
Paget MP, Almeric, 265
Parliamentary Recruitment Committee, 88
Patattivo, Alexander, 155
Patzig, Oberl. Helmut, 319, 320

Index

Pengilly, Mr - a Third Officer, 116
Perière, Kapitänleutnant Lothar von Arnauld de la, 10, 317, 331, 337
Pétain, General, 294
Phillips, Lieut. Cmdr.H, 114
Piercy, Lieut. Cmdr. Basil, 115
Pohl, Adm. Hugo von, 19, 39, 83, 84, 96, 97, 115, 150, 171, 345
Pohle, Kapt. Richard, 33
Polack, Cpt. Charles, 23
Pound, Cpt. Dudley, 288
Propert, Cpt. William, 91
Pustkuchen, Oberl. Herbert, 167, 168, 217, 222
Q-ships, 138, 140, 141, 150, 248, 253, 275, 277
Queenstown - patrol base, 140, 146, 147, 212, 241, 246, 258, 259, 273, 282, 323, 338
Radcliffe, Cpt Stephen, 281
Rae, Mr. - Radio officer, 318
Ramm, Oberl. Robert, 328
Rathenau, Walter, 160
Remy, Kaptl. Walter, 264, 319
Repington, Lieut Col Charles à Court, 14, 15, 51, 88, 264
Rhondda, 2nd Countess, 127
Richardson, Cpt. John, 57
Richardson, Frederick, 57, 58, 244
Richmond, Cpt Herbert, 18, 19, 20, 67, 230
Riddell, Lord (Press magnate), 173, 294
Ritschl, Prof. Albrecht, 29
Roberts, Lord, 28
Robertson, Sir William, 264
Robinson, Rev. George, 87
Rohrbeck, KapitL. Otto, 281
Room 40, 58, 59, 89, 164, 187, 215, 258, 260, 280, 296, 342
Rose, Kapt. Hans, 21, 192, 193, 194, 208, 323
Rosenberg-Gruszczynski, E von, 124
Roskill, Stephen, 290, 322
Ross, Harry, 144
Royal Norwegian Navy, 64

Rücker, Kaptl. Claus, 316
Rumbold, Horace, 17
Ryan, Cmdr. Cyril, 174
Ryan, William, 183
Saalwächter, Kaptl. Alfred, 272
Salisbury, Rev Homer, 162
Saltzwedel, Oberl. Reinhold, 215, 275, 276
Sanders, Lieut. Cmdr. William, 138, 145, 253, 254
Sanford, Lieut. Richard, 308
Saunders, M H, 310, 311
Scapa Flow, 15, 19, 31, 32, 33, 37, 38, 45, 48, 59, 61, 62, 74, 77, 78, 92, 164, 181, 185, 187, 231, 232, 235, 258, 300, 333
Scheer, Adm Reinhard, 19, 33, 76, 99, 171, 172, 173, 176, 177, 178, 179, 186, 187, 188, 195, 208, 249, 285, 298, 317, 325, 327, 331, 332, 333, 336, 345
Scheidemann, Philipp, 330
Schlieffen Plan, 64
Schlieffen, Field Marshal Alfred von, 12, 25, 46, 83
Schmettow, Kaptl. Matthias von, 251
Schneider, Kapt. Rudolf, 68, 86, 87, 88, 146, 148
Schrader, Kaptl. Otto von, 323, 324
Schröder, Adm. Ludwig von, 134
Schulthess, Kaptl. Hans, 139
Schweinitz, Kapt. Hans von, 32, 33
Schwieger, KorvK. Walther, 125, 127
Scott, Adm. Sir Percy, 48
Scrimgeour, Sub Lieut. Alexander, 21, 22, 24, 40, 41, 46, 61, 63, 67, 74, 92, 108, 112, 113, 345
Second Battle Squadron, 19, 70, 345
Second Cruiser Squadron, 62, 220
Selborne, Lord, 13, 175
Seventh Cruiser Squadron, 48
Ships - miscellaneous

Index

Augusto De Castilho (Portuguese), 331
Shoecraft, Eugene, 214
Sims, Rear Adm. William, 212, 240, 241, 242, 259, 273, 309, 321, 322, 324
Sinclair, Nurse Jeannie, 152
Sir John French, Field Marshal, 46, 48, 289
Smith, Harry S, 326
Smiths, Oberl. Wihelm, 173, 174
Smyth, Staff Surgeon Thomas, 43
Solomon, Skipper Ernest, 118
Spencer, Lieut. Herbert, 111, 139
Spiegel, Kaptl. Freiherr von, 106, 121, 240, 252, 253, 254
Spiess, Kapitanleutnant Johannes, 15, 20, 32, 50, 55, 56, 65, 158, 159, 239, 252, 254, 257, 258, 274, 275, 334, 335
Spragge, Sub Lieut. H E Spragge, 71
Stanley, Venetia, 51, 72, 73
Stapleton-Bretherton, Gertrude, 21
Steindorff, Oberl. Ernst, 315
Stephens, Mrs George, 127
Stevens, Bert, 188
Stoss, Kaptl. Alfred, 104, 105
Sturdee, Vice Adm. Sir Frederick, 37, 38, 345
Submarines - Allied
  C-24, 138
  C-3, 308
  D-4, 313
  E-19, 158
  E-3, 145
  E-9, 44, 45, 53, 54
Submarines - Central Powers
  Bremen, 13, 184
  Deutschland - later became *U-155*, 182, 183, 184, 260, 310
  U-103, 316
  U-12, 106, 107
  U-13, 32, 83
  U-135, 335
  U-139, 331, 332, 337
  U-140, 331

U-141, 331
U-15, 33, 83
U-151, 309, 310, 311
U-152, 311, 312
U-154, 314, 315
U-155 (ex-Deutschland), 260, 280, 310
U-156, 310
U-16, 98, 107
U-17, 56, 64
U-18, 78, 79, 80, 83
U-19, 30, 66, 257, 274, 275
U-20, 58, 125, 127, 149
U-21, 42, 44, 91, 92, 122, 123
U-23, 118, 139
U-24, 68, 86, 87
U-25, 11
U-27, 145, 146
U-28, 30, 58, 100, 116, 117, 149
U-29, 115
U-30, 124
U-32, 106, 121
U-33, 151, 152, 165, 185, 186
U-34, 264
U-35, 58, 151, 152, 166, 331
U-36, 58, 140
U-38, 79, 149, 150, 151, 155, 162
U-39, 58, 107, 149, 151, 152, 261
U-40, 138, 139
U-41, 58, 149
U-44, 107, 277
U-49, 210
U-50, 216
U-52, 188
U-53, 192, 193, 194, 195, 210, 323, 324
U-55, 10, 266, 267, 296
U-6, 103
U-61, 282, 283, 284
U-62, 216
U-63, 188, 245
U-64, 316
U-66, 188
U-70, 164, 217
U-75, 181
U-79, 281

363

Index

U-8, 104, 105, 106, 115
U-81, 221
U-82, 325, 326
U-83, 211, 212, 275
U-84, 277, 296
U-86, 320
U-87, 88
U-9, 10, 20, 32, 48, 49, 50, 51, 55, 158, 159, 239, 252, 332
U-90, 264, 319
U-93, 240, 252, 253, 254, 272, 296
U-95, 296
U-98, 8, 314
UB-103, 296
UB-115, 190
UB-116, 333
UB-123, 328
UB-14, 145
UB-23, 110
UB-26, 173, 174
UB-29, 167
UB-32, 263
UB-33, 309
UB-4, 120
UB-40, 245, 333
UB-48, 254
UB-50, 335
UB-51, 317, 318, 319
UB-55, 174, 309
UB-72, 312, 313
UB-81, 276
UB-85, 313
UC-25, 300
UC-26, 244, 251
UC-3, 252
UC-38, 244
UC-44, 277, 288, 292
UC-49, 190
UC-6, 100
UC-66, 222
UC-71, 215, 275, 276
UC-74, 243
UC-79, 309
Suchodoletz, Kapt. Ferdinand, 83
Sutton, Cpt. - Survivor in Leasowe, 318

Taussig, Vice Adm. Joseph, 246, 247
Taylor, Ltn Frederick, 138
Tenth Cruiser Squadron, 111, 161, 164
Thaer, General Albrecht von, 331, 353
Third Battle Cruiser Squadron, 119
Third Battle Squadron, 62, 345
Third Cruiser Squadron, 62
Thomas - Fireman, 221
Thompson, Lieut., 113
Thomson, Sir J J, 138
Thrasher, Leon, 118, 124
Tirpitz, Admiral Alfred von, 3, 12, 17, 19, 22, 33, 39, 45, 76, 86, 98, 115, 132, 150, 167, 171, 180, 345
Traeger, Oberl. Friedrich, 312, 313
Trayes, Frederick, 300, 301, 302, 303
Treaty of Brest-Litovsk 1917, 305
Treutler, Karl von, 132
Trewby, Cpt. George, 63
Trumbull, Frank, 213
Tucker, Cpt Allen, 215
Tumulty, Joseph, 208, 223
Tupper, Adm. Sir Reginald, 231
Turner, Cpt. William, 125
Turner, John, 153
Twelfth Cruiser Squadron, 41, 346
Tyrwhitt, Rear Admiral Reginald, 7, 9, 30, 36, 37, 38, 39, 187, 346
U-boat. *See* Submarines - German
U-boat School (Keil), 327
Valentiner, Kapt. Max, 79, 150, 151, 155, 156, 157
Vanderbilt Snr, Alfred, 126
Verney, Lieut Col. Sir Harry, 98
Vesco, Captain, 166
Victoria and Albert - HMS, 14, 17
Victoria, Queen, 12, 57
Wacker, Oberl. Karl, 263
Walney Island, 92
Wangenheim, Oberl.eutnaut zur See Freiherr von, 11

Index

War Office Research Department, 135
War Resources Board (German), 160
Wardlaw, Lieut. Mark, 139, 140
Wardle, Cpt. Thomas, 164
Warrender, Vice Adm. Sir George, 70
Warships - Allied
  Amiral Charner (French), 123
  Baralong (Q-ship), 145, 146
  Endurance - drifter, 173
  Garrigill - drifter, 153
  HMD Clover Bank, 297
  HMD *Gowanlea*, 255
  HMD Violet May, 297
  HMHS Glenart Castle, 305
  HMHS Llandovery Castle, 319, 320
  HMHS Soudan (hospital ship), 145
  HMS *Abdiel*, 304
  HMS *Aboukir*, 49, 50, 115
  HMS *Acheron*, 66, 107
  HMS *Achilles*, 220
  HMS *Ajax*, 33
  HMS *Alcantara*, 164
  HMS *Almanzora*, 114
  HMS Ambrose, 112
  HMS *Amphion*, 26, 27, 28, 29, 42
  HMS Antwerp, 150
  HMS *Arethusa*, 38
  HMS *Ariel*, 107
  HMS *Attack*, 107
  HMS *Audacious*, 70, 71, 72, 73, 74
  HMS *Badger*, 66
  HMS *Bayano*, 145
  HMS Birmingham, 33, 194
  HMS Boadicea, 41
  HMS Changuinola, 110
  HMS Charybdis, 45
  HMS *Cilicia*, 146
  HMS Commonwealth, 230
  HMS Courageous, 284
  HMS *Crescent*, 21, 22, 24, 40, 41, 56, 63, 67, 92
  HMS Cressy, 48, 49, 50, 115
  HMS Curacoa, 7
  HMS *Cyclops*, 300
  HMS Dorothy Gray, 79
  HMS Dragon, 7, 8
  HMS *Drake*, 61, 281, 282
  HMS Dreadnought, 115
  HMS *Dundee*, 220
  HMS *Dunraven*, 275, 276
  HMS Erne, 79
  HMS *Falmouth*, 61, 188
  HMS Farnborough, 211, 212, 275
  HMS *Filey*, 123, 124
  HMS Firedrake, 7, 8
  HMS *Formidable*, 87, 88, 89, 140, 146
  HMS Garry, 79
  HMS Ghurka, 105
  HMS *Glorious*, 315
  HMS *Hampshire*, 181
  HMS *Hawke*, 55, 56, 62, 115
  HMS Hermes, 145
  HMS Hind, 66
  HMS Hogue, 49, 50, 115
  HMS Hydra, 66
  HMS *Iago*, 123
  HMS Indomitable, 89
  HMS *Intrepid*, 308
  HMS Invincible, 119
  HMS *Iphigenia*, 308, 309
  HMS *Iron Duke*, 17, 18
  HMS *Jessamine*, 283
  HMS *King George V*, 15, 17, 147
  HMS *Lance*, 26
  HMS *Landrail*, 26
  HMS *Leda*, 62
  HMS *Leviathan*, 107
  HMS *Lion*, 75, 89
  HMS *Liverpool*, 71, 72, 75, 91, 92, 116, 129, 174, 199, 266, 319
  HMS *London*, 87
  HMS *Lorna*, 315
  HMS *Lychnis*, 316
  HMS Maidstone, 7
  HMS *Majestic*, 123
  HMS Maori, 105
  HMS *Monarch*, 33
  HMS *Morea*, 320

Index

HMS *New Zealand*, 89, 152
HMS *Nottingham*, 188
HMS *Obdurate*, 179
HMS *Oracle*, 107
HMS *Orotava*, 110, 113
HMS *Pargust*, 150, 212
HMS *Pathfinder*, 42, 43, 44, 56, 91
HMS Patia, 113
HMS *Patuca*, 103, 112
HMS *Penshurst*, 350
HMS *Primrose*, 147
HMS Prince Charles (Q-ship), 139, 140
HMS Prince of Wales, 22, 23
HMS Princess Royal, 89
HMS *Prize*, 252, 253
HMS Queen Elizabeth, 231, 232
HMS *Sandfly*, 304
HMS *Snowdrop*, 283
HMS *Southampton*, 67, 113, 176, 199, 222, 244, 345
HMS *Strongbow*, 281
HMS *Swift*, 62
HMS *Tamarisk*, 283
HMS Taranaki (Q-ship), 138, 139
HMS *Telemachus*, 303, 304
HMS *Termagant*, 297
HMS *Teviot*, 100
HMS *Theseus*, 57, 59
HMS *Thetis*, 308
HMS Thunderer, 31
HMS *Tiger*, 89, 90
HMS *Tokyo*, 78
HMS *Triumph*, 122, 123
HMS Viknor, 112, 113
HMS *Vindictive*, 307, 308
HMT *Arcadian*, 243
HMT *Leasowe Castle*, 317, 318, 319
HMT *Marquette*, 152
HMT Royal Edward, 143, 144, 145
HMT *Transylvania*, 245, 246
HMT *Wayfarer*, 121
HSMS *Salta*, 244, 245
La Provence (French troopship), 166

Orion, 19, 33
Portugal (Russian hospital ship), 165
USS *Cassin*, 282, 283, 284
USS *Mount Vernon*, 325, 326
USS *Parker*, 305, 323
USS *Porter*, 283
Warships - Allies
USS *Wilkes*, 323
Warships - Central Powers
UC-56, 304
Warships - German
Novara - Austrian cruiser, 255
S-126, 53, 54
SMS *Ariadne*, 39
SMS *Augsburg*, 58
SMS Baden, 334, 336
SMS *Bayern*, 187
SMS *Blücher*, 89, 90
SMS *Bremse*, 281
SMS *Brummer*, 281
SMS Cöln, 39
SMS Derfflinger, 89
SMS Frauenlob, 39
SMS Friedrich der Grosse, 269
SMS *Gneisenau*, 315
SMS *Greif*, 164
SMS Grosser Kurfürst, 187
SMS *Hela*, 44, 45
SMS *Helgoland*, 334, 335
SMS Kaiser Barbarossa, 13
SMS Kaiser Wilhelm der Grosse, 13
SMS Leopard, 219, 220
SMS *Magdeburg*, 58, 59
SMS *Mainz*, 39
SMS *Markgraf*, 187
SMS *Moltke*, 187
SMS *Pillau*, 269
SMS Prinzregent Luitpold, 269
SMS Scharnhorst, 315
SMS *Seydlitz*, 89
SMS Stettin, 39
SMS *Thüringen*, 334, 335
SMS *Undine*, 158
SMS Von der Tann, 187

366

Index

SMS *Wolf* - raider, 300, 301, 302, 303
SS Königin Luise, 26, 27, 28, 29
Warships - Norwegian
  Hai, 64
Warships - Russian
  Lieutenant Burakov, 59
Watt, Joseph, 255
Wawn, Cpt. Frederick, 120
Webb, Cpt. Richard, 163
Weddigen, Kapt. Otto, 20, 32, 48, 49, 50, 51, 55, 115
Wedel, Baron von, 112, 113
Wegener, Kaptl. Bernd, 145
Wellington, Duke of, 289
Wells, H G, 134, 135, 136
Wemyss, Vice-Adm. Wester, 21, 24, 41, 45, 54, 279, 289, 291, 296, 326, 346
Wenninger, KapitL. Ralph, 174, 309
Werner, KapitL. Wilhelm, 267
Whitehead, Cpt. Frederick, 248
Whitehead, Robert, 44
Wiegand, Karl von, 76
Wilhelm, Kaiser, 12, 13, 14, 15, 20, 25, 30, 39, 41, 46, 59, 83, 98, 100, 112, 132, 134, 149, 150, 156, 167, 176, 192, 195, 218, 241, 243, 251, 266, 302, 326, 327, 330, 334, 335, 336
Wilkins, Edith - nurse, 152
Williams, Cpt Hugh, 56
Williams, Walter, 245
Wilson, General Sir Henry, 305
Wilson, Havelock, 287
Wilson, President Woodrow, 56, 102, 124, 129, 132, 148, 154, 157, 162, 163, 169, 170, 189, 208, 210, 211, 213, 214, 216, 217, 218, 222, 223, 224, 242, 245, 259, 287, 305, 306, 324, 330
Wilson, Robert, 79
Wiseman, Sir William, 213
Wood, Albert, 174
X, 14, 15, 17, 93, 104, 140, 147, 172, 181, 204, 256, 265, 267, 287
Youngson, Alexander, 79
Zenker, Cpt., 83
Zeppelin *L-13*, 187
Zeppelins, 187, 252
Zimmermann, Arthur, 215, 346

References

Abbreviations
CAB: Cabinet
HC Deb: House of Commons Debates
NY Times: *New York Times*
ODNB: The Oxford Dictionary of National Biography
TNA The National Archives

---

[1] Keegan 1998. Hutchinson.
[2] King-Hall 1952, p. 161.
[3] https://rebeccajanemorgan.medium.com/the-forgotten-surrender-world-war-i-and-the-confiscation-of-the-german-u-boat-fleet-b589705ea248
[4] Manchester Guardian Nov 21, 1918.
[5] King-Hall 1936, p. 235.
[6] Ibid, p. 232.
[7] https://blog.nationalarchives.gov.uk/1918-submarine-surrender/
[8] Ibid.
[9] King-Hall 1936, pp. 235-6.
[10] Manchester Guardian, Nov 21, 1918.
[11] Hankey 1961, Vol I, p. 68.
[12] Tirpitz 1919, p. 105.
[13] Marder 1961, Vol I, p. 107.
[14] Ibid, p. 108.
[15] Ibid, pp. 108-9.
[16] Ibid, p. 109.
[17] *Blackwood's Magazine*, June 1910, p. 893.
[18] Ibid, p. 896.
[19] Ibid, p. 900.
[20] Moyer 1995, p. 61.
[21] Patterson 1966, pp. 31-6.
[22] Marder 1961, Vol. I, p. 364.
[23] Tirpitz 1919, p. 49.
[24] Churchill 1941, p. 109.
[25] Marder 1961, Vol I, p. 364.
[26] Scheer 1920, p. 25.
[27] Ibid, p. 10.
[28] Spiess 1927, p. 38.
[29] Watson 2015, p. 121.
[30] Hallam & Benyon 2008, pp. 31-2.
[31] Wemyss 1935, pp. 153-5.
[32] Hallam & Benyon 2008, p. 32.
[33] Beaverbrook 1928, pp. 35-6.

References

[34] http://www.bbc.co.uk/history/worldwars/wwone/mirror01_01.shtml
[35] Dewar 1939, p. 161.
[36] Wemyss 1935, p. 157.
[37] Hallam & Benyon 2008, p. 57.
[38] Marder 1961, Vol I, p. 332.
[39] https://www.forces-war-records.co.uk/blog/2014/08/06/on-this-day-6th-august-1914-the-hms-amphion-was-sunk-by-a-german-mine
[40] ibid.
[41] https://www.worldwar1postcards.com/the-lord-roberts-memorial-stamp-album.php
[42] HC Deb 07 August 1914 vol 65 cc2153-6.
[43] Hankey 1961, Vol I, p. 97.
[44] Churchill 1938, Vol I, p. 212.
[45] Oram 1974, p. 98.
[46] US Govt. 1915.
[47] Ibid.
[48] Spiess 1927, p. 4.
[49] Spiess 1927, p. 43.
[50] Scheer 1920, p. 36.
[51] Ibid, p. 40.
[52] Marder 1952, p. 309.
[53] Massie 2003, p. 98.
[54] Beatty report, Aug 28, 1914. http://www.gwpda.org/1914/helgo.html
[55] Churchill 1938, Vol I, p. 262.
[56] Ibid, p. 263.
[57] Chatterton 1932, p. 95.
[58] *Times* Aug 29, 1914.
[59] Roskill 1980, p. 84.
[60] Massie 2003, p. 116.
[61] Hallam & Benyon 2008, p. 46.
[62] Wemyss 1935, p. 168.
[63] Chalmers 1951, p. 154.
[64] Gretton 1968, pp. 165-6.
[65] https://www.surreyinthegreatwar.org.uk/story/lt-commander-ernest-torre-favell/
[66] http://www.scotlandswar.co.uk/hms_pathfinder.html
[67] https://www.belfasttelegraph.co.uk/news/northern-ireland/account-of-sailor-who-survived-torpedo-attack-on-hms-pathfinder-found-30553424.html
[68] http://www.scotlandswar.co.uk/hms_pathfinder.html
[69] Compton-Hall 1991, p. 127.
[70] Wemyss 1935, p. 161.

References

[71] Ibid, p. 168.
[72] Ibid, p. 164.
[73] Chalmers 1951, pp. 140-1.
[74] Tirpitz 1919, Vol II, p. 228.
[75] Hallam & Benyon 2008, p. 47.
[76] https://en.wikipedia.org/wiki/First_Battle_of_the_Marne#Aftermath
[77] *Times* June 5, 1914 quoted in Marder 1961, Vol I, p. 333.
[78] Corbett 1921, Vol I, p. 171.
[79] Lowell 1928, p. 25.
[80] http://historyhubulster.co.uk/tag/hms-aboukir/
[81] Ibid.
[82] Asquith 1982, p. 253.
[83] Hankey 1962, p. 180.
[84] *Times* Sept 23, 1914.
[85] Domville-Fife 1914, p. 33.
[86] David 1977, pp. 198-9.
[87] Lowell 1928, p. 29.
[88] http://historyhubulster.co.uk/hms-hawke-centenary/
[89] Ibid.
[90] Lowell 1928, p. 30.
[91] Hallam & Benyon 2008, pp. 78-9.
[92] https://www.theguardian.com/century/1910-1919/Story/0,,126442,00.html
[93] https://www.birminghammail.co.uk/news/ex-kings-norton-schoolboy-u-boat-tragedy-7533669
[94] King-Hall 1935, p. 394.
[95] David 1977, p. 199.
[96] https://www.aph.gov.au/About_Parliament/Parliamentary Departments/Parliamentary_Library/pubs/rp/rp1415/AustToWar1914
[97] Churchill 1938, Vol I, p. 415.
[98] Hallam & Benyon 2008, p. 87.
[99] King-Hall 1935, p. 394.
[100] Churchill 1938, Vol I, p. 349.
[101] Chalmers 1951, p. 158.
[102] Hallam & Benyon 2008, pp. 79-81.
[103] King-Hall 1935, p. 397.
[104] Ibid, p. 397.
[105] Marder 2013, Vol II, p. 50.
[106] https://doverhistorian.com/2016/10/02/captain-carey-and-the-queen/

References

[107] https://www.chippingcampdenhistory.org.uk/content/history/people-2/arts_artists_and_craftspeople/wentworth_huyshe
[108] Halpern 1994, p. 36.
[109] Gilbert 1971, p. 141.
[110] Asquith (ed Brock) 1982, pp. 287-8.
[111] Gilbert 1972, p. 222.
[112] Asquith (ed Brock) 1982, p. 290.
[113] *Times*, Nov 14, 1918.
[114] Hough 1974, pp. 302-3.
[115] Hallam & Benyon 2008, p. 87.
[116] Hough 1974, pp. 308.
[117] Chalmers 1951, p. 179.
[118] Ibid, p. 161.
[119] *Times*, Nov 3, 1914.
[120] https://norfolktalesmyths.com/2019/05/29/the-1914-raid-on-great-yarmouth/
[121] Pirzio-Biroli, 2016.
[122] Scheer 1920, p. 222.
[123] Lilley 2012, p. 33.
[124] Ibid, p. 34.
[125] Churchill 1938, Vol I, p. 343.
[126] https://www.orkanadventures.com/articles/the-loss-of-u-18
[127] https://www.naval-history.net/WW1NavyBritishLGDecorations1919.htm
[128] Andrew 2009, p. 63.
[129] http://www.gwpda.org/1915/usmarit.html
[130] Ibid.
[131] Bremer 2010, p. 17.
[132] Churchill 1938, Vol I, p. 499.
[133] Ibid.
[134] Jarausch 1973, pp. 272-3.
[135] Field 2021. Independently published.
[136] Churchill 1938, Vol I, p. 495.
[137] www.lincstothepast.com
[138] https://en.wikipedia.org/wiki/HMS_Formidable_(1898)
[139] Ibid.
[140] HC Deb 04 February 1915 vol 69 c164W.
[141] Hart 2015.
[142] *Times* Feb 12, 1915.
[143] Hurd 2006, Chpt. 7.
[144] Hallam & Benyon 2008, p. 142.
[145] US Dept of State 1915.
[146] Jameson 1965, pp. 159-60.

References

[147] Lilley 2012, p. 33.
[148] http://www.gwpda.org/naval/dc150204.htm
[149] https://wwi.lib.byu.edu/index.php/German_Admiralty_Declaration Regarding_Unrestricted_U-Boat_Warfare
[150] https://en.wikipedia.org/wiki/U-boat_Campaign
[151] *Times*, Feb 6, 1915.
[152] *Times* Feb 13, 1915.
[153] Scheer 1920, p. 230.
[154] Jameson 1965, p. 155.
[155] Scheer 1920, p. 230.
[156] Brock & Brock 2014, p. 77.
[157] HC Deb 11 February 1915 vol 69 cc744-5W.
[158] Scheer 1920, p. 227.
[159] Ibid, p. 229.
[160] https://www.wrecksite.eu/wreck.aspx?66227
[161] Forstner 1917, p. 81.
[162] HC Deb 01 March 1915 vol 70 cc589-623.
[163] https://en.wikipedia.org/wiki/Freedom_of_the_seas
[164] David 1977, p. 222.
[165] HC Deb 01 March 1915 vol 70 cc589-623
[166] Grattan 1929.
[167] Messimer 2001, p. 31.
[168] *Times* March 9, 1915.
[169] Spiegel 1976, pp. 68-70.
[170] Hallam & Benyon 2008, p. 134.
[171] https://www.naval-history.net/WW1Memoir-10CSNPatrol.htm#1
[172] Chatterton 1932.
[173] https://www.naval-history.net/OWShips-WW1-08-HMS_Changuinola.htm
[174] Hallam & Benyon 2008, p. 154.
[175] https://www.naval-history.net/OWShips-WW1-08-HMS_Patuca.htm
[176] Hallam & Benyon 2008, pp. 129-30.
[177] Ibid, p. 134.
[178] https://www.naval-history.net/OWShips-WW1-08-HMS_Patia.htm
[179] https://www.naval-history.net/OWShips-WW1-08-HMS_Orotava.htm
[180] King-Hall 1935, p. 412.
[181] https://naval-history.net/OWShips-WW1-08-HMS_Almanzora.htm
[182] Tirpitz 1919 Vol II, p. 168.
[183] Ibid, p. 321.

References

[184] Tirpitz 1919, Vol II, p. 168.
[185] http://archive.org/stream/shippingcasualti00grea/shippingcasualti00grea_djvu.txt
[186] Ibid. [186] 1988.
[187] https://www.stokesentinel.co.uk/news/history/tribal-chiefs-hero-grandson-saved-865929
[188] https://www.shropshirearchives.org.uk/wp-content/uploads/2018/10/wellington-remembers_Gough-Albert-James.pdf
[189] https://www.stokesentinel.co.uk/news/history/tribal-chiefs-hero-grandson-saved-865929
[190] http://ww1blog.osborneink.com/?p=6837
[191] https://www.cwgc.org/visit-us/find-cemeteries-memorials/cemetery-details/90002/tower-hill-memorial/
[192] Keegan, 1988.
[193] MaritimeQuest.com
[194] *Times* April 12, 1915.
[195] Spiegel 1976.
[196] *NY Times*, May 5, 1915.
[197] *Times* May 10, 1915.
[198] Bernstorff 1920, pp. 115-6.
[199] Churchill 1938 Vol II, p. 770.
[200] Lowell 1928, p. 95.
[201] Ibid, p. 97.
[202] https://www.archives.gov/exhibits/eyewitness/html.php?section=18
[203] Buffalo Evening News, Oct 22, 1928.
[204] Ibid.
[205] https://www.iwm.org.uk/history/voices-of-the-first-world-war-the-submarine-war
[206] *The Guardian*, May 1, 2014.
[207] Lowell 1928, p. 99.
[208] Bernstorff 1920, p. 121.
[209] Moyer 1995, p. 117.
[210] *Times* May 10, 1915.
[211] *NY Times*, May 9, 1915.
[212] https://en.wikipedia.org/wiki/U-boat_Campaign_(World_War_I)#First_attacks_on_merchant_ships
[213] Gerard 1917, pp. 240-1.
[214] House 1926 Vol I, p. 437.
[215] https://www.presidency.ucsb.edu/documents/address-naturalized-citizens-convention-hall-philadelphia
[216] http://liverpoolremembrance.weebly.com/
[217] Blücher 2019, p. 51.

References

[218] https://www.mylearning.org/resources/recruitment-poster-calling-on-the-men-of-hull-to-avenge-the
[219] https://www.mylearning.org/stories/first-world-war-propaganda-in-the-humber/755?
[220] http://www.gwpda.org/1915/lusitania1.html
[221] House 1926, Vol I, p. 446.
[222] Ibid, pp. 455-6.
[223] Tirpitz 1919, Vol II, pp. 156-7.
[224] Ibid, pp. 156-7.
[225] Bernstorff 1920, p. 141.
[226] Ibid, p. 129.
[227] Bernstorff 1920, p. 135.
[228] *Times* July 28, 1915.
[229] Peck 2018, p. 36.
[230] *Times* June 11, 1915.
[231] Tirpitz 1919, Vol II, pp. 168-9.
[232] *Times* June 15, 1915.
[233] *Times*, June 22, 1915.
[234] MacLeod & Andrews 1971, p. 7.
[235] Ibid, p.8.
[236] MacLeod & Andrews 1971, p. 7.
[237] https://www.historic-uk.com/HistoryUK/HistoryofBritain/Mystery-Ships/
[238] Bayly 1939, p. 196.
[239] Asquith 1968, p. 51.
[240] Hendrick 1923, pp. 66-7.
[241] Peck 2018, p. 137.
[242] https://imperialglobalexeter.files.wordpress.com/2014/01/mayoress-of-exeter-mothering-1915.jpg
[243] *Times*, August 18, 1915.
[244] HL Deb 08 November 1915 vol 20 cc181-230.
[245] https://www.warandson.co.uk/index.php/news/46-the-sinking-of-the-s-s-arabic-a-young-liverpudlian-lady-s-courage
[246] Fitch & Poirier 2014, p. 142.
[247] Hendrick 1923, p. 26.
[248] Bernstorff 1920, p. 146.
[249] House 1926, Vol II, pp. 29-30.
[250] Ibid, p. 66.
[251] Hendrick 1923, p. 27.
[252] Blücher 2019, p. 100.
[253] https://ww100.govt.nz/no-ordinary-transport-the-sinking-of-the-marquette
[254] https://ww100.govt.nz/no-ordinary-transport-the-sinking-of-the-marquette

References

[255] Hendrick 1923, Vol II, p. 32.
[256] Ibid, p. 30.
[257] Ibid, p. 40.
[258] Ibid, p. 38.
[259] Ibid, pp. 99-100.
[260] Fitch & Poirier 2014, p. 172.
[261] 'Submarine Warfare—Austria' *The American Journal of International Law*, Vol 11, No. 4, 1917, pp. 155–221.
[262] Manchester Guardian Nov 11, 1915.
[263] Times, Nov 11, 1915.
[264] House 1926, Vol II, p. 46.
[265] House 1926, Vol II, p. 49.
[266] Times Nov 8, 1915.
[267] House 1926, Vol II, p. 78.
[268] Beckett 2006, p. 110.
[269] Blücher 2019, pp. 100-1.
[270] Ibid, p. 83.
[271] Hendrick 1923, p. 114.
[272] https://ww1.habsburger.net/en/chapters/bells-bullets-metal-collection
[273] Berg 2013, pp. 383-4.
[274] *NY Times* Mar 31, 1916.
[275] Hendrick 1923, p. 48.
[276] Hendrick 1923, p. 49.
[277] Black 2005.
[278] http://ahoy.tk-jk.net/MaraudersWW1/Grief.html
[279] https://archive.org/details/waronhospitalshi00lond/page/5/mode/1up
[280] Reynolds, etc 1916.
[281] http://www.gwpda.org/1916/merchant.html
[282] US Govt 1929, pp. 250-1.
[283] *Times* Feb 10, 1916.
[284] Freeman 2020, p. 254.
[285] Asprey 1991, pp. 231-2
[286] *Times*, March 27,1916.
[287] Messimer 2001, p. 95.
[288] *Times* March 27, 1916.
[289] *NY Times* Mar 31, 1916.
[290] House 1926, Vol II, p. 227.
[291] *NY Times* Apr 20, 1916.
[292] *NY Times* April 22, 1916.
[293] Tirpitz 1919, Vol II, p. 180.
[294] Scheer 1920, p. 242.
[295] Max 1928, p. 34.
[296] King-Hall 1935, pp. 444-5.

References

[297] Ibid, p. 442.
[298] Ibid, p. 473.
[299] Winton 1981, pp. 222-3.
[300] Moyer 1995, p. 149.
[301] Keyes 1935, p. 69.
[302] https://www.ft.com/content/f3760af0-6545-11e4-91b1-00144feabdc0
[303] *Times*, June 7, 1916.
[304] https://history.blog.gov.uk/2016/06/06/hugh-obeirne-and-the-sinking-of-hms-hampshire-a-diplomat-remembered/
[305] *Times*, July 11, 1916.
[306] *NY Times* July 10, 1916.
[307] Blücher 2019, pp. 154-5.
[308] Keyes 1935, p. 73.
[309] https://en.wikipedia.org/wiki/Charles_Fryatt#U-boat_attack
[310] Ibid.
[311] US Govt 1929, pp. 430-431.
[312] George 1934, Vol III, p. 1131.
[313] Jellicoe 1934, pp. 2-3.
[314] Blake 1952, p. 186.
[315] http://www.gwpda.org/1916/uboot.html
[316] Ibid.
[317] Ibid.
[318] http://smallstatebighistory.com/a-german-u-boat-in-newport-harbor-during-world-war-i/
[319] Reynolds et al, Vol IV.
[320] Ibid.
[321] Bernstorff 1920, pp. 250-1.
[322] Keyes 1935, p. 163.
[323] Newbolt IV, p. 65.
[324] Marder 1949, Vol III, p. 381.
[325] HC Deb 15 November 1916 Vol 87 c757.
[326] Marder 1949, Vol III, p. 388.
[327] George 1934, Vol III, pp. 1139-40.
[328] Brittain 1978 ed, p. 297.
[329] https://archive.org/details/waronhospitalshi00lond/page/5/mode/1up
[330] George 1934, Vol III, p. 1201.
[331] Bertie 1924, pp. 66-7.
[332] George 1934, Vol III, p. 1131.
[333] Jellicoe 2006, p. 288.
[334] King-Hall 1935, p. 483.
[335] Bertie 1924, Vol II, p. 80.

References

[336] Blake 1952, p. 186.
[337] George1933, Vol II, p. 970.
[338] Jones 1969, p. 4.
[339] Hankey 1961, Vol II, p. 640.
[340] Taylor, 1965, p. 73.
[341] https://thehistoryofparliament.wordpress.com/
[342] Barnett 2000, p. 189.
[343] TNA CAB 23-1: Dec 22, 1916.
[344] Scheer 1920, pp. 249-50.
[345] http://www.gwpda.org/naval/hindtob.htm
[346] Asprey 1991, p. 267.
[347] Watson 2015, p.421.
[348] Taylor 1919, p. 305.
[349] Watson 2015, p. 421.
[350] Jameson 1965, p. 196.
[351] Stevenson 2017, p 32.
[352] Churchill 1938, Vol II, pp. 1116-17.
[353] Ibid.
[354] Watson 2015, p. 425.
[355] Ibid.
[356] Berg 2013, p. 423.
[357] Robinson & Robinson 2019, p. 138.
[358] Edwards 1963, p.108.
[359] Blücher 2019, p. 158.
[360] *Times* Nov 13, 1916.
[361] Berg 2013, p. 432.
[362] Stevenson 2017, p. 32.
[363] Campbell 1937, p. 276.
[364] Ibid, p. 240.
[365] Sims 1984, pp. 169-70
[366] https://millercenter.org/the-presidency/presidential-speeches/february-3-1917-message-regarding-us-german-relations
[367] Hendrick 1923, p. 215.
[368] Williams 2017, p. 69.
[369] https://www.wrecksite.eu/wreck.aspx?58893
[370] http://www.gwpda.org/1917/zimmerman.html
[371] *NY Times* Feb 27, 1917.
[372] https://www.spokesman.com/stories/2017/mar/01/100-years-ago-in-spokane-catholic-priest-recalls-d/
[373] *NY Times* Mar 1, 1917.
[374] https://www.naval-history.net/WW1Book-World_War_1_Timeline_or_Chronology_1916.htm
[375] https://magicmastsandsturdyships.weebly.com/a-german-u-boat-sinks-the-algonquin-and-bombs-america-into-world-war-i.html

References

[376] *NY Times*, March 15, 1917.
[377] Reynolds et al.
[378] Ibid.
[379] http://www.gwpda.org/1917/cabmtg.html
[380] Ibid.
[381] Hendrick 1923, p. 219.
[382] Gray 1994, pp. 174-5.
[383] *Times*, March 14, 1917.
[384] http://www.bandcstaffregister.com/page132.html
[385] https://avalon.law.yale.edu/20th_century/wilson2.asp
[386] https://millercenter.org/the-presidency/presidential-speeches/april-2-1917-address-congress-requesting-declaration-war
[387] Peck 2018, p. 90.
[388] Hendrick 1923, p. 230.
[389] Reynolds et al.
[390] Ibid.
[391] *Times*, April 7, 1917.
[392] Blake 1952, p. 240.
[393] Newbolt Vol IV, pp. 370-1.
[394] *Times*, Mar 7 & 14, 1917.
[395] Bilbrough 2014.
[396] Jellicoe 1920, Chpt 5.
[397] Jameson 1965, p. 215.
[398] Hankey 1961, Vol II, pp. 645-6.
[399] Ibid pp. 646-7.
[400] Roskill 1970, p. 356.
[401] Chalmers 1951 pp. 291-2.
[402] Ibid, p. 292
[403] Black 2005, p. 175.
[404] Newbolt Vol IV, pp. 382-4.
[405] George 1934, Vol III, p. 1158.
[406] Chalmers 1951, p. 292.
[407] Newbolt Vol 5, p. 16.
[408] TNA CAB 23-02, Mar 8, 1917.
[409] Black 2005, p. 176.
[410] Ibid.
[411] Black 2005, p. 177.
[412] Newbolt, Vol IV, p. 379.
[413] Marder 1917, p. 159.
[414] Newbolt Vol V, p. 24.
[415] Chalmers 1951, p. 312.
[416] TNA CAB 23-2. Apr 25, 1917.
[417] Hankey 1961, Vol I, p. 650.
[418] Dewar 1939, pp. 220–21.
[419] Jellicoe 1934, pp. 97-9.

References

[420] Bremer 2010, p. 60.
[421] Beesly 1982, p. 259.
[422] Hendrick 1923, pp. 278-9.
[423] TNA CAB 23-21, Apr 3, 1917.
[424] *Times* April 5, 1917.
[425] Watson 2015, p. 435.
[426] Ibid, p. 480.
[427] Hendrick 1923, p 275.
[428] Ibid, p. 275.
[429] Ibid, p. 275.
[430] Ibid, p. 276.
[431] Ibid, pp. 278-9.
[432] Ibid, p. 281.
[433] https://www.firstworldwar.com/diaries/torpedoed.htm
[434] Blücher 2019, p. 172.
[435] TNA CAB 23-21, May 4, 1917.
[436] Taffrail 1931, p. 327.
[437] Halpern 1994, p. 359.
[438] Roskill 1980, p. 221.
[439] TNA CAB 23, June 13, 1917.
[440] Jameson 1965, p. 222.
[441] Roskill 1980, p. 221.
[442] Blake 1952, pp. 229-30.
[443] Chalmers 1951, p. 318.
[444] Ibid, p. 321.
[445] ODNB: https://doi.org/10.1093/ref:odnb/33360
[446] Manchester Guardian, May 11, 1917.
[447] Maxwell 2014, p. 18.
[448] TNA CAB 23-31, June 15, 1917.
[449] Lowell 1928, p. 179.
[450] Spiess 1927, p. 133.
[451] Ibid, p. 134.
[452] *Times*, May 2, 1917.
[453] Hendrick 1923, Vol II, p. 240.
[454] Beckett 2006, p. 115.
[455] Hendrick 1923, Vol II, p. 243.
[456] Spiess 1927, p. 137
[457] Ibid.
[458] Blake 1952, p. 242.
[459] Hendrick 1923, p. 283.
[460] Ibid, p. 285.
[461] Padfield 1984, p. 71.
[462] Chalmers 1951, pp. 320-1.
[463] Halpern 1994, p. 367.
[464] TNA CAB 23-03, July 26, 1917.
[465] Ibid, June 15, 1917.

References

[466] Blake 1952, p. 239.
[467] Bacon 1919, p. 97.
[468] Blake 1952, p. 242.
[469] Ibid.
[470] Bertie 1924, Vol II, p. 148.
[471] https://www.wrecksite.eu/wreck.aspx?11964
[472] TNA CAB 23-3, August 3, 1917.
[473] Blücher 2019, pp. 183-4.
[474] Beaverbrook 1956, p. 170.
[475] TNA CAB 23-04, Sept 5, 1917.
[476] TNA CAB 23-04, Sept 7, 1917.
[477] Messimer 2001, pp. 153-4.
[478] Jameson 1965, p. 233.
[479] Chalmers 1951, p. 302.
[480] Newbolt IV, pp. 132-3.
[481] Jellicoe 1920.
[482] Keyes 1935, p. 117.
[483] TNA CAB 23-04, Oct 4, 1917.
[484] TNA CAB 23-04, Oct 29, 1917.
[485] Hendrick 1923, p. 324.
[486] Chalmers 1951, pp. 303-4.
[487] TNA CAB 23-04, Oct 29, 1917.
[488] TNA CAB 23-04, Nov 7, 1917.
[489] Blücher 2019, pp. 183-4.
[490] George 1934, Vol III, pp. 1188-9.
[491] Keyes 1935, p. 119.
[492] Marder 1959, Vol III, p. 502.
[493] Winton 1981, p. 259.
[494] Blake 1952, p. 240.
[495] Keyes 1935, p. 69.
[496] Roskill 1980, p. 242.
[497] Marder 1959, Vol III, p. 502.
[498] Keyes 1935, p. 135.
[499] Bacon Vol II, p. 509.
[500] TNA CAB 23-4, Dec 10, 1917.
[501] Wemyss 1935, p. 365.
[502] Blake 1952, p. 275.
[503] Keyes 1935, p. 154.
[504] TNA CAB 23-04, Nov 6, 1917.
[505] Blücher 2019, p. 185.
[506] Barnett 2000, p. 260.
[507] Riddell 1933, pp. 299-300.
[508] Aspinall-Oglander 1951, p. 221.
[509] HC Deb 05 March 1918 vol 103 cc1867-70.
[510] TNA CAB 23-05, Jan 15, 1918.

References

[511] https://trove.nla.gov.au/newspaper/article/4726055
[512] Keyes 1935, pp. 181-2.
[513] Gilbert 1971, pp. 269-70.
[514] Gilbert 1971, Companion Vol IV Part I, pp. 353-4.
[515] Padfield 1984, pp. 78.
[516] Trayes, F G 1919.
[517] Taffrail 1931, pp. 379-387.
[518] Churchill 1927, p. 411.
[519] Hendrick 1923, p. 364.
[520] Navy Department 1920, p. 141.
[521] https://en.wikipedia.org/wiki/USS_Ticonderoga_(1918)
[522] https://www.nzherald.co.nz/world/experts-move-a-step-closer-to-uncovering-the-mystery-of-the-german-submarine-attacked-by-a-sea-monster-in-ww1/BDBFBUGU7W4QBLYE3UPR7MJQQY/
[523] http://www.scotlandswar.co.uk/pdf_Leasowe_Castle.pdf (This site is no longer active.)
[524] https://en.wikipedia.org/wiki/HMHS_Llandovery_Castle
[525] Sims 1984, p. 307.
[526] Fitch & Poirier 2014, pp. 341-2.
[527] Bremer 2010, p. 65.
[528] TNA CAB 23-7, Sept 3, 1918.
[529] Sims 1984, p. 224.
[530] Ibid, pp. 230-1.
[531] Hendrick 1923, p. 388.
[532] *Times* Oct. 12, 1918.
[533] Op cit.
[534] TNA CAB 23-08, Oct 15,1918.
[535] *Times* Oct 16, 1918.
[536] Hankey 1961, Vol II, pp. 858-9.
[537] Von Thaer diary, October 1, 1918: http://www.gwpda.org/1918/thaereng.html
[538] https://www.workers.org/2018/10/39496/
[539] Ibid.
[540] Waldeyer-Hartz, 1933, p. 255.
[541] Spiess, 1927, p. 241.
[542] Ibid, p. 232.
[543] Spiess, 1927, p. 235.
[544] Ibid, p. 230.
[545] https://www.wereldoorlog1418.nl/revolte-duitse-marine-1917/index.html

References

[546] Scheer 1920, p. 358.
[547] Roskill 1980, p. 273.
[548] Philbin 1982, p. 173.
[549] *The Times* Nov. 12, 1918.
[550] Roskill 1980, pp. 275-6.
[551] Jameson 1965, p. 250.

Printed in Great Britain
by Amazon